☆☆Forbes
TRAVEL GUIDE

DATE DUE

D1005374

ACKNOWLEDGMENTS

We gratefully acknowledge the help of our representatives for their efficient and perceptive inspections of the lodgings listed. Forbes Travel Guide is also grateful to the talented writers who contributed to this book.

Front Cover image: ©iStockphoto.com
All maps: Mapping Specialists

ISBN: 9781936010929
Manufactured in the USA
10 9 8 7 6 5 4 3 2 1

CONTENTS

SOUTH

Acknowledgments	2
Star Attractions	4
Star Ratings	5-7
Your Questions Answered	8
Top Hotels and Restaurants	9

ALABAMA

WELCOME TO ALABAMA	10
Northern Cities	12
Central Cities	15
Black Belt	24
Mobile	31
Gulf Coast Towns	32

ARKANSAS

WELCOME TO ARKANSAS	39
Ozarks	39
Ouachitas	45
Little Rock	49

KENTUCKY

WELCOME TO KENTUCKY	55
Louisville	56
Northern Kentucky River Region	66
The Bluegrass Region	71
Appalachians	81
Daniel Boone Country	85

LOUISIANA

WELCOME TO LOUISIANA	88
Sportsman's Paradise	88
Cajun Country	93
Baton Rouge	101
New Orleans	108
Greater New Orleans	148

MISSISSIPPI

WELCOME TO MISSISSIPPI	152
Delta	152
Jackson	155
Capital/River	160
Coastal	169

TENNESSEE

WELCOME TO TENNESSEE	176
West Tennessee	177
Nashville	188
Middle Tennessee	203
East Tennessee	208
Great Smoky Mountains National Park	223

INDEX	230
MAPS	262

STAR ATTRACTIONS

If you've been a reader of Mobil Travel Guide, you will have heard that this historic brand partnered in 2009 with another storied media name, Forbes, to create a new entity, Forbes Travel Guide. For more than 50 years, Mobil Travel Guide assisted travelers in making smart decisions about where to stay and dine when traveling. With this new partnership, our mission has not changed: We're committed to the same rigorous inspections of hotels, restaurants and spas—the most comprehensive in the industry with more than 500 standards tested at each property we visit—to help you cut through the clutter and make easy and informed decisions on where to spend your time and travel budget. Our team of anonymous inspectors are constantly on the road, sleeping in hotels, eating in restaurants and making spa appointments, evaluating those exacting standards to determine a property's rating.

What kinds of standards are we looking for when we visit a property? We're looking for more than just high-thread count sheets, pristine spa treatment rooms and white linen-topped tables. We look for service that's attentive, individualized and unforgettable. We note how long it takes to be greeted when you sit down at your table, or to be served when you order room service, or whether the hotel staff can confidently help you when you've forgotten that one essential item that will make or break your trip. Unlike any other travel ratings entity, we visit each place we rate, testing hundreds of attributes to compile our ratings, and our ratings cannot be bought or influenced. The Forbes Five Star rating is the most prestigious achievement in hospitality—while we rate more than 5,000 properties in the U.S., Canada, Hong Kong, Macau and Beijing, for 2011, we have awarded Five Star designations to only 54 hotels, 23 restaurants and 20 spas. When you travel with Forbes, you can travel with confidence, knowing that you'll get the very best experience, no matter who you are.

We understand the importance of making the most of your time. That's why the most trusted name in travel is now Forbes Travel Guide.

STAR RATED HOTELS

Whether you're looking for the ultimate in luxury or the best value for your travel budget, we have a hotel recommendation for you. To help you pinpoint properties that meet your needs, Forbes Travel Guide classifies each lodging by type according to the following characteristics:

★★★★★These exceptional properties provide a memorable experience through virtually flawless service and the finest of amenities. Staff are intuitive, engaging and passionate, and eagerly deliver service above and beyond the guests' expectations. The hotel was designed with the guest's comfort in mind, with particular attention paid to craftsmanship and quality of product. A Five-Star property is a destination unto itself.

★★★★These properties provide a distinctive setting, and a guest will find many interesting and inviting elements to enjoy throughout the property. Attention to detail is prominent throughout the property, from design concept to quality of products provided. Staff are accommodating and take pride in catering to the guest's specific needs throughout their stay.

★★★These well-appointed establishments have enhanced amenities that provide travelers with a strong sense of location, whether for style or function. They may have a distinguishing style and ambience in both the public spaces and guest rooms; or they may be more focused on functionality, providing guests with easy access to local events, meetings or tourism highlights.

Recommended: These hotels are considered clean, comfortable and reliable establishments that have expanded amenities, such as full-service restaurants.

For every property, we also provide pricing information. All prices quoted are accurate at the time of publication; however, prices cannot be guaranteed. Because rates can fluctuate, we list a pricing range rather than specific prices.

STAR RATED RESTAURANTS

Every restaurant in this book has been visited by Forbes Travel Guide's team of experts and comes highly recommended as an outstanding dining experience.

★★★★★Forbes Five-Star restaurants deliver a truly unique and distinctive dining experience. A Five-Star restaurant consistently provides exceptional food, superlative service and elegant décor. An emphasis is placed on originality and personalized, attentive and discreet service. Every detail that surrounds the experience is attended to by a warm and gracious dining room team.

★★★★These are exciting restaurants with often well-known chefs that feature creative and complex foods and emphasize various culinary techniques and a focus on seasonality. A highly-trained dining room staff provides refined personal service and attention.

★★★Three Star restaurants offer skillfully prepared food with a focus on a specific style or cuisine. The dining room staff provides warm and professional service in a comfortable atmosphere. The décor is well-coordinated with quality fixtures and decorative items, and promotes a comfortable ambience.

Recommended: These restaurants serve fresh food in a clean setting with efficient service. Value is considered in this category, as is family friendliness.

Because menu prices can fluctuate, we list a pricing range rather than specific prices. The pricing ranges are per diner, and assume that you order an appetizer or dessert, an entrée and one drink.

STAR RATED SPAS

Forbes Travel Guide's spa ratings are based on objective evalua-tions of more than 450 attributes. About half of these criteria assess basic expectations, such as staff courtesy, the technical proficien-cy and skill of the employees and whether the facility is clean and maintained properly. Several standards address issues that impact a guest's physical comfort and convenience, as well as the staff's ability to impart a sense of personalized service. Additional criteria measure the spa's ability to create a completely calming ambience.

★★★★★Stepping foot in a Five Star Spa will result in an exceptional experience with no detail overlooked. These properties wow their guests with extraordinary design and facilities, and uncompro-mising service. Expert staff cater to your every whim and pam-per you with the most advanced treatments and skin care lines available. These spas often offer exclusive treatments and may emphasize local elements.

★★★★Four Star spas provide a wonderful experience in an invit-ing and serene environment. A sense of personalized service is evident from the moment you check in and receive your robe and slippers. The guest's comfort is always of utmost concern to the well-trained staff.

★★★These spas offer well-appointed facilities with a full com-plement of staff to ensure that guests' needs are met. The spa facil ties include clean and appealing treatment rooms, changing areas and a welcoming reception desk.

YOUR QUESTIONS ANSWERED

WHAT'S THE BEST PLACE FOR A SOUTHERN TREAT?

A number of mouth-watering dishes are Southern traditions, from grits to fried green tomatoes. But the best Southern treat can be found at a stand in New Orleans's French Market. Café du Monde (*81039 Decatur St., New Orleans*) turns out sinfully good beignets, hot fried square doughnuts sprinkled with powered sugar, that are best paired with a café au lait. The best part is if you get a craving for these addictive goodies, the original café is open 24 hours a day, seven days a week.

WHEN IS THE BEST TIME TO VISIT THE SOUTH?

The South's reliably warm climate makes it a great destination to visit no matter what season it is. But be prepared for brutal humidity if you decide to travel there in the summer. The perk is that although you'll be sweating buckets, fewer tourists travel to the region during that time. Another factor to consider when timing your Southern vacation is hurricanes. In the Gulf Coast, hurricane season runs from June through November.

WHAT IS THE MOST HISTORIC CIVIL WAR SITE?

The site of the Union's first major victory during the Civil War, Fort Donelson National Battlefield and Cemetery (*www.nps.gov/fodo*) in Dover, Tenn., is famous for General Ulysses S. Grant's demand for "unconditional and immediate surrender" when Confederate General Simon B. Bucker proposed a truce. Nothing helped Grant so much during this four-day battle as weak generalship on the part of Confederate Commanders John B. Floyd and Gideon J. Pillow. Although the Confederates repelled an attack by federal ironclad gunboats, bad decisions by the Confederate leaders left them with no choice but to surrender. Thanks to Grant's victory at Fort Donelson, coupled with the fall of Fort Henry 10 days earlier, the Union had passageways to the heart of the South: the Tennessee and Cumberland rivers. In Grant, northerners had a new hero. His terse surrender message stirred their imaginations, and he was quickly dubbed "Unconditional Surrender" Grant.

Today the fort walls, outer defenses and river batteries still remain and are well-marked to give the story of the battle. A visitor center features a 10-minute slide program, a museum and touch exhibits. A six-mile, self-guided auto tour includes a visit to the fort, the cemetery where Civil War soldiers and veterans since then rest and the Dover Hotel, where Buckner surrendered. The park is open year-round, dawn to dusk.

TOP HOTELS AND RESTAURANTS

HOTELS

★★★★★FIVE STAR
The Hermitage Hotel
(*Nashville, Tennessee*)

★★★★FOUR STAR
Blackberry Farm
(*Walland, Tennessee*)

The Peabody Little Rock
(*Little Rock, Arkansas*)

The Peabody Memphis
(*Memphis, Tennessee*)

The Windsor Court Hotel
(*New Orleans, Louisiana*)

RESTAURANTS

★★★★FOUR STAR
The Barn At Blackberry Farm
(*Walland, Tennessee*)

Bayona
(*New Orleans, Louisiana*)

Capitol Grille
(*Nashville, Tennessee*)

Chez Philippe
(*Memphis, Tennessee*)

The Grill Room
(*New Orleans, Louisiana*)

WELCOME TO ALABAMA

IF YOU'VE NEVER BEEN TO ALABAMA, YOU'RE IN FOR A SURPRISE. It is a scenic, versatile place marked by sophisticated cities, diverse geography and Southern charm. From postcard-perfect beaches to the gentle

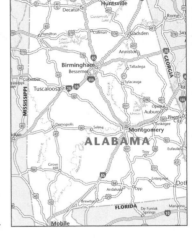

Appalachians, Alabama offers plenty of space for visitors to play outdoors, and its cities and towns chronicle the state's fascinating—if sometimes turbulent—history. Alabama's cultural offerings are as rich as anywhere else in the South: the state lays claim to the famed Alabama Shakespeare Festival, one of the nation's finest year-round theaters; the Birmingham Civil Rights Institute, a museum dedicated to civil-rights history; and countless art museums, musical venues and performing arts groups.

Alabama has the dubious honor of being the birthplace of both the Civil War and the civil-rights movement, separated by about 100 years. The order to fire on Fort Sumter—the first shots of the War Between the States—came in April 1861 from Confederate Gen. P.G.T. Beauregard in Montgomery. Alabama contributed between 65,000 and 100,000 troops to the South's efforts. (The white male population at the time was about 500,000.) The state did not see much fighting, and by the late 19th century, it was regaining its economic strength.

Nearly a century after the Civil War, a black seamstress named Rosa Parks refused to give up her bus seat to a white man, thereby sparking the Montgomery Bus Boycott that ignited the civil-rights movement, much of which played out on Alabama soil. Dr. Martin Luther King Jr. preached his first messages of nonviolence in a Montgomery church, and wrote his "Letter from Birmingham Jail," explaining the importance of street demonstrations to the movement.

Alabama preserves and tells its history with candor and compassion, but its historical legacy stretches beyond these events to quieter stories that bear telling. Helen Keller was born and raised in Tuscumbia, and visitors can see the water pump where her teacher, Anne Sullivan, finally broke through Keller's dark world and taught her how to communicate despite her inability to see, speak or hear. And W.C. Handy, a.k.a. "Father of the Blues," grew up

WHAT ARE THE BEST ATTRACTIONS IN ALABAMA?

CENTRAL CITIES
The main city—and the largest in the state—in this region is Birmingham, which is known for being the setting for the civil-rights movement. But it's also become an urban hot spot of great restaurants and cute boutiques.

BLACK BELT
The cities that make up middle Alabama have a rich history that dates back to the Civil War. The area is named for the thin layer of black topsoil that stretches through the region. Bone up on your history with visits to Selma and Montgomery.

MOBILE
For a dose of culture, visit Mobile, which teems with museums, gardens and other attractions. Don't miss the Mobile Museum of Art, the largest museum in the Gulf Coast.

GULF COAST TOWNS
Take a break from touring antebellum mansions and enjoy some sun and sand. Laying out on the Gulf Coast Towns that dot the area will make you forget you're in Alabama.

here, giving the South a powerful musical legacy.

Another of the state's important—and obvious—legacies is its link to sports. Bo Jackson, Hank Aaron, Willie Mays, Jesse Owens, Bobby Allison and many more sports icons perfected their swings, sprints and sacks in Alabama. Birmingham's Alabama Sports Hall of Fame celebrates stars from many different games, but football is king here, fueled by a healthy rivalry between Auburn University's Tigers and the University of Alabama's Crimson Tide. Certainly their annual clashes attract many visitors, but even after the season ends, the state has another unique sports draw: the Robert Trent Jones Trail, the largest golf construction project ever undertaken. The trail provides 378 holes stretching over more than 100 miles of golf.

So no matter what your pleasure, chances are you'll find it in the Heart of Dixie. History, culture, gorgeous scenery and plenty of places to play—it's all here.

NORTHERN CITIES

In northern Alabama, two small cities beckon travelers. Since Huntsville sits at the foot of a mountain, you might think tourists flock here for the scenery. Instead, they come for space exploration, thanks to NASA's Space and Rocket Center, which is headquartered here. Aspiring astronauts (or just curious earth-bound folks) head to Huntsville for Space Camp, where kids and families learn what it takes to cruise the universe. But rockets aren't the only attraction. Huntsville is rich in Civil War history, natural beauty and golf courses.

Head about 70 miles west of Huntsville to visit another small city that highlights the big names that have come out of Alabama. Tuscumbia is home to the Alabama Music Hall of Fame, which features natives such as Hank Williams and Lionel Richie, and Ivy Green, the birthplace of Helen Keller.

WHAT TO SEE

HUNTSVILLE
ALABAMA CONSTITUTION VILLAGE
109 Gates Ave., Huntsville, 256-564-8100; www.earlyworks.com

This re-created complex of buildings commemorates Alabama's entry into the Union at the 1819 Constitutional Convention. The village offers craft demonstrations and activities, and guides in period dress.

Admission: adults $10, seniors and youth $8, toddlers $4. March-October, Tuesday-Saturday 10 a.m.-4 p.m.

BURRITT MUSEUM & PARK
3101 Burritt Drive, Huntsville, 256-536-2882; www.burrittonthemountain.com

The 167-acre park atop Round Top Mountain offers a little something for everyone. The former home of eccentric Dr. William Henry Burritt, the mansion houses rotating exhibits, most of which have regional or local themes. The historic park has restored 19th-century buildings—including a blacksmith shop and a smokehouse—and volunteers in period dress. You'll also find nature trails, gardens and a panoramic view of the city.

Admission: adults $7, seniors and military $6, children 13-17 $5, children 3-12 $4, children under 2 free. April-October, Tuesday-Saturday 9 a.m.-5 p.m., Sunday 9 a.m.-noon; November-March, Tuesday-Saturday 10 a.m.-4 p.m., Sunday 9 a.m.-noon.

HUNTSVILLE DEPOT
320 Church St., Huntsville, 256-564-8100, 800-678-1819; www.earlyworks.com

Opened in 1860 as a "passenger house" and eastern division headquarters for the Memphis & Charleston Railroad Company, the Huntsville Depot was captured by Union troops and used as a prison; Civil War graffiti is still there. Kids can climb aboard real trains and Huntsville's first ladder truck.

Admission: adults $10, seniors and youth $8, toddlers $4. March-December, Tuesday-Saturday 10 a.m.-4 p.m.

HUNTSVILLE MUSEUM OF ART
300 Church St., Huntsville, 256-535-4350; www.hsvmuseum.org

Named one of the state's top 10 destinations by the Alabama Bureau of Tourism

HIGHLIGHT

WHAT ARE THE TOP THINGS TO DO IN THE NORTHERN CITIES?

SEE LOCAL ARTISTS AT THE HUNTSVILLE MUSEUM OF ART
This art museum, tucked in Big Spring International Park, focuses on the works of Southern artists. It's also known for its traveling exhibits.

EXPLORE THE TWICKENHAM HISTORIC DISTRICT
Walk around this historic district to see Alabama's largest concentration of antebellum architecture. You'll get a chance to see authentic Southern estates that look straight out of the movies.

BLAST OFF AT THE U.S. SPACE AND ROCKET CENTER
If you never got to attend space camp as a child, here's your chance. Go on the Space Spot ride, which simulates a rocket launch and shoots you into the air. Then tour the Marshall Space Flight Center, where real astronauts get their training.

CHECK OUT THE ALABAMA MUSIC HALL OF FAME
This Hall of Fame puts the spotlight on Alabama musicians in all genres, from Lionel Richie to Hank Williams Jr. If you get inspired from the music memorabilia, test your vocal chops in the onsite recording studio.

and Travel, the museum has seven galleries, which host traveling exhibits and display work from the museum's own collection. Tours, lectures, concerts and films round out the offerings.

Admission: adults $7, seniors, military and students $6, children 6-11 $3, children under 6 free. Tuesday-Wednesday, Thursday 10 a.m.-8 p.m., Friday-Saturday 10 a.m.-5 p.m., Sunday 1-5 p.m.

MONTE SANO STATE PARK
5105 Nolan Ave., Huntsville, 256-534-3757; www.dcnr.state.al.us

Spanish for "mountain of health," Monte Sano reaches 1,600 feet above sea level. Hiking trails, picnicking, a playground, concessions, camping, cabins and an amphitheater keep the park humming.
Daily.

TWICKENHAM HISTORIC DISTRICT
500 Church St., Huntsville, 256-551-2230; www.huntsville.org

A living museum of antebellum architecture, the district contains Alabama's largest concentration of prewar houses. Several of the homes are occupied by descendants of original builders or owners.
Daily.

SPECIAL EVENTS

BIG SPRING JAM

Big Spring International Park, 700 Monroe St., Huntsville, 256-533-1953;
www.bigspringjam.org
Three days, five stages, more than 80 musical acts—this annual festival has been taking place in Huntsville for two decades and everyone from Wynonna Judd to Lynyrd Skynyrd to Willie Nelson has performed for it. More than 200,000 fans come to enjoy the music. Late summer/early fall.

PANOPLY ARTS FESTIVAL

Big Spring International Park, 700 Monroe St., Huntsville, 256-519-2787;
www.panoply.org
A haven for art lovers of all kinds, the festival showcases work by visual artists, dancers, musicians and actors, and has become one of the biggest art events in the South in the last ten-plus years. During the three-day event, enjoy listening to music (including gospel, bluegrass and jazz), musical theater and hands-on children's activities, in addition to picking up great pieces of art to take home with you. You can also participate in various art workshops and there are several competitions, including a playwright competition and talent contest (sort of a Panoply's Got Talent, if you will). The Global Village highlights traditions from around the world.
Last weekend of April.

U.S. SPACE AND ROCKET CENTER
1 Tranquility Base, Huntsville, 256-837-3400, 800-637-7223; www.spacecamp.com

If you've ever dreamed of climbing aboard a rocket and blasting off, this is the place for you. Experience a rocket launch in Space Spot, a simulated ride that shoots riders 140 feet in the air in 2.5 seconds. Visit the Mars exhibit, where you can climb Olympus Mons, the tallest volcano in the solar system. In the museum, check out the Apollo capsule and space shuttle objects returned from orbit. The Omnimax Theater, with a tilted dome screen, seats 280 and shows 45-minute space shuttle and science flicks filmed by astronauts. NASA bus tours take visitors through Marshall Space Flight Center, featuring mission control, space station construction and the tank where astronauts simulate weightlessness. The U.S. Space Camp offers programs for children fourth grade and up, families and even corporate executives.
Daily 9 a.m.-5 p.m.

VON BRAUN CENTER
700 Monroe St., Huntsville, 256-533-1953; www.vonbrauncenter.com

This is the largest multipurpose complex in northern Alabama, named for noted space pioneer Dr. Wernher von Braun. But you won't find space-related offerings here; the center hosts concerts, touring Broadway performances, ballets and other shows.

TUSCUMBIA
ALABAMA MUSIC HALL OF FAME
617 Highway 72 W., Tuscumbia, 256-381-4417, 800-239-2643; www.alamhof.org

Rock on, Alabama: The Hall of Fame honors the contributions Alabamians have made to music of all genres—rock, rhythm and blues, gospel, contemporary and country music. Exhibits celebrate the accomplishments of performers such as Hank Williams, also Nat King Cole and Lionel Richie. Aspiring musicians can lay down a track or make a video at the recording studio.

Admission: adults $8, seniors and students $7, children 6-12 $5, children under 5 free. Monday-Saturday 9 a.m.-5 p.m., Sunday 1-5 p.m.

IVY GREEN
300 W. North Commons, Tuscumbia, 256-383-4066; www.helenkellerbirthplace.org

Helen Keller was born here in 1880. Deaf and blind from the age of 19 months, she learned to sign her first words at the water pump out back from her teacher Annie Sullivan. The play *The Miracle Worker* captures the turbulent and eventually triumphant relationship between Sullivan and Keller.

Admission: adults $6, seniors $5, children 5-18 $2, children under 5 free. Monday-Saturday 8:30 a.m.-4 p.m.

WHERE TO STAY

★★★HUNTSVILLE MARRIOTT
5 Tranquility Base, Huntsville, 256-830-2222; www.marriott.com

Rooms at this hotel are specifically designed for the business traveler, with large desks and high-speed Internet. But families will like its convenient location, since the Space and Rocket Museum is next door and hiking and biking trails abound nearby. Ask for one of the tower rooms so little ones can get a view of the Space Center.

290 rooms. Restaurant, bar. Business center. $61-150

CENTRAL CITIES

Alabama's largest city, Birmingham has found a way to preserve its history and still give off an air of urban sophistication—a combination that appeals to visitors and residents alike. Beautiful city streets, stylish boutiques and restaurants, and diverse cultural attractions make Birmingham a must-see stop on any trek through central Alabama.

Founded in 1871 and named for a British industrial city, Birmingham started out as a center of steel production. The late 19th century brought disease and a nationwide financial panic that almost ruined Birmingham, but the city boomed in the early years of the 20th century. Just as Birmingham was enjoying a streak of prosperity after the end of World War I, a secret white supremacist group, the Ku Klux Klan, garnered power, leading to violence against African-American citizens that lasted for decades.

Not surprisingly, Birmingham served as the setting for many battles during the civil-rights movement, including of course, Dr. Martin Luther King Jr.'s "Letter from Birmingham Jail," written April 16, 1963. In it, King explains why the demonstrations in the streets of Birmingham and other Southern cities were crucial to the fight for civil rights for African-Americans. Several months later, on September 15, 1963, a member of the Ku Klux Klan bombed Birmingham's 16th Street Baptist Church, killing four girls. The emotional response to the bombing galvanized the movement and helped lead to the passage of the 1964 Civil Rights Act.

By the 1970s, Birmingham was booming again, and in 1979, its citizens elected the city's first black mayor, Dr. Richard Arrington, Jr. Today, soak up Birmingham's history by day, and by night, swing by Five Points South, Birmingham's entertainment district, where you'll find great people-watching, fine dining and clubs to satisfy even the pickiest music aficionados.

NASCAR fans should head 55 miles west to Talladega, famous for its namesake speedway. If the great outdoors is more your speed, check out Logan Martin Lake to the northwest of Talladega and Talladega National Forest to the east.

WHAT TO SEE

BIRMINGHAM
ALABAMA SPORTS HALL OF FAME MUSEUM
2150 Richard Arrington Jr. Blvd. N., Birmingham, 205-323-6665; www.ashof.org
The museum celebrates sports heroes from the Heart of Dixie, including Willie Mays, Carl Lewis and Jesse Owens. See vintage equipment and uniforms, awards and photographs, and interactive kiosks and life-sized sculptures.
Admission: adults $5, seniors $4, students $3. Monday-Saturday 9 a.m.-5 p.m., Sunday 1-5 p.m.

ARLINGTON ANTEBELLUM HOME AND GARDENS
331 Cotton Ave. S.W., Birmingham, 205-780-5656; www.birminghamal.gov
Visit Birmingham's last-remaining antebellum house in the Greek Revival style, built circa 1850 on a sloping hill in Elyton. The oak and magnolia trees that surround the house suggest that Rhett Butler might stroll by at any minute.
Admission: adults $5, students $3. Tuesday-Saturday 10 a.m.-4 p.m., Sunday 1-4 p.m.

BIRMINGHAM BOTANICAL GARDENS
2612 Lane Park Road, Birmingham, 205-414-3900; www.bbgardens.org
Much more than just flowers, the botanical gardens offer tours, a garden maintained by the green thumbs at *Southern Living* magazine and a full calendar of events and classes. Don't miss the Japanese Garden, with its bonsai collection and authentic Japanese teahouse. And if you get hungry, there's a restaurant on the grounds.
Daily dusk-dawn.

BIRMINGHAM CIVIL RIGHTS INSTITUTE
520 16th St. N., Birmingham, 205-328-9696, 866-328-9696; www.bcri.org
Exhibits and multimedia presentations portray the struggle for civil rights in Birmingham and across the nation from the 1920s to the present. "The March" exhibit in the Movement Gallery is particularly poignant as it uses audio and video to examine the March on Washington.
Admission: adults $11, seniors and students $5, children 4-12 $3. Tuesday-Saturday 10 a.m.-5 p.m., Sunday 1-5 p.m.

HIGHLIGHTS

WHAT ARE THE TOP THINGS TO DO IN THE CENTRAL CITIES?

VISIT THE BIRMINGHAM CIVIL RIGHTS INSTITUTE
Find out how the fight for civil rights started on the streets of Birmingham. The museum's multimedia exhibits illustrate the struggle from the days of segregation to today's global human-rights issues.

SEE MASTERPIECES AT THE BIRMINGHAM MUSEUM OF ART
One of the best museums in the South sits in the middle of Birmingham's cultural district. And it's also free. Check out its vast collection of Asian art and its gallery devoted to African-American artists.

ZIP OVER TO BIRMINGHAM ZOO
Kids love watching the red panda and komodo dragon at this zoo. But they aren't the only ones; more than a half million people visit each year, making it the state's most popular destination.

GEEK OUT AT THE MCWANE SCIENCE CENTER
There's a five-story IMAX here, but before you catch a flick, check out the collection of dinosaur fossils found in Alabama and get up close to the sea animals at the aquarium, where you can pet sharks and rays.

RACE OVER TO TALLADEGA SUPERSPEEDWAY
If you have a need for speed, head to this track, which is said to be one of the world's fastest. Right next door is the International Motorsports Hall of Fame.

BIRMINGHAM-JEFFERSON CONVENTION COMPLEX
2100 Richard Arrington Jr. Blvd., Birmingham, 205-458-8400; www.bjcc.org
This complex covers seven square blocks and hosts events such as hunting expos, classic theatrical performances and sports tournaments. The center contains 220,000 square feet of exhibition space, a 3,000-seat concert hall, a 1,000-seat theater and an 18,000-seat coliseum.

BIRMINGHAM MUSEUM OF ART
2000 Rev. Abraham Woods Jr. Blvd., Birmingham, 205-254-2565; www.artsbma.org
Celebrated for its diverse collections, the museum is home to some 24,000 objects from almost every era of artistic production across the globe. Don't miss its collection of Asian art, including a 15th-century temple mural from China; its decorative arts, including the largest collection of Wedgwood outside of England; and the historical and contemporary work from Native American artists.
Tuesday-Saturday 10 a.m.-5 p.m., Sunday noon-5 p.m.

HIGHLIGHT

WHAT'S THE BEST WAY TO TOUR DOWNTOWN BIRMINGHAM?

Birmingham, home of the Civil Rights Institute, offers a powerful lesson about African-American history and culture.

Start at the **Historical Fourth Avenue Visitor Center** *(319 17th St. N., 205-328-1850)*, where you can pick up a map or take a guided tour of the historic African-American business district.

Across the street from the visitor center is the Alabama Jazz Hall of Fame, located within the historic **Carver Theater** *(1631 Fourth Ave. N., 205-254-2731)*. Exhibits cover the history of jazz and celebrate such artists as Dinah Washington, Nat King Cole, Duke Ellington and W.C. Handy, among others. The theater also hosts live performances. On the other side of the visitor center, the **Alabama Theater** *(1817 Third Ave. N.)* has been restored to its 1920s splendor and is now a cinema.

Head west along Third Avenue one block to **La Vase** *(328 16th St. N., 205-801-5165)*, a restaurant that serves hearty home-style soul food. After your meal, trek north up 16th Street three blocks to Kelly Ingram Park, the scene of civil-rights clashes in the 1950s and 1960s.

The **Birmingham Civil Rights Institute** *(520 16th St., 205-328-9696)*, across the street from the park, is the city's premier attraction. A short film introduces the city's history, and vintage footage illustrates the Jim Crow era and the development of the civil-rights movement. Exhibits emphasize Birmingham's role—positive and negative—in the civil-rights movement, and the bookshop has a good selection of African-American history and heritage titles.

Cross Sixth Avenue to reach the **16th Street Baptist Church** *(1530 Sixth Ave. N., 205-251-9402)*, where four girls were killed when a Ku Klux Klan member bombed the church in 1963. The rebuilt church hosts tens of thousands of visitors each year.

BIRMINGHAM ZOO

2630 Cahaba Road, Birmingham, 205-879-0409; www.birminghamzoo.com

Where else in Alabama can you see an Indo-Chinese tiger, a red panda and a host of sea lions within a few acres of one another? Check them out, along with nearly 800 other animals, at one of the state's most popular attractions.

Admission: adults $12, seniors and children 2-12 $7, children under 2 free. Daily 9 a.m.-5 p.m.

MCWANE SCIENCE CENTER

200 19th St. N., Birmingham, 205-714-8300; www.mcwane.org

A natural history museum on the slopes of Red Mountain, the McWane Science Center offers plenty of adventure: explore the universe at the Challenger Learning Center, catch a flick on the five-story IMAX screen or visit with sea creatures at the center's World of Water Aquarium. Don't miss the walkway carved into the face of the mountain above the expressway, where you'll see more than 150 million years of geologic history. You also can do some picnicking there.

Admission: adults $11, seniors and children 2-12 $8, children under 2 free. September-May, Monday-Friday 9 a.m.-5 p.m., Saturday 10 a.m.-6 p.m., Sunday noon-6 p.m.; June-August, Monday-Saturday 10 a.m.-6 p.m., Sunday noon-6 p.m.

OAK MOUNTAIN STATE PARK
200 Terrace Drive, Pelham, 205-620-2520; www.alapark.com
Peavine Falls and Gorge and two lakes sit amid 9,940 acres of the state's most rugged mountains. Enthusiasts cite Oak Mountain as one of the state's best places to mountain bike. Other activities include fishing, boating, hiking, backpacking, bridle trails, golf, tennis, picnicking, camping, cabins and a demonstration farm.
Admission: adults $2, seniors and children $1. Daily dawn-dusk.

RICKWOOD CAVERNS STATE PARK
370 Rickwood Park Road, Warrior, 205-647-9692; www.dcnr.state.al.us
Tour the "miracle mile," a stretch of colorful underground caverns that reveals 260-year-old limestone foundations. The 380-acre park also boasts an Olympic-sized swimming pool, hiking trails, a miniature train ride, carpet golf, a gift shop, concessions, picnic areas and camp sites.
Admission: $1, children under 6 free. Daily dawn-dusk.

RUFFNER MOUNTAIN NATURE CENTER
1214-81st St. S., Birmingham, 205-833-8264; www.ruffnermountain.org
A 1,011-acre natural retreat from the bustle of Birmingham, the mountain offers 11 miles of hiking trails. Learn about the mountain's biology, geology and history at the center and then venture out to see Alabama wildlife.
Tuesday-Saturday 9 a.m.-5 p.m., Sunday 1-5 p.m.

SLOSS FURNACES NATIONAL HISTORIC LANDMARK
20 32nd St. N., Birmingham, 205-324-1911; www.slossfurnaces.com
Don't let the name fool you: this industrial museum offers more than a glimpse at old furnaces. Here you'll find captivating stories about the economic and social growth of the South. But beware: paranormal investigators have suggested that it is one of nation's most haunted places, so watch out for the ghosts of old workers.
Tuesday-Friday 10 a.m.-4 p.m., Sunday noon-4 p.m.

SOUTHERN MUSEUM OF FLIGHT/ALABAMA AVIATION HALL OF FAME
4343 73rd St. N., Birmingham, 205-833-8226; www.southernmuseumofflight.org
View a full-size Wright Flyer replica, try your hand at flying in two U.S. Air Force fighter jet cockpit simulators and wander through flight-related memorabilia.
Admission: adults $5, seniors and students $4, military and children under 4 free. Tuesday-Saturday 9:30 a.m.-4:30 p.m.

VULCAN
1701 Valley View Drive, Birmingham, 205-933-1409; www.visitvulcan.com
Vulcan, Roman god of fire and forge and the legendary inventor of smithing and metalworking, stands as a monument to the city's iron industry atop Red Mountain. Since 1939, he has held a lighted torch aloft over the city from his perch on a 124-foot pedestal, making him the largest cast-iron statue in the world. A glass-enclosed elevator takes passengers to an observation deck. Vulcan's torch shines bright red for 24 hours after a traffic fatality in the city.
Admission: adults $6, seniors $5, children 5-12 $4, children under 5 free. Park: Daily 7 a.m.-10 p.m. Museum: Monday-Saturday 10 a.m.-6 p.m., Sunday 1-6 p.m.

HIGHLIGHTS

WHAT ARE SOME OF ALABAMA'S BEST PARKS?

BUCK'S POCKET STATE PARK
393 County Road 174, Guntersville, 256-659-2000; www.dcnr.state.al.us
A secluded natural pocket of the Appalachian mountain chain, this park offers breathtaking vistas. Fishing, a boat launch, hiking trails, picnic facilities, a playground, camping and a visitor center are all available at the park.
Daily dawn-dusk.

DESOTO STATE PARK
13883 County Road 89, Fort Payne, 256-845-5380; www.desotostatepark.com
This 3,502-acre park includes Lookout Mountain, Little River Canyon and DeSoto Falls and Lake. Twenty miles of hiking trails cross the mountaintop and a scenic drive skirts the canyon. Enjoy the wildflowers and waterfalls, both in abundance. The park also offers a swimming pool, a bathhouse, fishing, a hiking trail, tennis, a playground, picnicking, a restaurant, a country store, a resort inn, a nature center, camping and cabins.
Daily dawn-dusk.

EUFAULA NATIONAL WILDLIFE REFUGE
509 Old Highway 165, Eufaula, 334-687-4065; www.eufaula.fws.gov
Stretching from Alabama to Georgia, the refuge offers a feeding and resting area for waterfowl migrating between the Tennessee Valley and the Gulf Coast. See ducks, geese, egrets and herons—along with more than 275 other bird species. The grounds also boast an observation tower, a nature trail, hunting, and great photo ops.
Daily dawn-dusk.

HURRICANE CREEK PARK
22600 U.S. Highway 31, Vinemont, 256-734-2125;
www.hurricanecreek.homestead.com
Come see the park's 500-foot-deep gorge with an observation platform, trail over the swinging bridge, unusual rock formations, earthquake fault and waterfalls. Picnic tables are available if you want to make a day of it.
Admission: adults $3, children $2.50. Wednesday-Friday noon-5 p.m., Saturday-Sunday 9 a.m.-5 p.m.

LAKE GUNTERSVILLE STATE PARK
Highway 227, Guntersville, 256-571-5455, 800-548-4553; www.dcnr.state.al.us
Overlooking the Guntersville Reservoir, the 6,000-acre park is a nature lover's dream. A beach, waterskiing, a fishing center, boating, hiking, bicycling, golf, tennis, nature programs, picnicking, camping, a playground, a restaurant, chalets, lakeside cottages and a resort inn on Taylor Mountain keep the park busy.
Daily dawn-dusk.

NOCCALULA FALLS PARK

1500 Noccalula Road, Gadsden,
256-549-4663;
www.gadsden-etowahtourismboard.com
This 100-foot waterfall comes with a tale
of star-crossed love: according to local
legend, an Indian chief's daughter, named
Noccalula, leaped to her death instead
of betraying her true love and marrying
a man of her father's choosing. Lookout
Mountain Parkway, a scenic drive that
stretches all the way to Chattanooga,
originates here. A swimming pool, a
bathhouse, nature and hiking trails,
miniature golf, a picnic area, a playground, camping, a petting zoo and an
animal habitat house are all on offer.
There's also a pioneer homestead and
museum and botanical gardens.
Daily.

POINT MALLARD PARK

2901 Point Mallard Drive, Decatur,
256-341-4900, 800-350-3000;
www.pointmallardpark.com
On the Tennessee River, this 500-acre
park offers plenty of family fun. It
includes a swimming pool, wave pool,
water slide, beach, hiking and biking
trails, an 18-hole golf course, tennis
courts, an indoor ice rink, camping and a
recreation center.
Daily.

WHEELER NATIONAL WILDLIFE REFUGE

2700 Refuge Headquarters Road, Decatur,
256-353-7243; wheeler.fws.gov
At 34,500 acres, this is Alabama's oldest
and largest wildlife refuge. It's a wintering
ground for waterfowl and home to
numerous species of animal and plant
life. Fishing, boating, picnicking, bird
study and photography are available here.
There's a visitor center and Waterfowl
Observation Building as well.
March-September,   Tuesday-Saturday   9
a.m.-4 p.m.; October-February, daily 9
a.m.-5 p.m.

WILLIAM B. BANKHEAD NATIONAL FOREST

Highway 278, Double Springs, 205-489-
5111; www.fs.fed.us/r8/alabama
A place primed for adventure, the
180,000 acres contain bubbling streams,
diverse wildlife and plenty of space to
wander. The forest's crown jewel is Sipsey
Wilderness, often called the "Land of a
Thousand Waterfalls." Trek through the
Sipsey to find the state's last-remaining
stand of old-growth hardwood. There is
also swimming, fishing, boating, hiking
and horseback riding available.
Daily dawn-dusk.

SPECIAL EVENT

BIRMINGHAM INTERNATIONAL FESTIVAL

205 20th St. N., Birmingham, 205-252-7652; www.bic-al.org

Each year, the Birmingham International Festival highlights the culture of a different country to promote education as well as business and trade relationships between Alabama and the selected country. A party early in the year kicks off a series of events to take place in the months to follow, which includes a trade expo, conferences, art exhibits, lectures and a black-tie dinner. The free educational programs bring musicians, performers and storytellers to Alabama schools.

February-May.

TALLADEGA
CHEAHA STATE PARK
19644 Highway 281, Delta, 256-488-5111; www.dcnr.state.al.us

Visit the observation tower at the top of Mount Cheaha, the state's highest point at 2,407 feet. Nearly 2,800 acres of rugged forest country surround the mountain. But you may want to stick to the swimming in Lake Cheaha.

Daily dawn-dusk.

INTERNATIONAL MOTORSPORTS HALL OF FAME
3198 Speedway Blvd., Talladega, 256-362-5002; www.motorsportshalloffame.com

This is the official motor sports hall of fame, with memorabilia and displays of more than 100 vehicles. Try the racecar simulator and pick up a souvenir at the gift shop for the NASCAR fan in your family. The annual hall of fame induction ceremony takes place in late April.

Admission: adults $10, children 7-17 $5, children under 7 free. Daily 9 a.m.-5 p.m.

SILK STOCKING DISTRICT
25 W. 11th St., Talladega, 256-761-2108

Stroll by antebellum and turn-of-the-century houses along tree-lined streets. Talladega Square, in the heart of town, dates to 1834 and includes the renovated Talladega County Courthouse, the oldest courthouse in continuous use in Alabama.

TALLADEGA NATIONAL FOREST
Forest Supervisor, 2946 Chestnut St., Montgomery, 256-362-2909; www.fs.fed.us

On the Southern edge of the Appalachian Mountains, this forest comprises more than 360,000 acres of beauty. The forest has high ridges with spectacular views of wooded valleys, waterfalls and streams. There's lake swimming, fishing and hiking trails, including the 100-mile Pinhoti National Recreation Trail, a national byway extending from Highway 78 to Cheaha State Park.

Daily dawn-dusk.

TALLADEGA SUPERSPEEDWAY

5200 Speedway Blvd., Eastaboga, 256-362-5002, 877-462-3342;
www.talladegasuperspeedway.com

Race mavericks say this is one of the world's fastest speedways, with 33-degree banks in the turns. Stock-car races include the EA Sports 500, Aaron's 499, and Aaron's 312.
Ticket prices vary. Daily 8 a.m.-4 p.m.

WHERE TO STAY

★★★HAMPTON INN & SUITES BIRMINGHAM-DOWNTOWN-TUTWILER

2021 Park Place N., Birmingham, 205-322-2100, 877-999-3223; hamptoninn.hilton.com

The rooms in this comfortable hotel are big (choose between rooms with one king-sized bed or two queens) and pretty simple, with mahogany furniture and neutral colors on the walls, rugs and linens. Amenities include 32-inch TVs, DVD players and plush duvets. Each room has a different layout, but all have a view overlooking the city. Since the hotel is in the middle of downtown, you're near golfing and local attractions such as the Civil Rights Institute and the Alabama Sports Hall of Fame.

149 rooms. Restaurant, bar. Complimentary breakfast. Business center. Fitness center. $251-350

★★★HILTON BIRMINGHAM PERIMETER PARK

8 Perimeter Park S., Birmingham, 205-967-2700, 800-774-1500; www.hilton.com

Located in an up-and-coming business and entertainment area, this large hotel is near Birmingham's downtown cultural and corporate destinations, making it an ideal property for business travelers. The rooms are warm with shades of beige, olive and mustard and mahogany furniture. Among the amenities in the attractive rooms are work desks, dual phone lines and wireless Internet access. If you want a break from the business part of your trip, a hotel shuttle will drive you around to nearby attractions.

205 rooms. Restaurant, bar. Business center. Fitness center. Pool. $61-150

★★★MARRIOTT BIRMINGHAM

3590 Grandview Parkway, Birmingham, 205-968-3775, 800-228-9290; www.marriott.com

A mix of cozy and contemporary furnishings gives this hotel, just off Highway 280, an inviting and comfortable feel. Friendly staff, a huge array of amenities and a location close to many business headquarters and entertainment options make the Marriott a prime choice. Aside from the convenient location, business travelers will particularly like the large in-room work areas, the high-speed WiFi and the 24-hour business center.

295 rooms. Restaurant, bar. Business center. Fitness Center. Pool. $151-250

★★★SHERATON BIRMINGHAM HOTEL

2101 Richard Arrington Jr. Blvd. N., Birmingham, 205-324-5000, 800-325-3535;
www.sheraton.com

Located in downtown Birmingham, this hotel is a short stroll on the skywalk to the convention center, which makes the Sheraton Birmingham a great pick for conventioneers. But it's also close to fun spots such as the Birmingham Zoo, the Birmingham Museum of Art and the Five Points South historical district, which has tons of excellent restaurants. Inside the hotel, you'll find homey rooms done up in dark red, browns and tans. There's also an indoor heated pool, in case you want a quick break from the convention.

770 rooms. Restaurant, bar. Business center. Fitness center. Pool. $151-250

★★★THE WYNFREY HOTEL

1000 Riverchase Galleria, Birmingham, 205-987-1600, 800-996-3739; www.wynfrey.com

The Wynfrey Hotel is one of Birmingham's best lodging options. Located on the edge of the city, this gracious hotel combines Southern hospitality with European panache. The rooms and suites offer comfort and style, as curtains and bedding offer subtle ivory floral patterns that contrast with the dark wood furniture. The hotel is a favorite destination of shoppers because it's connected to the city's renowned Riverchase Galleria, which boasts more than 200 stores. After a day of bargain hunting, guests retire to the Spa Japonika or the rooftop pool to recharge and relax, or enjoy a meal at one of the hotel's three restaurants.

329 rooms. Restaurant, bar. Business center. Fitness center. Pool. Spa. $151-250

WHERE TO EAT

★★★HIGHLANDS

2011 11th Ave. S., Birmingham, 205-939-1400; www.highlandsbarandgrill.com

This French bistro has been one of Birmingham's premier restaurants for many years. The food has a Southern emphasis, which has become the chef's signature style. The duck two ways is particularly tasty, served with pearl onions, local turnips and sweet peas in a warm sherry sauce. For dessert, stick to the sweet Southern classics, like the hoe cakes with sorghum brown butter and bourbon ice cream.

French. Dinner. Closed Sunday-Monday. $36-85

BLACK BELT

The area in the middle of Alabama is called the Black Belt for its rich black soil. The Black Belt is dotted with towns big and small, and all of them have a history as rich as its soil. Known as the birthplace of the Civil War and civil rights, Montgomery is not just Alabama's state capital; it is a city that holds history important to the entire nation. It served as the Confederacy's first capital, from which Confederate leaders sent the "Fire on Fort Sumter" telegram that began the Civil War. About 100 years later, when black seamstress Rosa Parks refused to give up her bus seat to a white man, Montgomery again found itself embroiled in battle, this time for civil rights.

About 50 miles west is another Black Belt city that played a large role in the civil-rights movement: Selma. High on a bluff above the Alabama River, Selma has had a front-row seat to some of American history's most tumultuous battles. During the Civil War, Selma was one of the Confederacy's prime military manufacturing centers, which made it a target for Union armies. The city fell on April 2, 1865, during a bloody siege by Union forces, which destroyed Selma's arsenal and factories, along with much of the city. With defeat came an end to the era of wealthy plantation owners and leisurely living.

One hundred years after Selma was captured by Union forces, it was entangled in another battle. On March 7, 1965, nearly 600 African-American residents of Selma marched toward Montgomery. In the weeks before the protest, discrimination and intimidation had

HIGHLIGHT

WHAT ARE THE TOP THINGS TO DO IN THE BLACK BELT AREA?

HAVE A MOMENT OF SILENCE AT THE CIVIL RIGHTS MEMORIAL

The simple, elegant black granite Civil Rights Memorial honors those who died in the fight for civil rights. Its curved wall quotes King: "… until justice rolls down like waters and righteousness like a mighty stream."

GO BACK IN TIME AT OLD ALABAMA TOWN

Walk through this restored 19th-century village, which spans six blocks. The log cabin and schoolhouse show you what life was like back then. Catch demonstrations at the old-time drug store and print shop.

VISIT DEXTER AVENUE KING MEMORIAL BAPTIST CHURCH

Tour the church where Dr. Martin Luther King Jr. began a movement. Pastor King first preached from its pulpit and also organized the Montgomery bus boycott from the church.

PERUSE THE NATIONAL VOTING RIGHTS MUSEUM AND INSTITUTE

This museum documents America's tumultuous history with voting rights. Its location is key: it's near the Edmund Pettus Bridge, where civil-rights marchers were attacked by lawmen on Bloody Sunday.

TAKE SOME PICTURES AT THE FIRST WHITEHOUSE OF THE CONFEDERACY

This isn't the Whitehouse at 1600 Pennsylvania Avenue. During the Civil War, Confederate President Jefferson Davis set up camp at this mansion, which still has period furnishings.

GO TO THE TUSKEGEE INSTITUTE NATIONAL HISTORIC SITE

Originally a school for black teachers, this site pays homage to the visionaries who started it all. Visit the home of Booker T. Washington, the school's founder, and the George Washington Carver Museum, which honors one of its most prestigious teachers.

prevented much of Selma's black population from registering to vote, and the marchers hoped Gov. George Wallace would take notice of their plight when they arrived in the state's capital. Instead, Wallace declared the march a threat to public safety, and the marchers only made it as far as Selma's Edmund Pettus Bridge before they were driven back into town by police officers with clubs, whips and tear gas. This violence gave the day its name, "Bloody Sunday." Marchers, led by Dr. Martin Luther King Jr., tried again unsuccessfully two days later. They finally made it to Montgomery on their third attempt.

About 40 miles east of Montgomery is Tuskegee, a town that has witnessed great accomplishments by African-Americans. In 1881, Booker T. Washington founded the Tuskegee Normal School for Colored Teachers, which eventually became the Tuskegee Institute and then Tuskegee University. One of the institute's most famous instructors, George Washington Carver taught former slaves how to farm and be self-sufficient. In the early 1940s, the town's famous Tuskegee Airmen became America's first black military airmen.

WHAT TO SEE

MONTGOMERY
ALABAMA DEPARTMENT OF ARCHIVES AND HISTORY
624 Washington Ave., Montgomery, 334-242-4435; www.archives.state.al.us
This place houses a historical museum and genealogical research facilities. Artifact collections include exhibits on the 19th century, the military and early Native American pottery. It also has an interactive children's gallery.
Monday-Friday 8:30 a.m.-4:30 p.m.

ALABAMA SHAKESPEARE FESTIVAL
1 Festival Drive, Montgomery, 334-271-5353, 800-841-4273; www.asf.net
What started as a six-week summer festival held in a stuffy high school auditorium has become one the nation's finest year-round theaters. Each year, ASF actors perform three Shakespearean plays in addition to other classics by playwrights such as Tennessee Williams, George Bernard Shaw and Thornton Wilder. The company also produces musicals and commissions new works.

CIVIL RIGHTS MEMORIAL
400 Washington Ave., Montgomery
Designed by Vietnam Veterans Memorial artist Maya Lin, the touching memorial is inscribed with the names of people who lost their lives in the fight for civil rights.
Daily.

DEXTER AVENUE KING MEMORIAL BAPTIST CHURCH
454 Dexter Ave., Montgomery, 334-263-3970; www.dexterkingmemorial.org
See the pulpit from which Dr. Martin Luther King Jr. first preached his message of nonviolent activism. King directed the Montgomery bus boycott from this church, where he served as pastor from 1954 to 1960. The church is now home to the mural and original painting "The Beginning of a Dream." To see the church, go on a guided tour (Monday-Thursday 10 a.m., 2 p.m.), walk through (Friday 10 a.m.) or make an appointment (Saturday 10:30 a.m.-1:30 p.m.). Sunday worship is at 10:30 a.m.
Tuesday-Friday 10 a.m.-4 p.m., Saturday 10 a.m.-2 p.m.

F. SCOTT AND ZELDA FITZGERALD MUSEUM

919 Felder Ave., Montgomery, 334-264-4222

The famous *Great Gatsby* author and his wife lived in this house from 1931 to 1932. The museum contains personal artifacts detailing the couple's public and private lives. It includes paintings by Zelda, letters and photographs, plus a 25-minute video presentation.

Admission: adults $5, seniors and children $2. Wednesday-Friday 10 a.m.-2 p.m., Saturday-Sunday 1-5 p.m.

FIRST WHITE HOUSE OF THE CONFEDERACY

644 Washington Ave., Montgomery, 334-242-1861

Confederacy President Jefferson Davis and his family lived here while Montgomery was the Confederate capital. Moved from its original location at Bibb and Lee streets in 1920, it is now a museum containing period furnishings, Confederate mementos, personal belongings and paintings of the Davis family.

Monday-Friday 8 a.m.-4:30 p.m.

FORT TOULOUSE/JACKSON PARK NATIONAL HISTORIC LANDMARK

2521 W. Fort Toulouse Road, Montgomery, 334-567-3002; www.fttoulousejackson.org

At the confluence of the Coosa and Tallapoosa rivers, Fort Toulouse was originally a French fort, built in 1717 to keep those pesky Brits at bay. The French abandoned it in 1763, and more than 50 years later, Andrew Jackson built a fort on the same site. Today, you can see a reconstructed Fort Toulouse and a partially reconstructed Fort Jackson. Don't miss the mounds, which are nearly 1,000 years old. The park features a boat ramp, nature walks, picnicking, camping and a museum. A living-history program takes place the third weekend of each month.

Admission: adults $1, seniors and children $.50. Daily.

MAXWELL AIR FORCE BASE

55 S. LeMay Plaza, Montgomery, 334-953-1110; www.au.af.mil

Wilbur Wright began the world's first flying school here in 1910. His brother Orville made his first flight in Montgomery on March 26, 1910. Named in 1922 for Lt. William C. Maxwell, an Alabama man who was killed while serving in the Third Aero Squadron in the Philippines, it is now the home of Air University.

Daily.

MONTGOMERY MUSEUM OF FINE ARTS

1 Museum Drive, Montgomery, 334-244-5700; www.mmfa.org

The museum holds collections of 19th- and 20th-century American art, European works on paper, and regional and decorative arts. It also offers hands-on children's exhibits, lectures and concerts.

Tuesday-Saturday 10 a.m.-5 p.m., Sunday noon-5 p.m.

MONTGOMERY ZOO

2301 Coliseum Parkway, Montgomery, 334-240-4900; www.montgomeryal.gov

More than 500 animals from five continents reside here in natural, barrier-free habitats. The zoo's Overlook Café gives visitors a unique peek at the zoo, and a train ride helps them get a lay of the land.

Admission: adults $8, seniors and children 3-12 $5, children under 3 free. Daily 9 a.m.-5 p.m.

OLD ALABAMA TOWN

301 Columbus St., Montgomery, 334-240-4500, 888-240-1850; www.oldalabamatown.com

In the heart of historic Montgomery, this six-block stretch of restored 19th- and 20th-century buildings includes an 1820s log cabin, an urban church circa 1890, a country doctor's office and a corner grocer, among many others. Hosts in period dress give you an inside look into Alabama's history.

Admission: adults $8, children 6-18 $4, children under 6 free. Monday-Saturday 9 a.m.-3 p.m.

ST. JOHN'S EPISCOPAL CHURCH

113 Madison Ave., Montgomery, 334-262-1937; www.stjohnsmontgomery.org

Built in 1855, this church has seen much of Alabama's history up close. Confederate President Jefferson Davis worshipped here with his family. Today, visitors come to see the church's stained-glass windows, the Gothic pipe organ and Jefferson's pew.

Daily.

SELMA
BLACK HERITAGE TOUR

Chamber of Commerce, 513 Lauderdale St., Selma, 334-875-7241; www.selmaalabama.com

Learn about Selma's role in the fight for civil rights. Visit Brown Chapel A.M.E. Church (also a part of the Martin Luther King Jr. self-guided street walking tour), the Edmund Pettus Bridge, the National Voting Rights Museum, Selma University, the Dallas County Courthouse and the Wilson Building.

Daily.

CAHAWBA

9518 Cahaba Road, Selma, 334-872-8058; www.selmaalabama.com

This ghost town has a fascinating history. From 1820 to 1826, Cahawba served as Alabama's first permanent capital. Its low elevation made it vulnerable to frequent flooding, and the capital was moved to Tuscaloosa in 1826. The town survived until the Civil War, when the Confederate government tore up the railroad to extend a railroad nearby and established a lice-infested prison for captured Union troops. After the war, freemen used the courthouse as a meeting place to discuss how to gain political power, and former slave families created a new rural community. By 1900, the town was again abandoned and most of the buildings had collapsed or been burned. Today, visitors can stroll the deserted streets, chat with onsite archaeologists and view the town's ruins.

Daily.

NATIONAL VOTING RIGHTS MUSEUM AND INSTITUTE

1012 Water Ave., Selma, 334-418-0800; www.nvrm.org

Located near the foot of Edmund Pettus Bridge, this museum offers a pictorial history of the voting-rights struggle. It displays an exceptional record of events and participants, including Viola Liuzzo, who was killed by Ku Klux Klan members after the voting-rights march, and Marie Foster, who made history when she was brutally beaten in a protest march.

Admission: adults $6, seniors and students $4. Monday-Friday 9 a.m.-5 p.m., Saturday 10 a.m.-3 p.m.

OLD DEPOT MUSEUM
4 Martin Luther King Jr. St., Selma, 334-874-2197; www.selmaalabama.com

Visit this interpretive history museum to see artifacts from Selma and Alabama's "black belt" region, like a cameo belonging to Elodie Todd Dawson, a Confederate who also happened to be Abraham Lincoln's sister-in-law.

Admission: adult $4, seniors $3, students $2, children under 5 free. Monday-Saturday 10 a.m.-4 p.m.

OLD TOWN HISTORIC DISTRICT
Chamber of Commerce, 513 Lauderdale St., Selma, 334-875-7241; www.selmaalabama.com

Alabama's largest historic district, Old Town comprises more than 1,200 structures, including museums, specialty shops and restaurants. Daily.

STURDIVANT HALL
713 Mabry St., Selma, 334-872-5626; www.sturdivanthall.com

This beautiful home is an excellent example of Greek Revival architecture. Designed by Thomas Helm Lee, cousin of Robert E. Lee, it features massive Corinthian columns, original wrought iron on the balconies and belvedere on the roof. It's fully restored with period furnishings; the kitchen has slave quarters above; plus there's a smokehouse, wine cellar, carriage house and garden. One-hour guided tours are available.

Admission: adults $5, children $2. Tuesday-Saturday 10 a.m.-4 p.m.

TUSKEGEE

BOOKER T. WASHINGTON MONUMENT
Tuskegee, 540-721-2094; www.nps.gov

The larger-than-life bronze figure honors the institute's first principal, who advocated "lifting the veil of ignorance" from the heads of freed slaves.

Daily 9 a.m.-5 p.m.

CHAPEL, TUSKEGEE UNIVERSITY
Tuskegee University campus, Tuskegee, 334-727-8322; www.tuskegee.edu

Paul Rudolph designed this unusual structure with saw-toothed ceilings and deep beams. Adjacent are the graves of George Washington Carver and Booker T. Washington.

Daily.

GEORGE WASHINGTON CARVER MUSEUM
Tuskegee, 334-727-3200; www.nps.gov

Born a slave, George Washington Carver eventually earned an advanced degree in agriculture from Iowa Agricultural College. In 1896 he accepted a position at Tuskegee Institute, where he taught and researched for 47 years. The museum includes Carver's original laboratory, the array of products he developed, and his extensive collection of native plants, minerals, needlework, paintings, drawings and personal belongings. It's part of the Tuskegee Institute National Historic Site.

Daily 9 a.m.-5 p.m.

TUSKEGEE INSTITUTE NATIONAL HISTORIC SITE
1212 W. Montgomery Road, Tuskegee, 334-727-6390; www.nps.gov/tuin

The Tuskegee Institute opened on July 4, 1881—a date that celebrated freedom for all citizens, including the black students who enrolled. The institute focused on giving students the skills they would need to find work and on building their moral character. Many of these students went on to become educators who took their knowledge and skills to rural areas, where they taught people how to implement these ideas. The school's reputation as a progressive institution grew, and in 1974, Congress established Tuskegee Institute National Historic Site to include "The Oaks," home of Booker T. Washington; the George Washington Carver Museum; and the Historic Campus District. The 5,000-acre campus comprises more than 160 buildings.

Daily 9 a.m.-4:30 p.m.

TUSKEGEE NATIONAL FOREST
125 National Forest Road 949, Tuskegee, 334-727-2652; www.stateparks.com

This beautiful slice of southeastern country offers plenty of outdoor fun. There's fishing, hunting and hiking on Bartram National Recreation Trail; Atasi and Taska picnic sites; and camping. See the area's native animals at the Tsinia Wildlife Viewing Area.

Daily dawn-dusk.

WHERE TO STAY

RECOMMENDED
RENAISSANCE MONTGOMERY HOTEL & SPA
AT THE CONVENTION CENTER
201 Tallapoosa St., Montgomery, 334-481-5000; www.marriott.com

Located in downtown Montgomery at the Convention Center and near Alabama State University, this Marriott includes a rooftop pool with views of the city, comfortable and spacious rooms with colorful décor and bathrooms with separate tub and shower, and a well-equipped fitness center. Dining options include a Southern restaurant, oyster bar and pub.

290 rooms. Restaurant, bar. Fitness center. $151-250

WHERE TO EAT

★★★THE CHOPHOUSE VINTAGE YEAR
405 Cloverdale Road, Montgomery, 334-264-8463

Located in Montgomery's historic Cloverdale District, this restaurant serves unusual appetizers, like the duo of smoked salmon and Gulf crab meat taquitos with a habanero pepper jelly gastrique, and desserts, like the chocolate bread with crème anglaise and chocolate sauce. As for the entrées, you can't go wrong with either the seafood or a steak. The modern décor with intimate lighting makes it a great spot for a romantic dinner.

Seafood. Dinner. Closed Sunday-Monday. $16-35

MOBILE

Mobile, Alabama's largest port city, blends old Southern grace with new Southern enterprise. The city began in 1702 as the first capital of French Louisiana. Thanks to its prime location on the water and easy access to the Gulf of Mexico, it flourished. After the Civil War, Mobile grew into a shipbuilding port, and increased military production buoyed the town's economy during World War II. In fact, one of the nation's first submarines was built in Mobile. Today, the city is a vibrant industrial seaport that has preserved its air of antebellum graciousness. Its historic charm is on display in the Church Street, DeTonti Square, Oakleigh Garden and Old Dauphinway historical districts. So indulge in fresh Gulf seafood, enjoy the city's diverse architectural styles and breathe in the salty air of Alabama's "Port City."

WHAT TO SEE

BATTLESHIP MEMORIAL PARK, USS ALABAMA
2703 Battleship Parkway, Mobile Bay, 251-433-2703; www.ussalabama.com

Visitors may tour the 35,000-ton *USS Alabama,* which serves as a memorial to the state's men and women who served in World War II, the Korean conflict, Vietnam and Desert Storm. Don't miss the submarine *USS Drum,* World War II aircraft, a B-52 bomber and an A-12 Blackbird spy plane.

Admission: adults $12, children 6-11 $6, children under 6 free. October-March, daily 8 a.m.-4 p.m.; April-September, daily 8 a.m.-6 p.m.

BELLINGRATH GARDENS AND HOME
12401 Bellingrath Gardens Road, Mobile, 251-973-2217, 800-247-8420; www.bellingrath.org

Travels to world-famous gardens abroad inspired the Bellingraths to create these majestic gardens in the 1920s. Approximately 250,000 azalea plants of 200 varieties bloom on the estate alongside camellias, roses and water lilies. In the center of the gardens, you'll find the Bellingrath house, furnished with antiques, fine china and rare porcelain. The riverboat *Southern Belle* provides 45-minute cruises along the nearby Fowl River.

Garden admission: adults $11, children 5-12 $6, children under 5 free. Daily 8 a.m.-5 p.m.

BRAGG-MITCHELL MANSION
1906 Springhill Ave., Mobile, 251-471-6364; www.braggmitchellmansion.com

This Greek Revival 20-room mansion sits amid 12 acres of landscaped grounds. The restored interior includes extensive faux-grained woodwork and stenciled moldings as well as period furnishings. The dramatic circular staircase is not to be missed.

Admission: adults $5, children 6-18 $3, children under 6 free. Tuesday-Friday 10 a.m.-4 p.m.

CATHEDRAL OF THE IMMACULATE CONCEPTION
2 S. Claiborne, Mobile, 251-434-1565; www.mobilecathedral.org

Begun in 1835 and consecrated in 1850, the cathedral has German art-glass windows, a bronze canopy over the altar and hand-carved stations of the cross. *Daily.*

HIGHLIGHT

WHAT ARE THE TOP THINGS TO DO IN MOBILE?

CLIMB ABOARD THE USS ALABAMA

Pay homage to the Alabama servicemen and women who served in various wars at this memorial. You can also see a submarine and a bona fide spy plane.

WANDER THROUGH THE MOBILE MUSEUM OF ART

As the largest museum along the Gulf Coast, the Mobile Museum of Art offers an eyeful. Be sure to take a peek at the 19th-century American landscapes and the realist paintings from the WPA era.

STOP AND SMELL THE ROSES AT THE BELLINGRATH GARDENS AND HOME

Stroll through the lush 65-acre grounds of seasonal camellias, azaleas, chrysanthemums and award-winning roses. Then take a cruise along the nearby Fowl River and learn about the gardens and area.

GET GROSSED OUT AT THE MOBILE MEDICAL MUSEUM

This unusual museum showcases obscure medical artifacts, like Civil War amputation saws and bleeding bowls used to catch dripping blood during phlebotomies.

CONDE-CHARLOTTE MUSEUM HOUSE

104 Theatre St., Mobile, 251-432-4722; www.condecharlottemuseum.com

Mobile's first jail, the museum house now gives you a quick look at the city through its history. Check out a period kitchen and the walled Spanish garden. *Admission: adults $5, children 6-18 $2, children under 6 free. Tuesday-Saturday 10 a.m.-4 p.m.*

MALBIS GREEK ORTHODOX CHURCH

10145 Highway 90, Daphne, 251-626-3050

Inspired by a similar place of worship in Athens, Greece, this Byzantine church is a Greek wonder. Pentelic marble is from the same quarries that supplied the Parthenon. Skilled artists from Greece created the authentic paintings; hand-carved figures and ornaments were brought from Greece. Visitors enjoy the stained-glass windows, dome with murals and many works of art depicting the life of Christ. Guided tours are by appointment. *Daily.*

MOBILE MEDICAL MUSEUM

1664 Springhill Ave., Mobile, 251-415-1109; www.mobilemedicalmuseum.com

Prepare to be fascinated—and a little grossed out. The museum houses rare medical artifacts, tools and photographs. Imagine life as a Civil War solider when you see the tools a surgeon used back then, including bullet extractors and amputation saws. *Monday-Friday 10 a.m.-4 p.m.*

MOBILE MUSEUM OF ART

4850 Museum Drive, Mobile, 251-208-5200; www.mobilemuseumofart.com

The Gulf Coast's largest museum has a permanent collection that includes African and Asian art, contemporary glass as well as American and European 19th-century paintings and prints. It also houses traveling exhibits.

Admission: adults $10, children $6. Monday-Saturday 10 a.m.-5 p.m., Sunday 1-5 p.m.

MUSEUM OF MOBILE

111 S. Royal St., Mobile, 251-208-7569; www.museumofmobile.com

See 300 years of history in one place. You'll find artifacts from Mobile's French, British, Spanish and Confederate periods; costumes from Mardi Gras— Mobile claims to have celebrated the holiday first, even before New Orleans; and ship models and arms collection. It is all housed in the Bernstein-Bush House, an Italianate town house dating back to 1872.

Admission: adults $5, seniors $4, children 6-18 $3, children under 6 free. Monday-Saturday 9 a.m.-5 p.m., Sunday 1-5 p.m.

PHOENIX FIRE MUSEUM

111 S. Royal St., Mobile, 251-208-7569; www.museumofmobile.com

This museum, within a restored fire station from the 1800s, showcases firefighting equipment, memorabilia dating from Mobile's first volunteer company, steam fire engines and a collection of silver trumpets and helmets.

Tuesday-Saturday 9 a.m.-5 p.m., Sunday 1-5 p.m.

RICHARDS-DAR HOUSE

256 N. Joachim St., Mobile, 251-208-7320; www.richardsdarhouse.com

This restored Italianate town house features elaborate ironwork, a curved suspended staircase and period furniture. The elaborate white cast-iron façade depicts the four seasons and is stunning.

Admission: adults $5, children $2. Monday-Friday 11 a.m.-3:30 p.m., Saturday 10 a.m.-4 p.m., Sunday 1-4 p.m.

UNIVERSITY OF SOUTH ALABAMA

307 University Blvd., Mobile, 251-460-6101; www.southalabama.edu

Theater productions are presented during the school year at Laidlaw Performing Arts Center and at Saenger Theatre. Of architectural interest on campus are Seaman's Bethel Theater from 1860; the Plantation Creole House, a reconstructed Creole cottage dating back to 1828; and Mobile town house, an 1870 federal-style building showing Italianate and Greek Revival influences that also houses the USA campus art gallery.

Daily.

WHERE TO STAY

★★★GRAND HOTEL MARRIOTT RESORT, GOLF CLUB & SPA

1 Grand Blvd., Point Clear, 251-928-9201, 800-544-9933; www.marriott.com

Guests can indulge in fun and relaxation at this full-service beach resort on 550 landscaped acres along scenic Mobile Bay. History buffs will want to check out the historic Civil War cemetery onsite. Sporty types will take advantage of the beach's kayaking and sailing, while duffers will play a couple of rounds on the

SPECIAL EVENTS

AZALEA TRAIL RUN FESTIVAL AND FESTIVAL OF FLOWERS

1 S. Water St., Mobile, 800-566-2453; www.mobilebay.org

This pleasant—and fragrant—10K run through the oak-shaded streets of Mobile is a nice way to usher in spring. The smell of purple wisteria fills the air and pink azaleas and white dogwoods set the scene. You can also take in all the old stately homes along the way. The course is mostly flat (and is pretty fast) but if you're not much of a runner, a 35-mile-long driving tour winds through the floral streets in and around Mobile. The Convention & Visitors Corporation has further details and maps for self-guided tours of the Azalea Trail and local historic sites.

Late March.

BAY FEST

2900 Dauphin St., Mobile, 251-470-7730; www.bayfest.com

More than 200,000 fans spill into downtown Mobile to see more than 125 live music acts occupying nine stages during this three-day festival. Past performers have included Reba McEntire, The Temptations, Stone Temple Pilots, B.B. King, 3 Doors Down and Keith Urban. The festival offers music for every taste and spotlights local and upcoming talent, as well as drawing in big-name acts. Many say this is the event of the year in Alabama. Visit the website to purchase tickets far in advance.

First weekend in October.

36 championship holes that are part of the statewide Robert Trent Jones Golf Trail. Everyone will want to visit the 20,000-square-foot spa for a massage or facial. Guest rooms offer views of either the bay or the pool and verdant gardens.

371 rooms. Restaurant, bar. Business center. Fitness center. Pool. Spa. Beach. Golf. Tennis. $151-250

WHERE TO EAT

★★★THE GRAND DINING ROOM

1 Grand Blvd., Point Clear, 251-928-9201; www.marriott.com

Part of the Marriott's Grand Hotel Resort, Golf Club & Spa, this signature restaurant with a picture-perfect view offers generous buffet dining during breakfast and lunch and romantic, festive dinners. Fresh is the goal of this restaurant; dishes use local produce and herbs hand-picked daily from the chef's garden. Taste the bounty from the chef's adjacent garden in the cucumber bowl of baby mixed greens, enoki mushrooms, alfalfa sprouts, and carrot and beet threads doused with a housemade vinaigrette dressing. Or get some fresh local seafood with the pan-seared Gulf snapper with sun-dried tomato polenta, pickled baby vegetable jardinière and a Chianti sauce.

American. Breakfast, lunch, dinner. Closed Sunday-Monday. $16-35

★★★THE PILLARS

1757 Government St., Mobile, 251-471-3411; www.thepillarsmobile.com

Treat yourself to a delicious meal in a beautiful historic mansion. The menu reads like a surf-and-turf lover's dream: Gulf crab, shrimp, plenty of fresh fish and any cut of steak you could want. To see the culinary action, request a seat at the chef's table, which is smack-dab in the kitchen. At the chef's table, you'll get to nibble on many menu items; you'll receive a platter of favorite appetizers, a tasting of each soup, a salad sampler, fish and meat courses, a tasting of each dessert and wine with every course.

American. Dinner. Closed Sunday. $16-35

★★★RUTH'S CHRIS STEAK HOUSE

2058 Airport Blvd., Mobile, 251-476-0516; www.ruthschris.com

Now an international presence, this restaurant group started in New Orleans, so portions are generous and the menu is dotted with food inspired by the founder's hometown. But obviously the restaurant's main draw is the supreme cuts of juicy steak. Try the custom-aged Midwestern beef; it's never frozen and is cooked in a 1,800-degree broiler to customers' tastes.

Steak. Lunch, dinner. $36-85

GULF COAST TOWNS

Those looking for a sun-and-sand getaway in the Heart of Dixie should head south to the Gulf Coast. There, you'll find little beach towns like Dauphin Island, a barrier island with sandy beaches and a rich history. The Native Americans who first inhabited the island left their mark with the Shell Mound, made of middens from discarded oyster shells and other waste from the sea. East of Dauphin Island are the Gulf Shores, located on the aptly named Pleasure Island. Swimming and fishing in the Gulf are excellent, and golfers will find plenty of nearby courses to keep them busy. Nature lovers will enjoy bike paths, hiking trails and even a few prime spots for canoeing. Even further east is Orange Beach, a Gulf Coast town that offers plenty of white sand and warm breezes. Orange Beach and Gulf Shores make up one of Alabama's best playgrounds.

WHAT TO SEE

DAUPHIN ISLAND
DAUPHIN ISLAND CAMPGROUND

109 Bienville Blvd., Dauphin Island, 251-861-2742; www.dauphinisland.org

A private path leads to secluded Gulf beaches, fishing piers and boat launches. To see more nature, there's a hiking trail that brings you to the Audubon Bird Sanctuary, a 164-acre haven for local and migratory bird species. The campground also has recreation areas and tent and trailer sites.

Daily dawn-dusk.

FORT GAINES

51 Bienville Blvd., Dauphin Island, 251-861-3607; www.dauphinisland.org

Construction on this five-sided fort began in 1821 and was completed in the 1850s. Union forces captured the fort from the Confederates on August 23,

HIGHLIGHT

WHAT ARE THE TOP THINGS TO DO IN THE GULF COAST TOWNS?

CAMP OUT ON DAUPHIN ISLAND

Pitch a tent at the Dauphin Island Campground and you'll have easy access to the beach. Bird-watchers will want to bring their binoculars and head out on the hiking trail, which leads to the Audubon Bird Sanctuary.

CHECK OUT THE RESIDENT ANIMALS AT THE ALABAMA GULF COAST ZOO

Animal Planet junkies must stop at this animal house, which was featured in the series *The Little Zoo That Could*. Bonus: It's only blocks from the beach.

SEE WHERE THE WILD THINGS ARE AT BON SECOUR NATIONAL WILDLIFE REFUGE

You'll spot sea turtles, flocks of feathered flyers, and maybe red foxes, coyotes and armadillos at this 7,000-acre wildlife haven. It's one of the state's top 10 natural wonders.

HIT THE BEACHES AT GULF STATE PARK

Lay out on two miles of white sandy shores. After you get crispy, head into the water for some waterskiing or surfing— yes, surfing in Alabama.

1864. Check out the museum on the premises.
Daily dawn-dusk.

GULF SHORES

ALABAMA GULF COAST ZOO

1204 Gulf Shores Parkway, Gulf Shores, 251-968-5732; www.alabamagulfcoastzoo.com

Located a few miles from the beach, this zoo has endured violent visits from hurricanes Ivan, Dennis and Katrina in recent years, but its comeback landed it a television series called *The Little Zoo That Could* on Animal Planet.

Admission: adults $10, seniors $8, children 3-12 $7, children under 3 free. Daily 9 a.m.-4 p.m.

BON SECOUR NATIONAL WILDLIFE REFUGE

12295 State Highway 180, Gulf Shores, 251-540-7720; www.fws.gov/bonsecour

One of Alabama's 10 natural wonders, Bon Secour's 7,000 acres are home to endangered and threatened animals such as the nesting sea turtle and the Alabama beach mouse. You can commune with nature by swimming, hiking and even fishing here.

Schedule varies.

FORT MORGAN

51 State Highway 180 W., Gulf Shores, 251-540-7125

Fort Morgan's most famous moment came during the Civil War's Battle of Mobile Bay, when Union Admiral Farragut commanded his troops, "Damn the torpedoes, full speed ahead!" (Farragut was referring to the Confederates' use of mines, known then as torpedoes.) Following the battle, the fort withstood a two-week siege before surrendering to Union forces. The fort was used during the Spanish-American War, World War I and World War II.

Daily.

FORT MORGAN MUSEUM

51 State Highway 180 W., Gulf Shores, 251-540-7127

Just can't get enough military history? The museum, built in 1967 and designed after the 10-sided citadel damaged in 1864, displays military artifacts from the War of 1812 through World War II.

Daily.

FORT MORGAN PARK

51 State Highway 180, Gulf Shores

Explored by the Spanish in 1519, this area on the western tip of Mobile Point is a history buff's dream. Between 1519 and 1813, Spain, France, England and finally the U.S. held this strategic point. The park also has a fishing pier, picnicking and concessions.

Daily dawn-dusk.

GULF STATE PARK

20115 State Highway 135, Gulf Shores, 251-948-7275; www.dcnr.state.al.us

The 6,000-acre park boasts more than two miles of white-sand beaches on the Gulf and freshwater lakes. There's swimming, a bathhouse, waterskiing, surfing, fishing, a marina and boathouse, hiking, bicycling, tennis, 18-hole golf, a picnic area, a pavilion, grills, a restaurant, a resort inn, cabins and camping.

Daily dawn-dusk.

WHERE TO STAY

ORANGE BEACH

★★★PERDIDO BEACH RESORT

27200 Perdido Beach Blvd., Orange Beach, 251-981-9811, 800-634-8001;
www.perdidobeachresort.com

Directly on the Gulf of Mexico, this Mediterranean-style resort offers everything you need for a relaxing beachside vacation. Enjoy the white-sand beaches, boating, deep-sea fishing, parasailing and scuba diving. There are plenty of activities off the beach as well; the resort has an indoor and outdoor pool—the latter has its own bar in case you need a cocktail—and tennis courts that are lighted for nighttime play. Guest rooms are spacious but a better perk is that each comes with a balcony. From the outdoor perch, you'll get a panoramic view of either the pool or the Gulf.

346 rooms. Restaurant, bar. Fitness center. Pool. Beach. Tennis. $151-250

SPECIAL EVENTS

MARDI GRAS CELEBRATION

3150 Gulf Shores Parkway, Gulf Shores, 251-968-6904; www.gulfshores.com
New Orleans isn't the only place to celebrate Mardi Gras with parades, music and lots of revelers. In fact, Alabama was actually the site of the first Mardi Gras celebration. Since you're on the shores, the festivities here also include a parade of boats on the water.
Late February.

NATIONAL SHRIMP FESTIVAL

Highways 59 and 182, Gulf Shores, 251-968-6904; www.gulfshores.com
Although fresh seafood is the main draw at this long-held annual festival, visitors will also enjoy live music, a kids' art show and a sandcastle contest. The large event features over 300 vendors selling all kinds of arts and crafts, and of course, plenty of delicious shrimp. Admission to the festival is free.
Second weekend of October.

WHERE TO EAT

RECOMMENDED
HAZEL'S SEAFOOD RESTAURANT
25311 Perdido Beach Blvd., Orange Beach, 251-981-4628; www.hazelsseafoodrestaurant.com
Around since 1986, this restaurant is popular with locals and features a crowd-pleasing nightly buffet with seafood, ribs and fried chicken. The restaurant also specializes in fried egg omelets and poboys. Kids (and adults) will appreciate the free ice cream.
American. Breakfast, lunch, dinner. $16-35

WELCOME TO ARKANSAS

OUTDOOR ENTHUSIASTS OF EVERY STRIPE THINK

Arkansas is heaven on earth—and they just might be right. The Natural State has been well endowed by Mother Nature, and its beautiful terrain inspires people to trade in laptops and cell phones for mountain bikes and spelunking lanterns. The Ozark and Ouachita mountain ranges, separated by the Arkansas River, offer splendid forests. Pine and hardwood trees shade streams filled with enough black bass, bream and trout to restore any angler's faith. There are deer, geese, ducks and quail to hunt and feast on in season, and if you just want to see wildlife, the White River National Wildlife Refuge is a haven for a diverse population of animals and plants. Caves, springs, meadows, valleys, bayous, rice and cotton fields and magnificent lakes and rivers dot the state. For an enjoyable backwoods vacation, a visitor can't go wrong bunking in a quiet rustic resort or indulging in cosmopolitan Hot Springs National Park—the renowned spa dedicated to sophisticated pleasures and therapeutic treatment.

For much of its early American history, Arkansas was rugged land on the western frontier, and a spirit of adventure still lives here, as does an appreciation for the cultural offerings that make Arkansas unique. Bluegrass music rules, and it's almost as necessary as good food at many of the town's annual festivals.

Arkansas also has several great cities. Hot Springs, in the midst of wooded hills and valleys, has been a vacation hot spot—literally—since the 19th century. The town offers a mixture of spa-inspired luxury and hearty outdoor fun. Little Rock, the state's capital, enjoyed its time in the nation's spotlight when the 42nd president of the United States, Bill Clinton, once the governor, moved into the White House. Today, Little Rock—so named for its place on the Arkansas River—has a revived downtown scene that attracts fun-seekers looking for live entertainment, eclectic dining and a healthy dose of retail therapy. For a totally different scene, check out Eureka Springs, a tourist destination admired for its European flavor, Victorian homes and steep, winding streets.

People who have already discovered Arkansas' rich offerings don't want the secret to get out, but there's plenty of room in Arkansas' wide-open spaces for a few more guests. So regardless of whether you come to party at Little Rock's riverfront, indulge in a hot-spring-fed spa or wander along quiet mountain trails, you'll find a surprising slice of paradise in Arkansas.

OZARKS

The majestic Ozark Mountains in northern Arkansas are a perfect sightseeing destination. But the surrounding towns have their own attractions. Eureka Springs is one of the state's most popular tourist destinations. Visitors are drawn to its European

BEST ATTRACTIONS

WHAT ARE THE BEST ATTRACTIONS IN ARKANSAS?

OZARKS
Northern Arkansas' gorgeous Ozark Mountains are a picture-perfect backdrop to hiking, camping and any other outdoorsy activity.

RIVER VALLEY
Everything revolves around the Arkansas River in this region, where you'll find a national forest, a wildlife refuge and, of course, plenty of waterfalls and caverns.

LITTLE ROCK
The city may be most famous for its native son Bill Clinton, but Little Rock is building a name for itself with its revived downtown scene complete with river walks, great restaurants and more.

flavor, Victorian buildings and steep, winding streets. In the 19th century, Eureka Springs was a well-known health spa. Thousands of people flocked to the city because its springs, which gushed from limestone crevices, had a reputation for healing a wide variety of illnesses. Today, the town attracts tourists who simply want to enjoy the many art galleries, boutiques, restaurants and charm.

About 35 miles west is Rogers, a pleasant Ozarks town whose proximity to the mountains makes it a prime spot for outdoor sports year-round. It's also where Sam Walton built the first Wal-Mart. On the far east side of the Ozarks is Mountain View, a retreat that will provide a unique soundtrack to your vacation. The folk music heritage that early settlers brought to these mountains is still an important part of the community. Almost every night of the summer, if the weather is nice, people gather in Courthouse Square with chairs and instruments to hear and play music.

WHAT TO SEE

EUREKA SPRINGS
BIBLE MUSEUM
935 Passion Play Road, Eureka Springs, 866-566-3565; www.greatpassionplay.com
This museum carries rare Bibles, artifacts and more than 6,000 volumes in 625 languages, including works on papyrus, parchment and clay cylinders and cones dating from 2000 B.C.
Admission: adults $15, children 6-15 $10, children under 6 free. Daily noon-5 p.m.

CHRIST OF THE OZARKS

935 Passion Play Road, Eureka Springs, 866-566-3565; www.greatpassionplay.com

Erected in 1966, this seven-story-tall statue of Jesus weighs more than 1 million pounds and has an arm span of 65 feet.

Daily.

EUREKA SPRINGS & NORTH ARKANSAS RAILWAY

299 N. Main St., Eureka Springs, 479-253-9623; www.esnarailway.com

Travel through the hills of the Ozarks and imagine life in the 19th century, when the first settlers rode into Eureka Springs. Dining cars are available on certain trips.

Admission: adults $12, children 4-10 $6, children under 4 free. April-October, Tuesday-Saturday 10:30 a.m., noon, 2 p.m., 4 p.m.

EUREKA SPRINGS HISTORICAL MUSEUM

95 S. Main St., Eureka Springs, 479-253-9417; www.eshm.org

Eureka Springs has a history worth investigating, and the museum is a good spot to begin your exploration. Artifacts from the 19th century, including photographs and furniture, are on display in this beautiful house.

Admission: adults $5, students $2.50, children under 10 free. Monday-Saturday 9:30 a.m.-4 p.m., Sunday 11 a.m.-4 p.m.

FROG FANTASIES MUSEUM

151 Spring St., Eureka Springs, 479-253-7227; www.arkansas.com

This museum displays more than 7,000 man-made frog trinkets, from Christmas ornaments and plush toys to a diamond-encrusted pin. There's also a gift shop so you can pick up your own frog souvenirs.

Daily.

HAMMOND MUSEUM OF BELLS

2 Pine St., Eureka Springs

More than 30 lighted exhibits trace the history and structure of bells from 800 B.C. to the present. The collection of bells on display is impressive, from primitive antiques to examples of fine art. There's a narrated audio tour.

Admission: adults $3, children free. Monday-Friday 9:30 a.m.-5 p.m., Sunday 11:30 a.m.-4 p.m.

NEW HOLY LAND

935 Passion Play Road, Eureka Springs, 866-566-3565; www.greatpassionplay.com

Costumed guides lead you around Old and New Testament exhibits, including a full-size replica of Moses' tabernacle and a Last Supper re-creation.

Admission: adults $15, children 6-15 $10, children under 6 free. Monday-Saturday.

PIVOT ROCK AND NATURAL BRIDGE

1708 Pivot Rock Road, Eureka Springs, 479-253-8860; www.arkansas.com

Hidden in a forest, these unusual rock formations will surprise you. The top of Pivot Rock is 15 times as wide as the bottom, yet it is perfectly balanced. Nearby are a natural bridge and caves, where locals believe Jesse James once hid.

April-November, daily.

HIGHLIGHT

WHAT ARE THE TOP THINGS TO DO IN THE OZARKS?

CHECK OUT THORNCROWN CHAPEL

Architecture buffs will marvel at this gorgeous glass chapel nestled in the middle of the Ozark Mountains. To fit in with its rustic surroundings, the 48-foot-high structure is made with all organic materials.

VISIT PEA RIDGE NATIONAL MILITARY PARK

Pea Ridge was the site of a devastating battle in the Civil War that involved 26,000 troops. The park also contains a 2 1/2-mile section of the Trail of Tears.

GO INSIDE THE BLANCHARD SPRINGS CAVERNS

Take a guided tour through crystalline caverns and an underground river. At the visitor center, you can learn about the caverns by perusing the exhibits and watching the free movie.

ROSALIE HOUSE

282 Spring St., Eureka Springs, 479-253-7377; www.therosalie.com

The house was built of handmade brick with gingerbread trim, and it has its original interior, with gold leaf molding, ceiling frescoes, handmade woodwork and period furnishings. It is a popular destination for weddings and special events.

Thursday-Monday 11 a.m.-5 p.m.

THORNCROWN CHAPEL

12968 Highway 62 W., Eureka Springs, 479-253-7401; www.thorncrown.com

This sensational glass chapel structure is tucked in the woods in the Ozarks. It was designed by noted Arkansas architect E. Fay Jones.

April-November, daily 9 a.m.-5 p.m.; December, March, daily 11 a.m.-4 p.m.

WITHROW SPRINGS STATE PARK

Highway 23 N., Huntsville, 479-559-2593; www.arkansasstateparks.com

This 700-acre recreation area stretches across mountains and valleys along the bluffs of War Eagle River. The waters of a large spring gush from a shallow cave at the foot of a towering bluff. Get active canoeing, hiking, playing tennis, picnicking or camping.

Daily dawn-dusk.

ROGERS
BEAVER LAKE
2260 N. Second St., Rogers, 479-636-1210

A huge reservoir with a 500-mile shoreline is a prime spot for swimming, waterskiing, fishing and boating. The lake also offers hunting, picnicking, a playground and camping.

Daily.

DAISY INTERNATIONAL AIRGUN MUSEUM
202 W. Walnut, Rogers, 479-986-6873; www.daisymuseum.com

Daisy Outdoor Products, which manufactures the famed Red Ryder B-B Gun ("You'll shoot your eye out!"), established this museum, which has a large display of guns, some dating to the late 18th century.

Admission: adults $2, children under 16 free. Monday-Saturday 9 a.m.-5 p.m.

PEA RIDGE NATIONAL MILITARY PARK
15930 E. Highway 62, Garfield, 479-451-8122; www.nps.gov/peri

More than 26,000 troops clashed here on March 7-8, 1862, in a decisive Civil War battle that gave the Union control of Missouri. Three Confederate generals—McCulloch, McIntosh and Slack—died in the battle. The park preserves the battle's site and a 2 ½-mile section of the Trail of Tears.

Admission: $7. Daily 8 a.m.-5 p.m.

ROGERS HISTORICAL MUSEUM (HAWKINS HOUSE)
322 S. Second St., Rogers, 479-621-1154; www.rogersarkansas.com/museum

The museum shows exhibits on local history, re-created turn-of-the-century businesses and Victorian-era furnishings. There's also a hands-on children's discovery room.

Tuesday-Saturday 10 a.m.-4 p.m.

WAR EAGLE CAVERN
21494 Cavern Road, Rogers, 479-789-2909; www.wareaglecavern.com

The cavern's spectacular natural entrance leads to huge rooms full of interesting geologic formations. Learn about the cave's history and the bandits, warriors, squatters and draft dodgers who've holed up in the cavern over the years.

Admission: adults $11.50, children 4-12 $6.75, children under 4 free. Mid-March-November, daily 9:30 a.m.-5 p.m.

MOUNTAIN VIEW
BLANCHARD SPRINGS CAVERNS
Highway 14, Mountain View, 870-757-2211, 888-757-2246

These amazing living caverns feature crystalline formations, an underground river and huge chambers. Guided tours depart from the visitor information center, which has an exhibit hall and a free movie. There's a one-hour tour of the half-mile Dripstone Trail (year-round) and an almost two-hour tour of the more strenuous Discovery Trail (summer only).

Admission: adults $10, children 6-15 $5, children under 6 free. April-October, daily 9:30 a.m.-6 p.m.; November-March, Wednesday-Sunday 9:30 a.m.-6 p.m.

HIGHLIGHT

WHAT'S THE BEST WAY TO TOUR PRESDENTIAL LANDMARKS?

Former President Bill Clinton may reside in New York now, but much of his history lives in Arkansas. Little Rock is the place to learn about Clinton's political career, but to explore his life before he stepped into the limelight, you'll need to visit Hope, Clinton's birthplace, and Hot Springs, where he spent much of his childhood. So hop in the car for a driving tour of Clinton's life in Arkansas.

From Interstate 30 in Hope, follow signs to the visitor center at the train depot on Main and Division streets. (You might recognize the small depot with a large green "HOPE" sign from Clinton's presidential campaign videos.) Four blocks from the visitor center, Clinton's birthplace—a modest home on Hervey Street where he lived until he was eight years old—is now a historic site and museum. Stop by the gift shop to stock up on your Clinton magnets and mugs.

Next, head east on I-30 toward Hot Springs; once in town, go north on Highway 278 toward downtown. Clinton went to grade school and high school here, and the town is full of sites where he studied, worked and played long before he moved into the White House. Off Highway 7, at the south end of Bathhouse Row, a city visitor center distributes a map of 16 Clinton-related sites, including his church, a local bowling alley and his favorite hamburger joint. Hot Springs High School, from which Clinton graduated in 1964, is now the William Jefferson Clinton Cultural Campus, a residential community art center that features a restored theater and presidential museum from Clinton's high school days. And if you still haven't gotten enough presidential history, take I-30 east to Little Rock, where Clinton made his political debut as attorney general of Arkansas in 1976.

OZARK FOLK CENTER STATE PARK

Highway 382, Mountain View, 870-269-3851, 800-264-3655; www.ozarkfolkcenter.com

Established to preserve and share the crafts, music and heritage of the Ozark region, the park hosts events such as a cowboy folk humor and storytelling weekend and crafts workshops. In the living museum, artisans demonstrate basketry, quilt-making and woodcarving. The park also includes a lodge, a restaurant, a music auditorium and an outdoor stage with 300 covered seats. Special events are held all year.

Daily.

WHERE TO STAY

★★★1886 CRESCENT HOTEL & SPA

75 Prospect Ave., Eureka Springs, 877-342-9766, 800-342-9766; www.crescent-hotel.com

Built atop Eureka Springs' highest point, this grand hotel offers gorgeous views of the valley. Guests will feel as if they have traveled back in time when they pass through the front door into the opulent lobby. Victorian-style guest rooms are decorated with wallpaper and period furnishings. Stake out a spot by the pool or indulge in a spa treatment at the property's New Moon Spa and Salon. Adventure seekers will find plenty of activities in the area, such as ghost tours, fishing, hiking, kayaking, canoeing, and car and motorcycle tours. After a busy day, The Crystal Dining Room is the perfect spot for an elegant meal, followed by drinks at Dr. Baker's Lounge, where guests can enjoy panoramic views of the Ozarks and live entertainment on the weekends.

72 rooms. Restaurant, bar. Pool. Spa. $61-150

WHERE TO EAT

★★★THE CRYSTAL DINING ROOM

75 Prospect Ave., Eureka Springs, 479-253-9766, 800-342-9766; www.crescent-hotel.com/dining

Located off the lobby of the historic 1886 Crescent Hotel & Spa, The Crystal Dining Room offers beautiful Victorian-style surroundings with hardwood floors, high ceilings and sparkling chandeliers; formal but friendly service; and a stellar menu of inventive American cuisine. For dinner, try the espresso-glazed filet of sirloin or the mesquite-seared salmon. Breakfast, lunch and a Sunday champagne brunch are also served; dishes like three-layer pancakes with wild berry compote and a classic Reuben on marble rye satisfy every palate.

American. Breakfast, lunch, dinner, Sunday brunch. Reservations recommended. Children's menu. $36-85

OUACHITAS

The Ouachitas region may be rugged terrain, but it's a hot spot, literally. One of the most popular destinations in the United States, the colorful city of Hot Springs surrounds portions of Hot Springs National Park. Known as "America's spa," Hot Springs has long attracted vacationers in search of healing or relaxation.

Nearly 1 million gallons of thermal water flow daily from the 47 springs within the park. At an average temperature of 147 F, the water runs to a reservoir under the city's headquarters building; here it is distributed to bathhouses and spas through insulated pipes. Bathhouses mix cooled and hot thermal water to regulate bath temperatures.

Hot Springs, however, is more than a spa. It is a cosmopolitan city in the midst of beautiful wooded hills, valleys and lakes of the Ouachita region. The town's art scene is one of the best in the South, and its downtown area offers delicious restaurants and charming shops. Swimming, boating and water sports are available at nearby Catherine, Hamilton and Ouachita lakes. All three offer good year-round fishing for bream, crappie, bass and rainbow trout.

For more outside fun, the pretty little town of Mena sits at the base of Rich Mountain in the Ouachita Mountains. Outdoor enthusiasts flock here for the bounty of recreational activities.

HIGHLIGHT

WHAT ARE THE TOP THINGS TO DO IN OUACHITAS?

GET A GREAT VIEW AT HOT SPRINGS MOUNTAIN TOWER

A glass-enclosed elevator will lift you 1,256 feet above sea level for a vista of the Ouachita Mountains. Step out onto the open-air deck to breathe in that fresh mountain air and to snap some photos.

MID-AMERICA SCIENCE MUSEUM

Kids and adults can get a science lesson or two at this museum. Check out "Underground Arkansas," an interactive adventure with swinging bridges and rope ladders. And stop by the aquarium.

PLAY OUTDOORS AT OUACHITA NATIONAL FOREST

The forest's 1.8 million acres are an outdoor playground. You can hike or ride a horse through the numerous trails or you can canoe in one of its nine rivers.

SOAK IN A TUB AT THE ARLINGTON RESORT HOTEL AND SPA

Learn why the hot springs are such a hot commodity in this town. The Arlington's spa offers mineral-rich thermal baths that are supposed to help relax your body and mind.

HIT THE ROAD FOR THE TALIMENA SCENIC DRIVE

Make a do-it-yourself driving tour of this beautiful countryside. The 54-mile winding drive will take you over the tippy top of the Ouachita Mountains in eastern Oklahoma and western Arkansas.

WHAT TO SEE

HOT SPRINGS AND HOT SPRINGS NATIONAL PARK
ARKANSAS ALLIGATOR FARM & PETTING ZOO

847 Whittington Ave., Hot Springs, 501-623-6172; www.arkansasalligatorfarm.com

We're not sure you'll actually want to pet the alligators, but this stop has plenty for you to see. It's also home to rhesus monkeys, mountain lions, llamas, pygmy goats, ducks and other animals.

Admission: adults $6.50, children 3-12 $5.50, children 2 free. Daily 9:30 a.m.-5 p.m.

COLEMAN'S CRYSTAL MINE

5387 N. Highway 7, Jesseville, 501-984-5328; www.jimcolemancrystals.com

Visitors may dig for quartz crystals or just take a spin through the massive collection of already-found gems.

Admission: adults $10, children under 10 free. Daily 8 a.m.-5 p.m.

FORDYCE BATHHOUSE MUSEUM & HOT SPRINGS NATIONAL PARK VISITOR CENTER

300 Central Ave., Hot Springs, 501-624-2308; www.hotsprings.org

Multiple exhibits on the history of the Hot Springs are on display in this renovated 1915 original bathhouse structure with stained glass ceilings, marble walls and carved statues.

Daily 9 a.m.-7 p.m.

HOT SPRINGS MOUNTAIN TOWER

401 Hot Springs Mountain Drive, Hot Springs, 501-623-6035

The tower rises 216 feet above Hot Springs National Park. Ride its glass-enclosed elevator up 1,256 feet above sea level for spectacular views of the Ouachita Mountains. Enjoy the fully enclosed viewing area and higher up, an open-air deck.

Admission: adults $7, seniors $6, children 5-11 $4, children under 5 free. Daily.

JOSEPHINE TUSSAUD WAX MUSEUM

250 Central Ave., Hot Springs, 501-623-5836; www.rideaduck.com

Set in the former Southern Club, which was the city's largest casino and supper club until the late 1960s, this museum displays more than 100 wax figures, including beloved Arkansas couple Bill and Hillary Clinton. This Tussaud wax wonderland has no affiliation with the Madame Tussauds brand, though its namesake, Josephine, was the great-great-granddaughter to the real-life Madame Tussaud.

Admission: adults $9, children 3-12 $5.50, children under 3 free. May-September, Sunday-Thursday 9 a.m.-8 p.m., Friday-Saturday 9 a.m.-9 p.m.; October-April, Sunday-Thursday 9:30 a.m.-5 p.m., Friday-Saturday 9:30 a.m.-8 p.m.

MID-AMERICA SCIENCE MUSEUM

500 Mid-America Blvd., Hot Springs, 501-767-3461; www.midamericamuseum.org

Spend a day contemplating the wonders of the world—or at least, of Arkansas. Travel through "Underground Arkansas," an indoor cave with bridges, chambers, tunnels and slides. Catch the laser light show and trap your shadow—à la Peter Pan—in the Shadow Trapper. Before you leave, check out the 35,000-gallon freshwater aquarium.

Admission: adults $8, seniors, military and children 2-12 $7, children under 2 free. June-August, daily 9:30 a.m.-6 p.m.; September-May, Tuesday-Sunday 10 a.m.-5 p.m.

NATIONAL PARK DUCK TOURS

418 Central Ave., Hot Springs, 501-321-2911, 800-682-7044; www.rideaduck.com

The amphibious "Ducks" travel on both land and water. Board in the heart of Hot Springs and proceed onto Lake Hamilton and around St. John's Island. Ticket prices vary.

March-October, daily; November-February, weather permitting.

OUACHITA NATIONAL FOREST

100 Reserve St., Hot Springs, 501-321-5202; www.hotspringsar.com

The Ouachita ("WASH-i-taw") stretches across 1.8 million acres of natural beauty in west central Arkansas and southeast Oklahoma. Landlubbers can hike, mountain bike or ride horseback along the park's many trails. Seafarers can fish, swim or boat in any one of eight lakes, or canoe down one of its nine navigable rivers.

Daily dawn-dusk.

PARK HEADQUARTERS AND VISITOR CENTER

101 Reserve St., Hot Springs, 501-624-3383; www.nps.gov/hosp/index.htm

The center offers an exhibit on the workings and origin of the hot springs. A self-guided nature trail starts here and follows the Grand Promenade. The visitor center is in the Hill Wheatley Plaza at the park entrance.

Daily.

MENA

QUEEN WILHELMINA STATE PARK

3877 Highway 88 W., Mena, 479-394-2863, 800-264-2477; www.queenwilhelmina.com

With views fit for royalty, this park atop Rich Mountain is the perfect antidote to cabin fever or too much time in the office. The Kansas City Railroad Company built the original inn here in 1898 as a luxurious retreat; financed by Dutch investors, the inn was named for the reigning queen of the Netherlands, Queen Wilhelmina. The current building is a reconstruction of the original. The park also offers hiking trails, miniature golf, picnicking, a playground, a store, a restaurant, camping and shower facilities.

Daily dawn-dusk.

TALIMENA SCENIC DRIVE

524 Sherwood Ave., Mena, 501-394-2912; www.talimenascenicdrive.com

This 54-mile roller-coaster drive through the Ouachita National Forests to Talihina, Okla., passes through the park and other interesting and beautiful areas. In addition to campgrounds in the park, there are other camping locations along the drive. The trip may be difficult in the winter.

Daily.

WHERE TO STAY

★★★ARLINGTON RESORT HOTEL AND SPA

239 Central Ave., Hot Springs, 501-623-7771, 800-643-1502; www.arlingtonhotel.com

The big draw of the Arlington is its spa offerings. You will find total relaxation and enjoyment at this resort in the beautiful Ouachita Mountains of Hot Springs National Park. Unwind in twin cascading pools or in the refreshing outdoor mountainside hot tub. Or visit the mineral baths in the thermal water spa. The mineral-rich waters are supposed to penetrate your muscles and nerve centers to relax your body and mind, though the spa's massage therapists can lend a hand as well. The spa services aren't only for the ladies; baseball legend Babe Ruth soaked in the hotel's thermal baths.

484 rooms. Restaurant, bar. Pool. Spa. $151-250

★★★THE AUSTIN HOTEL & CONVENTION CENTER

305 Malvern Ave., Hot Springs, 501-623-6600, 877-623-6697; www.theaustinhotel.com

This wonderful getaway is in Hot Springs Park with a spectacular view of the Ouachita Mountains. Rejuvenate with a visit to the hotel's famous Spa in the Park, where you can soak in private thermal baths, or enjoy art galleries and music shows only a few miles away. Convenient for business travelers, the hotel is connected to the Hot Springs Convention Center via a covered walkway.

200 rooms. Restaurant, bar. Pool. Spa. $151-250

LITTLE ROCK

Little Rock, the state capital, got its name from French explorers who dubbed this site on the Arkansas River "La Petite Roche" to distinguish it from larger rock outcroppings up the river. By 1831, the town was incorporated.

More than 175 years later, Little Rock is a historic city with the sophistication and spunk of a metropolitan mecca. Little Rockers—as the city's residents are called—enjoy beautiful river walks, chic restaurants, fine museums and plenty of recreational and cultural activities. One of the hottest spots in town is River Market in downtown Little Rock, home to a large indoor market where shoppers can buy everything from fresh vegetables to instruments. At night, River Market is the place to find great live entertainment, often provided by the city's up-and-coming musicians.

Another lively neighborhood, the Heights on the north central side of town has a cool vibe. Exclusive boutiques, antique shops, coffee houses and cafés—all frequented by the yuppies who live nearby—are worth a visit. The area gets its name from the bluffs on which many of the posh residential homes sit.

WHAT TO SEE

ARKANSAS ARTS CENTER

MacArthur Park, 501 E. Ninth St., Little Rock, 501-372-4000; www.arkarts.com

Exhibits at this arts center include paintings, drawings, prints, sculpture and ceramics. One highlight is the collection of works on paper, which has pieces by Cézanne, Van Gogh, Jackson Pollock, Georgia O'Keeffe. The center also dabbles in performing arts, since it has a theater on its grounds. Plus, the facility also features a library and restaurant.

Tuesday-Saturday 10 a.m.-5 p.m., Sunday 11 a.m.-5 p.m.

BURNS PARK

1 Eldor Johnson Drive, North Little Rock, 501-791-8537; www.northlittlerock.ar.gov

One of the largest city-owned parks in the country, 1,500-acre Burns Park caters to all types of outdoorsy people. Fishing, boating, wildlife trails, 27-hole golf, miniature golf, tennis and even camping are available. The park's more unusual activities include amusement rides and nine-hole Frisbee golf.

Daily.

HIGHLIGHT

WHAT ARE THE TOP THINGS TO DO IN THE OZARKS?

STROLL THROUGH BURNS PARK
Burns is one of the biggest city-owned parks in the country. Its vast grounds aren't all greenery; you'll find amusement rides, miniature golf, fishing and wildlife trails.

VISIT THE CLINTON PRESIDENTIAL LIBRARY AND MUSEUM
This library and museum helps document our presidents with papers, photos and personal artifacts. Its collections are the largest within the presidential library system. Check out the re-created Oval Office.

WALK AROUND THE TOLTEC MOUNDS ARCHEOLOGICAL STATE PARK
Toltec Mounds is one of the biggest prehistoric Native American settlements in the Lower Mississippi Valley. See the original mounds built by the Native Americans when they lived here in A.D. 600.

COOL OFF AT WILD RIVER COUNTRY
If you need relief from the heat, head to Arkansas' biggest water park. It has everything for the family, from steep, fast waterslides for the adults to a special pool just for toddlers.

CLINTON PRESIDENTIAL LIBRARY AND MUSEUM
1200 Clinton Ave., Little Rock, 501-374-4242
The library and museum archives contain more than 76 million pages of documents, more than a million photographs and 84,600 artifacts that preserve the written record of our presidents. The museum also offers educational programs, exhibits and special events. Take a look at the replicas of the Oval Office and Cabinet Room from when Clinton was in office.
Admission: adults $7, seniors and students $5, children $3. Monday-Saturday 9 a.m.-5 p.m., Sunday 1-5 p.m.

HISTORIC ARKANSAS MUSEUM
200 E. Third St., Little Rock, 501-324-9351; www.arkansashistory.com
Built between the 1820s and 1850s, the restoration includes four homes, outbuildings and a log house arranged to give a realistic picture of pre-Civil War Arkansas. The museum houses Arkansas-made exhibits and a crafts shop.
Admission: adults $2.50, seniors $1.50, children $1. Monday-Saturday 9 a.m.-5 p.m., Sunday 1-5 p.m.

LITTLE ROCK ZOO

1 Jonesboro Drive, Little Rock, 501-666-2406; www.littlerockzoo.com

What began in 1926 with an abandoned timber wolf and a circus-trained brown bear has grown into one of Little Rock's best attractions. More than 700 animals live here, many of them on the endangered species list. Be sure to check out the antique Over-the-Jumps carousel that dates back to the 1880s.

Admission: adults $10, seniors and children 1-12 $8, children under 1 free. Daily 9 a.m.-5 p.m.

MUSEUM OF DISCOVERY

500 President Clinton Ave., Little Rock, 501-396-7050, 800-880-6475; www.amod.org

This hands-on museum houses exhibits that will fascinate you and your kids. Check out the eerily empty mummy's coffin; its owner hasn't been found. Or chill out with a tarantula, an alligator or even the famed blue-tongued skink. Other exhibits cover energy, technology, the human body, foreign nations and much more.

Admission: adults $8, seniors and children 1-12 $7, children under 1 free. Monday-Saturday 9 a.m.-5 p.m., Sunday 1-5 p.m.

OLD MILL

Lakeshore and Fairway avenues, North Little Rock, 501-791-8537; www.northlr.org

This scenic city park is famous for its cameo in the opening scene of *Gone with the Wind*. On the road to the mill are original milestones laid out by Confederate President Jefferson Davis.

Daily.

THE OLD STATE HOUSE

300 W. Markham St., Little Rock, 501-324-9685; www.oldstatehouse.com

Originally designed by Kentucky architect Gideon Shryock, this beautiful Greek Revival building was the capitol from 1836 to 1911. It now houses a museum of Arkansas history. See the restored legislative chambers, an exhibit on the state's First Families and a display of Arkansas' first ladies' gowns, one of the museum's most popular collections.

Monday-Saturday 9 a.m.-5 p.m., Sunday 1-5 p.m.

PINNACLE MOUNTAIN STATE PARK

9420 Highway 300, Roland, 501-868-5806; www.arkansasstateparks.com

A cone-shaped mountain juts 1,000 feet above this heavily forested, 1,800-acre park, bordered on the west by 9,000-acre Lake Maumelle. Fishing, boating, hiking, backpacking, picnicking and a playground provide lots to do. There's also a gift shop and visitor center with natural history exhibits.

Daily dawn-dusk.

QUAPAW QUARTER HISTORIC NEIGHBORHOODS

1315 Scott St., Little Rock and North Little Rock, 501-371-0075; www.quapaw.com

Named for Arkansas' native Quapaw Indians, this nine-square-mile area oozes charm and old-fashioned style. The neighborhoods contain sites and structures from the 1820s to the present. The original town of Little Rock grew up here, and you'll find more than 150 buildings listed on the National Register of Historic Places. A tour of historic houses in the area is held the first weekend of May.

Daily.

STATE CAPITOL

1 State Capitol, Little Rock, 501-682-5080; www.sosweb.state.ar.us

This slightly smaller replica of the nation's capitol has stood in for its big brother in several films, including the 1986 TV movie *Under Siege*. You can explore some of the grounds on your own, but you might opt for the free, guided tour to get the scoop on the building's history and some of the state's liveliest politicians. When the legislature is in session—beginning the second Monday in January of odd-numbered years—take a seat in the House or Senate chamber and watch the politicos debate. If you get tired of the wrangling, escape to the south lawn's 1,600-bush rose garden.

Monday-Friday 9 a.m.-5 p.m.

TOLTEC MOUNDS ARCHEOLOGICAL STATE PARK

490 Toltec Mounds Road, Scott, 501-961-9442; www.arkansasstateparks.com

The park is one of the largest and most complex prehistoric Native American settlements in the Lower Mississippi Valley. Native American inhabited this site from A.D. 600 to 1050, and the park preserves several mounds and a remnant of an embankment. Tours depart from the visitor center, which has exhibits that explain the site's history. The center also offers audiovisual programs and an archaeological laboratory.

Admission: adults $3, children 6-12 $2. Monday-Saturday 8 a.m.-5 p.m., Sunday noon-5 p.m.

WILD RIVER COUNTRY

6820 Crystal Hill Road, North Little Rock, 501-753-8600; www.wildrivercountry.com

Cool off in Arkansas' largest water park and scare yourself on rides with names like Vertigo, Vortex and Cyclone. There are also a few low-key offerings, like a lazy river and a Tad Pool for toddlers.

Admission: adults $29.99, children 2-12 $19.99, seniors and children under 2 free. June-August, Monday-Saturday 10 a.m.-8 p.m., Sunday noon-8 p.m.

WHERE TO STAY

★★★THE CAPITAL HOTEL

111 W. Markham St., Little Rock, 501-374-7474, 800-766-7666; www.capitalhotel.com

This historic downtown hotel earns high marks for its modern amenities, outstanding service and vintage Southern charm. First opened in 1872, the Capital

Hotel is located across the street from the Statehouse and a short stroll from the Clinton Library, the Arkansas Art Center, the River Market and other Little Rock must-sees. Bright, airy guest rooms benefit from neutral hues, floor-to-ceiling windows, flat-screen TVs and Frette bath linens. No visit is complete without a meal at Ashley's restaurant, where dishes such as rice grits with tasso and rock shrimp and chicken and parsnip bacon cornbread pudding remind you that there's more to Southern cooking than fried chicken.

125 rooms. Restaurant, bar. $151-250

★★★EMPRESS OF LITTLE ROCK

2120 S. Louisiana, Little Rock, 501-374-7966, 877-374-7966; www.theempress.com

Scarlett O'Hara would approve of this 1888 Queen Anne-style mansion which was originally built with all native Arkansas materials, including cypress and yellow pine. Carefully restored in the 1990s, this Victorian masterpiece offers antique-filled "bedchambers," or suites. They all have their own private bathrooms, some of which are bath spas, with a Jacuzzi, a steam shower, aromatherapy, a foot bath and a massage tower. Other than those modern amenities, the lovely, flowery rooms stick to Victorian décor. Don't forget to take advantage of the free gourmet two-course breakfast. And be sure to ask the innkeeper about the house's fascinating history.

8 rooms. Complimentary breakfast. $151-250

★★★★THE PEABODY LITTLE ROCK

Three Statehouse Plaza, Little Rock, 501-906-4000; www.peabodylittlerock.com

One of Little Rock's most unusual—and endearing—spectacles happens here: At 11 a.m. each day, the hotel's beloved ducks march on a red carpet from their duck palace in the lobby to the fountain, while John Philip Sousa's "King Cotton March" plays. At 5 p.m., they march back to their digs. If the ducks are treated this well, imagine how much pampering the hotel's human guests enjoy. Guest rooms are small and in need of a facelift, but the accommodating staff more than makes up for the tired décor. One treat not to be missed: gourmet dining at Capriccio, famous for steaks and Italian favorites.

417 rooms. Restaurant, bar. Business center. Fitness center. $151-250

RECOMMENDED

1620

1620 Market St., Little Rock, 501-221-1620; www.1620restaurant.com

This fine-dining restaurant specializes in seasonal, contemporary American fare. Chef Tim Morton shops the markets each morning to find the freshest ingredients. A prix-fixe menu is available for $36, which may feature items such as catfish mousseline, blackened rib eye steak and bread pudding with homemade ice cream for dessert.

Contemporary American. Dinner, brunch (Sunday). $16-35

ASHLEY'S

Capital Hotel, 111 West Markham, Little Rock, 501-374-7474; www. capitalhotel.com.com

Located just off the lobby of the lavishly restored Capital Hotel, Ashley's is much more than your typical biscuits and collard greens. This is serious

Southern food elevated to a finer playing field. The elegant dining room with large windows overlooking the street provides for a perfectly relaxed but dignified setting for chef Lee Richardson's carefully crafted farm-driven Southern cuisine. Chef Richardson combines seasonal ingredients with regional favorites to create dishes such as Arkansas rice grits with rock shrimp and tasso ham, and seared diver scallops with smoked pork shoulder and local apples. Diners have the choice of three courses for the bargain price of $49; adventurous types should go for the six pre-selected courses or try the surprise chef's degustation menu. The best part about Ashley's is that the addictive southern Americana food is not limited to the dinner hour but is also available for breakfast and lunch.

Contemporary American. Breakfast, lunch (Monday-Friday). Dinner (Monday-Saturday). Bar. $36-85

WELCOME TO KENTUCKY

FAMOUS FOR HORSERACING, MINT JULEPS AND

bluegrass, Kentucky spends a few minutes each May in the world's spotlight when all eyes turn to Louisville's Churchill Downs and the Derby. But the commonwealth offers much more than "the most exciting two minutes in sports." This is the place where President Abraham Lincoln was born, where explorer Daniel Boone carved out a path for pioneers on young America's western edge and where Harriet Beecher Stowe witnessed the auctioning of slaves and found inspiration for *Uncle Tom's Cabin*. It's also home to flourishing art communities, hip urban neighborhoods and an eclectic music scene. And even though the Derby might be Kentucky's biggest party, the rest of the year, Kentuckians celebrate everything from bluegrass music and barbecue to beauty queens and Scottish traditions. The pioneer spirit meets Southern charm in this diverse state. Kentucky stretches from Virginia to Missouri, a geographic and historic bridge in the westward flow of American settlement. The commonwealth can be divided into four sections: the Bluegrass, the south-central cave country, the eastern mountains and the western lakes. Each region will surprise visitors with its unique geography and culture. The Lexington plain, a circular area in the north-central part of Kentucky, is Bluegrass Country, home of fast horses and gentlemen farmers. South of this region is cave country, where you'll find Mammoth Cave National Park, the world's longest cave system. And outdoor enthusiasts will enjoy the Appalachian Mountains in the east, which provide a beautiful backdrop for outdoor activities, and the western lakes, an ideal place for boating, fishing and canoeing.

The Cumberland Gap, a natural passageway through the mountains that sealed the Kentucky wilderness off from Virginia, was the gateway of the pioneers. Dr. Thomas Walker, the first recorded explorer to make a thorough land expedition into the area, arrived in 1750. Daniel Boone and a company of axmen hacked the Wilderness Road through the Cumberland Gap and far into the wild. The first permanent settlement was at Harrodsburg in 1774, and less than 20 years later in 1792, Congress admitted Kentucky into the Union. During the Civil War, Kentucky supported the Union but opposed abolition, a position that highlights its place as a bridge between the Old South and the Yankee North. Ironically, President Abraham Lincoln and Confederate President Jefferson Davis were both born in Kentucky—less than one year and 100 miles apart. Countless museums, restored historical sites and festivals pay tribute to Honest Abe, the commonwealth's most famous native son.

Of course, Kentucky didn't just give the nation bourbon, horses and politicians. Heavyweight boxing champion Muhammad Ali, actor Johnny Depp, TV journalist Diane Sawyer and country music legend Loretta Lynn all hail from the Bluegrass State. As if that weren't enough, this is where Kentucky Fried Chicken, now dubbed KFC, got its start, where Louisville Slugger baseball bats were born and where all the Corvettes in the world are produced.

So if you miss the most exciting two minutes in sports each May, you'll still find plenty of ways to fill the time until the next Derby Day.

BEST ATTRACTIONS

WHAT ARE THE BEST ATTRACTIONS IN KENTUCKY?

LOUISVILLE
Big-hatted ladies sipping mint juleps fill the city each year for the Kentucky Derby. But an emerging arts community and an underground music scene make Louisville a safe bet outside of Derby Day as well.

DERBY REGION
If you want a taste of Kentucky's bourbon background, bring an empty glass to the Derby Region. You can fill it up at the Jim Beam American Outpost and then drink in information at a museum for whiskey history.

BLUEGRASS REGION
You'll find nods to Kentucky's equine history all over the Bluegrass Region. Its main hub, Lexington, is even called the "Horse Capital of the World." But you'll also find a swinging cultural scene here, with dance companies and theater troupes calling it home.

APPALACHIANS
The majestic Appalachian Mountains make this a scenic spot. This region is also home to a park that's considered the "Grand Canyon of the South." In other words, bring your camera.

LOUISVILLE

On the banks of the Ohio River, Louisville is sometimes called "the biggest small town in America." Its unique blend of Southern charm and urban sophistication is on display every year when the world watches the renowned Kentucky Derby, Louisville's biggest claim to fame. First run on May 17, 1875, and modeled after England's Epsom Derby, the Derby is the nation's oldest continually held race. The first Saturday in May each year, Churchill Downs hosts "the best two minutes in sports," played out against its backdrop of Edwardian towers and antique grandstands.

Louisville knows how to have a good time, and Derby festivities are the ultimate Southern party: they are a glamorous mélange of carnival, fashion show, spectacle and celebration of the horse. But if you can't make it to Louisville during these first days of May, you'll still find plenty to keep you entertained. Home to a growing art community and a hot underground music scene, the city takes its cultural life seriously. The public subscription Fund for the Arts subsidizes the Tony Award-winning Actors Theater, and the city boasts the Kentucky Center for the Arts, home of ballet, opera and music performances. For those interested in less formal entertainment, Louisville's Highlands neighborhood is a good bet. The funky district, which stretches along Bardstown Road, has nightclubs, upscale dining, art galleries and one-of-a-kind shops.

Part of Louisville's appeal comes from its ability to mesh its urban style with its colorful history. Founded in 1778 and named for French King Louis XVI for his help during the American Revolution, the city soon became a leader in the new nation's economic growth, thanks in part to its prime spot on the Ohio River. The city has been home to several giants of American history, too: President Zachary Taylor grew up nearby, and two Supreme Court justices—including Louis Brandeis—are from the city. F. Scott Fitzgerald was stationed at Camp Zachary Taylor during World War I and frequented the bar at the Seelbach Hotel, which was celebrated in *The Great Gatsby*.

WHAT TO SEE

AMERICAN PRINTING HOUSE FOR THE BLIND

1839 Frankfort Ave., Louisville, 502-895-2405; www.aph.org

Dating back to 1858, this is the largest and oldest publishing house for the blind in the nation. In addition to books and music in Braille, it issues talking books and magazines, large-type textbooks and educational aids.

Tours: Monday-Thursday 10 a.m. and 2 p.m.

CAVE HILL CEMETERY

701 Baxter Ave., Louisville, 502-451-5630; www.cavehillcemetery.com

This is the burial ground of George Rogers Clark, hero of the American Revolution and founder of the settlement that became Louisville. Colonel Harland Sanders, of fried chicken fame, is also buried here. The grounds have rare trees, shrubs and plants, as well as swans, geese and ducks.

Daily.

CHURCHILL DOWNS

700 Central Ave., Louisville, 502-636-4400; www.churchilldowns.com

Founded in 1875, this historic and world-famous thoroughbred racetrack is the home of the Kentucky Derby, held here the first Saturday in May. You can catch other races throughout the spring and fall.

E. P. "TOM" SAWYER STATE PARK

3000 Freys Hill Road, Louisville, 502-429-7270, www.parks.ky.gov

Named for Erbon Powers "Tom" Sawyer, a former county judge executive and

HIGHLIGHT

WHAT ARE THE TOP THINGS TO DO IN LOUISVILLE?

PLACE YOUR BETS AT CHURCHILL DOWNS

The ideal plan would be to visit Churchill Downs during the Kentucky Derby. But even if you miss the May event, you can catch spring and fall competitions at this racetrack.

PERUSE THE KENTUCKY DERBY MUSEUM

Get a lesson on Kentucky Derby history with the exhibits in this museum, which sits on the foot of Churchill Downs. After you're done with the learning part, head outside to the paddock to see some thoroughbreds.

GET ON DECK AT THE LOUISVILLE SLUGGER MUSEUM AND FACTORY

Hardcore baseball fans can tour the Slugger factory to see how its famous bats are made and then hit the museum, where you can see priceless items such as Babe Ruth's bat from his 60-home run season in 1927.

HURRY OVER TO THE SPEED ART MUSEUM

This art museum is Kentucky's oldest and largest. Among the more than 13,000 pieces in its permanent collection, you'll spot everything from ancient Egyptian art to contemporary works.

CHECK OUT THE THOMAS EDISON HOUSE

Visit the former home of Thomas Edison, a restored 1850 cottage that exhibits the inventor's phonographs, records and other memorabilia. The home also showcases an early light bulb collection.

father of television journalist Diane Sawyer, the park has 550 acres that make up one of Louisville's best playgrounds for outdoor enthusiasts. People come for the swimming, tennis, archery range, BMX track, ball fields, gymnasium and picnicking areas.
Daily.

FARMINGTON HISTORIC HOME

3033 Bardstown Road N., Louisville, 502-452-9920; www.historicfarmington.org

This federal-style house was built from plans drawn by Thomas Jefferson. Abraham Lincoln visited here in 1841. It's furnished with pre-1820 antiques, plus it has a hidden stairway, octagonal rooms, a museum room, a blacksmith shop, a stone barn and a 19th-century garden.

Admission: adults $9, seniors $8, children 6-14 $4, children under 6 free. Tuesday-Saturday 10 a.m.-4:30 p.m.

HISTORIC DISTRICTS
Old Louisville, between Breckinridge and Ninth streets, near Central Park

Old Louisville teems with historical districts. The West Main Street Historic District is a concentration of cast-iron buildings, many recently renovated, on Main Street between First and Eighth streets. Butchertown is a renovated 19th-century German community between Market Street and Story Avenue. Cherokee Triangle is a well-preserved Victorian neighborhood with diverse architectural details. And Portland is an early settlement and commercial port with Irish and French heritage.

JEFFERSON COUNTY COURTHOUSE
527 W. Jefferson St., Louisville

This Greek Revival-style courthouse was designed by Gideon Shryock. A cast-iron floor in the rotunda supports a statue of Henry Clay. The 68-foot rotunda also boasts a magnificent cast-iron monumental stair and balustrade. Statues of Thomas Jefferson and Louis XVI call the courthouse home, and there's a war memorial on the grounds. Guided tours are available by appointment.
Monday-Friday 9 a.m.-5 p.m.

KENTUCKY CENTER FOR THE ARTS
501 W. Main St., Louisville, 502-584-7777, 800-775-7777; www.kca.org

Three stages present national and international performers showcasing a wide range of music, dance and drama. A distinctive glass-arched lobby features a collection of 20th-century sculpture and provides a panoramic view of the Ohio River and Falls Fountain. There is also a restaurant and gift shop.

KENTUCKY DERBY MUSEUM
704 Central Ave., Louisville, 502-637-1111; www.derbymuseum.org

A tribute to the classic "run for the roses," the museum features exhibits on thoroughbred racing and the Kentucky Derby. Experience the excitement of Derby Day when you watch The Greatest Day, featured in high-definition on a 360-degree screen. Check out hands-on exhibits, artifacts, educational programs, a tour and special events. There's also an outdoor paddock area with thoroughbreds. In addition, there's a shop and a café serving lunch. Tours of Churchill Downs are available, weather permitting.
Monday-Saturday 8 a.m.-5 p.m., Sunday 8 a.m.-noon.

KENTUCKY FAIR AND EXPOSITION CENTER
937 Phillips Lane, Louisville, 502-367-5000; www.kyfairexpo.org

This gigantic complex includes a coliseum, exposition halls, a stadium and an amusement park. More than 1,500 events take place throughout the year, including basketball and the Milwaukee Brewers' minor league affiliate team's home games.

LOCUST GROVE
561 Blankenbaker Lane, Louisville, 502-897-9845; www.locustgrove.org

This was the home of Gen. George Rogers Clark from 1809 to 1818. The handsome Georgian mansion sits on 55 acres. It retains its original paneling, authentic furnishings and a lovely garden. There are eight restored outbuildings.

The visitor center offers an audiovisual program.
Monday-Saturday 10 a.m.-4:30 p.m., Sunday 1:30-4:30 p.m.

LOUISVILLE SCIENCE CENTER & IMAX THEATRE
727 W. Main St., Louisville, 502-561-6100; www.louisvillescience.org

You don't have to keep your hands to yourself in this museum. Designed to encourage exploration, the museum has exhibits that test visitors' creative-thinking skills, teach them about space travel and introduce them to natural wonders, such as a mummy, polar bears and a Gemini trainer. There's also a theater with a four-story IMAX screen.
Monday-Thursday 9:30 a.m.-5 p.m., Friday-Saturday 9:30 a.m.-9 p.m., Sunday noon-6 p.m.

LOUISVILLE SLUGGER MUSEUM & BAT FACTORY
800 W. Main St., Louisville, 610-524-0822; www.sluggermuseum.org

Buy me some peanuts and Cracker Jacks...or just take me to this museum, a haven for baseball fans. See memorabilia and tour the factory, where Louisville Slugger baseball bats and PowerBilt golf clubs are made. Tours are available, but no cameras are allowed.
Admission: adults $10, children $5, children under 6 free. Monday-Saturday 9 a.m.-5 p.m.; April-November, Sunday noon-5 p.m.

LOUISVILLE ZOO
1100 Trevilian Way, Louisville, 502-459-2181; www.louisvillezoo.org

More than 1,600 animals live in naturalistic settings here. Exhibits include Gorilla Forest, a 4-acre display that gives visitors a look into the world of the gorillas; Herp Aquarium, the home of King Louie, a rare white alligator; and Islands, which highlights endangered species and habitats. Camel and elephant rides are available.
Admission: adults $11.95, children $8.50, children under 3 free. September-March, daily 10 a.m.-4 p.m.; April-August, daily 10 a.m.-5 p.m.

RIVERBOAT EXCURSION
Riverfront Plaza, Fourth Street and River Road, Louisville, 502-574-2355;
www.belleoflouisville.org

Cruise the river during a two-hour afternoon trip on the sternwheeler Belle of Louisville or the Spirit of Jefferson.
Memorial Day-Labor Day, Tuesday-Sunday.

SIX FLAGS KENTUCKY KINGDOM
937 Phillips Lane, Louisville, 502-366-2231; www.sixflags.com

This amusement and water park is filled with more than 110 rides and attrac-tions, including five roller coasters.

SPEED ART MUSEUM
2035 S. Third St., Louisville, 502-634-2700;
www.speedmuseum.org

Kentucky's oldest and largest art museum, Speed has a collection that spans more than 6,000 years of human history. It provides traditional and modern art, an English Renaissance Room and a sculpture collection. The museum also highlights local artists. A café, shop and bookstore are on the premises; tours are available on request.

Tuesday-Wednesday, Friday 10:30 a.m.-4 p.m.; Thursday 10:30 a.m.-8 p.m.; Sunday noon-5 p.m.

THOMAS EDISON HOUSE
729-731 E. Washington St., Louisville, 502-585-5247; www.edisonhouse.org

This is the restored 1850 cottage where Edison lived while working for Western Union after the Civil War. The bedroom is decorated with period furnishings. Four display rooms have Edison memorabilia and inventions, including phonographs, records and cylinders as well as an early light bulb collection.

Tuesday-Saturday 10 a.m.-2 p.m., also by appointment.

UNIVERSITY OF LOUISVILLE
2301 S. Third St., Louisville, 502-852-5555, 800-334-8635; www.louisville.edu

This public university, home of the Cardinals, is known for its outstanding medical facilities, killer athletic programs and a recent boost in its endowment. If you tour the campus, don't miss the Ekstrom Library and the John Patterson rare book collection; the original town charter signed by Thomas Jefferson; and the Photo Archives, one of the largest photograph collections in the country. Also here is an enlarged cast of Rodin's sculpture The Thinker; a Foucault pendulum more than 73 feet high, which demonstrates the Earth's rotation; and one of the largest concert organs in the region. Two art galleries feature works by students and locals as well as national and international artists. The grave of Supreme Court Justice Louis D. Brandeis is under the School of Law portico.

WATER TOWER
Zorn Avenue and River Road, Louisville, 502-896-2146; www.cem.va.gov

A restored tower and pumping station was built in the classic style in 1860. The tower houses the Louisville Visual Art Association and the Center for Contemporary Art.

Daily.

ZACHARY TAYLOR NATIONAL CEMETERY
4701 Brownboro Road, Louisville, 502-893-3852

The 12th president of the United States is buried here, near the site where he lived from infancy to adulthood. Established in 1928, this national cemetery surrounds the Taylor family plot.

Daily.

WHERE TO STAY

★★★21C MUSEUM HOTEL
700 W. Main St., Louisville, 502-217-6300, 877-217-6400; www.21cmuseumhotel.com

This museum and hotel hybrid focuses on contemporary art and puts a premium on good design. Sprinkled throughout the boutique hotel are photographs, paintings and sculptures from some of the world's top contemporary artists and there's even a lounge offering video installations. The top-notch design doesn't stop in the hotel's public spaces; one guest room boasts a Chuck

Close portrait. Rooms are appropriately loaded with 21st-century amenities, including oversized plasma TVs and iPods (customized pre-arrival with your favorite music) as well as docking stations. The hotel includes an onsite spa and fitness center, and the acclaimed restaurant Proof on Main.

90 rooms. Restaurant, bar. Fitness center. Spa. $151-250

★★★THE BROWN HOTEL
335 W. Broadway, Louisville, 502-583-1234, 888-888-5252; www.brownhotel.com

The beautifully restored lobby of this hotel exudes Southern elegance, with intricate plaster moldings, polished woodwork, stained glass and crystal chandeliers. The rooms also go for classic décor, with poster beds and antique-looking furniture. The proper setting seems like an unlikely place for a suite devoted to Muhammad Ali, but the suite is decked out with memorabilia, including a photo and boxing gloves, signed by the boxer himself. The Louisville-born boxer even made an appearance at the hotel for the suite dedication in 2001. Built by philanthropist J. Graham Brown in 1923, the property's Georgian Revival-style building hosts many of Louisville's swankiest parties.

293 rooms. Restaurant, bar. $151-250

★★★HYATT REGENCY LOUISVILLE
320 W. Jefferson St., Louisville, 502-581-1234; www.hyatt.com

The hotel offers views of the Ohio River and the downtown area. It is connected to both the Commonwealth Convention Center and the Louisville Galleria mall, which is convenient for business travelers and tourists looking to go on a shopping binge. As far as perks within the hotel, you'll find tennis courts, a gym and an indoor heated pool. The rooms give a cozy feel with deep golds and blues, and with touches of black.

393 rooms. Restaurant, bar. Fitness center. Pool. Spa. $61-150

★★★THE SEELBACH HILTON LOUISVILLE
500 Fourth Ave., Louisville, 502-585-3200, 800-333-3399; www.seelbachhilton.com

Elegant and historic, the Seelbach Hotel provides a luxurious home away from home. Built in 1905 by brothers Otto and Louis Seelbach, this landmark in the heart of downtown Louisville is immortalized in F. Scott Fitzgerald's *The Great Gatsby* as the site of Tom and Daisy Buchanan's wedding. Magnificent belle époque architecture and glittering interiors reflect an era long past, but the Seelbach offers all the amenities a contemporary traveler could want. The rooms and suites are charming with period reproductions and rich fabrics. Don't miss the sensational Oakroom restaurant, a favorite of critics and sweetheart of "best of" lists.

321 rooms. Complimentary breakfast. Restaurant, bar. $151-250

WHERE TO EAT

★★★THE ENGLISH GRILL
335 W. Broadway, Louisville, 502-583-1234; www.brownhotel.com

This ornate dining room in the Brown Hotel has a decidedly refined English feel and a menu by chef Joe Castro to match. The sophisticated service and a wine list heavy on Bordeaux complete the experience, considered by many to be the best in town. Go light on dinner to save room for dessert. For an entrée, try the Hot Brown, which was invented at the hotel in 1926. It's a hot open-faced sandwich with roasted turkey breast and parmesan, slathered with mornay sauce and topped with tomatoes and bacon. To cap your meal, order the restaurant's saucy-sounding signature dessert, the chocolate striptease. The rich creation—dark chocolate cake with milk chocolate mousse covered with ganache and chocolate shavings—is quite the spectacle, as it's served flaming with rum.

American. Dinner. Closed Sunday. $36-85

★★★LE RELAIS

2817 Taylorsville Road, Louisville, 502-451-9020; www.lerelaisrestaurant.com

This romantic French bistro is tucked away in the historic administration building in Bowman Field. The comfortable and elegant Art Deco dining room, wonderful service and creative French menu have made Le Relais one of the most beloved restaurants in Louisville. Fresh, seasonal ingredients fill the menu in dishes such as herb-encrusted venison rack with braised cabbage, carrots and potatoes; certified Angus beef filet with roasted potato and root vegetables; and duck confit with sage polenta cake, flageolet beans and baby Brussels sprouts. A well-crafted wine list beautifully complements every dish.

French. Dinner. Closed Monday. $36-85

★★★LILLY'S

1147 Bardstown Road, Louisville, 502-451-0447; www.lillyslapeche.com

A brightly colored neon sign marks the window of chef Kathy Cary's innovative dining room—a hint to the Art Deco interior that lies beyond the red-brick entrance. Her menu changes seasonally and has an eclectic, urban edge with dishes such as seared scallops in beurre blanc served with basil couscous. Some of the fresh ingredients are picked only an hour before arriving on your plate. The restaurant uses produce from its own organic garden, which grows lettuces, herbs, tomatoes, peppers, eggplants and more.

International. Lunch, dinner. Closed Sunday-Monday. $36-85

★★★PROOF ON MAIN

702 W. Main St., Louisville, 502-217-6360; www.proofonmain.com

Art collectors and Kentucky philanthropists Steve Wilson and Laura Lee Brown (heir to a liquor fortune built by brands such as Jack Daniel's) launched this cutting-edge restaurant in 2006. Along with the adjacent 21c Museum Hotel, Proof on Main (the name is a nod to the owners' bourbon past) is a prime spot for showcasing top-notch contemporary art and food. Executive chef Michael Paley sources local ingredients and puts them to good use in dishes such as Kentucky bison tenderloin with buttered leeks and fingerling potatoes, or smoked chicken with grain mustard and roasted string beans. Desserts include twists on Southern classics such as chocolate bread pudding with sea salt caramel gelato.

American. Breakfast, lunch, dinner. $36-85

HIGHLIGHT

WHAT IS THERE TO SEE IN THE DERBY REGION?

When people hear "Derby," Louisville and its world-famous springtime horse race usually pop into their heads. There's more to the Derby Region than Louisville and Churchill Downs. Other cities in the area also offer history, culture and entertainment. Folks in Bardstown, just under an hour's drive from Louisville, are proud of their town's Southern charm, their beautiful city and their bourbon. In fact, Bardstown is the heart of the Kentucky Bourbon Trail, a standout experience. While you're here, be sure to pay a visit to the **Jim Beam American Outpost** (*149 Happy Hollow Road, Shepherdsville, 502-543-9877; www.jimbeam.com*), where visitors can tour the historic Beam family home and stroll the grounds. Check out the craft shop before enjoying a free tasting.

If you're here in mid-September, check out the **Kentucky Bourbon Festival** (*1 Court Square, Bardstown, 800-638-4877; www.kybourbonfestival.com*). Folks in Bardstown have been making bourbon since 1776, and at this annual festival, they celebrate their favorite spirit. For six full days, visitors can enjoy the smooth Bourbon that has been refined since the signing of The Declaration of Independence. As the Bourbon Capital of the World, it is no wonder why this festival is such a big hit. With plenty of entertainment, food, and of course, booze, you will want to scratch this festival off your bucket list. Each year, there is an official drink of the festival, the winner of the previous year's Mixed Drink Contest. After a few rounds of tasting the various Bourbons, you will feel the spirit of Kentucky too. Festivities include art exhibits, a black-tie gala and, of course, plenty of bourbon tasting.

With a starring role in Cameron Crowe's 2005 movie *Elizabethtown*, the eponymous town could have gotten a Hollywood-sized ego. Instead, Elizabethtown sticks to its roots. The little town plays a big role in President Abraham Lincoln's family story: Thomas Lincoln, the president's father, owned property and worked here, and he brought his bride Nancy Hanks to the area after their wedding. Honest Abe's older sister Sarah was born here, and after his first wife's death, Thomas returned here to marry Sarah Bush Johnston. History buffs who want to learn more about President Lincoln should also visit Hodgenville, where the 16th president of the United States was born in 1809. A museum in the town is dedicated to all things Abe. See the work of Thomas Lincoln, father of President Abraham Lincoln (he created the unusual trim work) at the **Lincoln Heritage House** (*Elizabethtown, one mile north on Highway 31 W., in Freeman Lake Park, 270-765-2175, 800-437-0092; www.touretown. com*), home of pioneer Hardin Thomas. The double log cabin showcases pioneer implements, early surveying equipment and period furniture.

The **Lincoln Museum** (*66 Lincoln Square, Hodgenville, 270-358-3163; www. lincolnmuseum-ky.org*) tells the story of President Lincoln's life, from his early childhood in Kentucky to his assassination at Ford's Theatre. The second floor holds rare newspaper clippings, memorabilia, campaign posters and an art gallery.

WHERE TO SHOP

CARMICHAEL'S BOOKSTORE
1295 Bardstown Road, Louisville, 502-456-6950; www.carmichaelsbookstore.com

In business since 1978—and family-run ever since—Carmichael's is a fixture in Louisville (and its oldest independent bookstore). Although it has moved a few times over the years, the people of Louisville have always followed (there is now a second location in Crescent Hill at Frankfort and Bayly avenues) and treated it as a sort of neighborhood gathering place. In addition to a wide selection of current sellers, the bookstore contains a good selection of books of local interest. The store also has a number of autographed books on hand for purchase. If you long for this type of old-fashioned bookstore where the staff has seemingly read everything and will eagerly point you to your next great read, you will enjoy a visit here.

Sunday -Thursday 8 a.m.-10 p.m., Friday-Saturday 8 a.m.-11 p.m. The Crescent Hill location is open seven days a week, 2720 Frankfort Ave., Louisville, Kentucky, 502-896-6950.

EUROPEAN ANTIQUE MARKET
933 Barret Ave., Louisville, 502-585-3111; www.euroantiquemarket.com

If you're looking for French and European antiques, pay a visit to the European Antique Market. You'll find all kinds of furniture and art pieces from the 17th century through the 20th century in the styles of Louis XV, Louis XVI, Louis Phillipe, Regency, Gothic, Painted and Country French, among others. Prices are fair and the inventory constantly changes.

Tuesday-Saturday 10 a.m.-4 p.m. and by appointment (call 502-553-4362).

HADLEY POTTERY COMPANY
1570 Story Ave., 502-584-2171, 866-584-2171; www.hadleypottery.com

Hadley Pottery is sold in retailers across the country but for the best selection, fans of the classic American pottery pay a visit to the factory. Hadley has been making beautiful handcrafted stoneware inspired by artist Mary Alice Hadley ever since 1940, and the pieces have a classic, whimsical appeal. All fifteen patterns are sold here; there are beach, western, nautical, fishing and other themes, as well as the simple, traditional ones. You can also get custom pieces for weddings or anniversaries, as well as name and address plates. The pottery is made from clay from Kentucky and Indiana; it is then painted, glazed and kiln-fired at 2,100 degrees Fahrenheit. The stuff is so sturdy, you can put it in the microwave or dishwasher (each piece is also lead free). The pieces are signed by an artist who has been trained by protégés of Hadley and have a hand-painted "M.A. Hadley" mark. Tours of the factory are available, where you can also purchase the plates, pitchers, bowls, mugs and tea pots.

Monday-Friday 8 a.m.-5 p.m., Saturday 9 a.m.-1 p.m. Saturday, until 4 p.m. from the second week in November until Christmas.

JOE LEY ANTIQUES, INC.
615 E. Market St., Louisville, 502-583-4014; www.joeley.com

This well-known antique shop—recommended by interior designers every-where and often written about in magazines—is filled to the brim with all sorts of finds, from doors and mantels to porcelain and sterling silver to vintage appliances and everything in between. You'll even find things like vintage typewriters and phone booths. You never know what you might come across here. It's a must-stop if you're in the area to find unique items for your home or business. The building housing this collection of treasures is an old 1890 schoolhouse. You can also order things from anywhere—browse all the items online and then just pick up the phone to purchase.

Tuesday-Saturday 8:30 a.m- 5:00 p.m.

MUTH'S CANDY

630 East Market St., Louisville, 1-800-556-8847; www.shop.muthscandy.com

Visitors should try some bourbon chocolates while they're in town, and there is no better place to do so than at Muth's, which has been making the treats since 1921. Muth's Kentucky Bourbons pack a real punch; each is made with 100 proof Kentucky bourbon and dipped in rich semi-sweet chocolate. Other special treats include the modjeskas, an interesting (and tasty) combination of marshmallow and caramel. Solid chocolate horseshoes make cute (and delicious) gifts to take back home to friends and family after a visit to the Kentucky Derby—and don't contain alcohol for those who are not of age or don't imbibe.

Tuesday-Friday 8:30a.m.-4 p.m., Saturday 10:00 a.m.-4 p.m.

RODES

4938 Brownsboro Road, Louisville, 502-753- 7633; www.rodes.com

The ever-elegant Rodes has been dressing the ladies and gents of Louisville since 1914 and is still family owned and operated. The store was located downtown for decades but eventually moved to a bigger 12,000-square-foot space on Brownsboro Road in the East End of Metro Louisville to accommodate its loyal customers. This is the place to visit if you're looking to browse designers clothing and receive superior service. There's a nice selection for both men and women. Designers for the ladies run the gamut from Burberry to Rebecca Minkoff to Ted Rossi. Guys may find Ferragamo, John Varvatos and Etro, among many others. Rodes is the style leader in the area and always has great pieces. Alternations are free and there's a custom tailoring department.

Monday-Saturday 10 a.m.-6 p.m., Thursday until 7 p.m.

NORTHERN KENTUCKY RIVER REGION

Five broad bridges spanning the Ohio River link Covington to Cincinnati, but this city doesn't need help from Ohioans to have fun. Covington, named for a hero of the War of 1812, has had a renaissance in the last 20 years. Real estate developers and the city government invested in the riverfront and infrastructure, and eclectic restaurants and unique shops followed. To experience this revival, check out Covington Landing, a floating restaurant and entertainment complex. This Ohio River town, first known as Limestone, was established by the Virginia Legislature. By 1792, it had become a leading port of entry for Kentucky settlers. Daniel Boone and his wife maintained a tavern in the town for several years.

HIGHLIGHT

WHAT ARE THE TOP THINGS TO DO IN THE NORTHERN KENTUCKY RIVER REGION?

WALK AROUND MAINSTRASSE VILLAGE

Go for a stroll in this old German neighborhood. In the historic district, you'll breeze past shops, homes and restaurants. Take a break at a little German pub for authentic fare and a beer.

VISIT THE VENT HAVEN MUSEUM

This unusual museum is dedicated to the art of ventriloquism. If you want to see the more than 700 ventriloquist dummies on display, plan ahead; museum visits are by appointment only.

HANG OUT AT NEWPORT ON THE LEVEE

Whether you need to find some souvenirs or while away an afternoon, you'll find something to do in this 10-acre riverside entertainment complex. Go shopping or check out the Newport Aquarium.

PLAY AROUND AT THE WORLD OF SPORTS

Athletes have their choice of games at World of Sports. There's 18-hole golf, miniature golf, basketball, billiards and more. The less active can stick to the video arcade.

Many buildings and sites in the eight-block historic district are included on the National Register of Historic places.

WHAT TO SEE

COVINGTON (CINCINNATI AIRPORT AREA)
CARROLL CHIMES BELL TOWER
Covington, west end of village
Completed in 1979, this 100-foot tower has a 43-bell carillon and mechanical figures that portray the legend of the Pied Piper of Hamelin.

CATHEDRAL BASILICA OF THE ASSUMPTION
1400 Madison Ave., Covington, 859-431-2060; www.covcathedral.com
Patterned after the Abbey of St. Denis and the Cathedral of Notre Dame in France, the basilica has massive doors, classic stained-glass windows (including one of the largest in the world), murals and mosaics by local and foreign artists.
Monday-Saturday 9:30 a.m.-4 p.m.

SPECIAL EVENTS

MAIFEST

MainStrasse Village, 605 Philadelphia St., Covington, 859-491-0458;
www.mainstrasse.org

Join in the traditional German welcoming of the first spring wines at this lively festival, which meshes traditional German fare—like polka bands and sauerkraut—with Kentucky treats, like Southern rock bands and artisans' crafts. (Of course, this being a German tradition, you can also enjoy some great beers.) The popular festival has been taking place in MainStrasse Village, a historic German neighborhood, for more than three decades and includes great food, arts and crafts and amusement rides for the kids.
Third weekend in May.

OKTOBERFEST

MainStrasse Village, 605 Philadelphia St., Covington

Any self-respecting German historic neighborhood must celebrate Oktoberfest, and MainStrasse doesn't disappoint. Grab a beer and a brat and enjoy the full schedule of German music, ranging from rock 'n' roll to oompah music. Each day begins with the legendary Keg Tapping Ceremony.
Early September.

RIVERFEST

Covington, banks of Ohio River, 859-581-2260; www.nkycvb.com

One of the largest fireworks displays in the country, Riverfest shoots its pyrotechnics from barges moored on the river. For more than thirty years, Riverfest has attracted people from Ohio and Kentucky for the all-day affair. The good old rivalry between Ohio and Kentucky can be seen, and definitely heard, at the Ohio/Kentucky Shout-Off right before the fireworks begin. This festival boasts all kinds of activities, including food and live entertainment. More than half a million people come out to this event every year, so if you don't feel like fighting the crowds, watch it from the comfort of your couch.
Labor Day weekend.

BEHRINGER-CRAWFORD MUSEUM
1600 Montague Road, Covington, 859-491-4003; www.bcmuseum.org

The museum keeps exhibits on local archaeology, paleontology, history, fine art and wildlife.

Admission: adults $7, seniors $6, children $4. Tuesday-Saturday 10 a.m.-5 p.m., Sunday 1-5 p.m.

MAINSTRASSE VILLAGE
406 W. Sixth St., Covington, 859-491-0458; www.mainstrasse.org

Approximately five square blocks in Covington's old German area make up this historic district of residences, shops and restaurants. It has more than 20 restored buildings dating back to the mid to late 1800s.

Monday-Saturday 11 a.m.-5 p.m., Sunday noon-5 p.m.

NEWPORT ON THE LEVEE

1 Levee Way, Newport, 859-750-4995; www.newportonthelevee.com

This 10-acre entertainment district on the river includes a trendy shopping center; 12 stylish restaurants; a state-of-the-art, 20-screen movie theater; and the acclaimed Newport Aquarium.

VENT HAVEN MUSEUM

33 W. Maple Ave., Fort Mitchell, 859-341-0461; www.venthavenmuseum.net

The only one of its kind in the world, this quirky museum houses more than 700 ventriloquist dummies who stare wide-eyed at visitors. The museum also contains pictures and collectibles.

Admission: $5. May-September, by appointment.

WORLD OF SPORTS

7400 Woodspoint Drive, Florence, 859-371-8255; www.landrumgolf.com

Grab your clubs and check out this family entertainment complex, which has an 18-hole golf course, a 25-station lighted practice range, nine covered tees and a miniature golf course. When you tire of the woods and irons, you can play at the billiard hall, video arcade, five racquetball/volleyball courts and three slam-dunk basketball courts. A snack bar is available for refueling.

Sunday-Thursday 9 a.m.-11 p.m., Friday-Saturday 9 a.m.-1 p.m.

MAYSVILLE

BLUE LICKS BATTLEFIELD STATE RESORT PARK

Highway 68 Maysville Road, Mount Olivet, 26 miles Southwest on Highway 68, 859-289-5507; www.parks.ky.gov

The park preserves about 150 acres along the site of one of the Revolutionary War's bloodiest battles, which occurred August 19, 1782, a year after Cornwallis surrendered. In this final battle in Kentucky, 60 Americans died, including Daniel Boone's son, Israel. A monument in the park honors pioneers killed in an ambush and a museum depicts the history of the area. Recreational facilities include a swimming pool, fishing, miniature golf and picnic shelters.

April-October, daily.

HISTORIC WASHINGTON

2215 Old Main St., Washington, 606-759-7411; www.washingtonky.com

The original seat of Mason County, Washington was founded in 1786 and soon was the second-largest town in Kentucky, with 119 cabins. Restored buildings include the Paxton Inn, Albert Sidney Johnston House, Old Church Museum and Cane Brake, thought to be one of the original cabins of 1790. Guided tours are available.

Mid-March-December, daily.

THE PIEDMONT ART GALLERY

115 W. Riverside Drive, Augusta, 606-756-2216

Located in one of the oldest settlements on the Ohio River, the gallery houses contemporary works by national and regional artists and craftspeople. It also spotlights antiques, paintings, sculpture, ceramics and American folk art.

Thursday-Sunday.

HIGHLIGHT

WHAT IS THERE TO SEE IN WESTERN KENTUCKY?

If you're driving through, you'll find pockets of beautiful landscapes on the western side of the state. The area inspired artist and naturalist John James Audubon, who lived in Henderson for nine years and painted life-size pictures of the wildlife nearby. Visit the **John James Audubon State Park** *(3100 I-41 North, Henderson, 270-826-2247; www.parks.ky.gov)* to see the massive hardwood forests, woodland plants and two lakes that inspired Audubon's writings. A museum holds the celebrated naturalist's art and personal memorabilia. The area even has its own Cave Country, cities with natural caverns that draw tourists. **Crystal Onyx Cave** *(8709 Happy Valley Road, Cave City, 270-773-2359; www.cavecity.com)* is filled with all kinds of geologic wonders, including helectites, stalagmites, stalactites, onyx columns and rare crystal onyx rim-stone formations that will amaze you. So will the knowledge that Native Americans used the 54-degree cave as a burial site more than 2,700 years ago. Guided tours depart every 45 minutes.

There's much more to do here than commune with nature. The region also is known for its speedy industry. Car enthusiasts race over to Bowling Green, the Corvette capital of the world, to visit the **National Corvette Museum** *(350 Corvette Drive, Bowling Green, 270-781-7973; www.corvettemuseum.com)* which has hands-on educational exhibits and displays about the history of this classic American car. Open since 1953, the museum also has an impressive collection of full-scale dioramas, advertisements and videos. More than 50 vintage vehicles are available for viewing. The city's only place that produces the cars.

Paducah has a growing underground music scene and a thriving arts community, thanks to its Artist Relocation Program. In the historic Lowertown Arts District, artists from across the country come to live and work together, and there are gourmet restaurants and funky coffee shops added to the mix. In addition, the towns have museums and other cultural offerings that'll keep you busy until your next nature hike.

WHERE TO STAY

★★★MARRIOTT AT RIVERCENTER
10 W. RiverCenter Blvd., Covington, 859-261-2900, 800-228-9290; www.marriott.com
Situated along the Ohio River, this soaring 14-story hotel offers close proximity to Cincinnati, as well as direct access to the Northern Kentucky Convention Center, a great perk for business travelers. They'll also appreciate the wireless Internet access in the rooms and the lobby. But it will be hard to stay on the computer for long when the spacious rooms boast waterfront views.
321 rooms. Restaurant, bar. Business center. Fitness center. $61-150

★★★RADISSON HOTEL CINCINNATI RIVERFRONT

668 W. Fifth St., Covington, 859-491-1200; www.radisson.com

The guest rooms supply vistas of the beautiful Ohio River, the lush wooded hills of northern Kentucky or scenic downtown Cincinnati. Ask for a room with a balcony so that you can enjoy the scenery. Aside from the view, sports fans will like that the hotel is near the Cincinnati Reds' Great American Ball Park and the Bengals' Paul Brown Stadium. The free wireless in all of the rooms and the Jacuzzis in the suites are nice perks as well.

220 rooms. Restaurant, bar. Fitness center. Pool. $61-150

WHERE TO EAT

★★★WATERFRONT

14 Pete Rose Pier, Covington, 859-581-1414; www.jeffruby.com

It's all about meat at this bustling restaurant, whether it be steak, lobster or sashimi from the sit-down sushi bar. If you can't decide on a dish, get surf and turf with Jeff Ruby's Jewel, a chili-rubbed, dry-aged bone-in rib with cipollini onions and sisho peppers, and a side of the lobster mashed potatoes. After the hearty meal, sit back and enjoy the stunning view of the Cincinnati skyline.

Steak. Dinner. Closed Sunday. $16-35

THE BLUEGRASS REGION

This region gets its name from the legendary steel-blue tint of the bluegrass that's visible only in May's early morning sunshine. Anchoring the central region is Lexington. It might be the "Horse Capital of the World," but don't mistake this city for a simple pony town. In the heart of Kentucky's Bluegrass region, Lexington benefits from smart urban planning, Southern sophistication and the allure of bourbon and horse racing. In 1775, an exploring party was camping here when members got news of the colonists' triumph at the Battle of Lexington in Massachusetts and decided to name their campsite in honor of the victory. Four years later, the city was established, and it quickly gained prominence in the expanding western territory. Pioneers who settled here brought their best horses from Maryland and Virginia, and as the citizens' wealth grew, they imported horses from abroad to improve the breed. The first races were held in Lexington in 1780, and the first jockey club was organized in 1797.

In the early 19th century, Lexington earned the nickname "Athens of the West," thanks to its vibrant cultural life—a spirit that continues today. The city's offerings include two ballet companies, a professional theater group and an outstanding opera program at the University of Kentucky.

The other Bluegrass cities have their own offerings as well. As the birthplace of Kentucky government, Danville has had a front-row seat for much of the state's history. Ten years after the city was founded, it became the first capital of the Kentucky district of Virginia. The state constitution was signed here in 1792, and in the years leading up to statehood, Danville was one of the largest settlements on the Wilderness Road. Danville is the site of the state's first college, first log courthouse, first post office, first

HIGHLIGHT

WHAT ARE THE TOP THINGS TO DO IN THE BLUEGRASS REGION?

GO TO ROYAL SPRING PARK

This may look like an ordinary spring, but it's also the spot of the first bourbon distillation in 1789. The site hosted a number of other firsts: the first Western paper mill and the state's first ropewalk.

EXPLORE SHAKER VILLAGE OF PLEASANT HILL

Shakers, a communal society that practiced celibacy and an ascetic lifestyle, settled here in 1805. Now the area is America's largest restored Shaker community. You can stay at the onsite inn and check it out.

VISIT THE AMERICAN SADDLEBRED MUSEUM

Kentucky's known for its horses, but the state only has one native breed.

This museum puts the spotlight on that breed, the American saddlebred. Exhibits look at the ways we use the horse.

TOUR THE HUNT-MORGAN HOUSE

A number of famous Kentuckians have called this manse home, including the state's first millionaire and a Nobel Prize-winning geneticist. Inside, you'll find early furniture, antique porcelain and 19th-century paintings.

TROT OVER TO THE KENTUCKY HORSE PARK

These vast grounds are devoted to everything equine. The International Museum of the Horse and the Parade of Breeds reside here. Mosey on over to the Hall of Champions stable that houses famous thoroughbreds and standardbreds.

school for the deaf and first law school.

Settled in 1774, Harrodsburg is another place with a lot of history. Named for pioneer James Harrod, Harrodsburg is Kentucky's oldest town. Its sulfur springs and historical sites make it a busy tourist center. Georgetown may be small, but it has one big claim to fame: this is the place where Kentucky bourbon whiskey was first produced. Baptist minister the Reverend Elijah Craig invented the spirit in 1789 using water from Royal Spring, which still flows in the center of the city.

Frankfort is one of the most picturesque state capitals in the country, with the Kentucky River running through the city and wooded hills rising up around it. But don't let the scenery fool you: against this serene backdrop, politics rule when the legislature is in session. Catch the politicos at play and tour the city's historic sites.

WHAT TO SEE

DANVILLE

CONSTITUTION SQUARE STATE SHRINE
134 S. Second St., Danville, 859-239-7089; www.parks.ky.gov

An authentic reproduction of Kentucky's first courthouse square stands at the site where the first state constitution was framed and adopted in 1792. The original post office is here as well as replicas of the jail, courthouse and meetinghouse. Governor's Circle has a bronze plaque of each Kentucky governor. A museum store and art gallery are also on the grounds.
Daily.

HERRINGTON LAKE
1200 Gwinn Island Road, Danville, 859-236-4286; gwinnmarina.com

Formed by Dix Dam, one of the world's largest rock-filled dams, Herrington has 333 miles of shoreline. A balanced fish population is maintained through a conservation program. Fishing, a boat launch, camping hookups and cabins are all available.
Daily.

MCDOWELL HOUSE AND APOTHECARY SHOP
125 S. Second St., Danville, 859-236-2804; www.mcdowellhouse.com

On Christmas Day 1809, Dr. Ephraim McDowell removed a 22.5-pound ovarian tumor from a woman without anesthesia or antisepsis, neither of which had been invented yet. Amazingly, the surgery was a success. McDowell's residence and shop are restored and refurbished with period pieces. You'll see a large apothecary-ware collection. The surrounding gardens include trees, wildflowers and herbs of the period.
Admission: adults $7, seniors $5, students $3, children 5-12 $2, children under 5 free. Monday-Saturday 10 a.m.-noon, 1-4 p.m., Sunday 2-4 p.m.

PERRYVILLE BATTLEFIELD STATE HISTORIC SITE
1825 Battlefield Road, Perryville, 859-332-8631; www.parks.ky.gov

A 300-acre park, once a field, appears much as it did on October 8, 1862, when Confederate forces and Union troops clashed. A total of 4,241 Union soldiers and 1,822 Confederate troops were killed, wounded or missing. Still standing are the Crawford House, used by Confederate General Bragg as headquarters, and Bottom House, the site of some of the heaviest fighting. A mock battle is staged each year (weekend nearest October 8). At the north end of the battle line is a 1902 memorial to remember the Confederate dead and one built in 1931 to honor the Union casualties. A museum houses artifacts from the battle. Take a gander at a 9-by-9-foot detailed battle map and battle dioramas.
April-October, daily; November-March, by appointment.

PIONEER PLAYHOUSE VILLAGE-OF-THE-ARTS
840 Stanford Road, Danville, 859-236-2747; www.pioneerplayhouse.com

This reproduction of an 18th-century Kentucky village features a drama school

and museum on a 200-acre site.
May-October, daily.

FRANKFORT

DANIEL BOONE'S GRAVE
215 E. Main St., Frankfort Cemetery, Frankfort, 502-227-2403

This monument is for Boone and his wife. Boone died in Missouri but his remains were brought here in 1845.
Daily.

FLORAL CLOCK
300 Capitol Ave., Frankfort, 502-564-3449

This functioning outdoor timepiece is adorned with thousands of plants and elevated above a reflecting pool. The mechanism moves a 530-pound minute hand and a 420-pound hour hand. Visitors toss thousands of dollars in coins into the pool, all of which are donated to state child-care agencies.
Daily.

KENTUCKY HISTORICAL SOCIETY
100 W. Broadway St., Frankfort, 502-564-1792; www.history.ky.gov

The center features exhibits pertaining to the history and development of the state and the culture of its people. The Historical Society's campus also includes the Old State Capitol, a library with an impressive genealogical archive and the Kentucky Military History Museum.
Admission: adults $4, children 6-18 $2, children under 6 free. Tuesday-Saturday 10 a.m.-5 p.m.

KENTUCKY VIETNAM VETERANS MEMORIAL
300 Coffee Tree Road, Frankfort; www.kyvietnammemorial.net

This unique memorial is a 14-foot sundial that casts a shadow across veterans' names on the anniversaries of their deaths. The memorial contains more than 1,000 names.

LIBERTY HALL
218 Wilkinson St., Frankfort, 502-227-2560; www.libertyhall.org

The first U.S. senator from Kentucky, John Brown, built this home near the end of the 18th century. It has been restored to its original state and furnished with family heirlooms. Take a stroll through the surrounding period gardens.
Admission: adults $4, seniors $3, children 4-18 $1, children under 4 free. Tuesday-Saturday, dawn-dusk.

OLD GOVERNOR'S MANSION
420 High St., Frankfort, 502-564-3449; www.kentucky.gov

The official residence of the governor is styled after the Petit Trianon, Marie Antoinette's villa at Versailles. The outfitted parlor and dining room have hosted such heavyweights as Theodore Roosevelt, Henry Clay and the Marquis de Lafayette.
Tours: Monday, Tuesday and Thursday 1:30-3:30 p.m.

OLD STATE CAPITOL BUILDING

Broadway and Lewis streets, Frankfort; 502-564-1792; www.history.ky.gov

Kentucky's third capitol building was used as the seat of state government from 1830 to 1909 and was the first Greek Revival statehouse west of the Alleghenies. Completely restored and furnished in period style, the building features an unusual self-supporting double stairway.

Admission: adults $4, children 6-18 $2, children under 6 free. Tuesday-Saturday 10 a.m.-4 p.m.

ORLANDO BROWN HOUSE

202 Wilkinson St., Frankfort, 502-227-2560; www.libertyhall.org

This early Greek Revival house was built for Orlando Brown, son of Sen. John Brown. The home has its original furnishings and artifacts.

Admission: adults $4, seniors $3, children 4-18 $1, children under 4 free. Tuesday-Saturday 10 a.m.-5 p.m.

STATE CAPITOL

700 Capitol Ave., Frankfort, 502-564-3449; www.finance.ky.gov/properties/capitol.htm

The stately Beaux-Arts building has French influences. The dome over the rotunda was designed to look like the one over Napoleon's tomb in Paris, and the Paris Grand Opera House inspired the massive marble stairways to the second floor. You can watch the politicians do their thing when the legislature is in session. Admire great men of history when you walk by the rotunda's statues of Abraham Lincoln, Jefferson Davis, Henry Clay, Dr. Ephraim McDowell and Alben Barkley, vice president under Harry S. Truman. Guided tours are available.

Monday-Friday 8:30 a.m.-3:30 p.m.

GEORGETOWN

ROYAL SPRING PARK

West Main and South Water streets, Georgetown, 502-863-2547; www.georgetownky.com

Kentucky's largest spring and the city's water source since 1775, Royal Spring is the site of the first bourbon distillation, which dates back to 1789. It's also the former site of McClelland's Fort 1776, the first paper mill in the West, a pioneer classical music school and state's first ropewalk. A cabin of a former slave was relocated and restored here for use as an information center.

Mid-May to mid-October, Tuesday-Sunday.

HARRODSBURG

MORGAN ROW

220-222 S. Chiles St., Harrodsburg, 859-734-5985

One of the oldest-standing row houses west of the Alleghenies, Morgan Row once was a stagecoach stop and tavern. Now it houses the Harrodsburg Historical Society Museum.

Tuesday 10 a.m.-4 p.m., Wednesday-Saturday 1-4 p.m.

OLD FORT HARROD STATE PARK

100 S. College, Harrodsburg, 859-734-3314; www.parks.ky.gov

This 28-acre park includes a reproduction of Old Fort Harrod, near where the original fort was built in 1774. Other structures on the site include pioneers' homes, which hold authentic cooking utensils, tools and furniture. The

Mansion Museum includes the Lincoln Room, the Confederate Room, a gun collection and Native American artifacts. Lincoln Marriage Temple shelters the log cabin in which Abraham Lincoln's parents were married on June 12, 1806 (moved from its original site in Beech Fork). Picnic facilities, a playground and a gift shop are there as well. Living history crafts programs are held in the fort.

OLD MUD MEETING HOUSE
Harrodsburg, four miles south off Highway 68, 859-734-5985
This is the first Dutch Reformed Church west of the Alleghenies. The original mud-thatch walls have been restored.
By appointment only.

SHAKER VILLAGE OF PLEASANT HILL
3501 Lexington Road, Harrodsburg, 859-734-5411; www.shakervillageky.org
What was once a flourishing society is now the nation's largest restored Shaker community. In the heart of horse country, this village has 34 buildings and 3,000 acres of farmland, much of which visitors can explore on foot, bike or horseback. Costumed interpreters in the village tell the stories of Shaker life. Craft shops offer reproductions of Shaker furniture and Kentucky craft items. A year-round calendar of special events includes music, dance and workshops.
April-October, daily 10 a.m.-5 p.m.

LEXINGTON
AMERICAN SADDLEBRED MUSEUM
4093 Iron Works Parkway, Lexington, 859-259-2746; www.americansaddlebredmuseum.org
The museum is dedicated to the American saddlebred horse, Kentucky's only native breed. Contemporary exhibits look at the development and uses of the American saddlebred. There's also a gift shop that sells everything equine, from hand-blown glass stemware to earrings.
Admission: adults $15, seniors $14, children 7-12 $8, children under 7 free. June-August 9 a.m.-6 p.m.; September-May 9 a.m.-5 p.m.

ASHLAND
Richmond and Sycamore roads, Lexington, 859-266-8581; www.henryclay.org
This estate on 20 acres of woodlands was the home of Henry Clay, statesman, orator, senator and would-be president. Occupied by the Clay clan for five generations, Ashland is furnished with family possessions. The estate was named for the ash trees that surround it. A number of outbuildings still stand.
Admission: adults $7, children 6-18 $4, children under 6 free. Tuesday-Saturday 10 a.m.-4 p.m., Sunday 1-4 p.m.

HEADLEY-WHITNEY MUSEUM
4435 Old Frankfort Pike, Lexington, 859-255-6653; www.headley-whitney.org
This museum exhibits decorative arts—furniture, metalwork, textiles and ceramics. Unusual buildings house displays of bibelots, (small decorative objects) created with precious metals and jewels, Oriental porcelains, paintings, decorative arts, a shell grotto and special exhibits.
Admission: adults $10, seniors and students $7, children under 5 free. Tuesday-Friday 10 a.m.-5 p.m., Saturday-Sunday noon-5 p.m.

SPECIAL EVENTS

TOYOTA BLUE GRASS STAKES

Keeneland Race Course, 4201 Versailles Road, Lexington, 859-254-3412; www.keeneland.com

Horse racing is to Kentucky as bull riding is to Texas. If you want to see the big leagues in their natural environment, pay a visit to the Toyota Blue Grass Stakes, where you can get in on the Derby action early on. Instead of picking the horse whose name you like best, make an educated guess by actually paying attention to who has a chance. What better way to learn about the contenders than to watch them race? The top contenders for the Derby face off in one of the last major prep races before Derby Day.
Mid-April.

FESTIVAL OF THE BLUEGRASS

Kentucky Horse Park, 4089 Iron Works Parkway, Lexington, 859-846-4995; www.festivalofthebluegrass.com

This is Kentucky's oldest bluegrass festival, and for a state known for their bluegrass, that means something. Taking place in the heart of where bluegrass (the actual grass) grows, the festival attracts top names in bluegrass music with more than 20 bands appearing and includes special shows for children and workshops with the musicians. Past performances have included bluegrass acts such as J.D. Crowe, Seldom Scene, and Mountain Heart.
Second weekend in June.

GRAND CIRCUIT MEET

The Red Mile Track, 1200 Red Mile Road, Lexington, 859-255-0752; www.theredmile.com

The Red Mile has been hosting harness racing since 1875, which makes it Lexington's oldest track and the second oldest track in America. The Grand Circuit Meet features the Kentucky Futurity race, the final leg of harness racing's Triple Crown. It's known for its red clay one-mile track—hence the red mile. Harness racing is an event unto its own. A bit like chariot racing, the horse pulls a two-wheeled cart called sulky. Just like the horse races we have all known and come to love, fans place bets on these races.
Late September-early October.

ROLEX KENTUCKY THREE-DAY EVENT

Kentucky Horse Park, 4080 Iron Works Parkway, Lexington, 859-233-2362; www.rk3de.org

This is a three-day endurance test for horses and riders in dressage, cross-country and stadium jumping. Day one, dressage, tests the fine-tuning of the horse—gait, suppleness and obedience. In other words, the horse is judged on the beauty of its movements. Day two, cross-country, exhibits the horse's stamina, speed, fortitude and ability to jump. Day two also tests the rider on his knowledge of the horse, personally and mechanically. Day three, jumping, examines more closely the athleticism—condition and training—of the horse. A single mistake in this series can make or break it for the rider and the horse. The fair also features boutiques.
Late April.

HORSE FARMS

Lexington

More than 400 horse farms are in the area, most of them concentrated in Lexington-Fayette County. Although the majority are thoroughbred farms, some farms breed other varieties, such as standardbreds, American saddle horses, Arabians, Morgans and quarter horses. You can see the farms by taking one of many tours offered by companies in Lexington.

HUNT-MORGAN HOUSE

201 N. Mill St., Lexington, 859-253-0362; www.bluegrasstrust.org

This mansion has been home to several of Kentucky's famous native sons. Built for John Wesley Hunt, the state's first millionaire, it was later occupied by his grandson, Gen. John Hunt Morgan, known as the "Thunderbolt of the Confederacy" for his guerilla tactics behind enemy lines. In 1866, Nobel Prize-winning geneticist Thomas Hunt Morgan was born in this house. Inside it, you'll see family furniture, portraits and porcelain. There's also a walled courtyard garden and gift shop.

Admission: adults $7, seniors $6, children $4. Wednesday-Friday 1-4 p.m., Saturday 10 a.m.-3 p.m., Sunday 1-4 p.m.

KENTUCKY HORSE PARK

4089 Iron Works Parkway, Lexington, 859-233-4303, 800-568-8813; www.imh.org

Dedicated to "man's relationship with the horse," this park has more than 1,000 acres of beautiful bluegrass. Its diverse offerings include the Man O' War grave and memorial, in honor of one of the world's greatest thoroughbred horses of all time. The visitor information center shows a widescreen film presentation, *Thou Shalt Fly Without Wings.* Also located within the park are the International Museum of the Horse, the Parade of Breeds, the Calumet Trophy Collection, the Sears Collection of hand-carved miniatures, the Hall of Champions stable which houses famous thoroughbreds and standardbreds, a walking farm tour and an antique carriage display. In addition, the park offers swimming, tennis, ball courts, picnic areas, playgrounds and a campground.

Admission: adults $15, children 7-12 $8, children under 7 free. Mid-March to October, daily 9 a.m.-5 p.m.; November to mid-March, Wednesday-Sunday 9 a.m.-5 p.m.

LEXINGTON CEMETERY

833 W. Main St., Lexington, 859-255-5522; www.lexcem.org

Buried on these 170 acres are Henry Clay, John C. Breckinridge, General John Hunt Morgan, the Todds (Mrs. Abraham Lincoln's family), coach Adolph Rupp (one of college basketball's most successful coaches) and many other notable persons, including 500 Confederate and 1,110 Union veterans. The grounds have sunken gardens, lily pools, a 4-acre flower garden, extensive plantings of spring-flowering trees and shrubs.

Daily.

MARY TODD LINCOLN HOUSE

578 W. Main St., Lexington, 859-233-9999; www.mtlhouse.org

The childhood residence of Mary Todd Lincoln is authentically restored and has period furnishings and personal items. The brick Georgian-style house was initially built as an inn in 1803.

Admission: adults $7, children 6-12 $4, children under 6 free. Mid-February-November, Monday-Saturday 10 a.m.-4 p.m.

VICTORIAN SQUARE

401 W. Main St., Lexington, 859-252-7575; www.victoriansquareshoppes.com

This shopping area is in the downtown restoration project. Head there for specialty stores, restaurants and a children's museum.

Daily.

WAVELAND STATE HISTORIC SITE

225 Waveland Museum Lane, Lexington, 859-272-3611; www.parks.ky.gov

For a glimpse into plantation life in the 19th century, visit this Greek Revival mansion. Slave quarters, outbuildings, an icehouse and a smokehouse remain standing. There's also a playground.

Daily.

WILLIAM S. WEBB MUSEUM OF ANTHROPOLOGY

S. Limestone Street and Euclid Avenue, Lexington, 859-257-8208; www.uky.edu

Exhibits include the cultural history of Kentucky and the evolution of man.

Monday-Friday 8 a.m.-4:30 p.m.

WHERE TO STAY

HARRODSBURG

★★★BEAUMONT INN

638 Beaumont Inn Drive, Harrodsburg, 859-734-3381, 800-352-3992; www.beaumontinn.com

Maintaining the style and tradition of the past, this property offers accommodations that reflect the area's rich heritage. The Beaumont has its own rich heritage, as it's the oldest family-operated country inn in the state and is listed on the National Register of Historic Places. The inn tries to keep its period details, so you'll see antiques from the original furnishings in the guest rooms and a proper parlor with a Steinway piano. But there are modern conveniences as well, like a spa. For a decadent Southern treat, head to dinner here for some country cooking, such as the yellow-legged fried chicken and the two-year-old cured ham.

31 rooms. Restaurant, bar. Spa. $61-150

LEXINGTON

★★★DOUBLETREE GUEST SUITES LEXINGTON

2601 Richmond Road, Lexington, 859-268-0060, 800-262-3774; www.doubletree.com

This French Quarter-styled property blends Southern hospitality with modern conveniences, including ample workspaces, luxury Sweet Dreams beds, Wolfgang Puck coffee makers and whirlpool-style tubs in each room. The outdoor pool is very refreshing in summer and the atrium is a nice place to relax. To kick back even more, visit Keeneland Race Course and Kentucky Horse Park, located minutes away.

155 rooms. Restaurant, bar. Business center. Fitness center. Pool. $61-150

HIGHLIGHT

HOW DO I TOUR THE COUNTRY MUSIC HIGHWAY?

A stretch of Highway 23 that runs almost the entire length of Eastern Kentucky is the perfect introduction to the state's rich history and musical heritage. Dubbed the "Country Music Highway," the path will take you by towns where country music stars such as Loretta Lynn, Wynona and Naomi Judd, Dwight Yoakam and Patty Loveless once lived. You'll also learn about Kentucky's fascinating history, so find a little country music on the radio and explore, y'all.

Begin in Ashland at the **Paramount Art Center** *(1300 Winchester Ave., 606-324-3175)*, where music legends such as Kentucky natives Billy Ray Cyrus and Wynona and Naomi Judd have played. Originally a movie house, this restored theater also hosts up-and-comers in its intimate space. Not far away, the **Highlands Museum and Discovery Center** *(1620 Winchester Ave., Ashland, 606-329-8888)* celebrates Eastern Kentucky heritage. Kids will enjoy the Karaoke Korner, where they can make their own music.

Head south to **Louisa and Kentucky Pavilion** *(606-638-9998)*, a shrine to country music. The five-story building houses country stars' costumes, signed guitars, photographs and random artifacts like Elvis Presley's Exxon gas card.

Continue south to the remote mining town of Butcher Hollow, where Loretta Lynn was born. Visitors can stop by the cabin where Lynn grew up. (Her autobiographical song "Coal Miner's Daughter" and subsequent movie is based on her life here.)

Your next stop is Prestonburg, about 15 miles from Butcher Hollow. Here you'll find the **Kentucky Opry** *(88 Chilton Lane, Benton, 888-459-8704)* at the Mountain Arts Center. Catch a country, bluegrass or gospel show by local favorites or national headliners to round out your trip along one of America's most historic highways.

★★★GRATZ PARK INN
120 W. Second St., Lexington, 859-231-1777, 800-752-4166; www.gratzparkinn.com

Just steps from many of Lexington's attractions and in the middle of the heart of the Gratz Park Historic District, this boutique inn pampers guests with distinctive charm. Each room is decorated differently with 19th-century antique reproductions, stately mahogany furniture and regional artwork. You can relax in the lobby, retreat to the library or take a stroll in the English garden. If hunger hits, enjoy a mouthwatering meal, like shrimp and white cheddar grits, at chef Lundy's acclaimed restaurant, Jonathan at Gratz Park Inn.
41 rooms. Restaurant. $151-250

★★★GRIFFIN GATE MARRIOTT RESORT AND SPA
1800 Newtown Pike, Lexington, 859-231-5100, 888-236-2427; www.marriott.com

This resort sits in the heart of Kentucky Bluegrass Country. Leisure seekers will enjoy the championship golf course, tennis courts and an indoor and outdoor pool. After a day of sporty fun, head back to your room to rest your weary body on the Tempur-Pedic mattress. For those who are no play and all business, the dataport-equipped phones, voicemail services and business center will be useful. For some pampering, head to the spa to lounge in the relaxation room and get a body scrub.

409 rooms. Restaurant, bar. Business center. Pool. Spa. Tennis. $61-150

★★★HILTON SUITES LEXINGTON GREEN

245 Lexington Green Circle, Lexington, 859-271-4000, 800-774-1500; www.hilton.com

This hotel features deluxe two-room suites. The suites are enveloped in warm yellows, reds and browns, along with horse-inspired accents and wall art to pay homage to the hotel's location in the Horse Capital of the World. If you're not in Lexington for the ponies, the hotel is next to a shopping mall with restaurants, shops and a comedy club. The hotel is also less than seven miles from Bluegrass Airport, which makes it a convenient choice for business travelers.

174 rooms. Restaurant, bar. Business center. Fitness center. Pool. $61-150

★★★HYATT REGENCY LEXINGTON

401 W. High St., Lexington, 859-253-1234; www.hyatt.com

This hotel is perfectly situated in the downtown business district at Triangle Park and Lexington Center, near shopping, restaurants, a convention center and entertainment. It's right next to the Rupp Arena, home of University of Kentucky men's basketball team. The modern rooms have a brown, red and gold palette and chestnut-colored furniture. They also include perks such as iPod docks and flat-screen TVs, but you'll likely be admiring the views of historic Triangle Park and the city skyline. To unwind, take advantage of the hotel's heated indoor pool and its outdoor sun deck.

366 rooms. Restaurant, bar. Business center. Fitness center. Pool. $151-250

WHERE TO EAT

★★★THE MANSION AT GRIFFIN GATE

1800 Newtown Pike, Lexington, 859-288-6142; www.mansionrestaurant.com

Antiques, paintings and crystal chandeliers fill this two-story antebellum mansion. The food is as elegant as the décor. Executive chef Brian Hove serves entrées such as Kurobuta pork chops served with baked grits and apricot bourbon glaze and sesame-crusted ahi with coconut risotto, pineapple salsa and a sesame-soy sauce. The wine list is extensive, and the service professional.

American. Dinner. $36-85

APPALACHIANS

As its name implies, the Appalachians region rests along the stunning Appalachian Mountains. Travelers make the trek to the northeastern Kentucky area to witness its natural beauty or to enjoy the great outdoors. Home to a site called the "Grand Canyon of the South," Breaks Interstate Park is a particularly scenic point at the Kentucky-Virginia border. In the highlands, you'll find Ashland, which enjoys a prime location on the Ohio River. The small town is the first unofficial stop on

HIGHLIGHT

WHAT ARE THE TOP THINGS TO DO IN THE APPALACHIANS?

GO SIGHTSEEING AT BREAKS INTERSTATE PARK

The canyons and gorge in this park have drawn comparisons to the Grand Canyon. See it for yourself and stop along the way to look at the caves, fields and the huge pyramid of rocks called the Towers.

VISIT CAVE RUN LAKE

Hit the beach here to soak up some rays. For more active pursuits, try horseback riding, fishing and boating on the park grounds.

EXPLORE CARTER CAVES STATE RESORT PARK

This park offers many sights to see, including cliffs, streams and caves. Don't miss the amazing 30-foot underground waterfall.

CHECK OUT GRAYSON LAKE STATE PARK

Grayson has almost 75 miles of shoreline. Follow it and you'll find canyons and slopes along Grayson Lake. Take a break from your hike to have a picnic along the water.

VISIT JENNY WILEY STATE RESORT PARK

There are tons of activities in this park. Take a hike through the terrain, go swimming in the 1,150-acre Dewey Lake or play a round on the disc golf course. You also can catch a show in the outdoor amphitheater.

the Country Highway, known less glamorously as U.S. Route 23. The highway celebrates country music history and the legends who came from this neck of the woods, including Loretta Lynn, Patty Loveless and the Judds.

If you're more interested in the stars in the sky than country music stars, head to Morehead or Olive Hill. Both offer more beautiful scenery that makes this part of Kentucky so appealing to those looking for recreation. If you can't find something to do in the thousands of acres of raw outdoors just waiting to be explored here, you're just not trying.

WHAT TO SEE

ASHLAND

BENNETT'S MILL BRIDGE
Ashland, eight miles west on Highway 125 off Highway 7

One of Kentucky's longest single-span covered bridges at 195 feet, Bennett's Mill Bridge was built in 1855 to serve mill customers. Its original footings and frame are intact, but it's closed to traffic.

Daily.

GREENBO LAKE STATE RESORT PARK
Ashland, 18 miles west via Highway 23 to Highway 1, Ashland, 606-473-7324; www.parks.ky.gov

Get active and enjoy the great outdoors at this popular state park, which offers plenty of activities, including swimming, fishing, boating, hiking, bicycle rentals and tennis. When you're ready to take it easy, an amphitheater offers concerts and shows. The park also offers a variety of recreational programs for children, as well as a lodge and campground.

Daily dawn-dusk.

HIGHLANDS MUSEUM & DISCOVERY CENTER
1620 Winchester Ave., Ashland, 606-329-8888; www.highlandsmuseum.com

Visit this interactive museum to learn about Kentucky's unique heritage. Exhibits include a tribute to country music's history in the state, a glimpse at life in the 19th century and a look at the Kentuckians who fought in the wars of the 20th century.

Admission: adults $5.50, seniors and children 2-18 $4.50, children under 2 free. Tuesday-Saturday 10 a.m.-5 p.m.

PARAMOUNT ARTS CENTER
1300 Winchester Ave., Ashland, 606-324-3175; www.paramountartscenter.com

This intimate theater hosts all kinds of performances, from country music concerts to touring Broadway shows. The center also prides itself on sharing the arts with the rest of the community, especially youths. The restored 1930s Art Deco theater was originally a movie house.

Daily.

MOREHEAD

CAVE RUN LAKE
2375 Highway 801 S., Morehead, 606-784-5624; www.caverun.org

Take advantage of the beach, the bathhouse and seasonal interpretive programs at Twin Knobs and Zilpo campgrounds. Or go fishing for bass and muskie, use the 12 boat ramps, visit the two marinas with boat rentals, go hiking or camp at Twin Knobs and Zilpo campgrounds.

Mid-April-October, daily.

MOREHEAD STATE UNIVERSITY
150 University Blvd., Morehead, 606-783-2221; www.moreheadstate.edu

On campus, see the historic one-room schoolhouse by appointment. The Folk Art Museum, on the first floor of Claypool-Young Art Building, is open

WHAT IS THERE TO SEE IN BREAKS INTERSTATE PARK?

This park's main attraction is the "Grand Canyon of the South," where the Russell Fork of the Big Sandy River plunges through the mountains. The 1,600-foot-deep gorge stretches for five miles through this park on the Kentucky-Virginia border. From the park's entrance, a paved road winds through an evergreen forest and then skirts the canyon rim. Overlooks along the route provide spectacular views of the "Towers," a huge pyramid of rocks. You'll also find caves, springs and fields of rhododendron in this natural wonder.

The visitor center houses historical and natural exhibits. Laurel Lake is stocked with bass and bluegill. It also has a swimming pool, pedal boats, hiking, and mountain bike trails, picnicking, playground and camping.

Monday to Friday. Don't miss the MSU Appalachian Collection, which includes books, periodicals, genealogical materials and government documents. Special holdings are devoted to authors James Still and Jesse Stuart, and there are displays of regional art.
Daily.

OLIVE HILL
CARTER CAVES STATE RESORT PARK
344 Caveland Drive, Olive Hill, 606-286-4411;
www.parks.ky.gov
This 1,350-acre park lies in a region of cliffs, streams and many caves, where you'll find a 30-foot underground waterfall, among other surprises. Activities abound: there's a swimming pool, boating, fishing, canoe trips, nine-hole and miniature golf, tennis, shuffleboard, picnicking, a playground, cottages, a lodge and tent and trailer sites. The park also hosts films, dances and festivals. Several guided cave tours are available.
Daily.

GRAYSON LAKE STATE PARK
314 Grayson Lake Park Road, Olive Hill, 606-474-9727;
www.parks.ky.gov
Nearly 75 miles of shoreline change from gentle slopes to canyons and offer a beautiful backdrop to a day on Grayson Lake. Fishing, boating, hiking, picnicking and camping all keep park visitors entertained.
Daily.

PRESTONSBURG
JENNY WILEY STATE RESORT PARK
75 Theatre Court, Prestonsburg, 606-886-1790,
800-325-0142; www.parks.ky.gov
This park has everything a nature lover could want: hiking trails through the mountainous terrain, water sports on 1,150-acre Dewey Lake, a disc golf course and even an outdoor amphitheater where guests can catch musical-theater hits. There's also a swimming pool, fishing, boating, nine-hole golf, shuffleboard, picnicking, a playground, cottages, a lodge and tent and trailer sites.

MOUNTAIN ARTS CENTER

1 Hal Rogers Drive, Prestonsburg, 606-886-2623; www.macarts.com

This performance theater seats 1,054. It's the home of the Kentucky Opry. A variety of entertainment is scheduled year-round.

DANIEL BOONE COUNTRY

The eastern highlands in southern Kentucky are named for the famous frontiersman. But he's not the only big name to come from this region. Colonel Sanders first introduced the world to finger-lickin' good chicken in Corbin, home to the first Kentucky Fried Chicken restaurant. The area is also home to some breathtaking sites, such as the picturesque Cumberland Gap National Historic Park, which offers a bevy of outdoor activities that will satisfy your inner Daniel Boone.

WHAT TO SEE

CORBIN

BLUE HERON MINING COMMUNITY

Cumberland, in Big South Fork National River/Recreation Area (Kentucky side), south via Highways 27 and 92 to Stearns, then nine miles west on Highway 742 (Mine 18 Road), 606-376-3787; www.nps.gov/biso/bheron.htm

Once a thriving mining community, Blue Heron was abandoned when the mine was closed in 1962. Today, the re-created town comprises metal-frame "ghost structures" that tell the stories of life here in the mid-20th century. Begin your tour at the depot, which has exhibits on the town's history. A scenic railway line connects Blue Heron with the town of Stearns.

Daily.

COLONEL HARLAND SANDERS' ORIGINAL RESTAURANT

Highway 25, Corbin, 606-528-2163; www.chickenfestival.com

There really was a Colonel Sanders. See this authentic restoration of his first Kentucky Fried Chicken restaurant. Displays include an original kitchen, artifacts and the motel where Sanders worked as a chef. The original dining area is still in use, so if the exhibits make you hungry, you can get a bucket of extra crispy.

Daily 10 a.m.-10 p.m.

CUMBERLAND GAP NATIONAL HISTORICAL PARK

Highway 25E, Corbin, 606-248-2817; www.nps.gov/cuga

The park captures the gap's history with several historic buildings and structures preserved on 22,000 acres. Visitors will be amazed by the park's dramatically beautiful countryside, ready to be explored on more than 70 miles of hiking trails. The park's main attraction is a magnificent waterfall, 65 feet high and 125 feet wide. Surrounded by Daniel Boone National Forest, this awesome waterfall is the second largest east of the Rockies. By night, when the moon is full and the sky clear, a mysterious moonbow appears in the mist—a phenomenon you can't find anywhere else in the Western Hemisphere. The park also

HIGHLIGHT

WHAT ARE THE TOP THINGS TO DO IN DANIEL BOONE COUNTRY?

EAT IN COLONEL HARLAND SANDERS' ORIGINAL RESTAURANT

Sit down to a plate of fried chicken bits in Colonel Sanders' first chicken restaurant, the precursor to KFC. Then check out displays of the original kitchen and various other chicken-related memorabilia.

GET ACTIVE IN CUMBERLAND GAP NATIONAL HISTORICAL PARK

There's much to see in this park's vast 20,000 acres. Don't miss the amazing waterfall, which at 65 feet high and 125 feet wide is the second largest east of the Rockies. The park's also the only place in the Western Hemisphere to see a moonbow.

SAVOR THE VIEW IN THE PINNACLE OVERLOOK

Situated in Cumberland Gap National Historical Park, this 2,440-foot overlook offers break-taking vistas of Kentucky, Virginia and Tennessee.

offers a swimming pool, fishing, nature trails, a nature center, riding, tennis, picnicking, a playground, a lodge, cottages, tent and trailer campsites. *Daily.*

HENSLEY SETTLEMENT

Cumberland Gap National Historical Park, Highway 25E, Corbin, 606-248-2817; www.nps.gov/cuga

An isolated mountain community until 1951, Hensley is now a restored historic site. To get here, hike 3 ½ miles up the Chadwell Gap trail or take the shuttle from the visitor center.

Daily 8 a.m.-5 p.m.

LAUREL RIVER LAKE

1433 Laurel Lake Road, London, 606-864-6412

A 5,600-acre lake offers fishing and boating. If you're more of a landlubber, take a hike on one of the many nature trails.

Daily.

HIGHLIGHT

WHAT ARE THE BEST ATTRACTIONS WITHIN DANIEL BOONE NATIONAL FOREST?

These 707,000 acres contain some of Kentucky's most spectacular scenery. Among the park's famous attractions is Red River Gorge Geological Area, known for its natural arches and colorful rock formations as tall as 300 feet. A scenic loop drive of the gorge begins north of Natural Bridge State Resort Park on Highway 77. The nearest camping facilities are at Koomer Ridge, on Highway 15 between the Slade and Beattyville exits of Mount Parkway.

Another must-see is the forest's section of Sheltowee Trace National Recreation Trail, which runs the length of the national forest (and stretches more than 260 miles from Morehead, Ky., to Pickett State Rustic Park in Tennessee). If you're looking for a spectacular drive, take Forest Development Road 918—the main route to Zilpo Recreation Area on Cave Run Lake. The 11.2-mile road winds through hardwood forests and offers great views of Cave Run Lake.

After glimpses of it from afar, don't miss Cave Run Lake. It has beaches, boat ramps and camping at Twin Knobs and Zilpo recreation areas. Laurel River Lake has boat ramps and camping areas at Holly Bay and Grove. Clay Lick (Cave Run Lake), Grove and White Oak (Laurel River Lake) have boat-in camping as well. Hunting and fishing are permitted in most parts of the forest under Kentucky regulations; backpacking is permitted on forest trails.

PINNACLE OVERLOOK

Cumberland Gap National Historical Park, Highway 25E, Corbin, 606-248-2817; www.nps.gov/cuga

The 2,440-foot overlook offers spectacular views into Kentucky, Virginia and Tennessee. To get there, take the Skyline Road up the mountain. Vehicles more than 20 feet in length and all trailers are prohibited.

Daily.

SHELTOWEE TRACE OUTFITTERS

117 Hawkins Ave., Somerset, 606-376-5567, 800-541-7238; www.ky-rafting.com

Go on river rafting, canoeing and "funyak" trips in the scenic Cumberland River below the falls. Appointments are required for the five- to seven-hour trips.

Prices vary. June-September, daily; March-May and October, Saturday-Sunday.

WELCOME TO LOUISIANA

BORN OUT OF SWAMPS AND BAYOUS, CRAFTED FROM

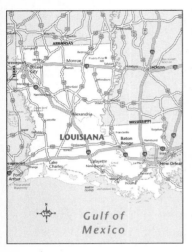

Gulf of
Mexico

the work and tradition of dozens of cultures and celebrated as the home of renowned music, food and legend, Louisiana is as colorful and varied as the characters on the streets of New Orleans during Mardi Gras.

Named by the French (for Louis XIV), Louisiana was settled by both the French and the Spanish. To prevent Louisiana from falling into the hands of the English, Louis XV of France gave it to his cousin, Charles III of Spain. In 1801, Napoleon regained it for France, though no one in Louisiana knew of this until 1803, only 20 days before the Louisiana Purchase made it U.S. territory. From its earliest days, the state was home to settlers of English, Irish and German origin.

The settlers were drawn to Louisiana for any number of reasons. For some, the unique landscape is a major selling point: Louisiana is semitropical, and beautifully unusual—a land of bayous with cypress and live oak overhung with Spanish moss. Today, some Louisianans live in isolation on the bayous and riverbanks, where they still fish, trap and do a little farming.

The northern and southern parts of the state are quite different topographically. In the southern area are fine old mansions and sugarcane plantation estates, many of which are open to the public. The north is more rural, with beautiful rivers, hills, forests and cotton plantation mansions. This is the area from which the colorful politician Huey Long came; he was born in Winnfield.

Hurricane Katrina hit Louisiana hard in 2005, but the affected cities and towns continue the hard work of rebuilding. The storm's floodwaters washed away homes, businesses and some of the state's most beloved landmarks but failed to touch Louisiana's charm. It remains the old Deep South at its best: gracious, cultured and hospitable.

SPORTSMAN'S PARADISE

Louisiana's northernmost region is all about the great outdoors. Bastrop boasts woodlands and bayous, while West Monroe and its smaller twin city, Monroe, have the Ouachita River as a backdrop. But you don't need to be a sportsman to enjoy Sportsman's Paradise. Minden, named after a town in Germany, hosted the wedding of country singer Hank Williams Sr. in 1952. Shreveport, founded in 1835 by river captain and steamboat inventor Henry Miller Shreve, is now best known for its multiple casinos and thoroughbred racing.

Businesses also have found this region to be an inviting place to set up shop; Monroe was the first location west of the Mississippi to brew Coca-Cola and the birthplace of Delta Airlines.

BEST ATTRACTIONS

WHAT ARE THE BEST ATTRACTIONS IN LOUISIANA?

CROSSROADS
If your vision of the South is Steel Magnolias, Crossroads is your place; the film was shot there. But it's also the setting for art museums, theater and proper Southern plantations.

CAJUN COUNTRY
Go down to the Louisiana bayou to see Cajun Country's spectacular swamps and marshes and to get a peek at real Cajun life and maybe an alligator or two.

BATON ROUGE
Beautiful antebellum mansions and gardens fill the neighborhoods of Baton Rouge. Stroll the city's Garden District to see some of the best homes in the city.

NEW ORLEANS
No trip to Louisiana is complete without visiting the Big Easy. Let your worries go and party it up on Bourbon Street, take in homegrown jazz, shop on Magazine Street or feast in the excellent restaurants.

WHAT TO SEE

BASTROP
CHEMIN-A-HAUT STATE PARK
14656 State Park Road, Bastrop, 318-283-0812, 888-677-2436; www.crt.state.la.us/parks
More than 500 wooded acres are found at the intersection of bayous Chemin-a-Haut and Bartholomew. A portion of the "high road to the South" was originally an Native American trail. Visitors can swim, fish, rent a boat, hike or spend the night at one of many tent and trailer sites.
Daily.

SNYDER MEMORIAL MUSEUM
1620 E. Madison Ave., Bastrop, 318-281-8760
The museum covers 150 years of Morehouse Parish history. See antique furniture, kitchen utensils, farm equipment, clothing and Native American artifacts. The gallery features changing art and photographic exhibits.
Daily.

HIGHLIGHT

WHAT ARE THE TOP THINGS TO DO IN SPORTSMAN'S PARADISE?

EXPLORE CHEMIN-A-HAUT STATE PARK

Originally a Native American trail, this park is a place to swim, fish or hike. There's plenty of nature eye candy as well: the 500 wooded acres are near two bayous.

GO TO THE GERMANTOWN MUSEUM

See what life was like back in the day for German settlers. This museum's three buildings were built in 1835 by Germans who were trying to escape persecution.

VISIT THE LOUISIANA PURCHASE GARDENS AND ZOO

Amble through the winding walkways in this garden, which is home to more than 850 animals. If you tire of walking through the 80-acre gardens, you can rest your feet and hop on a boat ride.

PERUSE THE WORKS AND GROUNDS AT THE R. W. NORTON ART GALLERY

This free museum focuses on American and European sculpture, paintings and decorative arts. Check out the pieces by Frederic Remington and Charles M. Russell and afterward take a stroll through the azalea gardens.

MINDEN

GERMANTOWN MUSEUM

120 Museum Road, Minden, 318-377-6061; www.mindenusa.com

The museum includes three buildings completed in 1835 by Germans seeking freedom from persecution. You'll find replicas of a communal smokehouse and a blacksmith shop, as well as records and artifacts used by settlers.
Wednesday-Sunday.

LAKE BISTINEAU STATE PARK

103 State Park Road, Minden, 318-745-3503, 888-677-2478; www.lastateparks.com

This 750-acre park in the heart of a pine forest includes a large lake. Head there for swimming, waterskiing, fishing and boating. Tent and trailer sites and cabins are among the other offerings.
Daily.

MONROE AND WEST MONROE

BRY HALL ART GALLERY

700 University Ave., Monroe, 318-342-1375

The gallery shows art exhibits, including photographs by American and foreign artists, students and faculty.

February-mid-December, Monday-Friday.

BIEDENHARN FAMILY HOUSE

2006 Riverside Drive, Monroe, 800-362-0983; www.bmuseum.org

This historic home is at the Biedenharn Museum & Gardens. Built by Joseph Biedenharn, the first bottler of Coca-Cola in 1914, the house contains antiques, fine furnishings, silver dating from the 18th century and, of course, some Coca-Cola memorabilia.

ELSONG GARDENS & CONSERVATORY

2006 Riverside Drive, Monroe, 800-362-0983; www.bmuseum.org

Located at the Biedenharn Museum & Gardens, these formal gardens enclosed within brick walls were originally designed to accommodate musical events. Today, visitors trigger background music when they amble through separate gardens linked by winding paths. There are four fountains, including one from the garden of Russian Empress Catherine the Great.

LOUISIANA PURCHASE GARDENS AND ZOO

1405 Bernstien Park Drive, Monroe, 318-329-2400; www.monroezoo.org

Formal gardens, moss-laden live oaks, waterways and winding paths surround naturalistic habitats for more than 850 exotic animals in this 80-acre zoo. Boat and miniature train rides are also available, as are areas for picnics and concessions.

Admission: adults $4.50, children $3, children under 3 free. Daily 10 a.m.-5 p.m.

MUSEUM OF ZOOLOGY

700 University Ave., Monroe, 318-342-1799

The fish collection at this intimate museum is one of the largest and most complete in the nation.

February-mid-August, mid-September-December, Monday-Friday.

SHREVEPORT

AMERICAN ROSE CENTER

8877 Jefferson-Paige Road, Shreveport, 318-938-5402; www.ars.org

The center consists of 60 individually designed rose gardens donated by rose societies from across the U.S.

April-October, Monday-Friday 9 a.m.-5 p.m., Saturday 9 a.m.-6 p.m., Sunday 1-6 p.m.

C. BICKHAM DICKSON PARK

2283 E. Bert Kouns Loop, Shreveport; 318-673-7808

Shreveport's largest park contains a 200-acre oxbow lake with a pier. The park offers fishing, hayrides, picnicking and a playground for kids.

Daily.

LOUISIANA STATE EXHIBIT MUSEUM

3015 Greenwood Road, Shreveport; 318-632-2020; www.sos.louisiana.gov

This museum showcases remarkable dioramas and murals of the prehistory and resources of the Louisiana area. It also has exhibits of antique and modern items and a historical gallery.

Monday-Friday 9 a.m.-4 p.m., Saturday-Sunday 9 a.m.-4 p.m.

R. S. BARNWELL MEMORIAL GARDEN AND ART CENTER

601 Clyde Fant Parkway, Shreveport, 318-673-7703; www.nwlagardener.org

The combination art and horticulture facility has permanent and changing exhibits. Flower displays include seasonal and native plantings of the area; the sculpture garden has a walk-through bronze statue; plus, there's a fragrance garden for the visually impaired.

Daily.

R. W. NORTON ART GALLERY

4747 Creswell Ave., Shreveport, 318-865-4201; www.rwnaf.org

The art gallery specializes in American and European paintings, sculpture, decorative arts and manuscripts from the 15th to 20th centuries. It also has a large collection of Western art by Frederic Remington and Charles M. Russell.

Tuesday-Friday 10 a.m.-5 p.m., Saturday-Sunday 1-5 p.m.

WATER TOWN USA

7670 W. 70th St., Shreveport, 318-938-5475; www.watertownusa.com

This 20-acre water theme park features speed slides, adventure slides and a wave pool, plus two other pools. You can take a break at the restaurant and concessions.

WHERE TO STAY

RECOMMENDED

HILTON SHREVEPORT

104 Market St., Shreveport, 318-698-0900

Located in downtown Shreveport, the Hilton is connected to the convention center and is just two blocks from the riverboat casinos. Guest rooms feature Hilton's Serenity bedding, flat-screen LCD televisions with on-demand movies and Nintendo, LaVazza coffee makers, work desks and complimentary Internet access. River Rock Grill serves breakfast with a huge buffet, lunch and dinner. There's also a lounge and coffee bar.

313 rooms. Restaurant, bar. Fitness center. Business center. $61-150

WHERE TO EAT

RECOMMENDED

SUPERIOR GRILL

6123 Line Ave., Shreveport, 318-869-3243; www.superiorgrill.com

Superior Grill has four locations in Baton Rouge, New Orleans and Birmingham, and serves up tasty Mexican food in a lively atmosphere (with a rollicking happy hour every night). The menu includes all of your Mexican favorites, from cheesy enchiladas to sizzling fajitas to crawfish quesadillas and fish tacos.

Mexican. Lunch, dinner. $16-35

CAJUN COUNTRY

Louisiana's famous swamps and marshes are the soul of Cajun Country. This is also where many of the state's Cajun population lives, so visitors get an authentic look at Cajun life here. Franklin, reportedly named by founder Guinea Lewis for Benjamin Franklin, on the Bayou Teche is in the center of Cajun Country. It has much of the beautiful scenery outsiders imagine when they think of Louisiana's coast. Boating, fishing and hunting are popular diversions at the nearby Atchafalaya Basin. Situated on Bayou Terrebonne and the Intracoastal Waterway, Houma is known as the "Venice of America," famous for its Cajun food and hospitality. Jennings, a small town known for its Cajun food, music and museums, is also notable for its outdoor recreational opportunities, including fishing, boating and hiking. The city hosts a farmers market every Saturday and live country music on the last Saturday of each month.

But the heart of Cajun Country lies in Lafayette, a city with French, Spanish and Caribbean traditions still present in the speech patterns, cooking and daily life of its residents. Lafayette is home to top-notch Cajun and Creole restaurants, historic homes and a backyard of outdoor activities worth exploring. Despite its urban rhythm and growing population, Lafayette has retained its small-town appeal. Live oaks and azaleas bloom all around town, as do clumps of native irises. These blooms offer color to an already vibrant place.

New Iberia is home to a variety of attractions ranging from farmers' markets to historic buildings (the city has the country's oldest rice mill) to the 200-acre Jungle Gardens. It's known for a few Louisiana classics: swamps, bayous and alligators.

For a dose of history, few towns in Louisiana have a more colorful past than St. Martinville. On the winding, peaceful Bayou Teche, St. Martinville was first settled around 1760. In the years thereafter, Acadians driven out of Nova Scotia by the British drifted into St. Martinville with the hope of finding religious tolerance. The town is the setting for part of Henry Wadsworth Longfellow's *Evangeline*, a poem about an Acadian girl who is separated from her beloved Gabriel when the British deport the Acadians from Canada during the 18th century. Evangeline eventually settles in Philadelphia, where, as an old woman, she finds her beloved in a hospital and he dies in her arms. Today St. Martinville is a quiet, hospitable destination for visitors who want to stop by the Evangeline Oak and Commemorative Area or sample the local cuisine. There many more towns in this region that offer a piece of Cajun Country, so go down to the bayou and see it for yourself.

WHAT TO SEE

FRANKLIN
CHITIMACHA CULTURAL CENTER
490 Decater St., Charenton, 504-589-3882; www.nps.gov

Museum exhibits, crafts and a 10-minute video focus on the history and culture of the Chitimacha tribe of Louisiana. Walking tours are available. This center is a unit of Jean Lafitte National Historical Park.
Daily.

CYPREMORT POINT STATE PARK
306 Beach Lane, Franklin, 337-867-4510; www.lastateparks.com

This 185-acre site offers access to the Gulf of Mexico. The man-made beach in the heart of a natural marsh affords fresh and saltwater fishing and other seashore recreation opportunities.
Daily.

GREVEMBERG HOUSE
St. Mary Parish Museum, 407 Sterling Road, Franklin, 337-828-2092; www.grevemberghouse.com

The Greek Revival house maintains a fine collection of antique furnishings dating from the 1850s, children's toys, paintings and Civil War relics.
Daily.

OAKLAWN MANOR PLANTATION
3296 E. Oaklawn Drive, Franklin, 337-828-0434; www.oaklawnmanor.com

Restored in 1927, this massive Greek Revival house has 20-inch-thick walls, is furnished with European antiques and is surrounded by one of the largest groves of live oaks in the U.S. It's also the home of former Louisiana Governor Mike Foster.
Admission: adults $10, students $6. Tuesday-Sunday 10 a.m.-4 p.m.

HOUMA
ANNIE MILLER'S SWAMP & MARSH TOURS
3718 Southdown Mandalay, Houma, 985-868-4758; www.annie-miller.com

Boat trips travel through winding waterways in swamps and wild marshlands. See birds, alligators, wild game, tropical plants and flowers.
March-October, daily.

SOUTHDOWN PLANTATION HOUSE/TERREBONNE MUSEUM
1208 Museum Drive, Houma, 985-851-0154; www.southdownmuseum.org

The first floor, Greek Revival in style, was built in 1859; the second floor, which has more of a late Victorian/Queen Anne look, was added in 1893. The 21-room house includes stained glass, a Boehm and Doughty porcelain bird collection, a Terrebonne Parish history room, a re-creation of Allen Ellender's Senate office, antique furniture and Mardi Gras costumes.
Tuesday-Saturday 10 a.m.-4 p.m.

HIGHLIGHT

WHAT ARE THE TOP THINGS TO DO IN CAJUN COUNTRY?

TAKE A DRIVE ON THE CREOLE NATURE TRAIL NATIONAL SCENIC BYWAY

Go for a leisurely car ride through this scenic trail. Aside from the lovely landscape, you'll see one of the largest gator populations in the world, four wildlife refuges and a bird sanctuary.

VISIT AVERY ISLAND

This island is a picturesque paradise with azaleas, Japanese camellias, Egyptian papyrus and other botanical blooms and wildlife like white-tailed deer and small black bears running around.

STOP BY JUNGLE GARDENS

One of Avery Island's best attractions, Jungle Gardens protects egrets and herons, among other animals, and offers trails through oak groves, manmade lagoons, an arch of old wisterias and flower orchards.

STOCK UP ON TABASCO AT THE McILHENNY COMPANY

This family-owned company created the ultimate hot sauce on Avery Island and continues to make it there. Tour the factory and then stop by the store to get some Tabasco lollipops and flash drives shaped like mini 'Basco bottles.

TOUR SHADOWS-ON-THE-TECHE

People like Walt Disney and D. W. Griffith hung out on this antebellum plantation. Four generations lived in this beautiful home, set on the banks of Bayou Teche with Spanish moss-covered oaks towering above.

JENNINGS

W. H. TUPPER GENERAL MERCHANDISE MUSEUM

311 N. Main St., Jennings, 337-821-5532, 800-264-5521; www.tuppermuseum.com

More than 10,000 items on display re-create the atmosphere of early-20th-century life in rural Louisiana. You'll see a toy collection, period clothing, drugs, toiletries and Native American basketry.

Admission: adults $3, students $1. Monday-Friday 9 a.m.-5 p.m.

ZIGLER MUSEUM
411 Clara St., Jennings, 337-824-0114

The museum contains galleries of wildlife and natural history, as well as European and American art.

Tuesday-Sunday.

LAFAYETTE

ACADIAN VILLAGE: A MUSEUM OF ACADIAN HERITAGE AND CULTURE
200 Greenleaf Drive, Lafayette, 337-981-2364, 800-962-9133; www.acadianvillage.org

This restored 19th-century Acadian village features fine examples of unique Acadian architecture with houses, a general store and a chapel. Crafts are on display and for sale.

Daily.

CHRÉTIEN POINT PLANTATION
665 Chrétien Point Road, Lafayette, 337-662-7050; www.chretienpoint.com

This restored 1831 Greek Revival mansion was the site of a Civil War battle.

Daily.

LAFAYETTE MUSEUM
1122 Lafayette St., Lafayette, 337-234-2208

Once the residence of Alexandre Mouton, the first Democratic governor of the state, the house is now a museum with antique furnishings, Civil War relics and carnival costumes.

Tuesday-Sunday.

LAKE CHARLES

BRIMSTONE HISTORICAL SOCIETY MUSEUM
800 Picard Road, Sulphur, 337-527-7142; www.brimstonemuseum.org

The museum commemorates the turn-of-the-century birth of the local sulfur industry with exhibits explaining the development of the Frasch mining process; other exhibits deal with southwest Louisiana.

Monday-Friday 10 a.m.-noon, 1-5 p.m.

CREOLE NATURE TRAIL NATIONAL SCENIC BYWAY
1205 N. Lakeshore Drive, Sulphur, 800-456-7952; www.creolenaturetrail.org

The nature trail follows Highway 27 in a circular route ending back at Lake Charles. It's a unique composite of wildflowers, animals, shrimp, crab and many varieties of fish. Plus, it has one of the largest alligator populations in the world; it's a winter habitat of thousands of ducks and geese; it has views of several bayous, the Intracoastal Waterway, oil platforms, beaches, four wildlife refuges and a bird sanctuary. Take the automobile nature trail or the walking nature trail.

Daily.

HISTORIC "CHARPENTIER"
Lake Charles

The district includes 20 square blocks of downtown area; architectural styles range from Queen Anne, Eastlake and Carpenter's Gothic (known locally as "Lake Charles style") to Western stick-style bungalows. Daily.

IMPERIAL CALCASIEU MUSEUM

204 W. Sallier St., Lake Charles, 337-439-3797; www.imperialcalcasieumuseum.org

Items of local historical interest, a toy collection and rare Audubon prints can be found at this museum. The Gibson-Barham Gallery houses art exhibits. On the premises is the 300-year-old Sallier oak tree.

Tuesday-Saturday.

SAM HOUSTON JONES STATE PARK

107 Sutherland Road, Lake Charles, 888-677-7264; www.lastateparks.com

The approximately 1,000 acres have lagoons in a densely wooded area at the confluence of the west fork of the Caslcasieu and Houston Rivers and the Indian Bayou. Fishing, boating, nature trails, hiking, picnicking, tent and trailer sites, and cabins provide lots of opportunities recreation.

NEW IBERIA

AVERY ISLAND

Highway 14

Surrounded by a bayou, the island is a haven for colorful wildlife, including blue herons, white-tailed deer and small black bears. This unusual Eden is also where Tabasco sauce has been made for nearly 140 years.

BOULIGNY PLAZA

Main Street, New Iberia

In the park are depictions of the history of the area as well as a gazebo, historic landmarks and a beautiful view along the bayou.

JUNGLE GARDENS

200 Center St., New Iberia, Avery Island, 337-369-6243; www.junglegardens.org

Avery Island's most spectacular feature was developed by the late Edward Avery McIlhenny of Tabasco fame. Camellias, azaleas, irises and tropical plants form a beautiful seasonal display. Enormous flocks of egrets, cranes and herons, among other species, are protected here and may be seen in early spring and summer; ducks and other wild fowl can be spotted in winter. The Chinese Garden contains a fine Buddha dating from A.D. 1000.

Admission: adults $8, children $5. Daily 9 a.m.-5 p.m.

KONRIKO RICE MILL AND COMPANY STORE

309 Ann St., New Iberia, 337-364-7242, 800-551-3245; www.conradricemill.com

Take a tour of the oldest rice mill in the U.S.; next door is a replica of the original company store, with antique fixtures and merchandise typical of Acadiana and Louisiana.

Monday-Saturday.

MCILHENNY COMPANY

Highway 329, Avery Island, 337-365-8173; www.tabasco.com

Spice up your day with a tour of the Tabasco factory and Country Store. The gift shop provides some good souvenir options.

Monday-Saturday.

RIP VAN WINKLE GARDENS

5505 Rip Van Winkle Road, New Iberia, 337-359-8525; www.ripvanwinklegardens.com

Stroll through 20 acres of landscaped gardens and nature preserves. Also on the premises is the Victorian residence of 19th-century actor Joseph Jefferson. Stop in the restaurant and gift shop.

Admission: adults $10, children $8. Daily.

SHADOWS-ON-THE-TECHE

317 E. Main St., New Iberia, 337-369-6446; www.shadowsontheteche.org

The red brick and white-pillared Greek Revival house was built on the banks of the Bayou Teche in 1834 by sugar planter David Weeks. Home to four generations of his family, it served as the center of an antebellum plantation system. The house was restored and its celebrated gardens were created in the 1920s by the builder's great-grandson, Weeks Hall. He used the estate to entertain such celebrities as D. W. Griffith, Anaïs Nin and Walt Disney. The house is surrounded by 3 acres of azaleas, camellias and massive oaks draped in Spanish moss. It's a National Trust for Historic Preservation property.

Daily 9 a.m.-4:30 p.m.

ST. MARTINVILLE

EVANGELINE OAK

On the bayou at end of Port Street

This ancient, moss-draped live oak is said to be the meeting place of the real Evangeline and her Gabriel.

LONGFELLOW-EVANGELINE STATE COMMEMORATIVE AREA

1200 N. Main St., St. Martinville, 337-394-3754; www.crt.state.la.us/parks

This 157-acre park on the banks of the Bayou Teche is a reconstruction of a typical 19th-century plantation. Begun around 1810 by Pierre Olivier du Clozel, a French Creole, the Olivier plantation employs wooden pegs; walls are made of Spanish moss-mixed bousillage and cypress; period furnishings fill the space; and there's a replica of an 1840s kitchen and a kitchen garden.

Daily.

ST. MARTIN OF TOURS CATHOLIC CHURCH

133 S. Main St., St. Martinville, 337-394-7334

Established in 1765 as the mother church of the exiled Acadians, the presently restored building contains stained-glass windows; an exquisite carved baptismal font, which was a gift of Louis XVI of France; a gold and silver sanctuary light; a painting of St. Martin de Tours by Jean Francois Mouchet; and other religious artifacts. Guided tours are available by appointment only.

PETIT PARIS MUSEUM

103 S. Main St., St. Martinville, 337-394-7334

This museum contains a collection of elaborate carnival costumes, local memorabilia and a gift shop.

Daily.

HIGHLIGHT

WHAT'S A GOOD DRIVING TOUR OF CAJUN COUNTRY?

Among the bayous and swamps west of New Orleans lies Cajun Country, a 22-parish region with a noticeably French accent. The area's vibrant history stretches back to the 18th century, when French refugees forced out of Nova Scotia by the British sought refuge in the French colony of New Orleans.

Although Lafayette, "the Capital of French Louisiana," can be reached in two hours from New Orleans by interstate, Highway 90 offers a leisurely introduction to Cajun Country that could take a half-day or more. You can catch Highway 90 just west of the French Quarter, but you're better off bypassing suburban congestion by taking I-10 west to the I-310 spur south. Here, the interstate bridge crosses a fierce bend of the Mississippi River barely contained by a high levee. West of the river, I-310 deposits you in the subtropical Cajun wetlands region onto Highway 90; follow this route west toward Gibson.

In New Iberia, a detour south on Highway 329 leads to Avery Island, home of the world-famous McIlhenny Tabasco Sauce, where you can visit the factory for free. After your detour, cross 90 and follow Bayou Teche ("Tesh") toward downtown New Iberia, settled by the Spanish in 1779. Here Shadows-on-the-Teche, built in 1834, opens a stately plantation house museum with an extensive garden of magnolias, oaks and Spanish moss on Highway 182 at 317 E. Main St.

Ten miles north of New Iberia on Highway 31, St. Martinville is famous for the live oak memorialized in Longfellow's epic poem *Evangeline*. The 1847 poem tells the story of Acadian lovers reunited under the venerable oak. A statue of Evangeline stands outside the St. Martin de Tours Church in the small downtown square nearby. At the Longfellow Evangeline Commemorative Area a mile north of town, guides offer tours of the 19th-century sugar plantation house.

Further up Bayou Teche via Highway 31, Breaux Bridge proclaims itself "Crawfish Capital of the World." The town's annual Crawfish Festival on the first full weekend in May features crawfish races, a crawfish-eating contest, the crowning of the Crawfish King and Queen and continuous Cajun and zydeco music. But at any time, you can find people dancing away at Mulate's ("MOO-lots"), 1/4 mile west of Highway 31, practically spitting distance south of I-10. Follow the signs.

In downtown Breaux Bridge, near the drawbridge over Bayou Teche, Cafe des Amis operates out of an old general store built in 1925, retaining the stamped tin ceiling, ceiling fans and brick walls.

To reach Lafayette, take State Road 94 south and west. Founded as Vermilionville alongside the Bayou Vermilion in 1821, Lafayette was later renamed in honor of the Marquis de Lafayette. Today the historic attraction of Vermilionville re-creates a 19th century village, with guides in period costume, craft demonstrations and Cajun music in the barn house. It's open daily at 1600 Surrey St. Across the bayou at **Jean Lafitte National Historic Park** *(501 Fisher Road, 337-232-0789)*, a 30-minute film dramatizes the story of the British removal of the Acadians from Nova Scotia in 1755.

You can find Cajun specialties right off I-49 at the popular **Prejean's** *(3480 N.E. Evangeline Trwy., Lafayette, 337-896-3247; www.prejeans.com)*. After a visit to Cajun Country, you can easily loop back to New Orleans along I-10 East. It's approximately 350 miles.

PRESBYTERE
133 S. Main St., St. Martinville, 337-394-7334

The priest's residence, Greek Revival in style, was constructed in 1856. According to legend, it was built in such a grand manner in the hope that St. Martinville would be designated as the seat of the diocese.

WHERE TO STAY

★★★HILTON LAFAYETTE AND TOWERS
1521 W. Pinhook Road, Lafayette, 337-235-6111; www.hilton.com

The Hilton Lafayette sits along the banks of the Vermilion Bayou. Park yourself in a chaise lounge on the hotel's outdoor pool deck for an excellent view of the river. Back in the room, enjoy amenities like a 37-inch flat-screen HD television, free HBO and other premium cable channels and wireless. The décor is inviting, with soft creams and tans on the walls and duvets and mahogany furniture. If you want to hit the town, the recommended Blue Dog Café and the Bella Notte Jazz Club are about a mile away.

327 rooms. Restaurant, bar. Fitness center. Pool. Pets accepted. $151-250

WHERE TO EAT

★★★RUTH'S CHRIS STEAK HOUSE
620 W. Pinhook Road, Lafayette, 337-237-6123; www.ruthschris.com

Prime steaks broiled in a custom-built oven and served sizzling in a pool of butter on a very hot plate are what you will find in this upscale steakhouse chain. À la carte vegetables include creamed spinach; asparagus with hollandaise sauce; and baked, mashed, lyonnaise, or au gratin potatoes are good meat-pairing options.

Steak. Lunch, dinner. $36-85

RECOMMENDED

BLUE DOG CAFE
1211 W. Pinhook Road, Lafayette, 337-237-0005; www.bluedogcafe.com

Satisfying dishes include Andouille sausage with Creole mustard, seafood gumbo and crawfish enchiladas. The popular Sunday brunch includes a huge buffet and live jazz. You'll also find live music in the bar every Thursday, Friday and Saturday evening.

Cajun, Creole. Lunch (Monday-Friday), dinner, Sunday brunch. $16-35

POOR BOY'S RIVERSIDE INN
240 Tubing Road, Lafayette, 337-235-8559; www.poorboysriversideinn.com

The large menu here features everything from alligator bits and gumbo to a variety of shrimp dishes and oysters. There's also fresh fish, crab and lobster. For dessert, try the sweet potato beignets with cinnamon and an orange-hazelnut glaze.

Cajun, seafood. Lunch, dinner. Closed Sunday. $16-35

BATON ROUGE

Named by its French founders for a red post that marked the boundary between the lands of two Native American tribes, Baton Rouge, the busy capital of Louisiana, is also a major Mississippi River port. Clinging to its gracious past, the area has restored antebellum mansions, gardens, tree-shaded university campuses, splendid Cajun and Creole cuisine, and historic attractions that reflect the culture and struggle of living under 10 flags over a period of three centuries.

When Hurricane Katrina hit the Gulf Coast in August 2005, Baton Rouge endured some minor damage, but the most pronounced effect from the storm was the influx of residents from New Orleans and other cities on the Gulf, causing a boost in population that remains today.

Baton Rouge is divided into distinct neighborhoods, each with its own flavor. One of the most popular is Spanish Town, near downtown, which attracts an eclectic crowd because of its restored historic buildings, big Mardi Gras parade and inclusive attitude. The Garden District is a good place for a casual stroll and a peek at some of the city's most beautiful historic homes, and Beauregard Town, in downtown Baton Rouge, is worth a visit; it one of the city's oldest neighborhoods.

WHAT TO SEE

BREC'S BATON ROUGE ZOO
3601 Thomas Road, Baton Rouge, 225-775-3877; www.brzoo.org
Walkways overlook 140 acres of enclosed habitats for more than 1,800 animals and birds. Take in views of some of the fish, reptiles and amphibians of Louisiana at L'aquarium de Louisiane or take the kids to the Safari Playground or a live elephant show.
Daily.

BREC'S MAGNOLIA MOUND PLANTATION
2161 Nicholson Drive, Baton Rouge, 225-343-4955; www.magnoliamound.org
An early-19th-century Creole-style building was restored to emphasize the lifestyle of colonial Louisiana. See more of that lifestyle with weekly demonstrations of open-hearth Creole cooking and costumed docents. Then meander over to the visitor center and gift shop.
Tuesday-Sunday.

COTTAGE PLANTATION
10528 Cottage Lane, St. Francisville, 225-635-3674; www.cottageplantation.com
The oldest part of the main house was built during Spanish control of the area. Outbuildings include a smokehouse, a school, kitchens and slave cabins. Accommodations and breakfast are available.
Daily.

GOVERNOR'S MANSION
1001 Capitol Access Road, Baton Rouge, 225-342-5855; www.lamansionfoundation.org
On a Greek Revival/Louisiana-style plantation, the mansion was built in 1963

HIGHLIGHT

WHAT ARE THE TOP THINGS TO DO IN BATON ROUGE?

GO TO HOUMAS HOUSE
Stars like Bette Davis, Chevy Chase and Susan Lucci shot on location at Houmas House. It's no wonder why when you see the restored sugar plantation's Greek Revival mansion and lush 38-acre grounds.

LEARN SOMETHING AT THE LOUISIANA ART AND SCIENCE MUSEUM
This former railroad depot is now a stop for fine art and sculpture as well as cultural and historical exhibits. Kiddies will like putting their paws all over the hands-on gallery and science displays.

GET SPOOKED AT MYRTLES PLANTATION
This French-inspired house has ornamental plasterwork and period furniture, but people don't come here to see the décor. They come because it's supposed to be one of the nation's most haunted mansions.

EXPLORE THE NOTTOWAY PLANTATION
You can spend the day exploring Nottoway, one of the largest remaining antebellum mansions in the South. But if it gets too late, stay overnight in one of its lovely Victorian rooms. Bonus: spend the night and you'll get a free tour of the plantation.

CLIMB ABOARD THE USS KIDD
Roam around on this World War II Fletcher-class destroyer. Make time to visit the adjacent museum. There you'll find a ship model collection, maritime artifacts and a restored P-40 Flying Tiger plane.

to replace an earlier official residence.
Tours: Monday-Friday.

HERITAGE MUSEUM AND VILLAGE
1606 Main St., Baker, 225-774-1776
The turn-of-the-century Victorian house showcases period rooms and exhibits. Also check out the rural village with a church, a school, a store and town hall replica buildings.
Monday-Saturday.

HOUMAS HOUSE

40136 Highway 92, Burnside, 225-473-9380, 888-323-8314; www.houmashouse.com

This large restored sugar plantation features a Greek Revival mansion with early Louisiana-crafted furnishings, a spiral staircase, a belvedere and hexagonal garconnieres in gardens. The house and grounds have been used as a set for films such as *Hush... Hush, Sweet Charlotte* starring Bette Davis and TV shows like *Top Chef*. *Monday-Tuesday 9 a.m.-5 p.m., Wednesday-Sunday 9 a.m.-7 p.m.*

LAURENS HENRY COHN, SR., MEMORIAL PLANT ARBORETUM

12056 Foster Road, Baton Rouge, 225-775-1006

This unusual 16-acre tract of rolling terrain contains more than 120 species of native and adaptable trees and shrubs; several major plant collections; an herb/ fragrance garden; and a tropical collection in a greenhouse.
Daily.

LOUISIANA ART & SCIENCE MUSEUM

100 S. River Road, Baton Rouge, 225-344-5272;
www.lasm.org

Originally a railroad depot, this building houses fine art, sculpture, cultural and historical exhibits, an Egyptian exhibition, Discovery Depot (for children ages 6 months to 9 years), hands-on galleries and science exhibits for kids. The Irene W. Pennington Planetarium features large-format films and laser shows. Outside, visitors can explore a sculpture garden and a restored five-car train. Additional fees are charged for Space Theater shows.
Tuesday-Saturday 10 a.m.-4 p.m., Sunday 1-4 p.m. Planetarium: Friday-Saturday 7-10 p.m.

LOUISIANA STATE LIBRARY

701 N. Fourth St., Baton Rouge, 225-342-4913; www.state.lib.la.us

The library houses some 350,000 books, including an extensive section of Louisiana historical tomes, maps and photographs.
Monday-Friday 8 a.m.-4:30 p.m.

INDIAN MOUNDS

Field House and Dalrymple drives, Baton Rouge

These mounds are believed to have served socio-religious purposes and date from 3300 to 2500 B.C.

LSU TIGERS

Nicholson and North Stadium drives, Baton Rouge, 800-960-8587; www.lsusports.net

Louisiana State University fields 20 athletic teams and draws some of the largest crowds in college athletics. The LSU mascots are Mike the Tiger, Mike VI (a live Bengal tiger that hosts daily feedings at the Tiger Cage) and Ellis Hugh (an inflatable acrobatic tiger). LSU adopted its Fighting Tigers nickname in 1896 from a Civil War volunteer company out of New Orleans called the Tiger Rifles.

MEMORIAL TOWER

Highland Road and Dalrymple Drive, Baton Rouge, 225-388-4003;
www.lsu.edu/campus/locations/MEMT.html

Built in 1923 as a monument to Louisianans who died in World War I, the tower houses the LSU Museum of Art and features original 17th- through mid-19th-century rooms from England and America.

MUSEUM OF NATURAL SCIENCE
119 Foster Hall, Baton Rouge, 225-578-2855; www.lsu.com

The museum features an extensive collection of birds from around the world; wildlife scenes include Louisiana marshlands and swamps, the Arizona desert, alpine regions and Honduran jungles.
Monday-Saturday.

THE MYRTLES PLANTATION
7747 Highway 61, St. Francisville, 225-635-6277; www.myrtlesplantation.com

Known as one of America's most haunted mansions, this carefully restored house of French influence boasts outstanding examples of wrought iron, ornamental plasterwork and period furniture. Visitors looking for signs of haunting can take a mystery tour on Friday and Saturday evenings.
Daily.

NOTTOWAY PLANTATION
30970 Highway 405, White Castle, 225-545-2730, 866-527-6884; www.nottoway.com

One of the South's most imposing houses, the 50,000-square-foot Nottoway has 64 rooms, 200 windows and 165 doors. In a near-perfect original state, the house is famous for its all-white ballroom. Also on the premises are a restaurant and overnight accommodations.
Daily.

OAKLEY HOUSE
Audubon State Historic Site, Highway 965, St. Francisville, 225-635-3739, 888-677-2838; www.nps.gov

While living at Oakley and working as a tutor, John James Audubon painted 32 of his Birds of America. Spanish colonial Oakley is part of the Audubon State Historic Site, a 100-acre tract set aside as a wildlife sanctuary.
Daily.

OLD ARSENAL MUSEUM
State Capitol Grounds, 900 Capital Lake Drive, 225-342-0401; www.sos.louisiana.gov

This one-time military garrison dates back to 1838. On the south side are formal gardens that focus on a sunken garden with a monumental statue erected over the grave of Huey P. Long, who was buried here in 1935 after being assassinated in the Capitol.

OLD GOVERNOR'S MANSION
502 North Blvd., Baton Rouge, 225-387-2464; www.oldgovernorsmansion.org

The mansion is restored to the period of the 1930s, when it was built for Gov. Huey P. Long. It includes original furnishings and memorabilia of former governors.
Tuesday-Friday 10 a.m.-4 p.m.

OLD STATE CAPITOL
100 North Blvd., Baton Rouge, 225-342-0500; www.nps.gov

Completed in 1849, Louisiana's old state capitol may be the country's most

SPECIAL EVENT

BLUES WEEK

730 North Blvd., Baton Rouge, 225-383-0968; www.louisianasmusic.com
Louisiana is known for its blues. What better place to have blues week than Baton Rouge? The events range from an entertainment business panel discussion to the Baton Rouge Blues Society all-star jam. The weeklong event features blues, jazz, Cajun, zydeco and gospel music. Previous years have included performers such as Grammy Award winner Chris Thomas King. A Louisiana blues festival is a must. Where else are you going to get the variety of music, events, and good Creole food? Traditional Louisiana cuisine is served. *Late April-early May.*

extravagant example of the Gothic Revival style popularized by the British Houses of Parliament. Located on a bluff overlooking the Mississippi River, the richly ornamented building was enlarged in 1881 and abandoned as the capitol in 1932. A major restoration project was begun in 1990 and re-opened later as the Center for Political and Governmental History. It is is now (at least, officially) referred to as the Museum of Political History
Tuesday-Sunday.

PARLANGE PLANTATION
8211 False River Road, Baton Rouge, 225-638-8410; www.nps.gov
Owned by relatives of the builder, this working plantation is a National Historic Landmark. It includes a French colonial home with a rare example of bousillage construction. Doorways and ceiling moldings are of hand-carved cypress; two octagonal brick dovecotes flank the driveway.
Daily.

PENTAGON BARRACKS MUSEUM
959 Third St., Baton Rouge, 225-342-1866; www.nps.gov
Built in 1822 as part of a U.S. military post, the columned, galleried buildings later became the first permanent home of Louisiana State University.

PORT HUDSON STATE HISTORIC SITE
236 Highway 61, Jackson, 225-654-3775, 888-677-3400; www.crt.state.la.us
This 650-acre area encompasses part of a Civil War battlefield, site of the longest siege in American military history. The site features a 40-foot viewing towers, Civil War guns and trenches and hiking trails. Interpretive programs tell the 1863 story of how 6,800 Confederates held off a Union force of 30,000 to 40,000 men.
Daily.

ROSEDOWN PLANTATION AND GARDENS
12501 Highway 10, St. Francisville, 225-635-3332, 888-376-1867; www.crt.state.la.us/parks
This magnificently restored 1835 antebellum mansion has many original furnishings. The 28 acres of formal gardens include century-old camellias and azaleas, fountains, gazebos and an allée of moss-draped live oaks.
Daily.

RURAL LIFE MUSEUM

4600 Essen Lane, Baton Rouge, 225-765-2437; www.rurallife.lsu.edu

The 3-acre museum complex of 25 buildings is divided into plantation, folk architecture and exhibits. The plantation includes a blacksmith shop, an open-kettle sugar mill, a commissary and a church.

Admission: adults $7, children $5, children under 5 free. Daily.

STATE CAPITOL

N. Third Street and State Capitol Drive, Baton Rouge, 225-342-7317,
800-527-6843;www.nps.gov

Built during Huey P. Long's administration, this 34-story, 450-foot moderne skyscraper is decorated with 26 different varieties of marble. The capitol's Memorial Hall floor is laid with polished lava from Mount Vesuvius; the ceiling is leafed in gold. An observation tower offers views of the city. The Lorado Taft sculpture groups on both sides of the entrance symbolize the pioneer and patriotic spirit.
Daily.

USS KIDD

305 S. River Road, Baton Rouge, 225-342-1942;
www.usskidd.com

Visitors may roam the decks of the World War II Fletcher-class destroyer and explore its interior compartments. A unique dock allows the ship to be exhibited completely out of water when the Mississippi River is in its low stages. The adjacent museum houses a ship model collection, maritime artifacts and a restored P-40 Flying Tiger plane. There's a visitor center and an observation tower that overlooks the river. The Memorial Wall is dedicated to service personnel.
Daily 9 a.m.-5 p.m.

WEST BATON ROUGE MUSEUM

845 N. Jefferson Ave., Port Allen, 225-336-2422;
www.westbatonrougemuseum.com

Exhibits include a large-scale 1904 model sugar mill, a bedroom featuring American Empire furniture and a sugar plantation slave cabin and French Creole house.
Tuesday-Saturday 10 a.m.- 4:30 p.m., Sunday 2-5 p.m.

WHERE TO STAY

★★★MARRIOTT BATON ROUGE

5500 Hilton Ave., Baton Rouge, 225-924-5000; www.marriott.com

Not far from Louisiana State University, this Baton Rouge hotel also is within walking distance of some shops and restaurants. Active types will appreciate its proximity to the 18-hole golf course at Webb Park, but they'll also enjoy the hotel's onsite pool and gym. The comfortable rooms have plush feather comforters and down pillows to ensure a good night's rest before hitting golf links.
299 rooms. Restaurant, bar. Business center. Fitness center. Pool. $61-150

★★★NOTTOWAY PLANTATION RESTAURANT & INN

31025 Louisiana Highway 1, White Castle, 225-545-2730, 866-527-6884; www.nottoway.com

This Victorian-style inn was built in 1859. Today, the home retains its original hand-painted Dresden doorknobs, elaborate plaster frieze work and marble fireplaces. The rooms in the mansion also seem frozen in that era, with mahogany four-poster and half-tester beds and antique furniture. Luckily, they aren't completely frozen in time; the rooms get an update with Internet access. The quaint cottages along the pond are popular new additions to the plantation. All rooms include a free tour of the beautiful estate, which is listed on the National Register of Historic Places. A lovely plantation-style restaurant serves Cajun and Southern cuisine.

15 rooms. Restaurant. Complimentary breakfast. $61-150

★★★SHERATON BATON ROUGE CONVENTION CENTER HOTEL

102 France St., Baton Rouge, 225-242-2600; www.sheraton.com

As its name implies, this Sheraton hotel is right next to an event and meeting facility, Baton Rouge River Center. But it's also steps away from the *USS Kidd* Naval Museum, the Louisiana Art and Science Museum and the Belle of Baton Rouge Casino, so there are plenty of options to keep you busy. But you'll likely make time to take a dip in the outdoor pool and whirlpool at the hotel. The atrium lobby and bar provide another sunny spot to relax. The rooms are equally relaxing, with soothing neutral colors and nice view of the river and city.

300 rooms. Restaurant, bar. Business center. Fitness center. Pool. $151-250

WHERE TO EAT

★★★JUBAN'S

3739 Perkins Road, Baton Rouge, 225-346-8422; www.jubans.com

Diners will find fine southern Louisiana cuisine with a Creole-American influence at this elegant, intimate restaurant. For a sure thing, order the veal T-bone with shiitake mushroom hash and a port wine demi-glace or the hallelujah crab topped with Creolaise sauce. Cap the meal with some housemade honey boubon—it will give you a real taste of Louisiana.

Creole. Lunch, dinner. Closed Sunday. $36-85

★★★RUTH'S CHRIS STEAK HOUSE

4836 Constitution Ave., Baton Rouge, 225-925-0163; www.ruthschris.com

The excellent service and atmosphere are on par with the steaks at this upscale national chain. The different cuts of meat are the stars of the menu, so try a bone-in cowboy ribeye or the classic T-bone. All steaks are seared at 1,800 degrees and topped with fresh butter. For an accompaniment, try the New Orleans au gratin twist on the traditional creamed spinach. For dessert, choose the bread pudding with whiskey sauce.

Steak. Lunch, dinner. Closed Sunday. $36-85

NEW ORLEANS

It is an exciting time to visit New Orleans. Like a phoenix rising from the ashes, or more aptly, the hapless Saints winning the 2010 Super Bowl, the city is experiencing a renaissance fueled by energetic newcomers and determined locals, both of whom are dedicated to making New Orleans a better place to live while preserving its heart and soul. As travelers who are lured back year after year for Mardi Gras, the Jazz Fest or the French Quarter Festival have learned, the music, cuisine and culture are a tasty, slow-cooked gumbo that can't be found anywhere else in the world.

The local music scene is jumping. Trumpeter Irvin Mayfield, the unofficial mayor of New Orleans, opened his swanky Jazz Playhouse smack in the middle of Bourbon Street, an area better known for less high-brow activities. The iconic Uptown club Tipitina's, a shabby clapboard building whose stage has seen a who's who of the world's most talented performers, is ensuring the city's homegrown musical future.

Not to be outdone, the city is teeming with new restaurants. Butcher Cochon, an urban love letter to Cajun country, and Domenica, a nouveau tribute to the city's Italian heritage, are just two of the restaurants that are providing foodies with more diverse choices. Also sprouting up are well-priced neighborhood eateries like Neyow's Creole Cafe in Mid-City. Its healthy helpings of delicious red beans and rice with grilled pork chops and other local standards may yet make it worth the trek across town.

But it is not out with the old and in the new. Many of the city's icons have been or are being lovingly restored. The Roosevelt, New Orleans' former grande dame of the hotel world, is back after a $145 million renovation. Splendid in her finery, she is poised to once again be the backdrop for high-society high jinks, as well as the luxurious place for notable jet-setters to call home. Also on the horizon is the Saenger Theater, listed on the National Register of Historic Places. Expected to open in 2011, it will be the anchor for an emerging live theater district on the edge of the Quarter.

Laissez les bon temps rouler once again. (Translation: let the good times roll!)

WHAT TO SEE

AMPERSAND
1100 Tulane Ave., New Orleans, 504-587-3737; www.clubampersand.com
Sophisticatedly naughty, this converted bank building features two levels, two bars, a huge dance floor, an outdoor courtyard and several sitting rooms, one in the former bank vault. Appealing to serious clubbers of all stripes, Ampersand offers DJs from around the world spinning music of the techno and industrial persuasion.
Friday-Saturday 11 p.m.

HIGHLIGHT

WHAT ARE THE TOP THINGS TO DO IN NEW ORLEANS?

HIGHTAIL IT TO THE AUDUBON ZOO

Audubon Zoo is a whimsical experience, with towering palms and gnarled live oak trees lining the pathways, and a fountain with bronze elephants spouting water. Don't miss the eerie white alligator at the Louisiana Swamp exhibit.

SEE A FLASH OF THE MAKING OF MARDI GRAS

Mardi Gras World gives non-natives an exciting behind-the-scenes peek at the floats that make Mardi Gras one of the greatest shows on earth. Watch the artisans in action and see some of the rolling works of art up close and personal.

TOUR THE MANSIONS IN THE GARDEN DISTRICT

The Garden District neighborhood has some of the South's grandest mansions and most carefully preserved architecture. Entertaining tales of the goings-on of noteworthy inhabitants over the decades accompany tours of the Greek Revival, Italianate and Queen Anne Victorian homes, many of which are owned by local luminaries such as Anne Rice.

HEAR THE RHYTHM OF THE CITY ON FRENCHMEN STREET

Frenchmen Street, just outside of the French Quarter, is the city's musical heart and soul. On any given night, about a dozen clubs along three blocks feature homegrown acts performing everything from jazz to rhythm and blues to rock, with street musicians adding to the lively scene as you navigate from blaring trumpet to the next.

VISIT FAMOUS GRAVES AT THE ST. LOUIS CEMETERY NO. 1

St. Louis Cemetery No. 1 is the final resting place of some of the city's most famous—first mayor and sugar pioneer Etienne de Boré—and infamous—voodoo queen Marie Laveau—residents. A tour of the above ground tombs is the quintessential creepy New Orleans thing to do.

AUDUBON AQUARIUM OF THE AMERICAS

1 Canal St., Riverfront Area, New Orleans, 504-861-2537, 800-774-7394; www.auduboninstitute.org

True to its name, this aquarium houses more than 10,000 aquatic creatures from all areas of the Americas. For total immersion without getting wet, walk through the aquatic tunnel in the Caribbean Reef section or catch a glimpse of a rare white alligator through the River View window in the Mississippi section. Boasting the largest collection of jellyfish in the world, the aquarium also houses penguins, sea otters and sharks—brave visitors can touch one.

Sunday-Tuesday 10 a.m.-5 p.m., Friday-Saturday 10 a.m.-7 p.m.

AUDUBON NATURE INSTITUTE

6500 Magazine St., New Orleans, 504-861-2537; 800-774-7394; www.auduboninstitute.org

This 400-acre park designed by the Olmsted brothers is nestled between St. Charles Avenue and the Mississippi River and is surrounded by century-old live oak trees. The park features a par-62, 18-hole golf course, bicycle and jogging paths, and tennis courts.

Daily.

AUDUBON ZOO

6500 Magazine St., New Orleans, 504-861-2537, 800-774-7394; www.auduboninstitute.org

More than 1,800 animals from every continent call this top-ranked zoo, part of the Audubon Nature Institute, home. Check out kangaroos from Australia, llamas from South America, white tigers from Asia and zebras from Africa, all in naturalistic habitats. Indigenous furry, feathered and scaly creatures are featured at the Louisiana Swamp Exhibit. You can get up close during the sea lion show and in the Embraceable Zoo. Discovery walks, the EarthLab and other interactive programs make the zoo an educational experience. Just don't tell the kids.

Daily 10 a.m-4 p.m.

BAYOU BARRIERE GOLF COURSE

7427 Highway 23, Belle Chasse, 504-394-9500; www.bayoubarriere.com

This course is fairly flat but strives to offer variety from hole to hole. The fairways differ in width and water comes into play, but at different points in each hole. The prices are reasonable, and the course is open year-round. With 27 holes onsite, the facility accommodates high levels of traffic well, and you can explore various combinations of holes to find your favorite 18. The most challenging nine is the third, as the tee boxes are mostly on the course's levee.

BEAUREGARD-KEYES HOUSE AND GARDEN

1113 Chartres St., New Orleans, 504-523-7257; www.neworleansmuseums.com

This Greek Revival, Louisiana-raised cottage was restored by its former owner, the novelist Frances Parkinson Keyes. Confederate Army Gen. Pierre G. T. Beauregard lived here for more than a year following the Civil War. Exhibits include the main house and servant quarters, which together form a handsome shaded courtyard. (Keyes lived informally in the servant quarters, which are filled with her books, antiques and family heirlooms.) To the side of the main house is a formal garden that is part of the guided tour conducted by costumed docents.

Admission: adults $5, seniors $4, children $2. Monday-Saturday 10 a.m.-3 p.m.

BOURBON STREET

French Quarter, New Orleans, 504-525-5801; www.bourbonstreetexperience.com

No place in the world can match Bourbon Street for round-the-clock fun. With elegant hotels next door to garish strip clubs, Bourbon Street contains the ever-beating heart of the French Quarter. Visit its shops and restaurants in the daytime if you're not up for the always-rowdy nighttime crowds. But if you're visiting the Big Easy to let the good times roll, there's no better place to start a night of rambunctious partying.

THE CABILDO

701 Chartres St., New Orleans, 504-523-3939; www.friendsofthecabildo.org

Part of the Louisiana State Museum, the Cabildo offers exhibits on life in early New Orleans, including plantation and slave life. Construction was completed in 1799 and the building housed the city council and the Louisiana Supreme Court at various times. In 1803, the transfer of the Louisiana Purchase took place here. The museum covers diverse topics, such as burial customs, women's roles in the South and immigrants' fate.

Admission: adults $12, seniors $10, children free. Tuesday-Sunday 10 a.m.-1.30 p.m.

CATHEDRAL GARDEN

615 Pere Antoine Alley, New Orleans, 504-525-9585; www.stlouiscathedral.org

The monument in the center of the garden was erected in honor of French marines who died while nursing New Orleans' citizens during a yellow fever outbreak. Picturesque, narrow Pirate's Alley, bordering the garden, is a favorite spot for painters. On the Alley is the house in which William Faulkner lived when he wrote his first novel. The garden is also called St. Anthony's Square in memory of a beloved priest known as Pere Antoine.

Daily.

CEMETERY & VOODOO HISTORY TOUR

334-B Royal St., New Orleans, 504-947-2120; www.tourneworleans.com

The two-hour tour features St. Louis Cemetery No. 1, the oldest and most significant burial ground in New Orleans; visits to a practicing voodoo priestess at her temple; Congo Square, the site of early slave gatherings; and a stop at the home of legendary voodoo queen Marie Laveau.

Monday-Saturday 10 a.m., 1 p.m., Sunday 10 a.m.

CITY PARK

1 Palm Drive, New Orleans, 504-482-4888; www.neworleanscitypark.com

The 1,500 acres of City Park provide room for all sorts of family fun. Step into Storyland to glide down the dragon-flame slide, board Captain Hook's ship or engage with actors portraying storybook characters. Hop aboard one of two minitrains and mount a steed on one of the oldest wooden carousels in the U.S. Get some spray from Popp Fountain, secure a license and catch some fish in one of the many lagoons, or bask in Marconi Meadow and catch some rays. Admire a range of architectural styles in various buildings and bridges. Appreciate the natural beauty in the Botanical Garden and see more mature oak trees than any other place in the world. Get active and rent a boat or play tennis, golf or softball in the park's facilities. The options are endless.

CONTEMPORARY ARTS CENTER

900 Camp St., New Orleans, 504-528-3805; www.cacno.org

Established in 1976, the Contemporary Arts Center is housed in an award-winning building that was renovated in 1990. Each year, CAC hosts as many as two dozen exhibitions in its 10,000 square feet of gallery space. Taking a multi-disciplinary approach, the center promotes art forms as traditional as painting, photography and sculpture, and as diverse as performance art, dance, music and video. Artists Studio Days offer children and their elders a glimpse into the creative process. CAC also hosts the annual Black Theater Festival during the first two weekends in October.

Tuesday-Sunday 11 a.m.-5 p.m.

CRESCENT CITY FARMERS MARKET

Various locations throughout New Orleans, 504-861-4488, 504-495-1459; www.crescentcityfarmersmarket.org

At this market, regional vendors offer fresh produce, seafood, baked goods and other edibles, as well as cut flowers and bedding plants. Each location hosts frequent cooking demonstrations with area chefs and a variety of food-related events. Market founders promote sound ecological and economic development in the greater New Orleans area. Choose the day and location to suit your needs.

Tuesday Market (between Levee and Broadway in the parking lot of Uptown Square at 200 Broadway): 10 a.m.-1 p.m. Wednesday Market (between French Market Place and Governor Nicholls Street): 10 a.m.-2 p.m. Thursday Market (American Can Company residential development at 3700 Orleans Avenue): 3-7 p.m. Saturday Market (Warehouse District, at Magazine and Girod streets, at 700 Magazine St): 8 a.m.-noon.

DESTREHAN PLANTATION

13034 River Road, Destrehan, 985-764-9315, 877-453-2095; www.destrehanplantation.org

Built in 1787, this is the oldest plantation house left intact in the lower Mississippi Valley, with ancient live oaks adorning the grounds.

Daily.

ENTERGY IMAX THEATRE

1 Canal St., New Orleans, 504-581-4327, 800-774-7394; www.auduboninstitute.org/imax

Adjacent to the Audubon Aquarium of the Americas and part of the Audubon Nature Institute, this theater showcases several films at a time in larger-than-life format and hosts a summer film festival.

Daily.

F & F BOTANICA

801 N. Broad St., New Orleans, 504-482-9142

The oldest and largest spiritual supply store in the French Quarter, F & F Botanica sells herbs, oils, potions, candles, incense—whatever you need to enhance your spiritual practice. The store offers free consultations to help you figure out how to find what your spirit seeks.

Monday-Saturday 8 a.m.-6 p.m.

FAIR GROUNDS RACE COURSE

1751 Gentilly Blvd., New Orleans, 504-944-5515; www.fairgroundsracecourse.com

The horses have been darting out of the starting gates at this Mid-City racetrack since 1852, making it the oldest track still operating in the United States. When you're not placing bets and watching the fast-paced action, wander through the Racing Hall of Fame, which honors 110 of the sport's most revered, such as Bill Shoemaker, the legendary jockey, and Duncan Kenner, the founding father of racing in this country. The 145-acre facility also hosts the city's annual Jazz and Heritage Festival.

Mid-November-March.

FRENCH MARKET

800 Decatur St., New Orleans, 504-525-4544; www.cafedumonde.com

A farmers' market since 1791, the market is also home to the popular Café du Monde, a famous coffee stand specializing in café au lait (half coffee with chicory, half hot milk) and beignets (square-shaped doughnuts sprinkled with powdered sugar). The café never closes (except December 25), and café au lait and beignets are inexpensive treats.

Daily.

FRENCH QUARTER

From Canal Street to Esplanade Avenue, and from Decatur Street on the Mississippi River to Rampart Street, 504-636-1020; www.frenchquarter.com

Whether you are in New Orleans to party, shop till you drop, soak up Creole (or voodoo) charms, sample Southern hospitality, delve into history or admire architecture, you can find what you want in the Vieux Carré. The oldest and only remaining French and Spanish settlement in the country, the Quarter offers sights, sounds, tastes and treasures to suit every interest.

FRENCH QUARTER WALKING TOURS

www.frenchquarter.com

Both the Friends of the Cabildo (*1850 House Museum Store, 523 St. Ann St. on Jackson Square, 504-523-3939*) and the French Quarter Visitor Center (*419 Decatur St., 504-589-2636*) offer walking tours that cover the Quarter's history and architecture. The pace is not strenuous, but factor in the heat and humidity and dress accordingly. Licensed guides conduct the two-hour Friends of the Cabildo tours, while interpreters from the National Park Service lead a 90-minute free tour, which is restricted to the first 25 people who show up each day. A Cabildo tour ticket entitles you to a discount on items at the 1850 House Museum Store.

Daily.

GALLIER HOUSE

1132 Royal St., New Orleans, 504-525-5661; www.hgghh.org

For a slice of pre-Civil War life in New Orleans, check out the architect James Gallier Jr.'s home, which he designed for himself in 1857. Thoroughly modern for its time, the house boasts hot-and-cold running water and an indoor bathroom. Painstakingly restored, the house is one of New Orleans' more beautiful historic landmarks.

Monday-Friday 10 a.m.-4 p.m.

THE GARDEN DISTRICT
Magazine Street and Washington Avenue, New Orleans

Once the social center of New Orleans' American (as opposed to Creole) aristocracy, the district has beautiful Greek Revival and Victorian houses with palms, magnolias and enormous live oaks on the spacious grounds in this area. Numerous celebrities have homes here.

GRAY LINE BUS TOURS
1 Toulouse St., New Orleans, 504-569-1401, 800-535-7786; www.graylineneworleans.com

View all of New Orleans' must-see sites from the comfort of an air-conditioned bus. Besides its comprehensive city tour, Gray Line offers numerous other sightseeing options, including tours of plantations, swamps and bayous; the Garden District; and cemeteries. An off-the-beaten-path trek takes you to such places as the childhood neighborhood of jazz great Louis Armstrong and Faubourg Marigny, one of the earliest Creole suburbs, where the striking architecture will surely grab your attention. The company also offers a Hurricane Katrina tour, highlighting the city before, during and after the storm.

HARRAH'S NEW ORLEANS
8 Canal St., New Orleans, 504-533-6000, 800-847-5299; www.harrahs.com

The oldest of New Orleans's land-based casinos, Harrah's is 115,000 square feet of nonstop gambling. More than 100 tables offer 10 different games, including poker, craps, baccarat and roulette. You can play the slots for a penny, a dollar or up to $500. Live jazz, Creole cuisine, Mardi Gras décor and an attached hotel round out the experience.

HERMANN-GRIMA HOUSE
820 St. Louis St., New Orleans, 504-525-5661; www.hgghh.org

The Georgian design reflects the post-Louisiana Purchase American influence on traditional French and Spanish styles in the Quarter; the furnishings typify a well-to-do lifestyle during the period of 1831-1860. The restored house has elegant interiors, two landscaped courtyards, slave quarters, a stable and a working period kitchen. Speaking of the kitchen, check out Creole cooking demonstrations on the open hearth.
Monday-Friday.

HISTORIC NEW ORLEANS COLLECTION
533 Royal St., New Orleans, 504-523-4662; www.hnoc.org

Established in 1966 by local collectors General and Mrs. Kemper Williams, the Collection comprises several historic buildings that house a museum and comprehensive research center for state and local history. The main exhibition gallery presents changing displays on Louisiana's history and culture. The 1792 Merieult House features a pictorial history of New Orleans and Louisiana; the Williams Residence shows the elegant lifestyle of the Collection's founders. There is also a touch tour for the visually impaired.
Tuesday-Saturday 9:30 a.m.-4:30 p.m.

HOUSE OF BLUES

225 Decatur St., New Orleans, 504-310-4999; www.hob.com

Even in the eye-catching French Quarter, it is hard to miss the gaudy, neon-lit entrance to the House of Blues. Past the wildly decorated porch, you will hear live music ranging from Cajun to country and reggae to rock 'n' roll, not to mention pure, soulful blues. The Sunday Gospel brunch is justly famous and surprisingly inexpensive.

THE HOWLIN' WOLF

907 S. Peters St., New Orleans, 504-522-9653; www.howlin-wolf.com

Arguably one of New Orleans' best clubs, the Howlin' Wolf offers up live music of all sorts. Sometimes it rocks and sometimes it's got the blues, but it is always a great place to see a show. The Howlin' Wolf is popular with college students and those looking for original music and up-and-coming acts. Check out the acoustic open-mike nights on Mondays.

JACKSON BREWERY

600 Decatur St., New Orleans, 504-566-7245; www.jacksonbrewery.com

This historic brewery was converted into a large retail, food and entertainment complex with 75 shops and restaurants, outdoor seating and a riverfront promenade. Shop for souvenirs at the Big Easy T-Shirt Company, which sells city-themed tees; Gumbo Kids, custom-painted clothing for little ones; and Street Scene, an art gallery specializing in New Orleans woodgraphs.
Monday-Saturday 10 a.m.-8 p.m., Sunday 10 a.m.-7 p.m.

JACKSON SQUARE

615 Pere Antoine Alley, New Orleans; www.jackson-square.com

Bordered by Chartres, St. Peter, Decatur, and St. Ann streets, this area was established as a drill field in 1721 and was called the Place d'Armes until 1848, when it was renamed for Andrew Jackson, hero of the Battle of New Orleans. The figure of Jackson, the focal point of the square, was the world's first equestrian statue with more than one hoof unsupported; the American sculptor, Clark Mills, had never seen an equestrian statue and therefore did not know that the pose was thought to be impossible. Today, the square and surrounding plaza is one of the best places in the Quarter to catch your breath, people-watch and listen to jazz. It attracts local artists, food vendors and street performers such as mimes, magicians and musicians.

JEAN BRAGG ANTIQUES & GALLERY

600 Julia St., New Orleans, 504-895-7375; www.jeanbragg.com

The focus of this shop and gallery is on Louisianan and Southern art, especially paintings, watercolors and etchings of the state and the French Quarter. Specializing in George Ohr pottery and Newcomb College pottery and craftwork, the shop also offers museum-quality pieces from the late-19th and early-20th centuries. Discover vintage linens, jewelry and glassware along with Victorian furniture.
Monday-Saturday 10 a.m.-5 p.m.

HIGHLIGHT

WHAT'S THE BEST WAY TO SEE THE FRENCH QUARTER?

New Orleans practically begs visitors to stroll her scenic streets, and the city's most prestigious addresses are all on Royal Street, which is lined with historic buildings, fine restaurants and some of the nation's most exclusive antique shops. The most refined road in the Quarter, Royal is only a block south and a world away from party-hearty Bourbon Street. Even if you cannot afford to buy the Louis XVI carved mahogany loveseat, this strip is a great place to wander and window-shop.

A good starting point for exploring this part of New Orleans is behind St. Louis Cathedral, a block up from Jackson Square, where a lush collection of tropical plants fills the compact St. Anthony's Garden. Follow the alleyway upriver to 324 Pirates Alley, where author William Faulkner lived in 1925. His fans still flock to that corner, now the home of a popular bookstore featuring the works of this bard of Southern letters. Continue down Pirates Alley and away from the river along St. Peter to return to Royal Street.

Near St. Peter and Royal streets, the brick LaBranche buildings, with their dramatic cast-iron galleries, were built starting in 1835. Proceed upriver along Royal Street. Beyond Toulouse Street, the 1798 Court of Two Lions at 541 Royal Street features marble lions atop the entry posts. The same architect built the neighboring house (527-533 Royal St.) in 1792. Now home to the Historic New Orleans Collection, the house museum displays exhibits on the city's history.

Between St. Louis and Conti streets, the huge State Supreme Court Building dominates the block; the baroque edifice is made of white Georgia marble. Further down, between Conti and Bienville streets, the block-long Monteleone Hotel is a posh, 600-room home-away-from-home.

Head north on Iberville to Bourbon Street, pass restaurants, nightclubs and saloons, and then drop down St. Ann Street back to Royal, where the Café des Exiles marks the historical gathering spot of French refugees from the Revolution. Further downriver, a detour down Dumaine lands you in front of Madame John's Legacy (632 Dumaine, 504-568-6968). This French cottage was one of the few structures to survive the fire that destroyed most of the city in 1794. Return to Royal and proceed downriver to the cornstalk fence at 915 Royal, a site that draws onlookers and carriage tours that stop to admire the intricate tasseled design of the ironwork.

The Gallier House (1118-32 Royal St.) was built in the 1860s by acclaimed local architect James Gallier Jr. Further down Ursulines Avenue is the old Ursulines Convent at the corner of Chartres Street. The 1745 convent is among the oldest structures in the city. Continue down Ursulines toward the river to visit the French Market, or return upriver along Chartres Street to get back to Jackson Square.

JOHN JAMES AUDUBON RIVERBOAT

2 Canal St., New Orleans, 504-586-8777, 800-233-2628; www.steamboatnatchez.com

The riverboat *John James Audubon* provides river transportation between the Aquarium of the Americas and the Audubon Zoo seven miles upriver, round-trip or one-way; return may be made via the St. Charles Avenue Streetcar. The round-trip ticket price includes admission to both the Audubon Zoo and the Aquarium of the Americas.

LAFAYETTE SQUARE

6000 St. Charles Ave., New Orleans

The square features statues of Benjamin Franklin, Henry Clay and John McDonough.

LAFITTE'S BLACKSMITH SHOP

941 Bourbon St., New Orleans

This popular bar is arguably the oldest French-style building left in the French Quarter. (After two fires in the 1700s destroyed much of the city, the Spanish style dominated rebuilding efforts.) Local lore has it that the original smithy, built sometime before 1772, served as a front for pirate Jean Lafitte's more notorious activities. The bar retains a dark, historical feel, although the local and exotic patrons lighten the atmosphere.

LAKE PONTCHARTRAIN

Lakeshore Drive, New Orleans

This is a favorite local spot for picnicking, fishing, running, cycling, skating or simply watching sailboats pass by.

LE CHAT NOIR

715 St. Charles Ave., New Orleans, 504-581-5812; www.cabaretlechatnoir.com

Get decked out—that is, no jeans or shorts—to check out the Cat (chat noir means "black cat") for an ever-changing schedule of cabaret, live theater and musical performances. The Bar Noir is a cozier room, perfect for a pre-show cocktail (try the house specialty, the Black Cat) or for quiet conversation with friends.

LONGUE VUE HOUSE & GARDENS

7 Bamboo Road, New Orleans, 504-488-5488; www.longuevue.com

A grand city estate furnished with original English and American antiques is on 8 acres of formal and picturesque gardens. Plus there are changing exhibits in galleries and seasonal horticultural displays in the gardens.

Admission: adults $10, students $5, children free. Monday-Saturday 10 a.m.-4:30 p.m., Sunday 1-5 p.m.

LOUIS ARMSTRONG PARK

800 block of N. Rampart St., New Orleans

To the left of the entrance—built to resemble a Mardi Gras float—is a stand of very old live oak trees. This area was originally known as Congo Square, where slaves were permitted to congregate on Sunday afternoons; it was also the scene of voodoo rites. After the Civil War, the square was named for General

P. G. T. Beauregard. Louis Armstrong Park, which includes an extensive water garden that focuses upon a larger-than-life-size statue of Armstrong, was expanded from the original square and contains the municipal auditorium and the Theatre of the Performing Arts.

LOUISIANA STATE MUSEUM

751 Chartres St., New Orleans, 504-568-6968, 800-568-6968; lsm.crt.state.la.us

The museum comprises five properties in the French Quarter and three sites outside of the city. Though only the residence is open to the public (a kitchen and servants' quarters complete the complex), Madame John's Legacy is a fine example of Creole architecture. Built in 1789 after the great fire of 1788, it is notable for surviving the subsequent 1795 fire. The 1850 House, named for the year it was built, holds an authentic collection of period furnishings. The Old U.S. Mint was the only mint in the country that printed currency for both the Confederacy and the U.S. government. The mint now holds state and local research materials and exhibits.

Admission: adults $6, seniors $5, children free. Tuesday-Saturday 9 a.m.-5 p.m., Sunday noon-5 p.m.

LOUISIANA SUPERDOME

Sugar Bowl Drive, New Orleans, 504-587-3663, 800-756-7074; www.superdome.com

The Dome is home field for the New Orleans Saints and the Tulane University Green Wave. It has also hosted a variety of other sports events, including college baseball and the 2003 NCAA men's basketball Final Four. The annual Endymion Extravaganza Mardi Gras Parade and Party happens here, as well as the New Orleans Home & Garden Show, the Boat & Sport Fishing Show, the Kid's Fair & Expo and numerous concerts and other special events. In the immediate aftermath of Hurricane Katrina, the Superdome became a temporary home to thousands of people who evacuated due to rising floodwaters.

LOUISIANA CHILDREN'S MUSEUM

420 Julia St., New Orleans, 504-523-1357; www.lcm.org

Catering to toddlers and the young at heart, this museum encourages hands-on exploration. Kids can take a ride in a simulated police cruiser in the Safety First area, anchor a newscast in the Kidswatch Studio or experience bayou life in the Cajun Cottage. Other areas include Waterworks, Big City Port and Art Trek.

Children under 16 must be accompanied by an adult. Tuesday-Saturday 9:30 a.m.-4:30 p.m., Sunday noon-4:30 p.m.

M. S. RAU ANTIQUES

630 Royal St., New Orleans, 504-523-5660, 800-544-9440; www.rauantiques.com

Founded in 1912, this family-owned and family-run business is so confident of its merchandise that it offers a 125-percent guarantee on all in-store purchases. Internationally known names such as Paul Revere, Meissen, Faberg, Wedgwood, Tiffany and Chippendale are represented in the 25,000-square-foot showroom and extensive catalog. You can also pick up diamonds, jewelry, silver and objects d'art among the vast array of American and European antiques.

Monday-Saturday 9 a.m.-5:15 p.m.

HIGHLIGHT

WHAT ARE THE SOME OF NEW ORLEANS' BEST MUSIC VENUES?

IRVIN MAYFIELD'S JAZZ PLAYHOUSE
(300 Bourbon St., French Quarter, 504-586-0300)

Real New Orleans jazz had been missing from Bourbon Street for many years, but it's back with the sounds of Grammy award-winning Irvin Mayfield and his namesake club. Seven nights a week, the plush, dimly lit club tucked inside the Royal Sonesta Hotel serves up a local showcase of some of the area's top talent. Try to go on a Wednesday night when Irvin himself performs with members of the New Orleans Jazz Orchestra (NOJO) or on Friday for contemporary burlesque with Trixie Minx and music by Leon "Kid Chocolate" Brown. No cover (one drink minimum) and celebrity sightings sweeten the deal. Patrons young and old are up on their feet by the end of the night.

VAUGHAN'S LOUNGE
(800 Lesseps St., Bywater, 504-947-5562)

Kermit Ruffins is an incredibly likeable local trumpet player now playing himself in the HBO drama *Treme*. This family run, former grocery store located off the beaten path in the Bywater (a neighborhood in the ninth ward; about a $10 cab ride from downtown) has become famous for an authentic New Orleans experience. Ruffins will play until he decides to stop and the place serves red beans and rice and inexpensive beer.

PRESERVATION HALL
(726 St. Peter St., French Quarter, 504-522-2841)

Located in the heart of the French Quarter, Preservation Hall is worth waiting in line for. Legendary as a venue for traditional New Orleans jazz, this small space reveals large sound and an unforgettable experience. Nightly performances include the Preservation Hall Jazz Band, but can also include anything from the Dirty Dozen Brass Band to 98 year-old trumpet player Lionel Ferbos.

FRENCHMEN STREET
While you won't catch many locals on Bourbon, you will on Frenchmen. Take a stroll down this street in the Faubourg Marigny near the Quarter and find yourself being drawn in by the sounds spilling out onto the street—from jazz, R&B, funk, blues, reggae, and rock n' roll. Highlights include Snug Harbor *(626 Frenchmen St., 504-949-0696)*, D.B.A. *(618 Frenchmen St., 504-942-3731)*, The Blue Nile Nightclub *(532 Frenchmen St., 504-948-2583)* and La Maison de la Musique *(508 Frenchmen St, 504-289-5648)*.

MAGAZINE STREET

Magazine Street, New Orleans, 504-342-4435, 866-679-4764; www.magazinestreet.com

Fun and funky, Magazine Street offers six miles of clothing retailers, antique establishments, gift shops, eateries and more. Most of the businesses are housed in 19th-century buildings or brick-faced cottages, which helps the area maintain its otherworldly charm. You can stroll from the French Quarter through Magazine Street to the Audubon Zoo, purchasing some jewelry, a piece of furniture, a book or a bite to eat along the way. Make a point to stop off at the Magazine Arcade, a mini-mall that houses eclectic shops offering antique music boxes and musical instruments, period medical equipment, dolls and their furnishings, as well as antique household items for real people.

Most shops open daily 10 a.m.-5 p.m.

MAISON LEMONNIER

640 Royal St., New Orleans

Built in 1811 and sometimes called the "Skyscraper," this was the first building in the Vieux Carré more than two stories high. This house was used as the setting of George W. Cable's novel *Sieur George*. Notice the YLR, for Yves LeMonnier, worked into the grillwork.

MARDI GRAS WORLD

233 Newton St., New Orleans, 504-361-7821, 800-362-8213; www.mardigrasworld.com

For a fascinating look at where about 75 percent of Mardi Gras props and floats are made, visit this unique establishment—the world's largest of its kind. You can try on costumes; watch painters, sculptors and carpenters at work; and tour rooms filled with props and Mardi Gras paraphernalia. The Kern family's business also provides floats and props for parades across the country.

Daily 9:30 a.m.-4:30 p.m.

MEMORIAL HALL—CONFEDERATE MUSEUM

929 Camp St., New Orleans, 504-523-4522; www.confederatemuseum.com

Louisiana veterans of the War Between the States founded the Hall as a repository for artifacts and memorabilia of the Confederate side of the Civil War. Opened in 1891, it is the nation's longest continuously operating museum. The museum houses flags, swords and uniforms from both officers and foot soldiers as well as an extensive collection of photographs. The widow of Confederate president Jefferson Davis donated many family items.

Monday-Saturday 10 a.m.-4 p.m.

METAIRIE CEMETERY

5100 Pontchartrain Blvd., New Orleans, 504-486-6331; www.lakelawnmetairie.com

On the former grounds of the Metairie Race Course, the largest and loveliest of New Orleans' cemeteries is home to a variety of eye-catching memorials and mausoleums. Do not miss the pyramid and sphinx Brunswig mausoleum or the former gravesite of Storyville madam Josie Arlington, whose family had her body moved when tourists flocked to the crypt. But keep your eyes open: At least one of the numerous bronze statues is said to wander the grounds, a lovely setting for a quiet stroll.

Daily 8:30 a.m.-5 p.m.

MOONWALK

615 Pere Antoine Alley, New Orleans, www.neworleansonline.com

Running the length of the French Quarter along the river levee, the Moonwalk is a pedestrian thoroughfare that connects many attractions along the water, including the Aquarium of the Americas and paddleboat cruises, as well as shops and restaurants. Or you can park yourself on a bench and watch the crowds and the river flow by. Locals and tourists make this a popular venue for an evening stroll, especially on a clear, moonlit night.

MUSÉE CONTI HISTORICAL WAX MUSEUM

917 Rue Conti, New Orleans, 504-581-1993, 800-233-5405; www.get-waxed.com

More than 150 wax figures illustrate the history of the city in this amazing—and sometimes eerie—museum. Catch Napoleon Bonaparte in his bath, voodoo queen Marie Laveau and her dancers and Duke Ellington playing some jazz. The figures are painstakingly constructed (even clean-shaven men have stubble) using a process that makes them seem nearly life-like, and they are set in historically accurate tableaux.

Admission: adults $7, seniors $6.25, children 4-7 $6. Monday, Friday, Saturday 10 a.m.-4 p.m.

NATIONAL D-DAY MUSEUM

945 Magazine St., New Orleans, 504-527-6012; www.ddaymuseum.org

Opened on June 6, 2000, the 16,000 square feet of gallery space houses exhibits that trace the political and economic events leading up to the D-Day invasion in 1944. Founded by the late historian and author Stephen Ambrose, the museum offers oral histories of the men and women who participated, as well as rare film footage that helps bring World War II to life. Free lunchbox lectures on Wednesdays give insight into specific topics or personalities.

Daily 9 a.m.-5 p.m.

NEW ORLEANS BOTANICAL GARDEN

1 Palm Drive, New Orleans, 504-483-9386

This beautiful public garden lost most of its collection when Hurricane Katrina landed, but it opened again to the public in March of 2006, and flowers and plants are blooming once more.

Admission: adults $6, children $3. Tuesday-Sunday 10 a.m.-4:30 p.m.

NEW ORLEANS GHOST TOUR

625 St. Phillip St., New Orleans, 504-861-2727, 888-644-6787; www.neworleansghosttour.com

New Orleans might never look the same after you've heard tales of her ghostly past on this walking tour. Hear about the mad butcher—who may have butchered more than beef—the sultan reportedly buried alive, and other supernatural stories that will leave you with goose bumps.

NEW ORLEANS HISTORIC VOODOO MUSEUM

724 Dumaine, St., New Orleans, 504-680-0128; www.voodoomuseum.com

Marie Laveau reigned as voodoo queen of New Orleans throughout much of the 19th century. The Voodoo Museum displays her portrait and memorabilia. Although it sells the stereotypical voodoo supplies, the museum also offers serious

HIGHLIGHT

WHAT DO CERTAIN TERMS MEAN IN NEW ORLEANS SPEAK?

Cajun: Nickname for a Louisianan descended from the French-speaking people who began migrating to Louisiana from Nova Scotia (then Acadia) in 1755.

Creole: A person descended from early French or Spanish settlers of the U.S. Gulf states who preserves their speech and culture. Also the term for a highly seasoned food typically prepared with rice, okra, tomatoes and peppers.

Fais-do-do: When Cajuns partied in days gone by, they would bring their children along, bundle them in their blankets at bedtime, put them to sleep and party into the wee hours. Fais-do-do means "put the kids to sleep."

Faubourg: (FOE-burg) Faubourgs are neighborhoods near the French Quarter. Literally, Faubourg means "suburb."

French Quarter: The 90 square blocks that used to be the entire city of New Orleans and today encompasses 2,700 European- and Creole-style buildings.

Gris-gris: Means "X marks the spot." An X on a tomb indicates a voodoo spell, like that on the tomb of the mysterious Marie Laveau, New Orleans hairdresser-turned-legendary-voodoo-queen.

Gumbo ya-ya: Everybody talking at once.

Jazz: Louis Armstrong said, "If you gotta ask, you'll never know." With apologies to Armstrong, jazz mixes African and Creole rhythms with European styles. Irish, Germans and Italians added the brass.

Krewe: Wealthy 19th-century New Orleans citizens who bankrolled Mardi Gras balls and parades were members of carnival organizations with names like Rex (King of the Carnival). Members were called Krewe of Rex, a variation of the word crew.

Pass a good time: Live it up.

Vieux Carré: Old Square or Old Quarter, referring to the French Quarter.

Voodoo: A combination of the West African Yoruba religion and the Catholicism of French colonists in Haiti. It means "god, spirit or insight" in the Fon language of Dahomey, a former country in West Africa on the Gulf of Guinea.

Yat: A citizen. This term comes from the Ninth Ward greeting, "Where yat?"

exhibits on voodoo history and its artifacts. You can also purchase your own gris-gris bag filled with herbs, bone and charms to bring luck or love into your life.
Admission: adults $7, seniors and college students $5.50, high school students $4.50, children under 12 $3.50. Daily 10 a.m.-6 p.m.

NEW ORLEANS HORNETS (NBA)
New Orleans Arena, 1501 Girod St., New Orleans, 504-301-4000; www.nba.com/hornets
The Hornets moved from Charlotte for the 2002-2003 NBA season to give New Orleans a National Basketball Association team for the first time since the Jazz moved to Utah in 1979. They play home games at the New Orleans Arena, where the Honeybees cheer them on and mascot Hugo the Hornet is a three-time NBA Mascot Slam Dunk Champion.

NEW ORLEANS MUSEUM OF ART
City Park, 1 Collins Diboll Circle, New Orleans, 504-658-4100; www.noma.org
Established in 1911, NOMA boasts more than 40,000 objects in its permanent collection. The strengths of the collection lie in its photography and glassware exhibits, as well as notable collections of American, African, Japanese and French art, including works by Edgar Degas, who visited New Orleans in the early 1870s. World-class traveling exhibits, extensive children's programs and a sculpture garden, which opened in 2002 in the adjacent City Park, round out the attractions.
Admission: adults $8, students $7, children $4, children under 3 free. Wednesday noon-8 p.m., Thursday-Sunday 10 a.m.-5 p.m.

NEW ORLEANS OPERA
1010 Common St., New Orleans, 504-529-2278, 800-881-4459;
www.neworleansopera.org
Operating from the Mahalia Jackson Theatre of the Performing Arts, the New Orleans Opera Association presents four operas each season, which runs from October through March. The association was founded in 1943 and stages high-quality performances of renowned operas as well as world premieres. The 2003-2004 season opened with the world premiere of *Pontalba*, an opera in honor of the Louisiana Purchase. English translations appear in subtitles above the stage.

NEW ORLEANS PHARMACY MUSEUM (LA PHARMACIE FRANCAISE)
514 Chartres St., New Orleans, 504-565-8027; www.pharmacymuseum.org
Louis Dufilho, the first licensed pharmacist in the U.S., operated an apothecary shop here from 1823 to 1855. The ground floor contains pharmaceutical memorabilia of the 1800s, such as apothecary jars filled with medicinal herbs and voodoo powders, surgical instruments, pharmacy fixtures and a black-and-rose Italian marble soda fountain dating back to 1855.
Admission: adults $5, seniors $4. Tuesday-Sunday 10 a.m.-5 p.m.

NEW ORLEANS SAINTS (NFL)
Louisiana Superdome, Sugar Bowl Drive, New Orleans, 504-731-1700;
www.neworleanssaints.com
One of the few NFL teams that remains in its original city, the Saints joined the National Football League in 1967. The team plays home games in the

Superdome, which also regularly hosts the Super Bowl. The Saints tasted sweet victory when they won that game of games in 2010.

NEW ORLEANS SCHOOL OF COOKING & LOUISIANA GENERAL STORE

524 St. Louis St., New Orleans, 504-525-2665, 800-237-4841; www.nosoc.com

After a session at the School of Cooking, you will be a convert to Louisiana cuisine. Make a reservation for a two- or three-hour lunch class to learn the basics of Louisiana cooking and, even better, to sample the four dishes you prepare. An early 1800s-era converted molasses warehouse is home to the school and to the Louisiana General Store, where you can buy ingredients, a cookbook and cooking utensils.

NEW ORLEANS STEAMBOAT COMPANY

2 Canal St., New Orleans, 504-586-8777, 800-233-2628; www.steamboatnatchez.com

Cruise from the heart of the French Quarter on the steamboat Natchez, the ninth steamer with that name. Launched in 1975, she's one of only six true steam-powered sternwheelers sailing on the Mississippi today. Cruises on the Natchez last two hours with an optional Creole lunch available for an additional fee. Each cruise features live narration of historical facts and highlights, jazz music in the main dining room and a calliope concert during boarding times. The Harbor/Jazz Cruises at 11:30 a.m. and 2:30 p.m. offer jazz by Duke Heitger and the Steamboat Stompers, while the 7 p.m. Dinner/Jazz Cruise features the world-renowned Dukes of Dixieland. The Dinner/Jazz Cruise offers buffet-style dining and indoor/outdoor seating. Cruises depart from the Toulouse Street Wharf.

OAK ALLEY PLANTATION

3645 Highway 18 (Great River Road), Vacherie, 225-265-2151, 800-442-5539; www.oakalleyplantation.com

This quintessential antebellum, Greek Revival 1839 plantation house has been featured in many films, including *Primary Colors* and *Interview with a Vampire*. An allée of 300-year-old live oaks leads to the mansion, which is surrounded by galleries supported by massive columns. The interior was remodeled in the 1930s with antiques and modern furnishings of the day. You have your choice of picnicking or dining at the onsite restaurant.

Admission: adult $15, students $7.50, children $4.50. Monday-Friday 10 a.m.-4 p.m., Saturday-Sunday 10 a.m.-5 p.m.

THE OLD U.S. MINT

400 Esplanade Ave., New Orleans, 504-568-6968; www.lsm.crt.state.la.us

Designed by William Strickland in 1835, the mint produced coins for both the U.S. and for the Confederate States. Today, the mint houses permanent exhibitions of jazz and the Louisiana State Museum's Historical Center, a research facility.

Tuesday-Sunday 9 a.m.-5 p.m.

PADDLE WHEELER CREOLE QUEEN AND RIVERBOAT CAJUN QUEEN

2 Canal St., New Orleans, 504-524-0814, 504-529-4567; www.creolequeen.com

The Creole Queen offers 2½-hour sightseeing cruises to Chalmette National Historical Park, the site of the Battle of New Orleans, as well as three-hour

HIGHLIGHT

WHAT IS JAZZ FEST ALL ABOUT?

Jazz is in the soul of New Orleans. Couple that soul with the intense quality and flavor of the food and you've got the key ingredients of the New Orleans Jazz & Heritage Festival. More commonly known as Jazz Fest, it has taken place at the Fairgrounds Race Course over two weekends (end of April and beginning of May) for over 40 years.

Truly a celebration of the city and Louisiana culture, the festival showcases local talent, arts and crafts, parades and food. With entry (tickets are cheaper when purchased in advance, and are available online through Ticketmaster), you get access starting at 11:00 a.m. each day to 12 stages or tents varying in size; the main stages are Acura and Gentilly for the headliners. For jazz, blues and gospel fans, the three tents are lined up next to each other. Overall, the festival is a brilliant representation of fans of all ages enjoying a range of musical acts. You might hear everyone from Lena Prima (the daughter of late singer, songwriter and trumpeter, Louis Prima) to Lionel Richie.

Come hungry, too, because the festival is a great way to sample local culinary delights, such as crawfish tails and pasta, meat pies, mango freezes, gator sticks (alligator meat covered in fried dough) and cochon de lait po-boy (the Cajun term for a roast suckling pig sandwich).

The last show of each day concludes at 7 p.m. Once you leave the fairgrounds, your musical appetite can still be indulged with the multitude of shows in the city that coincide with the festival. The hardest part is having to choose where to go and who to see: jazz/funk musicians Troy "Trombone" Shorty or Big Sam's Funky Nation? True New Orleans brass funk bands Rebirth Brass Band or Soul Rebels Brass Band? Some nights you may not need to make a decision—2 a.m. shows are not uncommon and some artists will appear at multiple venues in one night.

The general rule for attire is function over fashion. Rain usually appears at least once during the Festival—you'll get lucky if you stay dry for an entire weekend. You can also expect temperatures in the mid-to-high 80s. Portable chairs slung over shoulders and small backpacks are common. Comfortable shoes, flip flops or rain boots, hats and sunglasses are almost a must.

Take a tip from locals, rather than trying to stick to solid plans about what you'll hear or taste while at Jazz Fest, arrive and see what is appealing in the moment. As New Orleanians say "During Jazz Fest, one never plans, we just go with the flow."

HIGHLIGHT

WHAT ARE SOME MARDI GRAS HIGHLIGHTS?

Mardi Gras is both a carnival and a holiday, the day before Ash Wednesday and the Lenten season of fasting and repentance. Contrary to what you might have seen on TV or read in the news, Fat Tuesday is more than the salacious frat-boy party you might imagine. It is a bash—a huge bash—but there are plenty of ways to celebrate in New Orleans, especially when the party is as big as Mardi Gras. The Mardi Gras season begins on Twelfth Night—January 6, a time when the festive holiday season traditionally ends. In New Orleans, Twelfth Night kicks off a season of merriment. Festivities reach fever pitch 12 days before Mardi Gras and peak on the Saturday prior to Fat Tuesday, when the city celebrates with four days of nonstop jazz, food, drink and masked balls. Perhaps most closely associated with the celebrations—aside from mayhem in the French Quarter—are the colorful parades where marchers in elaborate costumes toss plastic purple, green and gold beads to onlookers. If your visit falls during Mardi Gras, be sure to hit the highlights: On Fat Tuesday, the French Quarter is alive with visitors in mysterious, beautiful masks. Accent Annex (1420 Sams Ave.), is a good place to check out costumes, beads, doubloons and other Mardi Gras items. Be sure to taste a traditional king cake, a large cake, plain or filled with fruit or cream cheese, coated with purple, green and gold sugar and with a tiny plastic baby hidden inside). It's custom that whoever gets the slice with the baby provides the king cake for the next party.

At 6 p.m. on Fat Monday (Lundi Gras), the King of Rex lands at the riverfront near the French Quarter. The mayor turns over the city to him for the duration of Mardi Gras. Earlier that day, the Zulu King arrives at the riverfront and the Zulus celebrate in Woldenberg Park. The meeting of the two kings is widely celebrated.

dinner jazz cruises. The riverboat *Cajun Queen* offers harbor cruises from the Aquarium of the Americas.

PITOT HOUSE

1440 Moss St., New Orleans, 504-482-0312; www.pitothouse.org

This is one of the last remaining French colonial/West Indies-style plantation houses along Bayou St. John. Built in 1799, it was the residence of James Pitot, the first elected mayor of incorporated New Orleans. Inside the restored home you'll find antiques.

Admission: adults $7, students and children $5, children under 6 free. Wednesday-Saturday 10 a.m.-3 p.m.

PONTALBA BUILDING

523 St. Anne St., New Orleans, 504-524-9118

Completed in 1850 and 1851 by the Baroness Pontalba to beautify the square,

the building is still occupied and used as intended (with duplex apartments above ground-floor offices and shops). The buildings are now owned by the city and the Louisiana State Museum. The 1850 House is furnished in the manner of the period.
Tuesday-Sunday 9 a.m.-5 p.m.

THE PRESBYTERE
751 Chartres St., New Orleans, 504-568-6968, 800-568-6968;
www.lsm.crt.state.la.us/presbex.htm
Built to house clergy serving the parish church, the Presbytere was never used for that purpose, thanks in part to a series of fires that kept it incomplete until 1813, when it was finished by the U.S. government. It is now a museum with a permanent exhibit on the history of Mardi Gras. The Presbytere, like the Cabildo, is part of the Louisiana State Museum complex.
Tuesday-Sunday.

PRESERVATION HALL
726 St. Peter St., New Orleans, 504-522-2841; www.preservationhall.com
Since 1961, people have been filing into this rustic music hall in the French Quarter for one reason: to hear traditional New Orleans jazz. The building is not much to look at, but do not let that deter you. You will sweat—no air-conditioning—and the space is basically standing room only. But this place is worth it and the music here is enough to make you glad you came. Even if you're no jazz fan, you will still want to nod your head to the beat. Bring the kids, too; the hall welcomes people of all ages.
Daily 8 p.m.-midnight.

RIVER CRUISES
2 Canal St., New Orleans, 504-586-8777, 800-233-2628; www.steamboatnatchez.com
Daily excursions depart from the riverfront.

RIVERFRONT STREETCAR LINE
504-248-3900; www.norta.com
Vintage streetcars follow a 1½-mile route along the Mississippi riverfront from the Esplanade past the French Quarter to the World Trade Center, the Riverwalk, Convention Center and back.

RIVERWALK
1 Poydras St., New Orleans, 504-522-1555; www.riverwalkmarketplace.com
This ½-mile-long festival marketplace, converted from World's Fair pavilions, has more than 140 national and local shops, restaurants and cafés.
Monday-Saturday 10 a.m.-7 p.m., Sunday noon-6 p.m.

SAN FRANCISCO PLANTATION
2646 Highway 44 (River Road), Garyville, 985-535-2341, 888-322-1756;
www.sanfranciscoplantation.org
You cannot miss this colorful mansion, a far cry from what most Americans imagine when they think of plantations. The house, with its Creole structure, is a remarkable example of the "Steamboat Gothic" style. Authentically restored, the

interior features five decorated ceilings, two of which are original. The house was used as the setting of Frances Parkinson Keyes's novel *Steamboat Gothic*.

Daily 9:30 a.m.-4:40 p.m

SHOPS AT CANAL PLACE

333 Canal St., New Orleans, 504-522-9200; www.theshopsatcanalplace.com

More than 50 stores, many of them high-end retailers, give this shopping center a lot of cachet. Saks Fifth Avenue anchors the mall, and Gucci, Kenneth Cole and Betsey Johnson contribute to the swanky vibe. Additional amenities include a fitness club and a post office. The Southern Repertory Theater stage is here, too.

Monday-Saturday 10 a.m.-7 p.m., Sunday noon-6 p.m.

SOUTHERN REPERTORY THEATER

365 Canal St., New Orleans, 504-522-6545, 504-891-8332; www.southernrep.com

Permanently housed in The Shops at Canal Place mall since 1991, the Southern Repertory Theater was founded in 1986 to promote Southern plays and playwrights. Plays by luminaries such as Tennessee Williams, Pearl Cleage, Beth Henley and SRT founding member Rosary H. O'Neill form the basis of the theater's September-to-May season.

Days and times vary.

ST. BERNARD STATE PARK

501 St. Bernard Parkway, Braithwaite, 504-682-2101, 888-677-7823; www.lastateparks.com/stbernar

The park is approximately 358 acres near the Mississippi River, with many viewing points of the water and a network of artificial lagoons. Swimming, picnicking, a playground, trails and camping are all available.

ST. CHARLES AVENUE STREETCAR

6700 Plaza Drive, New Orleans, 504-827-7802; www.norta.com

The streetcars (never call them trolleys!) were added to the National Register of Historic Places in 1973. A ride is a quaint and relaxing way to view the varied architecture and exotic greenery of the aptly named Garden District. The 13.2-mile route can take you to tour Tulane University, drop you off at Audubon Park (where the zoo is located) and provide you with safe transport after imbibing in the French Quarter.

ST. LOUIS CATHEDRAL

615 Pere Antoine Alley, New Orleans, 504-525-9585; www.stlouiscathedral.org

The oldest continuously active cathedral in the United States, the St. Louis Cathedral is not much to see, but its history is worth noting. It is the third church to stand on the site; the first was destroyed by a hurricane in 1722, and the second burned to the ground on Good Friday 1788. In 2005, two large oaks fell during Hurricane Katrina and amputated a finger and a thumb of the statue of Jesus that stood near them. Stop inside for a chat with docents, who can tell you about the church's history, murals and windows and about why the church is sinking.

U.S. CUSTOM HOUSE

423 Canal St., New Orleans, Decatur and Canal Streets

Begun in 1848, interrupted by the Civil War and completed in 1881, the Greek Revival building with neo-Egyptian details was used in part as an office by Major General Benjamin "Spoons" Butler during Union occupation, and in part as a prison for Confederate soldiers. A great dome was planned but the excessive weight of the existing building caused the foundation to settle and the dome was never completed. (In 1940, the building had sunk 30 inches, while the street level had been raised three feet.) Of particular interest is the famed Marble Hall, an architectural wonder.

Monday-Friday.

WASHINGTON ARTILLERY PARK

Frenchman and Royal, New Orleans

Between the muddy Mississippi and elegant Jackson Square lies this park, named for the 141st Field Artillery, which has fought in every major conflict since the 1845 Mexican War. Broad steps serve as an amphitheater from which you can catch the escapades of the kids in the playground, the antics of the street performers, the lazy flow of the river or a great view of the French Quarter.

WOLDENBERG RIVERFRONT PARK

1 Canal St., New Orleans, 504-565-3033; www.auduboninstitute.org

Covering 17 acres on the riverfront, Woldenberg Park offers the city its first direct access to the river in 150 years; ships and paddle wheelers dock along the park. Visitors can choose from a variety of riverboat tours.

Sunday-Thursday 6 a.m.-10 p.m., Friday-Saturday 6 a.m.-midnight.

WORLD TRADE CENTER OF NEW ORLEANS

2 Canal St., New Orleans, 504-529-1601; www.wtcno.org

This center houses the offices of many maritime companies and foreign consulates involved in international trade. Top of the Mart, a revolving restaurant and cocktail lounge on the 33rd floor, offers fine views of the city and the Mississippi River.

WHERE TO STAY

★★★CHATEAU BOURBON, A WYNDHAM HISTORIC HOTEL

800 Iberville St., New Orleans, 504-586-0800, 800-996-3426;
www.chateaubourbonneworleans.com

Ideally situated in the heart of the French Quarter, the Chateau Bourbon was the backdrop for the book *Confederacy of Dunces*, the colorful story of eccentric, fictional Ignatius J. Reilly, and the city of New Orleans. This should give guests an inkling of what to expect at this historic hotel, once the home of the preeminent D. H. Holmes Department Store where New Orleanians from all walks of life shopped from 1842 to 1989. Rooms, the largest in the city, are made to feel even more spacious with 12-foot ceilings and floor-to-ceiling drapes. While the hotel itself is ready for a renovation, all rooms have new mattresses, starched white linens and flat-screen televisions. Looking for a bird's-eye view of the action? Request one of the rooms with a wrought-iron balcony overlooking

SPECIAL EVENTS

ALLSTATE SUGAR BOWL COLLEGE FOOTBALL CLASSIC

Louisiana Superdome, Sugar Bowl Drive, New Orleans, 504-525-8573; www.allstatesugarbowl.org

Each year, two top-ranked college football teams compete in this prestigious bowl game, part of the Bowl Championship Series. From 4 p.m. to kickoff, all football lovers can party at Fan Jam, on the Gate C Bridge on the Superdome's east side. The spirited event features live music, contests, hot food and ice-cold beverages. Sugar Bowl week also includes a basketball classic and a regatta on Lake Pontchartrain.

January.

BRIDGE CITY GUMBO FESTIVAL

Gumbo Festival Park on Angel Square, 1701 Bridge City Ave., New Orleans, 504-436-4712; www.hgaparish.org/gumbofestival.htm

In the Gumbo Capital of the World, festival organizers cook up more than 2,000 gallons of chicken, sausage and seafood gumbos. Jambalaya, another local specialty, is also available, along with a variety of accompaniments. You can enter a cooking contest, listen to live music, enjoy carnival rides and participate in many other activities.

Early November.

FRENCH QUARTER FESTIVAL

French Quarter, 100 Conti St., New Orleans, 504-522-5730, 800-673-5725; www.fqfi.org

Fabulous and free, the French Quarter Festival showcases local musicians on 15 stages throughout the Vieux Carré. Take in the sounds of marching bands, brass bands, jazz and Dixieland bands, Cajun, country, zydeco and anything else you can imagine. Music stages are at Jackson Square, Woldenberg Riverfront Park, Bourbon Street, Royal Street, the French Market, Le Petit Theatre at St. Peter and Chartres, and Louisiana State Museum's Old U.S. Mint at Esplanade and Decatur. Don't miss the "World's Largest Jazz Brunch"—booths can be found in Jackson Square, Woldenberg Riverfront Park and the Louisiana State Museum's Old U.S. Mint.

April.

LOUISIANA SWAMPFEST

6500 Magazine St., New Orleans, 504-581-4629, 866-487-2966; www.auduboninstitute.org/swampfest

Sample fried alligator tidbits while listening to local bands play Cajun and zydeco tunes. You may want to participate in the 5K run before indulging in the food and music treats, checking out the craft village or getting some hands-on experience with live creatures in the swamp exhibit.

Early-mid November.

MARDI GRAS FESTIVAL

Main parade route travels down St. Charles Ave. and Bourbon St., 504-566-5011; www.mardigras.com, www.mardigrasday.com

The biggest party of the year offers something for everyone. The party starts weeks before the actual date of Mardi Gras. Parades and bashes are scheduled throughout the weeks leading up to Ash Wednesday and Lent. Though most of the balls are invitation-only, you pay nothing to watch the numerous parades sponsored by the secret societies that organize the festivities. And of course, Bourbon Street is open to all revelers who want to party.

Early January-late February.

NEW ORLEANS JAZZ & HERITAGE FESTIVAL

Fair Grounds Racetrack, 1751 Gentilly Blvd., New Orleans, 504-522-4786, 504-410-4100; www.nojazzfest.com

Each year, Jazz Fest draws 500,000 visitors from around the world for an experience that sums up the best of New Orleans—music, food and culture—in one big party. The music is eclectic: the acts on any given day can include national headliners, local zydeco musicians and regional rockabilly and country bands. The main action is at the Fair Grounds, but the fun spreads to venues throughout the city. New Orleans' own Neville Brothers are always a big draw.

Late April-early May.

SPRING FIESTA

826 St. Ann St., New Orleans, 504-581-1367; www.springfiesta.com

For two weekends every year, New Orleans celebrates its unique heritage with this springtime festival. The fun-packed festivities include a parade of horse-drawn carriages through the French Quarter, the coronation of the festival's queen at Jackson Square, and tours of private homes, courtyards and the historic Metairie Cemetery.

Late March-April.

TENNESSEE WILLIAMS NEW ORLEANS LITERARY FESTIVAL

Le Petit Theatre du Vieux Carré, 616 St. Peter St., French Quarter, New Orleans, 504-581-1144, 800-965-4827; www.tennesseewilliams.net

Born in Mississippi, playwright Tennessee Williams adopted New Orleans as his spiritual home. The city honors him with an annual festival held around his March 26th birthday. The five days of the fest are filled with workshops on writing and publishing, a one-act play competition and a book fair, as well as performances of some of Williams's plays. You can join a literary walking tour or compete in a "Stanley and Stella" contest. Le Petit Theatre du Vieux Carré is the festival headquarters, but other venues also house activities.

Late March.

WHITE LINEN NIGHT

900 Camp St., New Orleans, 504-528-3805; www.cacno.org

Catch some culture during this annual art walk and street party. August in the bayou is always hot and humid, so patrons and partiers don their coolest clothes and stroll through the Arts District, popping into galleries that stay open late, catching live dance and theater performances, and ending up at the Contemporary Arts Center for a party that goes on until the wee hours.

First Saturday in August.

Bourbon Street. Must do: Dine on award-winning barbecue oysters at Ralph Brennan's Red Fish Grill and have your picture taken with a bronzed Riley "under the clock," the famous meeting place for the character and his mother.

251 rooms. Restaurant, bar. Business center. Fitness center. Pool. $251-350

★★★DAUPHINE ORLEANS HOTEL

415 Dauphine St., New Orleans, 504-586-1800, 800-521-7111;
www.dauphineorleans.com

Just a block away from Bourbon Street's madness, this boutique hotel spread among one main building and two 18th century townhouses is one of the better values in the French Quarter for both the location and quality of accommodations. Dauphine Orleans has successfully updated the interiors of the rooms, giving them a fresh feel and more sophisticated look while not compromising the hotel's historic charm. The small bathrooms sparkle with polished chrome and granite vanity tops, while spacious wrought-iron balconies off of some rooms provide an ideal vantage point to spy the occasional brass band marching by. There is a saltwater pool in the interior courtyard, which is leafy and cool with a variety of tropical foliage. In a nod to its infamous past, a red light shines outside of the dark, slightly garish Mae Bailey's, a former bordello and now the hotel bar where a welcome house wine or draft beer is complimentary. In a stark contrast to the former, the hotel also boasts Audubon Cottage, where John J. Audubon painted his famous "Birds of America" series.

111 rooms. Bar. Complimentary breakfast. Pool. $151-250

★★★HILTON NEW ORLEANS RIVERSIDE

Two Poydras St., New Orleans, 504-561-0500; www.neworleans.hilton.com

The standing joke among frequent visitors who return year after year to partake in French Quarter revelry is that no matter how many libations you may have, with the Hilton logo a beacon, blazing in red neon at the top of this 29-story building, you will always be able to find your way home. With its multiple levels, intimate sitting areas, soaring ceilings, long crosswalk and entrances in several different lobbies, the Hilton New Orleans Riverside lives up to its claim to be a city-within–a-city. This is not a quaint, cozy hotel. It's a busy place, frequented by families who are looking for activities to keep the kids happy and by travelers drawn to the amenities. Privileges to a nearby racquet and health club are available to guests for a small fee.

1,659 rooms. Restaurant, bar. Business center. Fitness center. Pool. Pets accepted. $151-250

★★★HOTEL LE CIRQUE

2 Lee Circle, New Orleans, 504-962-0900, 800-684-9525;
www.lecirqueneworleans.com

The ever-changing, festive combination of lights—purple, gold and green for Mardi Gras; black and gold for the Saints; red and green for Christmas—that illuminate the façade of the Hotel Le Cirque sets the tone for this design hotel. Located in the funky Arts and Warehouse District, the hotel appeals to travelers seeking chic sleep and urban surroundings. The Ogden Museum of Southern Art, the National World War II Museum and the Contemporary Arts Museum are just around the corner, while the Julia Street art galleries and some of the city's most innovative restaurants are a short stroll away. Facing

Lee Circle, the hotel is one of the best spots for watching the cavalcade of Mardi Gras parades roll by.

137 rooms. Restaurant, bar. Spa. Pets accepted. $61-150.

★★★HOTEL MONTELEONE

214 Royal St., New Orleans, 504-523-3341, 866-338-4684; www.hotelmonteleone.com

The Monteleone family has owned the French Quarter's oldest and largest hotel since 1886. Its guests have included some of the South's literary titans, such as Eurdora Welty, Tennessee Williams and William Faulkner, to name a few. The professional staff, some of whom have worked for the hotel for as long as 50 years, provide the most gracious service in the city. The lobby, with its dazzling chandelier, marbled floors and elaborate crown molding, makes for a grand entrance. Rooms vary in size and style, some more traditional, some with parlors, but they're all comfortable and well appointed. At the hotel's Carousel Bar, a favorite local watering hole, the circular bar rotates. The rooftop pool is an inviting respite after a day taking in the French Quarter sites.

570 rooms. Restaurant, bar. Business center. Fitness center. Pool. Spa. Pets accepted. $151-250

★★★INTERCONTINENTAL NEW ORLEANS

444 St. Charles Ave., New Orleans, 504-525-5566, 888-424-6835;
www.new-orleans.intercontinental.com

With translation services available, a foreign currency exchange on the premises, a global newspaper service and a multi-lingual staff, the InterContinental New Orleans can't help but have a European flair. The furnishings are modern and the business accoutrements are top-notch, as are the elements that bring pleasure to travel, including a terrific health club and a great location in the Central Business District. The Veranda, the hotel's in-house restaurant located in a lovely atrium setting, serves a taste of New Orleans for breakfast, lunch and dinner, and is renowned for its traditional jazz Sunday brunch,

479 rooms. Restaurant, bar. Business center. Fitness center. Pets accepted. $151-250

★★★INTERNATIONAL HOUSE

221 Camp St., New Orleans, 504-553-9550, 800-633-5770; www.ihhotel.com

Just two blocks from the French Quarter, the International House is one chic nest. It oozes sophistication the second you walk through the oversized doors of the beautiful Beaux-Arts building into the lobby. Three contemporary, hand-rubbed nickel chandeliers hang from the soaring ceiling while an array of whimsical furniture is artfully laid out below. Thanks go to owner Sean Cummings, who conspired with designer to the stars LM Pagano to create a unique urban offering in the heart of this historic city. While the emphasis may be modern, the décor throughout is a tribute to traditional New Orleans. The pilasters along the lobby walls were re-created using original drawings from 1906. Local photographers shot the black-and-white photos of the jazz greats who grace the walls. The armoires in the rooms, stylish and comfortable, were inspired by the handmade cherry, cypress and mahogany armoires of local craftsmen. The bar Loa, with its innovative libations menu, is a favored cocktail spot for the entrepreneurs who have flocked to the city and are helping fuel its renaissance.

119 rooms. Restaurant, bar. Fitness center. $151-250

★★★LAFAYETTE HOTEL
600 St. Charles Ave., New Orleans, 504-524-4441, 888-856-4706; www.thelafayettehotel.com

The Lafayette Hotel, a small, charming hotel in a lovely Beaux-Arts building, has been welcoming guests since 1916. Located on Lafayette Square in the Central Business District, it often hosts executives who are in town on business. Its Old World-style rooms and suites are individually decorated and come well appointed; many have French doors and wrought-iron balconies, and all have English botanical prints, overstuffed easy chairs and marble bathrooms with French-milled soaps and thick terry bathrobes. In contrast to the historic surroundings, Twist, the über-trendy, see-and-be-seen cocktail lounge facing St. Charles Avenue, is the perfect spot to sip a Cosmopolitan while watching the rattling street cars.

44 rooms. Restaurant, bar. $61-150

★★★LAFITTE GUEST HOUSE
1003 Bourbon St., New Orleans, 504-581-2678, 800-331-7971; www.lafitteguesthouse.com

Want to feel like you're visiting friends in the mid-19th century? This three-story bed and breakfast should do the trick. Each room has its own distinct Victorian flair, and the Victorian ground-floor sitting room will make you want to sip a cup of afternoon tea by the crackling fireplace. Best of all, breakfast is delivered to wherever you choose: your room, your balcony or the courtyard. Most of the guest rooms have private balconies with views of Bourbon Street or the French Quarter. The hotel's location can't be beat.

14 rooms. Complimentary breakfast. $151-250

★★★LE PAVILLON HOTEL
833 Poydras St., New Orleans, 504-581-3111, 800-535-9095; www.lepavillon.com

With four towering columns on one side of the porte-cochere and two statues on the other, Le Pavillon Hotel certainly makes a grand first impression. This historic hotel has seen it all: wars, prohibition and the birth of the horseless carriage. Through it all, it has kept its reputation as a Great Lady of New Orleans. In 1970, the Hotel Denechaud, as it was called, passed into new hands and was renamed Le Pavillon, receiving a facelift and some spectacular accoutrements: crystal chandeliers from Czechoslovakia, railings from the lobby of Paris Grand Hotel, and fine art and antiques from around the world. The Crystal Suite contains a hand-carved marble bathtub, a gift from Napoleon to a wealthy Louisiana plantation owner—just like the one in the Louvre. But this hotel isn't too stuffy; peanut-butter-and-jelly sandwiches, milk and chocolates are offered in the lobby after hours.

217 rooms. Restaurant, bar. Business center. Fitness center. Pool. $151-250

★★★LE RICHELIEU IN THE FRENCH QUARTER
1234 Chartres St., New Orleans, 504-529-2492, 800-535-9653; www.lerichelieuhotel.com

This family-owned hotel offers an amenity you won't find at any other place of lodging in the French Quarter: free self-parking. As good as that sounds, many guests keep coming back to this people-pleaser for other reasons: affordable rates; comfortable, homey rooms decorated in Creole style; a cozy bar and café; an attractive courtyard with a pool; and the great location. All these pluses got the attention of ex-Beatle Paul McCartney, who checked in here for two months in the late 1970s while he was in town doing some recording work. A suite is now named after him.

86 rooms. Restaurant, bar. Pool. $61-150

★★★OMNI ROYAL CRESCENT HOTEL

535 Gravier St., New Orleans, 504-527-0006, 800-843-6664;www.omniroyalcrescent.com

Just a short stroll from the French Quarter, this completely non-smoking hotel is in a good location at a good value. The hotel lobby is a blend of modern and traditional, with shiny brass elevators, a concierge stand and colorful fresh flowers, refined artwork and potted palms. The comfortable guest rooms feature touches of wood and brass. In a city overflowing with gumbo, Dress It, the hotel's gourmet burger joint, might be a welcome change for some.

97 rooms. Restaurant. Fitness center. Pets accepted. $151-250

★★★OMNI ROYAL ORLEANS

621 St. Louis St., New Orleans, 504-529-5333; www.omniroyalorleans.com

For royal treatment in the French Quarter, settle into one of the many plush rooms at this luxury hotel, which has been pampering visitors to the city since 1960. In the comfort of your room, this chain property will spoil you with Irish linen sheets, marble baths and windows overlooking all the action in the Quarter. Dine on steak and seafood in the Rib Room, a local favorite for decades; or refresh yourself with a mint julep or two at the Touche Bar or the Esplanade Lounge. Up on the rooftop, go for a relaxing swim in the pool, work up a sweat in the fitness center or just take in the sensational views.

346 rooms. Restaurant, bar. Business center. Fitness center. Pool. Pets accepted. $151-250

★★★RENAISSANCE PERE MARQUETTE HOTEL

817 Common St., New Orleans, 504-525-1111, 800-372-0482; www.marriott.com

Though it's housed in a historic building, this hotel has a contemporary look that appeals to those who like chic décor. Given its location in the Central Business District, the Renaissance attracts business travelers, especially because every room comes with high-speed Internet access, two-line phones with data ports and work desks with lamps. But leisure travelers book rooms here, too, for its close proximity to some of the city's best shopping, restaurants and attractions, including the French Quarter. Mila, which serves innovative dishes from seasonal sourced ingredients, has rocketed to the top of the city's list of must-visit restaurants.

272 rooms. Restaurant, bar. $151-250

★★★THE RITZ-CARLTON, NEW ORLEANS

921 Canal St., New Orleans, 504-524-1331, 800-542-8680; www.ritzcarlton.com

For a global brand, The Ritz-Carlton, New Orleans has managed to capture the spirit of the Big Easy. Bellmen decked out in seersucker welcome you like they were inviting you into their home. Entertaining trumpeter Jeremy Davenport belts out jazz standards at the deservedly named Davenport Lounge, where locals and tourists dance to an era of live music they thought had gone the way of the telegraph. The M Bistro pays homage to local cuisine, offering a cochon de lait po' boy, as well as the standard cheeseburger. The rooms, luxurious and comfortable, are divided between two buildings. The main building has a combination of rooms and suites, and the tasteful traditional décor was inspired by New Orleans. Elevating club level to, well, an all-new level, the adjoining Maison Orleans building offers six floors of exquisitely decorated rooms with private check-in and access to the nonstop tasty treats being served on the club floor. Dark wood, gorgeously upholstered overstuffed furniture, and carefully selected books on New Orleans throughout the rooms and common areas truly make you feel as if you were staying at your well-heeled friend's Garden District mansion. With 22 treatment rooms, a hair salon, the Spa Café and a boutique, The Ritz-Carlton Spa, New Orleans is unrivalled.

527 rooms. Restaurant, bar. Business center. Fitness Center. Spa. Pets accepted. $251-350

★★★ROYAL SONESTA HOTEL NEW ORLEANS

300 Bourbon St., New Orleans, 504-586-0300, 800-7663782; www.royalsonesta-neworleans.com

The location, pool and Irvin Mayfield's Jazz Playhouse more than make up for what the comfortable rooms at the Royal Sonesta Hotel New Orleans may lack in style. Walk out the front door and you spill right out to Bourbon Street. On a New Orleans bluebird-sky day, there is nowhere you'd rather be than lounging around the third-floor pool, cocktail in hand, ideally positioned to soak up the sun on your chaise lounge. When the sun sets, there's no need to go any further than downstairs to Irvin's, a sophisticated music venue that harkens back to another era, a rare find these days in the Quarter.

484 rooms. Restaurant, bar. Business center. Fitness center. Pool. Pets accepted. $151-250

★★★SONIAT HOUSE HOTEL

1133 Chartres St., New Orleans, 504-522-0570, 800-544-8808; www.soniathouse.com

If you are a sophisticated traveler who likes to fly under that radar screen, then check into the Soniat House Hotel. This boutique hotel has a repeat clientele that includes celebrities, rock stars and captains of industry who appreciate being treated as if they were a guest in an elegant French Quarter home. The hotel has a secured front entrance (you either must have a key or be buzzed in), and an out-of-the-way location. The rooms and suites are divided between two townhouses, both of which have brick courtyards overflowing with citrus trees and a variety of palms. All rooms are individually decorated and vary in size, but they are chock-full of antiques and historic features like beamed ceilings and crown molding; some have expansive balconies. The rooms in the building across the street are particularly large and grand, with voluminous floor-to-ceiling drapes and four-poster beds. The only meal served is breakfast, but who needs a croissant when you can have one of the fresh baked biscuits?

30 rooms. Children over 12 years only. $151-250

★★★ST. JAMES HOTEL

330 Magazine St., New Orleans, 504-304-4000, 888-856-4485; www.saintjameshotel.com

Even though the St. James opened just a few years ago, it has the look of a distinguished older property because it occupies a renovated building from the 1850s. The hotel looks vintage New Orleans, with wrought-iron balconies and some rooms with exposed-brick walls. Business travelers like the downtown location. Rooftop terraces overlook a small pool in a charming courtyard. Cuvee restaurant offers contemporary Creole cuisine and more than 500 wine choices.

86 rooms. Restaurant, bar. $151-250

★★★ST. LOUIS HOTEL
730 Bienville St., New Orleans, 504-581-7300, 888-535-9111; www.stlouishotel.com

All guest rooms in this French Quarter boutique hotel overlook a lovely Mediterranean courtyard lush with tropical greenery, banana trees, flowering plants and a baroque fountain. Inside, the rooms are decked out in French period reproductions, and fabulous French cuisine is featured in the Louis XVI Restaurant, a New Orleans tradition. At breakfast, the hotel serves eggs Sardou and other local favorites in its courtyard.

97 rooms. Restaurant. $61-150

★★★W NEW ORLEANS
333 Poydras St., New Orleans, 504-525-9444, 800-522-6963; www.whotels.com

There's no doubt that when you pass through the floor-to-ceiling curtains to enter the reception area at the W New Orleans, you are indeed in a W Hotel. There's an oversized red velvet chaise angled in front of a mammoth mirror. The polished chrome fans whirl overhead like an airplane propeller, and there's a library, replete with groovy leather chaises and faux books stacked on the shelves (really, who has time to read in New Orleans?). This W is über-hip, which is why it attracts everyone from rocker Tommy Lee to Anderson Cooper. The cool vibe wafts through the rooms with taupe, chrome and dark wood furnishings, as well as through the Whiskey Bar, and the Wet Area (the rooftop pool with teak chaises and cabanas). The nod to N.O.? Chef Christopher Brown, a native, whips up Southern-inspired cuisine at Zoë Restaurant. One of the hotel's best amenities is complimentary rides to anywhere within a six-mile radius in an Acura MDX (be sure to reserve).

423 rooms. Restaurant, bar. Business center. Fitness center. Pool. Pets accepted. $251-350

★★★THE WHITNEY
610 Poydras St., New Orleans, 504-581-4222; www.wyndham.com

This building used to house a grand old bank, and the revived space is worth a stop, even if you're not a guest here. The lobby has beautiful plasterwork and distinguished pillars, and the private dining room used to be the bank's vault. The public dining room was the actual bank space and the hotel's impossibly thick doors, we assume, kept out robbers. Rooms boast a traditional décor with corners room among the favorites.

93 rooms. Restaurant, bar. Business center. Fitness center. $61-150

★★★★WINDSOR COURT HOTEL
300 Gravier St., New Orleans, 504-523-6000, 888-596-0955; www.windsorcourthotel.com

Seasoned travelers doing business in New Orleans or just enjoying its riches have long sought the Old World ambience and superior service of the Windsor Court Hotel. Overstuffed chairs in the lobby's Le Salon, which serves afternoon tea as well as cocktails, lend a European feel, as does the world-class art collection that is sprinkled throughout the hotel. The tinkling of ivories can be heard nightly at the clubby Polo Lounge, all dark wood and leather, and a favorite of guests and locals alike. The rooms, the majority of which are suites and junior suites, are comfortable yet luxurious, full of antiques and chintz fabrics. The club-level floor is especially nice with wonderful views of the city and a sun terrace overlooking the mighty Mississippi. Come 2011, the Windsor Court

Hotel will be poised to become the crown jewel of both the city and the South when it completes major renovations to rooms and public spaces, though one could make the argument that the hotel is perfectly lovely as is.

322 rooms. Restaurant, bar. Business center. Fitness center. Pool. Pets accepted. $251-350

RECOMMENDED

THE ROOSEVELT NEW ORLEANS

123 Baronne St., New Orleans, 504.648.1200; www.therooseveltneworleans.com

This icon reopened its doors in 2009, much to the pleasure of New Orleanians who had longed for festive evenings at the Sazerac Bar, as well as travelers who wanted to stay in the grande dame that has been the setting for some of New Orleans' tallest tales. Governor Huey Long may or may not have shot the bar, but one thing is for certain, The Roosevelt is poised to give the city's other luxury hotels a run for their money. Gleaming chandeliers shine above the terrazzo floors in the elaborate lobby. The tasteful rooms are a contemporary interpretation of the originals. With legendaries like Pete Fountain performing at the Blue Room, there is always something happening at the hotel. One major difference from the former days is that this time around, the place is all non-smoking.

504 rooms. Restaurant, bar. Business center. Fitness center. Pool. Spa. Pets accepted. $251-350

W NEW ORLEANS FRENCH QUARTER

316 Chartres St., New Orleans, 504-581-1200, 800-522-6963; www.whotels.com

Unlike other W hotels, the French Quarter location departs from the brand. While the rooms have modern furnishings in a neutral palette, the historic buildings that house the hotel dictate a cozier feel. The alluring and large Italianate courtyard, with a pool and cabanas, is truly one of the loveliest in the city, anchoring the hotel and giving it a more welcoming feel. There is also an annex made up of four carriage houses with oversized rooms, exposed brick and local art, and with Jacuzzis in the two ground-floor rooms and balconies off the two upstairs rooms. The location, close enough to yet far enough away from the action, provides a peacefulness that many Quarter hotels lack.

98 rooms. Restaurant, bar. Fitness center. Pool. Pets accepted. $251-350

WESTIN NEW ORLEANS CANAL PLACE

100 Rue Iberville, New Orleans, 504-566-7006; www.westin.com

The Westin's downtown location isn't the only reason business travelers give this upscale hotel a thumbs-up. They also like the oversized guest rooms and the work-friendly amenities, including direct high-speed Internet access, ergonomic work chairs and cordless telephones. The Westin's convenient location also appeals to leisure travelers. In fact, the hotel is located in the Canal Place Tower, home to the Shops at Canal Place, where visitors and locals like to go on spending sprees in the many top-name stores, including Saks Fifth Avenue. Everyone who beds down here appreciates the stellar views of the city from both the marble-adorned lobby (on the tower's 11th floor) and the rooms that rise above it.

438 rooms. Restaurant, bar. Business center. Fitness center. Pool. $151-250

WHERE TO EAT

★★★ANTOINE'S

713 Rue St. Louis, New Orleans, 504-581-4422; www.antoines.com

Located in the French Quarter, just a short distance from Bourbon Street, Antoine's has been a fixture since 1840. The classic cavernous New Orleans dining room is replete with white tablecloths and black-and-white-tiled floors, and this Creole/classic French dining spot still exudes quality. The locals know which entrées are the best: the filet and any oyster dish—Rockefeller, Bienville and Foch included. Take time to peruse the memorabilia lining the walls of some of the smaller side dining rooms.

Creole. Lunch, dinner (Monday-Saturday), Sunday brunch. $36-85

★★★ARNAUD'S

813 Rue Bienville, New Orleans, 504-523-5433, 866-230-8891; www.arnauds.com

In the French Quarter near Bourbon Street, waiters who have dedicated their careers to this exquisite restaurant heap refined service on loyal diners. The speckled trout meunière is a classic, as is the shrimp rémoulade, which is delicious but spicy enough to make your eyes tear. Leaded glass windows and crystal chandeliers make Arnaud's a wonderful choice for a romantic dinner. Lagniappe (New Orleans for "an unexpected but nice surprise"): the exhibit of Mardi Gras ball gowns upstairs.

French, Creole. Dinner, Sunday brunch. $36-85

★★★BACCO

310 Chartres St., New Orleans, 504-522-2426; www.bacco.com

Located at the W Hotel in the French Quarter, Bacco is the Creole/Italian member of the Ralph Brennan family of restaurants. Executive Chef Chris Montero fuses seasonal local products with traditional Italian recipes, creating innovative dishes such as crawfish tomato bisque and Maine lobster and Gulf shrimp ravioli at this upscale eatery.

Italian, Creole. Lunch, dinner. $36-85

★★★★BAYONA

430 Dauphine St., New Orleans, 504-525-4455; www.bayona.com

A little slice of the romantic Mediterranean awaits you at Bayona, a restaurant tucked into a 200-year-old Creole cottage on a quiet street in the French Quarter. There are three cozy rooms, each with its own charms—abundant fresh flowers, stained-glass windows, a tromp l'oeil of the Mediterranean countryside—as well as a magical outdoor patio that is open most of the year. Renowned chef Susan Spicer serves up her own interpretation of New Orleans cuisine, blending the ingredients of the Mediterranean with the flavors of the Far East, North Africa and the United States. The waitstaff is eager to guide you and answer questions about the menu. A great selection of beers, including several local brews, plus an extensive wine list, round out the experience.

International. Lunch (Wednesday-Saturday), dinner. Closed Sunday. $36-85

★★★BRENNAN'S

417 Royal St., New Orleans, 504-525-9711; www.brennansneworleans.com

Located in the heart of the French Quarter, breakfast may be king at this sister restaurant to Commander's Palace, but guests will enjoy the classic upscale Creole cuisine any meal of the day. For first-timers, eggs Husard—poached eggs atop Holland rusks, Canadian bacon and Marchand de Vin sauce and topped with hollandaise sauce—are not to be missed. Even at breakfast, it is perfectly acceptable to start with a traditional Brandy milk punch.

French, Creole. Breakfast, lunch, dinner, brunch. $36-85

★★★BRIGTSEN'S

723 Dante St., New Orleans, 504-861-7610; www.brigtsens.com

Frank Brigtsen is the chef/owner of this delightful Uptown spot with superb food and service to match. It is a favorite with both locals and visitors in the know. Brigsten's Creole dishes, prepared from fresh seasonal ingredients, include broiled Gulf fish with crabmeat Parmesan crust, mushrooms and a tangy lemon mousselline sauce. The menu changes daily. Order the seafood platter and you will be rewarded with an oceanic feast that may include items such as grilled drum fish with crawfish and pistachio lime sauce, shrimp cornbread with jalapeño smoked corn butter, baked oysters and more.

Creole. Dinner. Closed Sunday-Monday. $36-85

★★★BROUSSARD'S

819 Conti St., New Orleans, 504-581-3866; www.broussards.com

This old-time restaurant has been family-owned for 75 years, albeit by different families. The current owners run things with as much care and attention to detail as the Broussards did in the early 1800s. Classically French-trained chef Gunter Preuss expertly executes stellar Creole dishes. Start with the trio of New Orleans oysters, which is three fried oysters prepared three delectable ways (Rockefeller, Bienville and Broussard's style), and then switch gears with the glazed maple leaf duckling Charlotte. Wine aficionados, prepare for the 20-page wine list.

French, Creole. Lunch (Monday-Friday), dinner. $36-85

★★★COMMANDER'S PALACE

1403 Washington Ave., New Orleans, 504-899-8221; www.commanderspalace.com

In the center of the Garden District stands this turquoise and white Victorian monument to Creole cuisine. The famed Brennan family has presided over the dining room since 1974, but Emile Commander originally founded it in 1880 as a fine restaurant for distinguished neighborhood families. The lush garden setting hosts live Dixieland music for the lively Saturday and Sunday jazz brunches. The set brunch menu, which includes a Bloody Mary, a smoked duck and foie gras gumbo, eggs cochon de lait and Creole bread pudding soufflé, is a delectable and affordable way to dine.

Creole. Lunch (Monday-Friday), dinner, Saturday-Sunday brunch. $36-85

★★★CUVEE

322 Magazine St., New Orleans, 504-587-9001; www.restaurantcuvee.com

Foodies love this restaurant for its innovative menu and excellent advice on

HIGHLIGHT

WHAT ARE SOME CLASSIC NEW ORLEANS FOODS?

MUFFULETTA
Find the best at: Central Grocery
You can't go wrong with the original home of the muffuletta. This feast of a sandwich consists of a Sicilian loaf sprinkled with sesame and layered inside with a marinated olive salad, capicola, salami, mortadella, emmentaler and provolone.
(Central Grocery, 923 Decatur St., French Quarter, 504-523-1620)

BEIGNETS
Find the best at: Café du Monde
You can find beignets all over town, but there is no place on the planet that prepares beignets like these—delicately fried, perfectly puffed and just the right amount of powered sugar dusted on top. Marry them with a steaming cup of café au lait and sit back and savor.
(Café du Monde, French Market, 800 Decatur St., French Quarter, 504-525-4544)

GUMBO
Find the best at: Dooky Chase Restaurant
Gumbo brings together the best flavors of New Orleans. The hearty stew consisting of a mixture of meat, fish or chicken with spices, vegetables and accompanied by rice is filling and satisfying. The legendary Dooky Chase makes the best.
(Dooky Chase Restaurant, 2301 Orleans Ave., Treme, 504-821-0535)

PO-BOYS
Find the best at: Parasol's
The key to a good po-boy is quality Louisiana French bread. The main contents inside are up to you, but some of the best local choices include shrimp, catfish or roast beef. Getting the po-boy "dressed" means adding lettuce, tomato and mayonnaise. Parasol's in the Irish Channel serves up a messy, home-roasted beef po-boy that's best paired with some gravy fries.
(Parasol's, 2533 Constance St., Irish Channel, 504-899-2054)

BBQ
Find the best at: Squeal Bar-B-Que
Take the St. Charles streetcar for a real visual treat beyond the Quarter and into the Garden District. Almost at the end of the line you'll hit Squeal Bar-B-Que. In-house smoked meats and ribs that fall off the bone are the draw and the sauce is made fresh and smoked daily.
(Squeal Bar-B-Que, 8400 Oak St, Uptown, 504-302-7370)

JAMBALAYA
Find the best at: Mother's
This Creole mixture of meats, vegetables and rice originated in New Orleans. You'll find different varieties elsewhere, but New Orleans jambalaya includes tomatoes. Try Jerry's Jambalaya at Mother's
(401 Poydras St., French Quarter, 504-523-9656)

wine-and-food pairings. Opened in 1999 and considered an upstart in this city of decades-old dining establishments, Cuvee has gained a reputation as one of New Orleans' finest gourmet restaurants. With just 85 seats, the intimate restaurant is housed in a landmark 1833 building whose age strangely complements its nouveau New Orleans cuisine. Dishes might include sugarcane-smoked duck breast and crispy confit leg served with Hudson Valley foie gras and Roquefort-pecan risotto. *Creole. Lunch (Wednesday-Thursday), dinner (Monday-Saturday). $36-85*

★★★EMERIL'S RESTAURANT
800 Tchoupitoulas St., New Orleans, 504-528-9393, 800-980-8474; www.emerils.com

There is a reason that "touristy" Emeril's continues to pack 'em in. This well-oiled machine consistently offers innovative and delicious food prepared and served by one of the most professional staffs in the business. Stylish with lofty ceilings, an open kitchen and a towering wooden wine wall, the restaurant is a dynamic space that suits its urban Warehouse District neighborhood. The slick food bar is a fun spot to take in the kitchen action. The room can get loud, but the vibe is festive. The menu employs a world of herbs, spices and chilies that awaken the palate with a delicious jolt. *Cajun,Creole. Lunch (Monday-Friday), dinner. $36-85*

★★★GALATOIRE'S
209 Bourbon St., New Orleans, 504-525-2021; www.galatoires.com

Jean Galatoire, a Frenchman from the foothills of the Pyrenees, founded this landmark French Quarter restaurant in 1905, and it is still one of New Orleans' most popular old-line restaurants. It's a favorite dining spot for New Orleans society, especially at Friday lunch when you will find ladies wearing hats, men in seersucker suits and the cocktails flowing (arrive early, as no reservations are accepted and the line is long). The traditional New Orleans menu includes specialties such as poisson meunière amandine and soufflé potatoes with béarnaise sauce, and it never changes. *Cajun, Creole. Lunch, dinner. Closed Monday. $36-85*

★★★GAUTREAU'S
1728 Soniat St., New Orleans, 504-899-7397; www.gautreausrestaurant.com

The only sign that there might be something afoot at this exquisite restaurant located in a small Uptown house is the cabs coming and going. Inside you will find a healthy serving of society folks who practically view the enchanting little eatery as their own private club. Chef Sue Zemanick consistently outdoes herself as she finds creative news ways to use seasonal produce and locally sourced meats and seafood.

American, seafood. Dinner. Closed Sunday. $36-85

★★★★THE GRILL ROOM
Windsor Court Hotel, 300 Gravier St., New Orleans, 504-522-1994, 888-596-0955; www.windsorcourthotel.com

Dining at The Grill Room inside the Windsor Court Hotel may be one of the most luxurious ways to spend an evening in the city. The Grill Room is known for its consistent contemporary American cuisine, and it has a menu that features locally grown and organic foods whenever possible. It is also a particularly romantic place to dine, with cozy banquettes in the main dining room, views of the twinkling light-wrapped palm trees from the Terrace, and live piano music for some dancing between courses.

American. Breakfast, lunch (Monday-Friday), dinner, Saturday-Sunday brunch. $36-85

★★★MILA
817 Common St., New Orleans, 504-595.6774; www.milaneworleans.com

Dining is fun and interesting at this upscale gem located in the Renaissance Pere Marquette Hotel in the Central Business District. Chefs Alison Vines-Rushing and Slade Rushing (from Louisiana and Mississippi, respectively) crank out delectable dishes creatively presented using locally sourced ingredients from Lujele farm. With appetizers such as New Orleans lobster with lemon confit and thyme, and entrées such as sweet tea-brined rotisserie duck with wilted spinach, both contemporary and Southern influences can be found in the menu.

Contemporary, Southern. Lunch (Monday-Friday), dinner. Closed Sunday. $36-85

★★★MR. B'S BISTRO
201 Royal St., New Orleans, 504-523-2078; www.mrbsbistro.com

This famous Brennan-family institution in the French Quarter offers contemporary Creole cuisine made with local and organically grown products. It's known for being the power-lunch spot in the Quarter, and its very popular for dinner. The bistro is also a comfortable place to dine at the bar if you find yourself traveling alone. Try the signature dish, Mr. B's barbecue shrimp.

Contemporary, Creole. Lunch (Monday-Saturday), dinner, Sunday brunch. $36-85

★★★NOLA
534 St. Louis St., New Orleans, 504-522-6652; www.emerils.com

As the most casual and accessible of Emeril Lagasse's restaurants, this French Quarter location offers innovative cuisine, such as hickory-roasted duck with whiskey caramel glaze and sweet barbecue Atlantic salmon with Creole maque choux, that will please guests. As with all of Lagasse's restaurants, there is an extensive wine list.

Creole. Lunch (Friday-Sunday), dinner. $36-85

★★★PALACE CAFÉ

605 Canal St., New Orleans, 504-523-1661; www.palacecafe.com

Owned by famous restaurateur, Dickie Brennan, The Palace Café on the edge of the French Quarter may look like a tourist trap from the outside, but the proof is in its white chocolate bread pudding—this cavernous bistro cranks out some delectable eats. Peering through the windows into the busy kitchen, you see a blackboard with a list of the "local groceries" that make up the evening's ingredients for the contemporary and Creole dishes, which might include the P&J oysters used in the pan roast and the Gulf shrimp found in the seafood fra diavolo.
Contemporary, Creole. Lunch (Monday-Saturday), dinner, Sunday brunch. $36-85

★★★PELICAN CLUB

312 Exchange Place, New Orleans, 504-523-1504; www.pelicanclub.com

For fine dining in the French Quarter, look no further than this cosmopolitan restaurant tucked away in a converted townhouse. The creative menu incorporates local seafood, prime meats and game, and fresh produce. Professional service and a smart setting round out the experience.
International, Southern. Dinner. $36-85

★★★RESTAURANT AUGUST

301 Tchoupitoulas St., New Orleans, 504-299-9777; www.restaurantaugust.com

Step into this converted 18th-century townhouse and you're sure to be greeted with a hearty welcome. With exposed-brick, vaulted ceilings and Old World antiques, August's dining room is one of the prettiest in town. Chef John Besh, who still cooks despite his celebrity status, does a wonderful job in the kitchen, with an innovative and delicious menu of dishes that marry robust ingredients from Spain and France with regional flavors. His menu changes seasonally, but his execution is as flawless as the wine list. It's a pampering culinary experience.
French. Lunch (Monday-Friday), dinner. $86 and up

★★★UPPERLINE

1413 Upperline St., New Orleans, 504-891-9822; www.upperline.com

The gracious service—owner JoAnn Clevenger makes a point to stop by every table to welcome guests and see how they are enjoying the meal—and excellent Creole food make this Uptown neighborhood restaurant a local favorite. Located just a block from St. Charles Avenue, it is an easy street car ride for tourists who want to sample the original fried green tomato with shrimp rémoulade. Be sure to check out the extensive collection of regional art hanging throughout the restaurant while you're there.
Creole. Dinner. Closed Monday-Tuesday. $36-85

★★★VERANDA

Intercontinental New Orleans, 444 St. Charles Ave., New Orleans, 504-525-5566; www.ichotelsgroup.com

On the second floor of the InterContinental New Orleans, opening onto the hotel's enormous faux-street, lamp-lined atrium, Veranda is an airy arena for a calming meal. Regional fare is the ticket here; gumbo, crawfish and other New Orleans cuisine are prepared in imaginative ways. Veranda is known primarily for its lavish breakfast and lunch buffets, and the Sunday champagne jazz brunch draws both locals and visitors to its tables.

American, Creole. Breakfast, lunch, dinner, Sunday brunch. $36-85

RECOMMENDED

COCHON BUTCHER

930 Tchoupitoulas St., New Orleans, 504-588-7675; www.cochonbutcher.com

There is no place quite like Cochon Butcher in or out of New Orleans. The industrial-looking space, cool in its urban sparseness, houses both a butcher shop and small restaurant that is really no more than a few tables with stools, and the aptly named Swine Bar. Chef Donald Link is the brainchild behind the concept. A native of southwest Louisiana, he decided it was time to bring authentically smoked and cured pork, game and duck to big-city dining. The result: some of the most delicious food for the price in the city. Sharing a selection of small plates is the way to go, because you don't want to miss anything. Sample the specials of the day, but be tempted by the duck pastrami sliders and the pork belly on white bread with mint and cucumbers. There is a surprisingly respectable, if limited, wine list, as well as a terrific selection of beers and a full bar.

Cajun. Lunch, dinner, Sunday brunch. $15 and under

DOMENICA

The Roosevelt, 123 Baronne St., New Orleans, 504-648-6020; www.domenicarestaurant.com

Located in The Roosevelt hotel, the contemporary Italian Domenica is the latest feather in chef John Besh's hat. His executive chef, Alon Shaya, spent a year traveling throughout Italy's countryside, learning firsthand from culinary artisans how to cure meats, prepare fresh pasta and make limoncello so that it tastes like it comes from the old country. Pizzas baked in a rotating wood oven, the only one in the United States, are a specialty. The salumi, featuring house-cured meats, are creatively served on a cypress plank with or without imported cheeses, olives and roasted vegetables. The option of small plates provides an opportunity to sample a few dishes, especially if you're sharing. Try the meatballs on polenta (a not-too-dense veal pork combo); delicately fried squash blossoms stuffed with local goat cheese; or a classic veal with lemon and arugula. The almost exclusively Italian wine list is carefully laid out by region and reasonably priced. The modern Venetian glass chandeliers, brown leather chairs and artfully divided space makes Domenica a chic dining experience.

Italian. Lunch, dinner, brunch. $36-85

HERBSAINT

701 St. Charles Ave., New Orleans, 504-524,4114; www.herbsaint.com

Herbsaint chef Donald Link is arguably the best in town, a claim the restaurant could also make. The food, with nods to both New Orleans and France, is absolutely delicious. There are standout dishes throughout the menu, such as Louisiana shrimp with tasso and grits, and a grilled and sliced rib-eye with sea salt and steak frites. The cool bistro vibe matches the urban location in the Warehouse District. The professional waiters are knowledgeable and friendly.

French, Southern. Lunch, dinner. Closed Sunday. $36-85

LE MERITAGE

1001 Toulouse St., New Orleans, 504-586-8000; www.lemeritagerestaurant.com

Located in the Maison Dupuy hotel away from the din of the Quarter, Le Meritage is the perfect combination of terrific wine, food and atmosphere. The option of small plates paired with half pours of suggested wines makes for a fun night of dining. The delicious menu includes P&J fried oysters, jumbo lump crab cakes with crawfish and Creole spices, and Gulf Coast tuna tartare.

Contemporary, Creole. Dinner. Closed Sunday-Monday. $36-85

LILETTE

3837 Magazine St., New Orleans, 504-891-3377; www.liletterestaurant.com

About all one needs to know about this impeccable Uptown French bistro is that it is one of renowned chef Donald Link's favorites. With pressed tin ceilings and white-paper tablecloths, it is a beautiful space, and it has a distinctly different feel from most New Orleans restaurants. There are daily specials written on a chalkboard, but you can always count on the duck confit with arugula and Banyul's vinaigrette, and bouillabaisse in saffron broth. The wine list is one of the best.

French. Lunch, dinner. Closed Sunday-Monday. $36-85

MR. JOHN'S STEAKHOUSE

2111 St. Charles Ave., New Orleans, 504-679-7697; www.mrjohnssteakhouse.com

The Crescent City has its share of steakhouses, but one of the standouts, at least according to frequent diner James Carville, is Mr. John's. The juicy, succulent steaks are served sizzling on your plate in the classic New Orleans' dining room. Of course, there are delicious accompaniments such as creamed spinach and potatoes au gratin, as well as an array of other choices if someone in your group is not in the mood for a steak. Be sure to make time for a pre-dinner cocktail in the gorgeous dark wood bar, where the bartender just might share tantalizing tales of the New Orleans of yore.

Steak. Lunch (Friday), dinner. Closed Sunday-Monday. $36-85

NAPOLEAN HOUSE

500 Chartres St., New Orleans, 504-524-9752; www.napoleonhouse.com

This 200-year-old landmark is a French Quarter icon. The building's first resident, Nicholas Girod, the mayor of New Orleans from 1812 through1815, offered up his home to Napoleon. Frankly, it doesn't look like there has been much done to the establishment since then. Walls, stripped of wallpaper and weathered with age, wood tables and chairs, and classical music create a charming ambience that transports you back in time. It is a simple menu with Creole, French and Italian dishes served by seasoned waiters wearing bow ties, black pants and white shirts. Don't miss the muffuletta with a side of jambalaya accompanied by the best Sazerac in town.

Creole, Italian. Lunch, dinner. Closed Sunday. $15 and under

SPA

★★★THE SPA AT THE RITZ-CARLTON, NEW ORLEANS

921 Canal St., New Orleans, 504-670-2929, 800-241-3333; www.ritzcarlton.com

Soft lighting, gleaming marble, brass chandeliers and gentle colors set a regal tone for the Spa at The Ritz-Carlton, New Orleans. This tranquil spa lets you relax and indulge like royalty—the treatment menu was inspired in part by favorite practices of French aristocrats. The Napoleon royal massage is a signature treatment that includes a heavenly citrus-smelling bath prior to a lemon-verbena-scented Swedish rubdown. The body treatments are superb, and the spa's magnolia sugar scrub gently exfoliates and polishes skin while the scent of Louisiana's luscious magnolias blend with botanical extracts for further relaxation.

SHOPPING

AIDAN GILL

2026 Magazine St., New Orleans, 504-587-9090; 550 Fulton St., New Orleans, 504-566-4903; www.aidangillformen.com

Being greeted by a well-coifed man in a bow tie sets the tone for this men's grooming store. Rows of expensive colognes from Scotland, England and Europe, shaving lotions, and boxed bars of luxurious soaps neatly line the shelves. Glass display cases showcase cufflinks, elegant ties and other must-haves for the proper gentleman. Be sure to make time for a hot towel shave in the shop's retro barbershop.

MARIE LAVEAU'S HOUSE OF VOODOO

739 Bourbon St., New Orleans, 504-581-3751; www.voodooneworleans.com

This little shop in the heart of throbbing Bourbon Street has a variety of voodoo-related items for those who really want to bring back quintessential New Orleans souvenirs such as handmade voodoo dolls and gris-gris bags. It is also a museum, so you can learn a little bit about what to do with those souvenirs when you get them home.

MIGNON FAGET

3801 Magazine St., New Orleans, 504-891-2005; Canal Place Shops, 504-524-2973; www.mignonfaget.com

Local designer Mignon Faget's sterling silver and gold jewelry is often inspired by New Orleans. A piece of wrought iron becomes a scroll cuff bracelet. A musical note becomes a pendant. A street car becomes a charm. But after 40 years of designing, Faget has moved beyond the fleur-de-lis, creating non-New Orleans jewelry collections, as well as adornments for the home. The common thread? All of her designs are exquisitely crafted and sophisticated in their simplicity.

PERLIS

6070 Magazine St., New Orleans, 504-895-8661; www.perlis.com

Perlis is the kind of place where a man can walk in during the height of carnival season, purchase a tuxedo the day before a ball and pick it up the next afternoon, expertly tailored. Its service and exquisite selection of high-quality clothes and shoes—Robert Graham shirts, seersucker and other summer suits, and its own line of crawfish logo polo shirts and shorts—have not gone unnoticed. Perlis consistently gets listed as one of the top men's stores in the country (even though it does sell women's clothes, too).

PLUM

5430 Magazine St., New Orleans, 504-897-3388; www.plumneworleans.com

Plum sits plum in the middle of a two-block stretch of some of the best boutiques in the city. The artfully displayed array of whimsical jewelry, gifts and housewares captures the spirit of New Orleans, whether it is fleur-de-lis cufflinks made by a local artisan, a set of goldfish tumblers made by one of the oldest glass blowers in France or a lamp shade designed like a vintage New Orleans postcard from Found Images in Texas. Plum is the ideal place to look for unique New Orleans mementos and other fun stuff.

GREATER NEW ORLEANS

New Orleans overshadows most of eastern Louisiana, but there are a number of great towns outside of it that warrant some attention. Since the late 19th century, Abita Springs has been a popular resort getaway for New Orleans residents. Today it is best known for the Abita Brewing Company, which brews beer with water from the city's artesian wells. Covington is in a wooded area north of Lake Pontchartrain, which is crossed via the 24-mile Lake Pontchartrain Causeway from New Orleans. With mild winters and semitropical summers, Covington is a town of vacation houses, recreational opportunities and pecan, pine and oak woods.

Slidell offers natural attractions and scenery in southeast Louisiana. The Honey Island Swamp encompasses the parish's eastern border. Slidell's historic district, called Olde Town, is filled with antique shops and restaurants.

WHAT TO SEE

ABITA SPRINGS
ABITA MYSTERY HOUSE/UCM MUSEUM

22275 Highway 36, Abita Springs, 985-892-2624; www.ucmmuseum.com

Looking for something off the beaten path? Check out the comb collection, popsicle-stick marble machine or "Aliens vs. Airstream Trailer" exhibits in this museum, which bills itself as Louisiana's "most eccentric."

Daily 10 a.m.-5 p.m.

COVINGTON
FONTAINEBLEAU STATE PARK

67825 Highway 190, Mandeville, 985-624-4443, 888-677-3668; www.lastateparks.com

A live oak allée forms the entrance to this 2,700-acre park on the north shore of Lake Pontchartrain. On the grounds are the ruins of a plantation brickyard and sugar mill. Swimming, fishing, boating and picnicking are available.

Daily.

PONTCHARTRAIN VINEYARDS & WINERY

81250 Highway 1082 (Old Military Road), Bush, 985-892-9742; www.pontchartrainvineyards.com

About an hour from New Orleans, the Pontchartrain Vineyards & Winery

HIGHLIGHT

WHAT ARE THE TOP THINGS TO DO IN GREATER NEW ORLEANS?

UNCOVER THE ABITA MYSTERY HOUSE/UCM MUSEUM

There's no stuffiness or pretension at this eclectic museum. Instead you'll find folk art, found objects and homemade inventions. The odd collections are among the most amusing, with a whole display dedicated to motel postcards.

KNOCK BACK SOME BEERS AT THE ABITA BREW PUB

You can get a burger at this brewpub, but the real reason to dine here is to get a cold Louisiana-made Abita beer. It's hard to choose from the beers on tap and those bottled, so go for the sampler, which will give you five pours of the company's most popular brews.

TAKE A GAMBLE ON TREASURE CHEST CASINO

Climb aboard this riverboat, which is docked in Lake Pontchartrain, in hopes of winning big at the blackjack table or the 1,000 slot machines.

produces wines to complement the unique cuisine of Southern Louisiana. You can buy a case of wine at a local spirits shop or order a bottle with your meal in any number of fine New Orleans restaurants, but it's more fun to drive out to the winery for a tasting.

Wednesday-Sunday noon-4p.m.

TAMMANY TRACE

Highway 59, Covington, 800-438-7223, 985-867-9490; www.tammanytrace.org

This follows the old Illinois Central Railroad corridor for 31 miles, ending in Slidell. There's a paved hiking/biking trail and an unpaved equestrian trail.

KENNER
TREASURE CHEST CASINO

5050 Williams Blvd., Kenner, 504-443-8000, 800-298-0711; www.treasurechest.com

This 25,767-square-foot riverboat docked in Lake Pontchartrain holds 1,000 slot machines and table games ranging from blackjack to Caribbean stud. Food choices are an all-you-can-eat buffet or the upscale Bobby G's restaurant, while the Caribbean Showroom offers live entertainment.

SLIDELL

FORT PIKE STATE COMMEMORATIVE AREA

Highway 90, Slidell, 504-662-5703, 888-662-5703; www.lastateparks.com/fortpike

The fort was constructed in the 1820s to defend navigational channels leading to New Orleans. Visitors can stroll through authentic brick archways and stand overlooking the Rigolets as sentries once did.

OAK HARBOR GOLF COURSE

201 Oak Harbor Blvd., Slidell, 985-646-0110; www.oakharborgolf.com

Oak Harbor requires smart, often conservative play to score well, with water on 12 holes and challenging approaches to many greens. Designed in the style of Pete Dye, with railroad ties and bulkheads along the course, Oak Harbor is still only a touch more than 6,200 yards from the men's tees. A GPS system in each cart helps players estimate distances and speed play.

WHERE TO STAY

KENNER

★★★HILTON NEW ORLEANS AIRPORT

901 Airline Drive, Kenner, 504-469-5000, 800-872-5914; www.hilton.com

The Hilton's location adjacent to the Louis Armstrong International Airport makes it a convenient choice for those who fly into town for work. But with a 21-station fitness center, an outdoor pool and whirlpool, tennis courts and a putting green, it is great for leisure travelers as well.

317 rooms. Restaurant, bar. Business center. Fitness center. Pool. Tennis. Golf. $61-150

WHERE TO EAT

RECOMMENDED
ABITA SPRINGS
ABITA BREW PUB

72011 Holly St., Abita Springs, 985-892-5837; www.abitabrewpub.com

Since 1986, the Abita Brewery has been gaining a following across the state with its five flagship brews and seasonal favorites. Today, the company brews more than 62,000 barrels of beer each year, including some sold in the brewery's pub. Try the Turbodog, a dark brown ale with a sweet chocolate-toffee flavor, or Purple Haze, a crisp wheat beer with raspberry purée.

American. Lunch, dinner. $16-35

LACOMBE
★★★LA PROVENCE

25020 Highway 190, E. Lacombe, 985-626-7662; www.laprovencerestaurant.com

For three decades, residents of New Orleans (and beyond) have been treated to the rustic, traditional cuisine of Southern France at this warm and satisfying place. The restaurant was opened in 1972 by innovative chef Chris Kerageorgiou, and La Provence and has paid homage to Kerageorgiou's Mediterranean cooking ever since with steaming dishes brimming with garlic, tomatoes, olives and fresh herbs. The restaurant is now famously run by chef

John Besh, widely considered one of the top chefs in America.
French. Lunch, dinner, brunch. Closed Monday-Tuesday. $16-35

MANDEVILLE
★★★TREY YUEN
600 N. Causeway, Mandeville, 985-626-4476; www.treyyuen.com/treyyuenmandeville.htm
Fresh local seafood defines the restaurant's unorthodox Chinese menu, which includes alligator dishes, soft-shell crab items and crawfish creations. Koi ponds, footbridges and custom-built carvings outside give diners a hint of Asia.
Chinese. Lunch, dinner. $16-35

WELCOME TO MISSISSIPPI

MISSISSIPPI IS A LAND OF GREAT AND TRAGIC STORIES.

Here, the blues were born on a large cotton plantation in the early 20th century; many of the Civil War's bloodiest battles were fought; and some of the nation's most celebrated storytellers, including Tennessee Williams, William Faulkner and Eudora Welty, found their inspiration. It's no surprise that history is a part of the lore for the state's visitors, who will find beautifully preserved antebellum homes and tributes to the state's famous sons and daughters at almost every stop. Mississippians know how to celebrate their history: All year long, cities and towns host festivals when locals and visitors can hear the blues, honor Native American traditions or tour some of the South's most beautiful buildings.

Mississippi's recorded history begins when Hernando De Soto trekked across this land looking for gold 80 years before the Mayflower landed in Massachusetts. In 1699, French settlers established Mississippi's first permanent settlement near Biloxi. There was no gold to be found, but the Mississippi River had created something as valuable: immense valleys of rich soil on which cotton could be grown. Cotton plantations became common sights and eventually Mississippi joined other Southern states in fighting against all attempts to abolish the plantations' primary source of labor: slavery.

The Civil War brought fierce battles to Mississippi. Many historians believe the 47-day Siege of Vicksburg sealed the South's fate. In the late 19th and early 20th centuries, the state had adopted Jim Crow laws that left Mississippi racially segregated. Nearly 100 years after the Civil War's end, the state found itself in the midst of a set of battles during the civil-rights movement, making the state a representative of the scourge of racial oppression that has stained American history.

Today the Magnolia State is still recovering from Hurricane Katrina's destructive visit in late August of 2005. Its famous Gulf Coast, a popular destination, was ravaged by the storm, though much of the shoreline is repaired and ready for tourists.

Sandy beaches and fresh seafood aren't all Mississippi has to offer. The John C. Stennis Space Center in Gulfport is NASA's largest rocket engine test facility and offers tours and exhibits about aerospace. In Tupelo, Elvis Presley fans can visit the small white frame house in which the King was born, and travelers who stop in Oxford, home of the University of Mississippi, will find a town that worships Ole Miss football, good food and local literary greats like Faulkner, who based his Yoknapatawpa County on surrounding Lafayette County.

In short, what Mississippi provides is a powerful character, captivating settings and stories that will amaze visitors. It ultimately offers an opportunity to see the country from a new perspective, through the stories and characters that have shaped not just this scenic land, but the nation, too.

BEST ATTRACTIONS

WHAT ARE THE BEST ATTRACTIONS IN MISSISSIPPI?

JACKSON
You'll have your choice of attractions in Jackson, whether you want to see art from Georgia O'Keeffe, a forest of petrified wood or bloom-filled gardens.

THE DELTA
The blues began in the Mississippi Delta. Muddy Waters and John Lee Hooker grew up here and helped create a thriving blues music scene that continues there today.

CAPITAL/RIVER REGION
The Mighty Mississippi runs through the Capital/River region, which makes it ideal for fishing and other water-based activities. The area also has two national forests for landlubbers.

DELTA

Explore the western Delta region and you'll find everything from quaint towns to hopping casinos. What may not be immediately noticeable is that it's the birthplace of the blues. In the early 20th century, fieldworker Henry Sloan showed Charley Patton how to play the guitar, and Patton went on to become the "Father of the Delta Blues." Muddy Waters grew up here, as did John Lee Hooker. Actor Morgan Freeman chose Clarksdale as the site of his celebrated Ground Zero blues club and his Madidi restaurant.

If the musical attractions don't move you, the Delta has other offerings. In Greenville, visit Lake Ferguson, an oxbow lake created by levees on the Mississippi River. There you'll find beautiful cypress groves, lively juke joints and the bright lights of casinos on the lake. Railroad aficionados should roll down to Yazoo City, home of the Casey Jones Railroad Museum, the site of the 1900 train wreck.

WHAT TO SEE

CLARKSDALE
DELTA BLUES MUSEUM
1 Blues Alley, Clarksdale, 662-627-6820; www.deltabluesmuseum.org
This museum features blues memorabilia, including video and audio recordings, sheet music, posters, photographs, costumes and folk art. Be sure to check out the collection of guitars that were played by blues legends like B.B. King,

HIGHLIGHT

WHAT ARE THE TOP THINGS TO DO IN THE DELTA?

HEAD TO THE DELTA BLUES MUSEUM

Blues was born in the Delta, and this museum pays homage to the musical genre with displays of video and audio recordings, sheet music, photos and costumes. Guitars strummed by blues greats are also on display.

HOP OVER TO THE BIRTHPLACE OF THE FROG EXHIBIT

In this display, the Washington County Tourist Center showcases everything Muppets. See Kermit, Miss Piggy and Fozzie memorabilia from collectors and the family of the late Jim Henson, the Muppets master.

SEE THE ALLIGATORS AT LEROY PERCY STATE PARK

Hang out with live gators in Mississippi's oldest state park. You can watch the creatures in their pond from the boardwalk. Take some time to appreciate the park's cypress trees and moss-covered oaks as well.

John Lee Hooker and Big Joe Williams.
March-mid-October, Monday-Saturday 9 a.m.-5 p.m.; mid-October-February, Monday-Saturday 10 a.m.-5 p.m.

GREENVILLE

BIRTHPLACE OF THE FROG EXHIBIT

South Deer Creek Drive, East Leland, 662-686-2687; www.lelandms.org/kermit.html

This exhibit, in the Washington County Tourist Center, houses Muppet memorabilia from collectors and the family of the late Jim Henson, the creator of Kermit, Miss Piggy and the rest of the Muppet gang.
September-May, Monday-Saturday 10 a.m.-4 p.m. June-August, daily 10 a.m.-5 p.m.

LEROY PERCY STATE PARK

Highway 12 , W., Hollandale, 662-827-5436; www.mdwfp.com

The oldest of Mississippi's state parks comprises approximately 2,400 acres of artesian springs, cypress trees and ancient oaks covered in Spanish moss. One of the four hot artesian wells provides water for an alligator pond, which can be viewed from the boardwalk. Nature trails lead through the Delta lowlands and a live alligator exhibit.

JACKSON

Jackson sits on the bluffs above the Pearl River, a site chosen by French Canadian pioneer Louis LeFleur for its proximity to navigable water. Named for Major General Andrew Jackson, the hero of the South who would become the seventh president of the United States, the growing town became the capital of Mississippi in 1821.

In 1868, the "Black and Tan" convention that met in Jackson was the first political organization in Mississippi with black representation. Its attendees framed a state constitution that gave black citizens the right to vote and enabled a few to attain high political office. However, Jackson was not immune from the increased racial tensions that plagued the nation and especially the South. During the civil-rights movement, clashes between white supremacists and black activists came to a head here, when Ku Klux Klan member Byron de la Beckwith murdered civil-rights leader Medgar Evers in 1963.

In the second half of the 20th century, Jackson's population grew steadily and the city established itself as a main metropolis of the South. Art galleries, museums, historic homes, theaters and blues and jazz clubs line city streets.

Jackson is Mississippi's most populated city, but it feels smaller because the population is relatively spread out. Most of the city's cultural offerings are downtown, but visitors trek to Jackson's different neighborhoods to get a real feel for the city. Ridgeland, a few miles from the city center, is a hotbed of restaurants, hotels and shops. Farish Street, west of downtown, was a center of African-American culture, politics and business after the Civil War. Once a vibrant community, Farish Street is now economically depressed but full of fascinating sites and stories.

WHAT TO SEE

BATTLEFIELD PARK
Porter Street and Langley Avenue, Jackson
The site of a Civil War battle, the park contains an original cannon and trenches.

GOVERNOR'S MANSION
300 E. Capitol St., Jackson, 601-359-6421; www.mdah.state.ms.us
Restored to its original Greek revival style, the mansion houses antiques and period furnishings. The grounds occupy an entire block and feature gardens and gazebos.
Tours: Tuesday-Friday 9:30-11:30 a.m. (every half hour).

MANSHIP HOUSE
420 E. Fortification St., Jackson, 601-961-4724; www.mdah.state.ms.us
This restored Gothic revival cottage circa 1855 was the residence of Charles Henry Manship, mayor of Jackson during the Civil War. Here you'll find period furnishings as well as fine examples of wood graining and marbling.
Tuesday-Friday 9 a.m.-4 p.m., Saturday 10 a.m.-4 p.m.

MISSISSIPPI AGRICULTURE & FORESTRY MUSEUM AND NATIONAL AGRICULTURAL AVIATION MUSEUM

1150 Lakeland Drive, Jackson, 601-713-3365, 800-844-8687; www.mdac.state.ms.us

This complex, covering 39 acres, includes a museum exhibit center, a forest trail, a 1920s living history town and farm.

Monday-Saturday 9 a.m.-5 p.m.

MISSISSIPPI MUSEUM OF ART

380 South Lamar St., Jackson, 601-960-1515; www.msmuseumart.org

Exhibitions of 19th- and 20th-century works by local, regional, national and international artists are on display here. The museum's collection also includes African-American folk art, photographs, a sculpture garden, a hands-on children's gallery and a restaurant.

Tuesday-Saturday 10 a.m.-6 p.m., Sunday noon-6 p.m.

MISSISSIPPI PETRIFIED FOREST

124 Forest Park Road, Flora, 601-879-8189; www.mspetrifiedforest.com

Surface erosion has exposed giant trees up to six feet in diameter. In the forest, you'll find petrified logs that were deposited in the Mississippi area as driftwood by a prehistoric river; a self-guided nature trail; and a museum at the visitor center that has a gift shop and dioramas as well as wood, gem, mineral and fossil displays.

Admission: adults $7, seniors and children $6. Daily.

MISSISSIPPI SPORTS HALL OF FAME AND MUSEUM

1152 Lakeland Drive, Jackson, 601-982-8264, 800-280-3263; www.msfame.com

The museum celebrates great athletes who hail from Mississippi, including Walter Payton, Archie Manning and George "Boomer" Scott. Touch-screen television kiosks play archival sports footage. Through interactive technology, visitors can play championship golf courses, kick soccer balls into "goals" and throw a baseball into a "field."

Admission: adults $5, seniors and children 6-17 $3.50, children under 5 free. Monday-Saturday 10 a.m.-4 p.m.

MUSEUM OF NATURAL SCIENCE

2148 Riverside Drive, Jackson, 601-354-7303; www.mdwfp.com/museum

This science museum encourages you to learn about Mississippi's wildlife and natural habitats by perusing exhibits both indoors and outdoors. Inside, check out the 100,000-gallon aquarium with 200 species of native fish, reptiles, amphibians and aquatic invertebrates. A greenhouse called "The Swamp" has another aquarium that provides a home for alligators and turtles. For some fresh air, head outside to the 300-acre natural area with trails that meander through wooded bluffs, river bottoms, lakes, and scenic swamplands.

Admission: adults $8, seniors $4, children 3-18 $3, children under 3 free. Monday-Friday 8 a.m.-5 p.m., Saturday 9 a.m.-5 p.m., Sunday 1-5 p.m.

MYNELLE GARDENS

4736 Clinton Blvd., Jackson, 601-960-1894

This 7-acre display garden has thousands of azaleas, camellias, daylilies, flowering trees and other perennials, as well as reflecting pools, a statuary, an

HIGHLIGHT

WHAT ARE THE TOP THINGS TO DO IN JACKSON?

LOOK AROUND IN THE MISSISSIPPI MUSEUM OF ART

This museum concentrates on 19th- and 20th-century art from artists of every stripe. You can spot works from notable artists like Georgia O'Keeffe and Andy Warhol. Check out its collection of art from Mississippians.

EXPLORE THE MISSISSIPPI PETRIFIED FOREST

Take a walk down the nature trail at this National Natural Landmark to see stone logs that were live trees about 36 million years ago. There's also a museum that has a cool black light display with fluorescent minerals.

HEAD OVER TO THE MISSISSIPPI SPORTS HALL OF FAME AND MUSEUM

Walter Payton and Archie Manning are the heroes at this museum, which honors Mississippi athletes. A section is dedicated to Dizzy Dean memorabilia, including his 1934 World Series and Hall of Fame rings.

SEE SCIENCE IN ACTION AT THE MUSEUM OF NATURAL SCIENCE

Go inside to see the museum's aquariums filled with native fishes, reptiles, amphibians and alligators. Then head outside to walk the museum grounds and see nature up close.

STOP AND SNIFF THE FLOWERS AT THE MYNELLE GARDENS

Mississippi is known for its beautiful landscape, so go enjoy it at these gardens. Admire the azaleas, camellias, daylilies and other blooms, as well as reflecting pools, a statuary, an Oriental garden and an all-white garden.

Oriental garden and an all-white garden. The turn-of-the-century Westbrook House is open for viewing.

OLD CAPITOL

100 S. State St., Jackson, 601-576-6920; www.mdah.state.ms.us/museum

The State Historical Museum traces Mississippi history in a restored Greek revival building that was the state capitol from 1839 to 1903. There's also a collection of Jefferson Davis memorabilia.

Monday-Friday 8 a.m.-5 p.m., Saturday 9:30 a.m.-4:30 p.m., Sunday 12:30-4:30 p.m.

SMITH ROBERTSON MUSEUM

528 Bloom St., Jackson, 601-960-1457; www.city.jackson.ms.us

This museum highlights the history and culture of African-American Mississippians from pre-slavery times to the present. There's s a large collection of photos, books, documents, arts and crafts.

Monday-Friday 9 a.m.-5 p.m., Saturday 10 a.m.-1 p.m., Sunday 2-5 p.m.

STATE CAPITOL

400 High St., Jackson, 601-359-3114

Impeccably restored in 1979, the lavish, Beaux-Arts-style capitol building was patterned after the national capitol in Washington. When the legislature is in session, visitors can take a seat in the chamber of the state House or Senate to watch some political wrangling. On the first floor, the Hall of Governors holds portraits of the state's governors since Mississippi Territory was created in 1798.

Tours can be arranged by appointment only.

THE OAKS HOUSE MUSEUM

823 N Jefferson St., Jackson, 601-353-9339; www.theoakshousemuseum.org

This Greek revival cottage, built of hand-hewn timber by James H. Boyd, former mayor of Jackson, was occupied by Gen. Sherman during the siege of 1863. The house contains period furniture.

Tuesday-Saturday 10 a.m.-3 p.m.

WHERE TO STAY

★★★HILTON JACKSON

1001 E. County Line Road, Jackson, 601-957-2800, 888-263-0524; www.hilton.com

The hotel tries to make you feel like you're at home with plush-top mattresses and 32-inch high-definition flat-screen televisions in every room. But there are some nice amenities that you definitely won't find at home: a full-service restaurant, a courtyard pool and Jacuzzi, a poolside fitness center, a complimentary airport shuttle and more. The Jackson property is near many of the local area attractions.

276 rooms. Restaurant, bar. Business center. Fitness room. Pool. $61-150

HIGHLIGHT

WHAT IS THERE TO SEE IN THE HILLS REGION?

The foothills of the Applalachians spill over to Mississippi's northernmost section, appropriately called the Hills region. It makes for some great scenery. Take Grenada, for instance. Its Grenada Lake attracts fishermen, boaters and campers who want to relax on its shores, while an 18-hole lakeside golf course gives duffers a chance to get in on the action as well.

This part of the state is also known for its rich history. Corinth preserves and celebrates its Civil War history. The town's location as a major railroad junction made it an important strategic site during the war. Between 1861 and 1865, as many as 300,000 soldiers from the north and the south occupied the town. In a struggle for control of the area, 65,000 Union troops met 44,000 Confederate troops in the Battle of Shiloh; the Confederate soldiers lost and evacuated the city. Six months later, they attempted (but failed) to reclaim the city in the Battle of Corinth, the bloodiest clash of the Civil War in Mississippi. The union fort **Battery Robinett** (*102 Linden St., Corinth, 662-287-9273*) was constructed on inner defense lines during the Battle of Corinth in 1862. Monuments mark the spots where Confederate soldiers died, and headstones commemorate color-bearers who fell while trying to plant a flag during battle. **Curlee House** (*705 Jackson St., Corinth, 662-287-9501; www.verandahhouse. org*) is a restored antebellum house that served as headquarters for Generals Bragg, Halleck and Hood during the Civil War.

Holly Springs crowns the ridge along which a Native American trail once led from the Mississippi to the tribal home of the Chickasaw Nation. The town has a reputation for preserving its historical buildings, including the antebellum homes that rose during a prosperous era in the 19th century. Perhaps its most remarkable attraction lately is the kitschy **Graceland Too** (*200 E. Gholson Ave.*), a "museum" full of Elvis memorabilia, open 24 hours a day. It's actually a fan's shrine to all things Elvis Presley. Presley fans stop here on their way from his childhood home in Tupelo to Graceland.

Elvis Presley was born in a two-room house in Tupelo in 1935. All these years later, the **Elvis Presley Park and Museum** (*306 Elvis Presley Drive, Tupelo, 662-841-1245; www.elvispresleybirthplace.com*) sees more than 50,000 die-hard Elvis fans every year, who make a pilgrimage to the small white frame house where the King lived for the first three years of his life. The museum houses a collection of Elvis memorabilia as well as a chapel.

While Elvis' birthplace is a big attraction, many people come to the Hills to visit Oxford. The town was named for the English university city in an effort to lure the University of Mississippi to the site. It worked. In 1848 the university opened. Today, "Ole Miss," with its forested, hilly campus, dominates the area, and Oxford relishes its role as a college town.

The city knows how to have a good time, but it also has a certain appeal for writers. William Faulkner, Nobel Prize-winning author, lived near the university at "Rowan Oak," and many landmarks of his fictional Yoknapatawpha County can be found in surrounding Lafayette County. John Grisham keeps a house here, too. Find out what makes the Hills so inspiring to writers and those who visit.

CAPITAL/RIVER

The Capital/River region is perhaps best known because of the state's capital city, Jackson. But the region offers so much more. The Mississippi River runs through this southwestern corner of the state, with historic towns near the water. Fish, fish and more fish is one reason to visit Mendenhall, a small city, home to lakes and 178,000 acres of forest. Natchez delivers the enchantment of the Old South, with a plantation atmosphere where everything seems beautiful and romantic. Greek revival mansions, manicured gardens and lawns, tree-shaded streets and hospitality abound in this museum of the antebellum South.

Port Gibson is where the Blues Highway and the Natchez Trace meet, which makes it a good place to begin an adventure in western Mississippi. Many antebellum houses and buildings remain in Port Gibson, lending support to the story that during the Civil War, Union General Grant spared the town on his march to Vicksburg with the words, "It's too beautiful to burn."

Originally an important river port, Vicksburg has a fascinating riverfront along the Mississippi River and the Yazoo Canal. Part of the town sits on a high bluff overlooking the river, a location that led to what is perhaps Vicksburg's biggest role in America history: the Civil War's Siege of Vicksburg.

Modern Vicksburg is nearly surrounded by the Vicksburg National Military Park, which is as much a part of the town as the streets and antebellum houses. The downtown district has art galleries, shops, restaurants, museums and antique stores, and Vicksburg's natural beauty makes it a haven for visitors who want to spend time outdoors.

If you'd rather spend time indoors, head to Woodville. The town has many beautiful 19th-century houses and some of the state's first churches, including Woodville Baptist, 1809; Woodville Methodist, 1824; and St. Paul's Episcopal 1823, which has an Erben organ from 1837.

WHAT TO SEE

MENDENHALL
BIENVILLE NATIONAL FOREST
3473 Highway 35 S., 601-469-3811; www.fs.fed.us
Fish-filled lakes, beautiful pine woods and well-maintained campsites make Bienville an ideal place to play outdoors. The forest's 178,000 acres attract hunters, fishermen, hikers, mountain bikers and anyone who just needs to find peace, quiet and a beautiful setting. Activities include swimming, boating, hiking, horse back riding, picnicking and camping.

D'LO WATER PARK
Highway 49, Mendenhall, 601-847-4310; www.dlowaterpark.com
This park is spread out over 85 acres. Activities include swimming, canoeing and fishing, while facilities include a playground, playing fields, a snack bar, picnicking shelters, boat ramps and rentals, campgrounds and cabins.
Daily.

HIGHLIGHT

WHAT ARE THE TOP THINGS TO DO IN CAPITAL/RIVER?

GET TO BIENVILLE NATIONAL FOREST

Located 45 miles east of Jackson, this is a good spot to enjoy horseback riding, swimming or picnicking on a warm summer day. But your best bet is to enjoy the local fly-fishing in the fish-filled lakes.

VISIT THE HISTORIC SPRINGFIELD PLANTATION

This is a must-see Southern plantation, the first mansion erected in the state. The site of Andrew Jackson's wedding, the mansion has beautiful woodworking and has been kept nearly intact since the 19th century.

HOOF IT TO HOMOCHITTO NATIONAL FOREST

This forest offers some of the best trails for hikers and bikers in the state. The trails are well maintained, though anyone with a hook and line will want to head to the Okhissa Lake Recreation Area, a prime spot for bass fishing.

STOP FOR A DRINK AT THE BIEDENHARN MUSEUM OF COCA-COLA MEMORABILIA

Stop here and take a step back in time to the 1890s, when this building was the site of the first Coca-Cola bottling factory. There's the expected collection of Coca-Cola kitsch, but the restored candy store offers an old-fashioned soda fountain that will make you rue the day you ever drank Coke from a can.

EXPLORE THE ROSEMONT PLANTATION

No visit to the state is complete without a stop at one of its historic plantations. The main house was the home of Jefferson Davis and generations of his family, and the mansion contains many of the family furnishings in their original state, giving you a sense of the man who was the Confederacy's first (and last) president.

NATCHEZ
CANAL STREET DEPOT

Canal and State streets, Natchez

Located one block from the Mississippi River, the Depot houses the Natchez Pilgrimage Tour and Tourist Headquarters, a children's factory outlet and old-fashioned shops. Here you can also take a carriage tour through the Natchez Historic District, presented with a 35-minute overview of the town's antebellum history along, with tours of Victorian townhouses and churches.

EMERALD MOUND

2680 Natchez Trace Parkway, Natchez, 601-442-2658; www.cr.nps.gov

One of the largest mounds in North America, Emerald Mound was a ceremonial center for ancestors of the Natchez Indians between A.D. 1250 and 1600. *Daily.*

GRAND VILLAGE OF THE NATCHEZ

400 Jefferson Davis Blvd., Natchez, 601-446-6502; www.mdah.state.ms.us

Here you'll find a museum, an archaeological site, nature trails, a picnic area and a gift shop.

Monday-Saturday 9 a.m.-5p.m., Sunday 1:30-5 p.m.

HISTORIC JEFFERSON COLLEGE

16 Old North St., Washington, 601-442-2901; www.mdah.state.ms.us

The Jefferson College campus was the site of the first state Constitutional Convention in 1817. Jefferson Davis was among the famous Mississippians who attended the school. No longer used as a college, it is now listed on the National Register of Historic places. A museum interprets the early history of the territory. The site includes nature trails and an area for picnicking.

Monday-Saturday 9 a.m.-5 p.m., Sunday 1-5 p.m.

HISTORIC SPRINGFIELD PLANTATION

Highway 553, Natchez, 601-786-3802

Believed to be the first mansion erected in Mississippi, the main house remains nearly intact with little remodeling over the years. Built for Thomas Marston Green, Jr., a wealthy planter from Virginia, and the site of Andrew Jackson's wedding, the mansion displays original hand-carved woodwork, Civil War equipment, railroad memorabilia and a narrow-gauge locomotive.

Daily.

HOMOCHITTO NATIONAL FOREST

Natchez, 601-965-4391, 601-384-5876; www.fs.fed.us

This 189,000-acre forest was the first of Mississippi's six national forests, established in 1936. Camp in any of the three recreation areas, and hike through the eastern half of the park, renowned among hikers for its irregular terrain and excellent trail system. Activities include swimming, fishing and camping.

Daily.

THE HOUSE ON ELLICOTT HILL

211 N. Canal St., Natchez, 601-442-2011

This is the site where, in 1797, Andrew Ellicott raised the first American flag in the lower Mississippi Valley. Built in 1798, the house overlooks both the Mississippi and the terminus of the Natchez Trace. The house is fully restored and authentically furnished.

Daily.

LONGWOOD
140 Lower Woodville Road, Natchez, 601-442-5193

This enormous, Italianate-detailed "octagon house" is crowned with an onion dome. Because the house was under construction at the start of the Civil War, its interiors were never completed above the first floor. Containing 1840 furnishings, Longwood is owned and operated by the Pilgrimage Garden Club. *Daily.*

MAGNOLIA HALL
South Pearl and Washington, Natchez, 601-442-6847; www.natchezgardenclub.com

The last great mansion to be erected in the city before the outbreak of the Civil War, Magnolia Hall is an outstanding example of Greek revival architecture. The mansion contains period antiques and a costume museum. *Daily.*

MELROSE ESTATE HOME
1 Melrose Ave., Natchez, 601-446-5790; www.nps.gov/natc

The National Park Service oversees this historic mansion and its grounds and tells the plantation story from a national perspective. The house is open for guided tours only, with self-guided tours available for the slave quarters. *Daily.*

MONMOUTH
36 Melrose Ave., Natchez, 601-442-5852; www.monmouthplantation.com

Registered as a National Historic Landmark, the monumental Greek revival house and auxiliary buildings, once owned by Mexican War hero General John Anthony Quitman, have been completely restored, with antique furnishings and extensive gardens. Monmouth also has guest rooms and tours available. *Daily.*

MOUNT LOCUST
2680 Natchez Trace Parkway, Natchez, 601-445-4211

One of Mississippi's oldest structures, Mount Locust was built in the 1780s and used as an inn on the Natchez Trail.

NATCHEZ STATE PARK
230B Wickliff Road, Natchez, 601-442-2658; www.mdwfp.com

The park's horse trails are believed to be abandoned plantation roads that lead to Brandon Hall, home of the first native Mississippi governor, Gerard Brandon, who served 1826-1831. Activities here include fishing, boating, picnicking and camping. *Daily.*

NATCHEZ VISITOR CENTER
640 S. Canal St., Natchez, 800-647-6742; www.cityofnatchez.com

This spacious visitor center on the bluff above the Mississippi River offers tourist services, including a film on the city's history and heritage. *Daily.*

ROSALIE

100 Orleans St., Natchez, 601-445-4555; www.rosaliemansion.com

This red brick Georgian mansion with a Greek revival portico served as the headquarters for the Union Army during occupation of Natchez. The original furnishings date from 1857, and the grounds contain gardens overlooking the Mississippi River.

Daily 9:30 a.m.-4:30 p.m.

STANTON HALL

401 High St., Natchez, 601-446-6631

This elaborate antebellum mansion is surrounded by giant oaks and contains original chandeliers, marble mantels, Sheffield hardware and French mirrors.

Daily 9 a.m.-4:30 p.m.

PORT GIBSON

GRAND GULF MILITARY PARK

Grand Gulf Road, Port Gibson, 601-437-5911; www.grandgulfpark.state.ms.us

The park, officially opened in 1962, commemorates the former town of Grand Gulf, which lost 55 of 75 city blocks to Mississippi floods between 1855 and 1860, as well as the battle that was fought here. During the Civil War, the town's population was waning when Confederate troops and Union forces clashed here, first in the spring of 1862 and again in the spring of 1863. The park today includes fortifications, an observation tower, a cemetery, a memorial chapel, a carriage house with vehicles used by the Confederates, a four-room cottage reconstructed from the early days of Grand Gulf and several other pre-Civil War buildings. A museum in the visitor center displays unique Civil War, Native American and prehistoric artifacts. You'll also find hiking trails and picnic areas.

Daily 8 a.m.-5 p.m.

OAK SQUARE PLANTATION

1207 Church St., Port Gibson, 601-437-4350

This restored 30-room mansion has six fluted, Corinthian columns, each standing 22 feet tall, as well as antique furnishings from the 18th and 19th centuries. There are extensive grounds, a courtyard and a gazebo. Guest rooms are available and tours can be made by appointment.

ROSSWOOD PLANTATION

Highway 552, Lorman, 800-533-5889; www.rosswood.net

This classic Greek revival mansion designed by David Shroder, architect of the nearby Windsor ruins, features columned galleries, 10 fireplaces, 15-foot ceilings, a winding stairway and original slave quarters in the basement. The home is beautifully restored and is furnished with antiques. Rosswood served as a cotton plantation on 1250 acres even before the Civil War. The first owner's diary has survived and offers details of antebellum life on a cotton plantation. The 14 rooms are furnished with antiques. Guest rooms are available.

March-November.

THE RUINS OF WINDSOR
Old Rodney Road, Port Gibson, 601-437-4351; home.olemiss.edu

These 23 stately columns are all that is left of a grand four-story mansion built in 1860 by a cotton plantation businessman at a cost of $175,000 and destroyed by fire in 1890. Its proximity to the river and size made it a natural marker for Mississippi River pilots, including Samuel Clemens, better known by his pen name, Mark Twain.

VICKSBURG

ANCHUCA HISTORIC MANSION AND INN
1010 First East St., Vicksburg, 601-661-0111, 888-686-0111; www.anchucamansion.com

This restored Greek revival mansion is furnished with period antiques and gas-burning lanterns. The site also includes guest rooms, landscaped gardens and a brick courtyard.
Daily.

BIEDENHARN MUSEUM OF COCA-COLA MEMORABILIA
1107 Washington St., Vicksburg, 601-638-6514; www.biedenharncoca-colamuseum.com

This is the building in which Coca-Cola was first bottled in 1894. The museum includes a restored candy store, an old-fashioned soda fountain and a collection of Coca-Cola advertising and memorabilia.
Daily.

CEDAR GROVE
2200 Oak St., Vicksburg, 601-636-1000, 800-862-1300; www.cedargroveinn.com

This mansion was shelled by Union gunboats during the Civil War. Though it's restored, a cannonball is still lodged in the parlor wall. The site includes a roof garden with view of the Mississippi and Yazoo rivers, a tea room, many original furnishings, more than 4 acres of formal gardens, courtyards, fountains, guest rooms and gazebos.
Daily.

DUFF GREEN
1114 First East St., Vicksburg, 601-636-6968, 800-992-0037; www.duffgreenmansion.com

This mansion features Palladian architecture. Shelled by Union forces during the Civil War, the site was then used as a hospital for Confederate and Union troops. The house is now restored with antique furnishings. Guided tours, guest rooms and high tea are available by reservation.
Daily.

MARTHA VICK HOUSE
1300 Grove St., Vicksburg, 601-638-7036; www.marthavickhouse.com

Built by the daughter of the founder of Vicksburg, Newit Vick, the house features a Greek revival façade, a restored interior furnished with 18th-and 19th-century antiques and an outstanding art collection.
Daily.

MCRAVEN HOME
1445 Harrison St., Vicksburg, 601-636-1663; www.mcraventourhome.com

This home was the heaviest-shelled house during the Siege of Vicksburg.

HIGHLIGHT

WHAT IS THE BEST WAY TO TOUR THE NATCHEZ HISTORIC DISTRICT?

Visit Natchez for a glimpse of the antebellum South. Built on a high bluff overlooking the Mississippi River, the town has a compact downtown area that history buffs will want to explore. Many of the historic buildings now house museums, where visitors can learn more about the town's fascinating history, and there are plenty of restaurants, cafés and shops to break up a day of sightseeing. Start upriver and work your way back down. The oldest house in town, built in 1799, is the small two-story **House on Ellicott Hill** (*North Canal at Jefferson, 601-442-2011*). Settler Andrew Elliott raised the American flag here in defiance of Spain, which claimed the broad plain along the Gulf to the Mississippi River as Spanish West Florida.

Walk away from the river down Jefferson, then up Pearl Street a block to **Stanton Hall** (*601-442-6282*). A stately mansion built in 1857, Stanton Hall fits the classic image of opulent antebellum architecture. Find fine dining and theater in the cottage house. Keeping strolling down Pearl Street toward the commercial district.

Two blocks down, carriage tours depart from the entranceway of the **Natchez Eola Hotel** (*110 Pearl St., 601-445-6000*). Around the corner on Main Street, in the old Post Office building, the **Museum of Afro-American History and Culture** (*601-445-0728*), provides an important reminder of the other side of the town's antebellum history.

Two blocks farther south along Pearl, **Magnolia Hall** (*215 S. Pearl St., 601-442-6672*), a Greek revival mansion, built in 1858, is now a house museum. A block west toward the river is the **Governor Holmes House** (*207 S. Wall St., 601-442-2366*). Home of the last governor of the Mississippi Territory, Holmes became the first state governor when Mississippi joined the Union in 1817. Like many of the historic houses in town, it also operates as an inn.

At Wall Street and Washington, get a bite to eat at one of the cafés or pop into a great area bookshop. Cross Canal Street and skip down a block to visit Rosalie, on the bluff at South Broadway, a lovely brick mansion that served as Union Army headquarters during the Civil War.

Walk upriver a couple of blocks until you see the steep road leading down the bluff. This leads to **Natchez Under-the-Hill,** once the neighborhood that catered to the seedier side of the steamboat trade. Today it is harmless, though it retains the look and spirit of the Old West frontier. There are several family restaurants and a tavern called the Saloon, all with great river views. Down at the water, the Lady Luck riverboat casino operates around the clock. If you've parked at the visitor center, your car is right up the hill from here.

Visitors can take a view of the architectural record of Vicksburg history, from frontier cottage 1797 to Empire 1836 and finally to elegant Greek revival townhouse 1849, as well as many original furnishings. Original brick walks surround the house, as does a lovely garden with magnolia and many plants. *Daily.*

OLD COURT HOUSE MUSEUM

1008 Cherry St., Vicksburg, 601-636-0741; www.oldcourthouse.org

Built with slave labor, this building offers a view of the Yazoo Canal from its hilltop position. Here, Grant raised the U.S. flag on July 4, 1863, signifying the end of fighting after 47 days. The courthouse now houses an extensive display of Americana. The Confederate room contains weapons and documents on the siege of Vicksburg. There is also a pioneer room, a furniture room as well as Native American displays and objets d'art.

Monday-Saturday 8:30 a.m.-4:30 p.m., Sunday 1:30-4:30 p.m.

VICKSBURG NATIONAL MILITARY PARK & CEMETERY

3201 Clay St., Vicksburg, 601-636-0583; www.nps.gov/vick

This historic park, the site of Union siege lines and a hardened Confederate defense, borders the eastern and northern sections of the city. A visitor center is at the park entrance, on Clay Street at Interstate 20. The site also contains a museum with exhibits and audiovisual aids. Take a self-guided 16-minute tour. *Daily 8 a.m.-5 p.m.*

WHERE TO STAY

NATCHEZ

★★★DUNLEITH PLANTATION

84 Homochitto St., Natchez, 601-446-8500, 800-433-2445; www.dunleith.com

This luxurious home has been restored to its pre-Civil War style. The gorgeous Greek revival manse, with 26 Tuscan columns surrounding it, sits at the edge of Natchez's historic district. If you want to relax on the plantation, check out the library or play some bocce ball on the onsite court. Or you can find some peace in the rooms, many of which have either claw-foot tubs or Jacuzzis. For dinner, head to the 1790s carriage house and stables, which have been converted into Castle Restaurant and Pub. There, you can get a Southern-influenced American meal along with an excellent pour from the impressive wine list.

9 rooms. No children under 14 years. Complimentary breakfast. $151-250

★★★MONMOUTH PLANTATION

36 Melrose Ave., Natchez, 601-442-5852, 800-828-4531; www.monmouthplantation.com

Visitors might expect to see Scarlet O'Hara herself gliding through the vast courtyards of this beautiful plantation home. During the day, stroll or take a carriage ride through the historic site; in the evening, enjoy a five-course dinner served in the elegant dining room. In fact, the plantation offers a lot of activities that will keep you busy: you can take one of its signature mint julep tours of the grounds, go fishing using the hotel's equipment, do a wine tasting, hear some great music during the Sunday jazz brunches or even go on a hot-air balloon

---

HIGHLIGHT

WHAT IS THE NATCHEZ TRACE?

One of the earliest "interstates," the Natchez Trace stretched from Natchez, Miss., to Nashville, Tenn., and was the most heavily traveled road in the Old Southwest from approximately 1785 to 1820. Boatmen floated their products downriver to Natchez or New Orleans, sold them and walked or rode home over the Natchez Trace. It was still in use, to some extent, as late as the 1830s, though its importance diminished after the invention of the steam engine.

Today the 444-mile-long parkway closely follows the original trace, often crossing over it and passing many points of historic interest, including Emerald Mound. The parkway headquarters and visitor center are five miles north of Tupelo, at junction Highway 45. Interpretive facilities include a visitor center with exhibits depicting the history of the area. Park Service personnel can provide information about self-guided trails, wayside exhibits, interpretive programs, camping and picnicking facilities along the parkway.

---

ride, which takes off from the front lawn.
30 rooms. No children under 14 years. Complimentary breakfast. $151-250

VICKSBURG

★★★ANCHUCA
1010 First E. St., Vicksburg, 888-686-0111, 800-469-2597; www.anchucamansion.com

Anchuca, a Choctaw word that means "happy home," was the first columned mansion in Vicksburg and it's listed on the National Register of Historic Places. Climb the narrow, greenery-lined steps to this pre-Civil War mansion and you'll find lovely guest rooms with private baths, a full breakfast and afternoon tea. Built around 1830 in Greek revival style, the hotel has common rooms that are furnished with period antiques and romantic, gas-burning chandeliers. Only a few blocks away from the "happy home" is a quaint downtown area full of antique shops and other little stores.
7 rooms. Complimentary breakfast. $61-150

★★★CEDAR GROVE MANSION INN
2200 Oak St., Vicksburg, 601-636-1000, 800-862-1300; www.cedargroveinn.com

This 5-acre, garden-like property includes guest rooms, cottages and suites. The inn was built in 1852, and luckily it was mostly unharmed during the Civil War because it was used as a Union hospital. The only evidence you'll see of the war is the cannon ball that's still lodged in the parlor wall. All accommodations include a full breakfast and afternoon tea. The lodgings also include a complimentary nightly turndown service that comes with a shot of sherry and chocolates, a sweet way to end the day. The inn's chef, Andre Flowers, turns out New Orleans cuisine at Andre's Restaurant.
34 rooms. Restaurant. Complimentary breakfast. $61-150

★★★DUFF GREEN MANSION

1114 First E. St., Vicksburg, 601-638-6662, 800-992-0037;
www.duffgreenmansion.com

This large 1856 Palladian mansion was used as a hospital for both Confederate and Union soldiers during the Siege of Vicksburg. The mansion served in many different capacities after the war, including as an orphanage and a retirement home, but it was eventually restored to its former glory with an emphasis on accurate period detail. Each of the bedrooms has a fireplace and porch and is furnished in period antiques and reproductions. The hotel also offers several entertainment options; there's a complimentary bar during happy hour in one of the reception rooms, a swimming pool with a secluded patio and daily tours of the property.

7 rooms. Complimentary breakfast. Business center. $61-150

WOODVILLE

ROSEMONT PLANTATION

Main Street, Woodville, 601-888-6809; www.rosemontplantation1810.com

This was the home of Jefferson Davis and his family. His parents, Samuel and Jane Davis, moved to Woodville and built the house when he was 2 years old. The Confederate president grew up here and returned to visit his family throughout his life. Many family furnishings remain, including a spinning wheel that belonged to Jane. Five generations of the Davis family are buried on this 300-acre plantation.

Tuesday-Saturday 10 a.m.-5 p.m.

COASTAL REGION

The Coastal region juts out of the southeastern part of the state and encompasses Laurel to the north and the Gulf Coast to the south. Its location along the water makes it a place of beauty, but it also made the region vulnerable when Hurricane Katrina struck in August 2005. The storm battered the Coastal towns, but they have worked hard to overcome the destruction.

The region's most popular town is also the oldest in the Mississippi Valley. Biloxi has been a hopping resort area since the 1840s. While the town has changed greatly since then, many of its prized possessions are still here. Fresh seafood is always available, and visitors who want to catch their own can choose from fresh-water, salt water and deep-sea fishing. The beaches are open for visitors who just want to relax on the sand or swim in the surf, and spas, shops and restaurants entice visitors to indulge.

Gulfport is another resort town that draws sun-and-sand types. Its proximity to lakes, rivers, bays and bayous make it an angler's paradise. The city has boutiques, colorful casinos and several 18-hole golf courses open to the public.

The little town of Pass Christian has drawn some big names; it has hosted six vacationing U.S. presidents: Andrew Jackson, Zachary Taylor, Ulysses S. Grant, Theodore Roosevelt, Woodrow Wilson and Harry Truman. And as if that weren't enough, the world's largest oyster reef is offshore.

HIGHLIGHT

WHAT ARE THE TOP THINGS TO DO ON THE COAST?

TAKE IN HISTORY AT THE JEFFERSON DAVIS HOME AND PRESIDENTIAL LIBRARY

You don't need to be a Civil War buff to visit the home of the first and last Confederate president. Damaged in Hurricane Katrina, the estate was restored in 2008 and contains important artifacts from the Confederate period.

MAKE A LAST STOP BEFORE THE FINAL FRONTIER AT THE JOHN C. STENNIS SPACE CENTER

The lesser-known cousin of the Johnson (Texas) and Kennedy (Florida) space centers, the John C. Stennis Space Center is still a must-stop-and-wonder spot for anyone who dreamed of flying to outer space or tried out astronaut food as a kid. The center was the main home for rocket testing for the Apollo missions, and you won't leave here without a sense of the thrill of strapping oneself to a fueled-up rocket to escape the Earth's gravity.

SET SAIL ON SHIP ISLAND EXCURSIONS

Here you can catch a ferry that leaves for Ship Island, which offers the best beaches in Mississippi. Once you get to the island, spend the day snorkeling or simply lazing in the sand.

EXPLORE THE LAUREN ROGERS MUSEUM OF ART

This is a great stop to make in Laurel's historic district. The museum has a solid collection of 19th- and 20th-century American and European paintings, but its highlights are the works of Winslow Homer and Thomas Moran.

STOP FOR A LISTEN AT THE SINGING RIVER

After a long day at one of the area parks, this is a perfect place to rest and listen to the sounds of nature, and what a sound. No one knows the source, but there's an eerie song from the river that is best heard on late summer and autumn evenings.

If you want a break from the water activities, try out Hattiesburg, which boasts a booming arts scene and one of the largest historic districts in southeast Mississippi. The buildings reflect architectural styles from 1884 to 1930. Laurel is another charming Southern town with oak-lined streets and historic homes.

WHAT TO SEE

BILOXI
BEAUVOIR—JEFFERSON DAVIS HOME AND PRESIDENTIAL LIBRARY
2244 Beach Blvd., Biloxi, 228-388-4400; www.beauvoir.org

Hurricane Katrina damaged much of Beauvoir, but this historic estate was restored in mid-2008. Confederate President Jefferson Davis spent the last 12 years of his life here, writing *The Rise and Fall of the Confederate Government* and *A Short History of the Confederate States of America*. The adjoining museum holds artifacts from Davis and the Confederate states. Here, too, is a cemetery with the Tomb of the Unknown Soldier of the Confederate States of America and a Presidential Library dedicated to Jefferson's tenure.

BILOXI CITY CEMETERY
1166 Irish Hill Drive, Biloxi; www.biloxi.ms.us

Across the rolling grass here are the burial grounds of the French pioneer families of Biloxi and the Gulf Coast. John Cuevas, hero of the Cat Island War of 1812, is buried here.

HARRISON COUNTY SAND BEACH
842 Commerce St., Biloxi, 228-896-0055; www.co.harrison.ms.us

This 300-foot-wide white-sand beach stretches the entire 26-mile length of the county, with a seawall separating the beach from the highway.

SMALL CRAFT HARBOR
Main Street and Highway 90, Biloxi

Visitors can view fishing boats unloading the day's catch of Gulf game fish or chart their own deep-sea fishing boat to make the big catch themselves.

GULFPORT
JOHN C. STENNIS SPACE CENTER
NASA Space Center, Gulfport, 228-688-2370; www.ssc.nasa.gov

In the 1960s and 1970s, locals would quip, "If you want to go to the moon, you have to go through Hancock County, Mississippi." It's part of the Gulfport-Biloxi metro area and home to the Stennis Space Center. NASA's largest rocket engine test facility, the Stennis Space Center was the testing site for Saturn V and for the first and second stages of the Apollo-manned lunar program, which landed the first men on the moon in 1969. The Stennis Space Center hosts NASA and 18 federal and state agencies involved in oceanographic, environmental and national defense programs. There is a visitor center with a 90-foot Space Tower, films, demonstrations, indoor and outdoor exhibits and guided tours.
Daily.

SPECIAL EVENTS

BLESSING OF THE FLEET

177 First St., Biloxi, Gulf of Mexico; www.biloxiblessing.com

Hundreds of vessels manned by descendants of settlers participate in this ritual of European origin. It is an unusual event, especially if you live in a landlocked area. The Blessing of the Fleet in Biloxi began in 1929. Participating boats are decorated to the nines. Shrimp is boiled. There is even a crowned Shrimp King and Queen, who rule over the blessing and the festivities that come along with it. For towns that relied on fishing, or in this case shrimp fishing, having the boats blessed with good luck was vital. The tradition, and superstition, is still carried on and is a great local event.

First weekend in June.

MARDI GRAS

2501 Beachview Drive, Biloxi

The biggest party of the year, Mardi Gras includes a carnival and parade with colorful, festive floats. Not quite on the same level as the Mardi Gras celebration next door in Louisiana, the Gulf Coast Mardi Gras parade still draws a large crowd. Judged to be one of the best parades on the Mississippi Gulf Coast. The first parade was held in 1908 and the French tradition has been carried on over the years. The parade features A Grand Marshal, Mayor and the councilmen of Biloxi. A king and queen are crowned to reign over the parade and become part of the history that makes this event so important to the town of Biloxi.

March.

SEAFOOD FESTIVAL

Point Cadet Plaza, 120 Cadet St., Biloxi

Visitors in the early fall can catch this festival, which includes an arts and crafts show, entertainment, seafood booths and contests. This particular festival attracts more than 25,000 people in its two-day stint. From the Gumbo Championship to the Kids Village, there is something for the whole family to do. With perpetual live entertainment throughout the weekend, plenty of seafood to munch on and countless activities for everyone, this festival draws in quite a crowd for this Gulf Coast town.

Mid-September.

PORT OF GULFPORT

Mississippi Technical Center, 200 E Main St., Starkville, 662-324-7776; www.starkville.org

The 1,320-foot-wide harbor separates the port's two parallel piers, which includes one of the largest banana import facilities in the U.S.

Daily.

SHIP ISLAND EXCURSIONS

Gulfport Yacht Harbor, Highway 90, Gulfport, 228-864-1014; www.msshipisland.com

Come here to catch a passenger ferry that leaves from the Gulfport Yacht Harbor for a one-hour trip to Ship Island, 12 miles off the coast. You can spend as much time on the island as you like, as long as you catch the last ferry of the day, at either 2:30 or 5 p.m., depending on the day and time of year.

HATTIESBURG
DE SOTO NATIONAL FOREST
654 W. Frontage Road, Chickasaw Ranger District, Wiggins, 601-965-4391, 601-528-6160; www.fs.fed.us

At approximately 500,000 acres, the park includes the Black Creek Float Trip, which offers 50 miles of scenic streams, and the Black Creek Trail, which has 41 miles of woodland paths, 10 of which go through 5,000 acres of Black Creek Wilderness. You can do swimming, fishing, hiking, horse riding, picnicking and primitive camping on these grounds.
Daily.

LAUREL
LANDRUM'S HOMESTEAD
1356 Highway 15 S., Laurel, 601-649-2546; www.landrums.com

This re-creation of a late-1800s settlement includes a blacksmith shop, a grist mill, a display of gem mining and a general store.
Monday-Saturday 9 a.m.-5 p.m.

LAUREN ROGERS MUSEUM OF ART
565 N. Fifth Ave., Laurel, 601-649-6374; www.lrma.org

Art lovers visit this museum each year to see its 19th- and 20th-century American and European paintings, 18th-century Japanese woodblock prints, English Georgian silver and Native American baskets. Works from the likes of Thomas Moran, Winslow Homer and Romare Bearden are on display.
Tuesday-Saturday 10 a.m.-4:45 p.m., Sunday 1-4 p.m.

PASCAGOULA
MISSISSIPPI SANDHILL CRANE NATIONAL WILDLIFE REFUGE
7200 Gautier Vancleave Road, Pascagoula, 228-497-6322; www.fws.gov

Established to protect endangered cranes, the refuge has three units that total 18,000 acres. Also here is a three-quarter-mile wildlife trail with interpretive panels, an outdoor exhibit and areas for bird-watching. The visitor center has slide programs by request, a wildlife exhibit, paintings and maps.
Monday-Friday 8 a.m.-4 p.m.

OLD SPANISH FORT AND MUSEUM
4602 Fort St., Pascagoula, 228-769-1505

Built by the French, later captured by the Spanish, the fort has walls of massive cypress timbers cemented with oyster shells, mud and moss that are 18 inches thick. Said to be the oldest structure in the Mississippi Valley, the site contains a museum with Native American relics as part of its collection.
Daily.

SCRANTON NATURE CENTER
IG Levy Park at Pascagoula River, Pascagoula, 228-938-6612; www.cityofpascagoula.com

The Center, surrounded by a lake and nature trails, houses owls and other

wildlife, assorted sea animals, plants and more.
Tuesday-Saturday. 10 a.m.-5 p.m.

SINGING RIVER
Pascagoula River, Pascagoula

There is indeed a singing sound from the river, which is best heard on late summer and autumn nights. The sound seems to get louder, coming nearer until it seems to be underfoot. Scientists have made several guesses about the sound's source: It could be made by fish, sand scraping the hard slate bottom, natural gas escaping from the sand bed or a current sucked past a hidden cave. No one has ever confirmed the exact source.

PASS CHRISTIAN

THE FRIENDSHIP OAK
University of Southern Mississippi's Gulf Park campus, Pass Christian, 228-865-4500; www.usm.edu

The Oak has become a symbol of the Gulf Coast's strength in the wake of Hurricane Katrina. It has been standing since 1487, five years before Columbus arrived in the new world. The oak has a 16-foot trunk, limbs larger than 5 feet in diameter and a root system that held fast enough to keep the tree standing through the storm. Legend says that people who stand together in the tree's shadow will remain friends forever.

WHERE TO STAY

★★★BEAU RIVAGE RESORT AND CASINO
875 Beach Blvd., Biloxi, 228-386-7444, 888-567-6667; www.beaurivage.com

Las Vegas meets the French Riviera of the South at Beau Rivage. A world of its own, the resort has a 31-slip marina, a casino and other recreational and entertainment choices. The guest rooms, decorated in styles that evoke the English countryside, offer great views of the bay or ocean, and eight restaurants serve cuisine inspired by places across the globe. Sports enthusiasts charter boats for relaxing rides or sport-fishing adventures, while the spa and salon lure landlubbers with a penchant for pampering.
1,780 rooms. Restaurant, bar. Spa. Casino. $151-250

★★★GRAND CASINO HOTEL BILOXI
265 Beach Blvd., Biloxi, 228-432-2500, 800-946-2946

Visitors head to this hotel to hit the casino floor. After you're exhausted or broke from gaming, you can retire to your room and rest your head on a pillow-topped bed and relax in front of the plasma-screen TV. You can also play a round on the 18-hole championship Jack Nicklaus golf course or go to the huge outdoor pool with its luxury cabanas.
491 rooms. Restaurant, bar. Pool. Casino. Golf. $61-150

WHERE TO EAT

★★★MARY MAHONEY'S OLD FRENCH HOUSE

Magnolia and Water streets, Biloxi, 228-374-0163; www.marymahoneys.com

The restaurant's namesake Mary Mahoney, daughter of Yugoslavian immigrants, founded this Gulf Coast landmark in 1964. The design of the restaurant has a French flavor, with high ceilings and other traits common in French Quarter apartments. The menu is full of fresh-from-the-Gulf seafood dishes. Start off with an appetizer that President Reagan enjoyed, appropriately called the Presidential Platter, with crab claws and petite soft-shell crabs. For your entrée, stick with seafood and go for the crabmeat au gratin and fried oysters.

American. Lunch, dinner. Closed Sunday. $36-85

WELCOME TO TENNESSEE

TENNESSEE WILL DELIGHT VISITORS WITH THE different landscapes that compose its parallelogram-esque shape. Along its border with North Carolina, the eastern third of the state is dominated by the Blue Ridge Mountains,

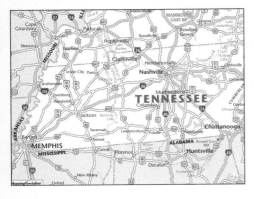

which include the subranges of the Great Smoky Mountains, the Bald Mountains, the Unicoi Mountains, the Unaka Mountains and Roan Highlands, and the Iron Mountains. Clingman's Dome, which at 6,643 feet is the highest point on the Appalachian Trail and in the state, sits among these mountains.

From the mountains in the east, the elevation decreases to create the Tennessee Valley before climbing up again to form the Cumberland Plateau. On the western side of the plateau in Middle Tennessee are the Nashville Basic and the Highland Rim that surrounds it.

West Tennessee is dominated by the Gulf Coastal Plain, which extends from the western Tennessee River (the Tennessee River crosses through the state in the east and again in the west) to the Mississippi River along Tennessee's western border. Outdoor activities on both land and water abound throughout the state, with 54 state parks offering recreation opportunities.

In 1796, Tennessee became the 16th state to join the Union. Before statehood, pioneers crossed the mountains from North Carolina into the eastern part of what would become Tennessee. Sycamore Shoals was an important frontier hub for pioneers moving west from Virginia and North Carolina. Elizabethton's Sycamore Shoals State Historic Park commemorates the site of the first permanent American settlement outside the original 13 colonies.

Tennessee earned its nickname "the Volunteer State" during the War of 1812, when thousands of Tennesseans responded to Governor Willie Blount's call for volunteer soldiers. In honor of this moniker, the University of Tennessee's mascot is the Volunteer. Though the university is in Knoxville, passionate fans of Vols football cover the entire state.

Tennessee's place in the nation's music history covers the width of the state. Bristol, located in the upper northeastern corner on the border with Virginia, is acknowledged as the birthplace of country music. Nashville, in the center of the state, is called "Music City, USA" because of its role in churning out music–industry stars, but it also gets the nickname because the historic Grand Ole Opry, the world's longest-running live radio program, airs from Nashville. Memphis, anchoring the southwestern corner of Tennessee, is famous for its roots in blues music and for Sun Records, where famous performers such as Elvis Presley, Johnny Cash and Roy Orbison recorded timeless hits.

From its urban to its rural areas, Tennessee offers plenty of enjoyable options for those who visit.

BEST ATTRACTIONS

WHAT ARE THE BEST ATTRACTIONS IN TENNESSEE?

WEST TENNESSEE
A number of cities make up Western Tennessee, but the most well known is Memphis. People flock to the metropolis for its civil-rights sites, the live blues music along Beale Street and, of course, Graceland.

NASHVILLE
For country music fans, there's no place like Nashville. Country's biggest stars either get their start in Music City or at least end up performing on the storied stage at the Grand Ole Opry.

EAST TENNESSEE
East Tennessee does it up big, from the sprawling Dollywood amusement park to the larger-than-life Smoky Mountains.

WEST TENNESSEE

When people think of West Tennessee, only one place comes to mind: Memphis. Old South meets modern metropolis in Memphis, thanks in part to a renaissance of the downtown area. This rebirth has given Memphis a shiny new face to go with its epic musical legacy and prime location on the banks of the Mississippi River.

Named after the Egyptian city, Memphis means "place of good abode," a translation that rings true for Elvis fans, who make Graceland the second most-visited home in the U.S. (Only the White House attracts more visitors each year.) If you have no interest in searching for the King's ghost, Memphis is still a hot destination, especially for music lovers.

Don't let Nashville fool you: American music owes a lot of its success to Memphis. "Father of the Blues" W.C. Handy scribbled the first written blues music here, Elvis made his first recording on Beale Street, and legends such as B.B. King and Muddy Waters gave life to the blues. Rock 'n' roll grew up here, too, when Sam Phillips of Sun Studio recorded musicians who fused country music and blues into rockabilly, the precursor to rock 'n' roll.

Though its rich musical past is Memphis' prime draw, the city offers more. It is home to more than a dozen institutions of higher learning, including the University of Memphis and Rhodes College. A civic ballet, a symphony orchestra, an opera company, a repertory theater and art galleries help create the city's rich cultural life.

Memphis may get the top billing for must-visit West Tennessee destinations, but there are smaller cities that warrant exploring. Located between Memphis and Nashville, Jackson is named for President Andrew Jackson; many of the president's soldiers and his wife's relatives settled here. The city's other famous son, John Luther "Casey" Jones, a railroad engineer, died in 1900 trying to stop his train from hitting a stopped freight train in Mississippi. Jones was the only one to die in the crash, making him a hero immortalized in ballads and legends.

WHAT TO SEE

JACKSON
BROOKS SHAW & SON OLD COUNTRY STORE
56 Casey Jones Lane, Jackson, 731-668-1223; www.caseyjonesvillage.com
This turn-of-the-century general store, located in Casey Jones Village, keeps more than 15,000 antiques on display. If you get hungry, there's also a restaurant, an ice-cream parlor and a confectionery shop.

CASEY JONES HOME AND RAILROAD MUSEUM
30 Casey Jones Lane, Jackson, 731-668-1222; www.caseyjones.com
See the original house of the high-rolling engineer who, on April 30, 1900, climbed into the cab of "Old 382" on the Illinois Central Railroad and took his "farewell trip to that promised land"—and a place in American folklore. On display are Jones' personal and railroad memorabilia, including railroad passes, timetables, bells and steam whistles; also check out the type of steam locomotive that was driven by Jones and restored 1890s coach cars.

CASEY JONES VILLAGE
56 Casey Jones Lane, Jackson, 731-668-1223; www.caseyjones.com
This complex of turn-of-the-century shops and buildings focuses on the life of one of America's most famous railroad heroes.
Daily 6:30 a.m.-9 p.m.

CYPRESS GROVE NATURE PARK
866 Highway 70 W., Jackson, 731-425-8316; www.jacksonrecandparks.com
A boardwalk winds through a 165-acre cypress forest. There's also an observation tower, a nature center and a picnic shelter.

PINSON MOUNDS STATE ARCHAEOLOGICAL AREA
460 Ozier Road, Pinson, 731-988-5614; www.state.tn.us
The area contains the remains of ancient mounds of the Middle Woodland Mound period and more than 10 ceremonial and burial mounds of various sizes, including Sauls, which towers at 72 feet tall. There's also a nature trail, picnicking and a museum.
Monday-Saturday 8 a.m.-4:30 p.m., Sunday 1-5 p.m.

MEMPHIS
BEALE STREET
203 Beale St., Memphis, 901-526-0110; www.bealestreet.com

This is part of a seven-block entertainment district stretching east from the Mississippi River bluffs with restaurants, shops, parks and theaters. There's a statue of W. C. Handy in Handy Park (Third and Beale streets).

THE CHILDREN'S MUSEUM OF MEMPHIS
2525 Central Ave., Memphis, 901-458-2678; www.cmom.com

This hands-on discovery museum has created an interactive "kid-sized city," including a bank, grocery store and skyscraper, among others. Other exhibits include "Art Smart," where kids sculpt, paint and draw; "Going Places," where children "fly" a real airplane and watch a hot-air balloon ride. Save time to explore other special workshops and exhibits.

Monday-Saturday 9 a.m.-5 p.m., Sunday noon-5 p.m.

CHUCALISSA ARCHAEOLOGICAL MUSEUM
1987 Indian Village Drive, Memphis, 901-785-3160; www.cas.memphis.edu

The archaeological project of the University of Memphis sits at the site of an Native American village founded about A.D. 900 and abandoned circa 1500. Native houses and temples have been reconstructed; archaeological exhibits are on display. The museum showcases artifacts and dioramas, and there's a 15-minute slide program.

Tuesday-Sunday.

CRYSTAL SHRINE GROTTO
5668 Poplar Ave., Memphis, 901-767-8930

This cave made of natural rock, quartz, crystal and semiprecious stones was carved out of a hillside by naturalistic artist Dionicio Rodriguez in the late 1930s. There are also scenes by the artist depicting the life of Jesus and biblical characters.

W. C. HANDY'S HOME
352 Beale St., Memphis, 901-522-1556

W. C. Handy wrote "Memphis Blues," "St. Louis Blues" and other classic tunes here. It also houses a collection of Handy memorabilia.

Tuesday-Saturday 11 a.m.-4 p.m.

DIXON GALLERY AND GARDENS
4339 Park Ave., Memphis, 901-761-5250; www.dixon.org

Hugo Norton Dixon and Margaret Oates Dixon, philanthropists and community leaders, left their home, grounds and a large portion of their estate to fund this museum and garden complex for the enjoyment and education of Memphis residents and visitors. The museum is surrounded by 17 acres of formal gardens with a camellia house and garden statuary. The exhibition galleries display American and French Impressionist and post-Impressionist art, British portraits and landscapes, and 18th-century German porcelain.

Tuesday-Friday 10 a.m.-4 p.m., Saturday 10 a.m.-5 p.m.

HIGHLIGHT

WHAT ARE THE BEST MUSEUMS IN MEMPHIS?

CASEY JONES HOME AND RAILROAD MUSEUM
This is the best stop for those interested in the legend of famed train engineer Casey Jones. The museum is full of all the bells and whistles, and features a steam locomotive driven by Jones and fully restored.

THE CHILDREN'S MUSEUM OF MEMPHIS
This is a wonderful stop for kids and those who want to act like them. There's plenty of hands-on exhibits and there's a cheery kid-sized city, but the best is "Art Smart," where adults can catch a break while the kids paint, draw and sculpt.

MEMPHIS BROOKS MUSEUM OF ART
This is Tennessee's largest art museum, with more than 7,000 pieces from across the globe. There are rare pieces by Georgia O'Keeffe and Auguste Rodin, and the museum's restaurant offers perhaps the best framed site in the building, with terrific views of Overton Park through its floor-to-ceiling windows.

NATIONAL CIVIL RIGHTS MUSEUM
The nation's first civil-rights museum is on the site of the old Lorraine Motel, where Dr. Martin Luther King Jr. was assassinated in 1968. It recognizes the darker side of the legacy of the South and the actions of those who made an indelible difference on the American landscape.

GRACELAND
3734 Elvis Presley Blvd., Memphis, 901-332-3322, 800-238-2000; www.elvis.com
No visit to Memphis is complete without a stop at Graceland to pay homage to the King of Rock 'n' Roll. The main attraction is the 60- to 90-minute tour of the home, where visitors swoon over the King's living room, dining room, music room, jungle room and kitchen, among other spaces. You'll also see the trophy room, where Elvis' gold records and awards are kept, and the Meditation Garden, where Elvis' own eternal flame blazes. Here, too, see Elvis' gravesite, likely covered in flowers and mementos from devoted fans. You can take separate tours of the Automobile Museum, which features Elvis' collection of Cadillacs—including the famous 1955 pink Caddy—and other cars and motorcycles; his custom jets, the Lisa Marie and the Hound Dog II; and Sincerely Elvis, a small museum of fan-related items. Don't miss the nearby gift

shops for an amazing assortment of Elvis-related kitsch.
March-October, Monday-Saturday 9 a.m.-5 p.m., Sunday 10 a.m.-4 p.m.; November-February, Monday, Wednesday-Sunday 10 a.m.-4 p.m.

LICHTERMAN NATURE CENTER
5992 Quince Road, Memphis, 901-767-7322; www.memphismuseums.org
The 65-acre wildlife sanctuary includes a 12-acre lake, greenhouse and hospital for wild animals. There are also three miles of hiking trails and places for picnicking.
Tuesday-Sunday.

MEEMAN-SHELBY FOREST STATE PARK
910 Riddick Road, Millington, 901-876-5215, 800-471-5293; www.state.tn.us
This 13,467-acre pristine state park features two lakes, a campground, fishing, boating and a swimming pool and is a beautiful setting for a leisurely hike or walk. Meeman-Shelby Forest State Park has more than 20 miles of hiking trails. However, since some of the trails are in the Mississippi River bottom, they are off limits during managed hunts.
Daily 7 a.m.-10 p.m.

MEMPHIS BOTANIC GARDEN
750 Cherry Road, Memphis, 901-576-4100; www.memphisbotanicgarden.com
The garden encompasses 96 acres; 20 formal gardens here include the Japanese Garden of Tranquility, the Rose Garden and the Wildflower Garden. A special Sensory Garden stimulates all five senses.
Days and times vary.

MEMPHIS BROOKS MUSEUM OF ART
1934 Poplar Ave., Memphis, 901-544-6200; www.brooksmuseum.org
The largest art museum in Tennessee has more than 7,000 pieces in its permanent collection, including drawings, paintings, sculpture, prints, photographs and decorative arts, such as glass and textiles. Its collections contain three centuries' worth of works from Africa, Asia, Europe and North and South America, with an emphasis on European and American art of the 18th through 20th centuries. Highlights include paintings by Andrew Wyeth, Winslow Homer and Georgia O'Keeffe; sculptures by Auguste Rodin; and prints by Thomas Hart Benton. The museum's Brushmark Restaurant, with terrific views of Overton Park through the floor-to-ceiling windows or on the outdoor terrace, serves lunch.
Tuesday-Friday 10 a.m.-4 p.m., Thursday 10 a.m.-8 p.m., Saturday 10 a.m.-5 p.m., Sunday 11:30 a.m.-5 p.m.

MEMPHIS PINK PALACE MUSEUM AND PLANETARIUM
3050 Central Ave., Memphis, 901-320-6320; www.memphismuseums.org
Exhibits at this recently expanded and remodeled museum focus on the natural and cultural history of the Mid-South. Visitors might enjoy the full-scale reproduction of an original Piggly Wiggly grocery store and a replica of an old-fashioned pharmacy with a soda fountain. The themes of the exhibits reflect the area's diversity: insects, birds, mammals, geology, pioneer life,

See the tailor shop, two houses and the burial place of the 17th president of the United States. Apprenticed to a tailor during his youth, Andrew Johnson came to Greeneville, Tenn., from his native Raleigh, N.C., in 1826. After years of service in local, state and federal governments, Senator Johnson remained loyal to the Union when Tennessee seceded. After serving as military governor of Tennessee, Johnson was elected vice president in 1864. On April 15, 1865, he became president following the assassination of Abraham Lincoln. Continued opposition to the radical program of Reconstruction led to his impeachment in 1868. Acquitted by the Senate, he continued to serve as president until 1869. In 1875, Johnson became the only former president to be elected to the U.S. Senate.

medical history and the Civil War. The museum also has a planetarium and an IMAX Theater.
Monday-Thursday 9 a.m.-4 p.m., Friday-Saturday 9 a.m.-9 p.m., Sunday noon-6 p.m.

MEMPHIS QUEEN LINE RIVERBOATS
45 Riverside Drive, Memphis, 901-527-5694; www.memphisqueen.com
Troll the river on one of the sightseeing or evening music cruises aboard a Mississippi riverboat.
Sightseeing: March-November, daily. Evening cruises: April-October, Friday-Saturday.

MEMPHIS ROCK 'N' SOUL MUSEUM
FedExForum, 191 Beale St., Memphis, 901-205-2533; www.memphisrocknsoul.org
Showcasing Memphis as the crossroads of blues, rock 'n' roll and country music, this museum features exhibits such as B. B. King's first "Lucille" guitar and Dick Clark's podium from *American Bandstand*.
Daily 10 a.m.-7 p.m.

MEMPHIS ZOO
2000 Galloway Ave., Memphis, 901-333-6500, 800-290-6041; www.memphiszoo.org
The Memphis Zoo houses more than 3,500 animals in naturalistic habitats. Two of the most popular animals at the zoo are Ya Ya and Le Le, the giant pandas from China—do not miss them. The zoo is large, but it's easy to get around, especially if you board the tram and cruise around the park. Take a break from viewing the animals to go for a ride on the carousel or get a bite to eat at the café.
March-October, daily 9 a.m.-6 p.m.; November-February, daily 9 a.m.-5 p.m.

MUD ISLAND RIVER PARK
125 N. Front St., Memphis, 901-576-7241, 800-507-6507; www.mudisland.com
This 52-acre island, accessible by monorail or pedestrian walkway, is a unique park designed to showcase the character of the river. The River Walk is a five-block-long scale model of the lower Mississippi River from Cairo, Ill., to the Gulf of Mexico (guided tours are available). The River Museum features 18 galleries that chronicle the development of river music, art, lore and history. Also here are films, a playground, riverboat excursions, shops, restaurants and a 5,400-seat amphitheater.

HIGHLIGHT

WHAT ARE THE BEST MUSIC DESTINATIONS IN MEMPHIS?

BEALE STREET
Memphis-style blues is unmistakable, and its raw energy can be felt on the street most nights of the year. Bring your harmonica or your sad story, because there's always room for more of the blues on Beale Street.

W. C. HANDY'S HOME
Dubbed the "Father of the Blues," Handy wrote the "Memphis Blues" and the "St. Louis Blues," along with other classics, in this house. See where a legend got his start.

GRACELAND
Old Elvis or Young Elvis, you'll find all the kitsch and wonder surrounding the late King of Rock 'n' Roll at Memphis' best-known attraction. When you need a breather from the gemstones and ostentatious inner quarters, visit the Meditation Garden, where Elvis' eternal flame beckons.

MEMPHIS ROCK 'N' SOUL MUSEUM
Featuring Dick Clark's podium from *American Bandstand* and B.B. King's "Lucille" guitar, the museum gives you a good taste of the history behind the Memphis mix of blues, rock 'n' roll and country music.

STAX MUSEUM OF AMERICAN SOUL MUSIC
The careers of Otis Redding, Isaac Hayes and other stars were launched at Stax. You can catch a glimpse of their style, including Hayes' gold-trimmed, peacock-blue "Superfly" Cadillac, among the 2,000 exhibits.

SUN STUDIO
This is perhaps the most famous little studio in the world. Here music legends such as Johnny Cash, B.B. King and Elvis Presley first recorded, and the studio itself is the place of many legendary stories from these stars' early days. You don't have be a legend to get a record deal here: after the tour, you can make your own recording.

SPECIAL EVENTS

BEALE STREET MUSIC FESTIVAL

Memphis; www.memphisinmay.org
One of the country's best blues events, the festival happens in what blues buffs consider the center of the universe. This three-day event hosts some of the biggest names in the blues industry. Past performances have included GooGoo Dolls, Hall & Oates, Earth, Wind & Fire, Limp Bizkit, and Colbie Caillat. Musicians from around the world come to Memphis for this musical family reunion, part of the "Memphis in May" festivities. *Early May.*

ELVIS PRESLEY INTERNATIONAL TRIBUTE WEEK

3734 Elvis Presley Blvd., Memphis, 901-332-3322, 800-238-2000; www.elvis.com
Thousands of people come to Memphis from all around the world for this event-packed week to celebrate and remember the King of Rock 'n' Roll. More than 30 events—including concerts, tours, vigils, street parties, fan forums and even an Elvis fashion show—take place during the week-long tribute to The King. *Mid-August.*

MEMPHIS IN MAY INTERNATIONAL FESTIVAL

88 Union Ave., Memphis, 901-525-4611; www.memphisinmay.org
The month-long community-wide celebration focuses on the cultural and artistic heritage of Memphis while featuring a different nation each year. Major events occur weekends, but activities are held daily. It includes the Beale Street Music Festival, World Championship Barbecue Cooking Contest and Sunset Symphony. As the honored nation changes, so do the cuisine and speakers and basically the whole event. Although the Beale Street Music Festival, BBQ Contest and Sunset Symphony don't rely solely on the cultural standpoint, they may feature an act or two specific to that culture. There are exhibits around Memphis that are worth visiting to learn a bit more about the country featured in the festival, as well as speakers, usually from the culture in the festival, to share more about life and various aspects of the nation. It offers something for everyone—arts, music, cuisine, education and more. *May.*

ZYDECO FESTIVAL

Beale Street, Memphis
Cajun-Creole and zydeco blues bands fill Beale Street clubs. Zydeco is heavily influenced by the Creole culture. It tends to be fast tempo and often dominated by the piano accordion and a form of the washboard. Zydeco keeps up with time by integrating hip-hop, ska, and reggae and even rock into its usual beats. This Cajun-themed festival could be pulled right out of the streets of New Orleans. Take Memphis, the blues capital, and add a little Cajun and Creole into the mix and you get Zydeco. *Late February.*

NATIONAL CIVIL RIGHTS MUSEUM

450 Mulberry St., Memphis, 901-521-9699; www.civilrightsmuseum.org

Opened in 1991, this is the nation's first civil-rights museum. It honors the American civil-rights movement and the people behind it, from colonial to present times. The museum is at the former Lorraine Motel, where Dr. Martin Luther King Jr. was assassinated in 1968. Exhibits include sound and light displays, audiovisual presentations and visitor participation programs. There is also an auditorium, a gift shop and a courtyard.

June-August, Monday, Wednesday-Saturday 9 a.m.-6 p.m., Sunday 1-6 p.m.; September-May, Monday, Wednesday-Saturday 9 a.m.-5 p.m., Sunday 1-5 p.m.

PYRAMID ARENA

1 Auction Ave., Memphis, 901-521-9675

This 32-story, 22,500-seat stainless-steel and concrete pyramid, which overlooks the Mississippi River, is fashioned after the ancient Egyptian Great Pyramid of Cheops. It's used as a multi-sports and entertainment arena. The NBA's Memphis Grizzlies left the Pyramid for the FedEx Forum in the 2006-2007 season. Tours are not available.

RACE-ON DRIVING EXPERIENCE

3638 Fite Road Millington, Memphis, 901-527-6174, 866-472-2366; www.4raceon.com

If you are jealous of watching the pros have all the fun, test your skills behind the wheel of a NASCAR vehicle around the ¾-mile paved tri-oval track at Memphis Motorsports Park (on non-race days, of course). The season runs from March to November, but times and dates vary, so call for a schedule.

STAX MUSEUM OF AMERICAN SOUL MUSIC

926 E. McLemore Ave., Memphis, 901-946-2535; www.soulsvilleusa.com

This museum is built on the original site of Stax Records, the Memphis-based record label that launched the careers of Otis Redding, Isaac Hayes, Sam and Dave and other stars of the 1960s and 1970s. Featured here are more than 2,000 exhibits, including Hayes' gold-trimmed, peacock-blue "Superfly" Cadillac.

March-October, Monday-Saturday 9 a.m.-4 p.m., Sunday 1-4 p.m.; November-February, Monday-Saturday 10 a.m.-4 p.m., Sunday 1-4 p.m.

SUN STUDIO

706 Union Ave., Memphis, 901-521-0664, 800-441-6249; www.sunstudio.com

Music legends such as Elvis Presley, Jerry Lee Lewis, Johnny Cash, B. B. King, Roy Orbison and Carl Perkins made their first recordings in this small studio. The 45-minute tour is worth the stop, and you can even make your own custom recording.

Daily 10 a.m.-6 p.m.

T. O. FULLER STATE PARK

1500 Mitchell Road, Memphis, 901-543-7581

This 384-acre park is where Spanish explorer Hernando De Soto is believed to have crossed the Mississippi. It has a swimming pool, a bathhouse, golf, picnicking and campsites.

Daily 8 a.m.-sunset.

VICTORIAN VILLAGE
600 Adams Ave., Memphis

These 18 landmark buildings, either preserved or restored, range in style from Gothic Revival to neo-classical.

Daily.

WHERE TO STAY

★★★HILTON MEMPHIS
939 Ridge Lake Blvd., Memphis, 901-684-6664, 800-445-8667; www.hilton.com

Towering 27 stories above the Memphis area, this hotel looks ultramodern on the outside but is bright and roomy on the inside. Though the rooms do have modern conveniences, such as flat-screen HD televisions and wireless Internet. The hotel is in the entertainment and the East Memphis business district, just minutes from downtown Memphis.

405 rooms. Restaurant, bar. Fitness center. Pool. $151-250

★★★MADISON HOTEL
79 Madison Ave., Memphis, 901-333-1200; www.madisonhotelmemphis.com

You can feel the jazzy spirit of Memphis at the Madison Hotel. The hotel's striking interiors use deep colors, geometric patterns and modern furnishings. The Madison is in the heart of the city's business and entertainment districts and is within walking distance to the famed Beale Street and Orpheum Theatre. Guest rooms are fitted with state-of-the-art technology for those traveling on business, while luxurious Italian bed linens, duvets and whirlpool baths appeal to all visitors. What also has mass appeal is the hotel's heated indoor pool and the rooftop garden that offers lovely views of the Mississippi River and downtown.

110 rooms. Complimentary breakfast. Restaurant, bar. Business center. Fitness center. Pool. $251-350

★★★MARRIOTT MEMPHIS EAST
2625 Thousand Oaks Blvd., Memphis, 901-362-6200, 800-627-3587; www.marriott.com

Although this isn't the Heartbreak Hotel, Elvis fans will like the Marriott Memphis East's proximity to Graceland. Shoppers will like that it's close to the Mall of Memphis. Kids will like the indoor and outdoor pools, as well as the video arcade games in the pool area. Rooms are spacious and include amenities like down comforters, duvets and fluffy pillows for a comfortable stay.

320 rooms. Restaurant, bar. Pool. $61-150

★★★MARRIOTT MEMPHIS DOWNTOWN
250 N. Main St., Memphis, 901-527-7300, 888-557-8740; www.memphismarriottdowntown.com

This hotel is the largest in town, so you know you'll get an excellent view from the spacious guest rooms. Its location is convenient for travelers, since it is 20 minutes from the Memphis International Airport and near shopping, museums, the world-famous Beale Street and Mud Island. It's only a mile and a half from the Children's Museum of Memphis, which makes it a good family pick. Business travelers will find it an ideal hotel because it's connected to the

Memphis-Cook Convention Center.
600 rooms. Restaurant, bar. Pool. $151-250

★★★★THE PEABODY MEMPHIS
149 Union Ave., Memphis, 901-529-4000, 800-732-2639;
www.peabodymemphis.com

The Peabody is a Memphis landmark. Perhaps best known for its signature ducks that march through the hotel twice daily to splash in the hotel's fountain, this grand hotel is also a shopping destination. It's the home of Lansky's, Elvis' favorite clothing store. Its location only blocks from Beale Street, the National Civil Rights Museum and more make it ideal for tourists. The hotel's impressive array of amenities includes a comprehensive health club, an indoor pool and Gould's Day Spa and Salon. The hotel's popular Capriccio Restaurant, Bar and Café serves delicious Italian dishes, while Chez Philippe adds a little twist to traditional French cuisine.
464 rooms. Restaurant, bar. Fitness center. Pool. Spa. $251-350

★★★SHERATON CASINO AND HOTEL
1107 Casino Center Drive, Robinsonville, 800-391-3777;
www.harrahs.com

Try your luck at blackjack, roulette, craps, Caribbean stud poker or slots at this hotel's 92,000-square-foot casino. The Tudor-style mansion houses 40 table games and 1,300 slot and video poker machines, an adjoining hotel, a restaurant, a spa and live entertainment seven days a week.
134 rooms. Restaurant, bar. Spa. $151-250

WHERE TO EAT

★★★★CHEZ PHILIPPE
The Peabody Memphis, 149 Union Ave., Memphis,
901-529-4000, 800-732-2639; www.peabodymemphis.com

For more than a decade, this sophisticated restaurant in the historic Peabody Memphis hotel has been a favorite of foodies, movie stars, celebrity chefs and well-heeled locals. Like clockwork, the crowds show up every evening, filling Chez Philippe's stunning dining room for the opportunity to feast on the culinary artwork on display. The service is efficient and unobtrusive, and the atmosphere is hushed, elegant and refined. Chef Reinaldo Alfonso applies simple, seasonal ingredients to the delicate dishes of French and Asian origin, which are occasionally

---

WHAT ARE TENNESSEE'S BEST OVERALL RESTAURANTS?

The Barn:
The visually stunning Barn restaurant at Blackberry Farm allows guests to sample regionally-inspired dishes using the freshest ingredients.

Capitol Grille:
Located in the elegant Hermitage Hotel, executive chef Tyler Brown oversees the creative Southern cuisine at this classic restaurant.

Chez Philippe:
This sophisticated restaurant in the historic Peabody Memphis hotel features a stunning dining room, lovely service, and wonderful cuisine using simple, seasonal ingredients.

accented with regional flair, like the lamb ragout with white corn polenta, broccoli rabe and tomato jus. Leave room for dessert: Chez Philippe is known for its soufflés.

French. Dinner. Closed Sunday-Monday. $36-85

★★★ERLING JENSEN
1044 S. Yates Road, Memphis, 901-763-3700; www.ejensen.com

This cutting-edge restaurant is one of the most popular in Memphis. Savor the seared ahi tuna over roasted corn and edamame risotto with teriyaki sauce, the black Angus filet with red wine demi glace and foie gras butter, or the rich creamy bisques and foie gras preparations.

International. Dinner. $36-85

★★★GRILL 83
83 Madison Ave., Memphis, 901-333-1224; www.grill83.com

Uniquely decorated, this chic restaurant is a good choice for a romantic evening or a special occasion. All the mouth-watering steak selections are accompanied with cabernet reduction, maitre d' butter and tobacco onions. Enticing non-steak options, such as pan-seared salmon and pan-roasted breast of Ashley Farms chicken, are also offered. Conveniently located in the heart of downtown Memphis, Grill 83 is close to historic Beale Street, entertainment and the Mississippi River, in case you need other options to cap off your date night.

Steak. Breakfast, lunch, dinner. $36-85

★★★RINALDO GRISANTI AND SONS
2855 Poplar Ave., Memphis, 901-323-0007

Everything is freshly prepared at this restaurant, which is tucked in a small strip mall east of downtown. Specialties of the northern Italian menu include gorgonzola-stuffed filets, fresh sea bass and buttered pasta la elfo with shrimp, garlic, white pepper and mushrooms.

Italian. Dinner. Closed Sunday. $36-85

NASHVILLE

Best known as Music City for its deep and long roots as a hub of country music, Nashville has evolved into a multi-faceted Southern city that retains the charm and friendliness of the small-town South. Sweet tea, iced of course, and smiles are aplenty here. You'll find Nashville residents eager to help with directions or provide other tips for enjoying their city.

Nashville is Tennessee's capital and the second-largest city by population, though its metropolitan area claims the state's top metro-area population with more than 1 million residents. The city began as a settlement called Fort Nashborough, established between 1779 and 1780 on the banks of the Cumberland River, which borders the present-day downtown area. Within 10 years the name was changed to Nashville.

Because of its diverse business climate, Nashville has weathered the country's recession well. In addition to music production, major industries include heathcare management, printing and publishing, finance, insurance, automobile production and tourism. Nashville is also home to numerous colleges and universities, including Vanderbilt University and Fisk University, prompting another of the city's old nicknames: Athens of the South. You'll even find the world's only full-scale replica of the Parthenon and its 42-foot statue of Athena in Centennial Park, Nashville's premier urban park.

Nashville is within 600 miles, or a day's drive, of 50 percent of the U.S. population, making the city easily accessible by air or road. Weather in Nashville is typically mild and pleasant according to the season, resulting in only rare snowfall in winter and allowing for outdoor activities to be enjoyed through much of the year.

Top attractions in the city's diverse music scene include the historic Ryman Auditorium, the Grand Ole Opry, Country Music Hall of Fame and Museum, Bluebird Café, Music Row and the Schermerhorn Symphony Center. With a city full of established and up-and-coming songwriters and musicians, excellent live music venues abound.

For history buffs, Nashville and the surrounding area offer numerous sites important in the Civil War. Visitors can check out The Hermitage, home of Andrew Jackson, the Tennessee State Museum; Belle Meade Plantation; Travellers Rest Plantation and Museum; and Downtown Presbyterian Church.

Sports fans will have plenty to cheer about when they visit Nashville, which is home to the NFL's Tennessee Titans and the NHL's Nashville Predators, as well as the Nashville Sounds, the Triple-A affiliate of MLB's Milwaukee Brewers.

Nashville also has a growing arts culture, from established venues such as the Frist Center for the Visual Arts to Cheekwood Botanical Gardens and Museum of Art, to an increasing number of small galleries. The city's restaurant scene is also increasingly diverse, ranging from traditional meat-and-threes to upscale dining options and ethnic restaurants.

Step foot in Music City and you'll sense the vibrancy created by the energetic rhythms of growth and change grounded by the strong notes of a city with a rich history.

WHAT TO SEE

ADVENTURE SCIENCE MUSEUM
800 Fort Negley Blvd., Nashville, 615-862-5160; www.adventuresci.com

Kids will love this hands-on science museum. There are six main areas to explore here: Earth Science, Creativity and Invention, Sound and Light, Air and Space, Health and Energy. You can find all of these concepts represented on the Adventure Tower, a 75-foot-tall structure with seven levels of activities. In it, you can lift a car, crawl through a beating heart and scale a giant glass pyramid. The interactive "Mission: Possible" exhibit allows children to experience the everyday obstacles for people with physical disabilities.

Admission: adults $12, seniors and children 3-12 $9, children under 3 free. Monday-Saturday 10 a.m.-5 p.m., Sunday 12:30-5:30 p.m.

BELLE MEADE PLANTATION
5025 Harding Road, Nashville, 615-356-0501, 800-270-3991; www.bellemeadeplantation.com

The antebellum mansion and outbuildings were once part of a 5,300-acre working plantation. At the turn of the 20th century, John Harding's Belle

HIGHLIGHT

WHAT ARE THE TOP THINGS TO DO IN NASHVILLE?

LEARN WEIRD SCIENCE AT THE ADVENTURE SCIENCE MUSEUM

Kids can lift a car and climb a giant glass pyramid all in the name of scientific investigation at this hands-on museum. There's also a planetarium on the premises in case you want to do some star-gazing.

EXPLORE THE BELLE MEADE PLANTATION

This former working plantation was considered the country's preeminent thoroughbred-breeding farm. But its winning trait is the authentic 14-room antebellum mansion filled with Victorian and Empire furnishings.

WALK THE GROUNDS OF THE CHEEKWOOD BOTANICAL GARDEN AND MUSEUM OF ART

Those with an eye for art and a green thumb will love this combination art museum and garden. There is a permanent exhibit of 19th- and 20th-century American art and numerous gardens filled with roses and tulips.

VISIT THE HERMITAGE, THE HOME OF A FORMER PRESIDENT

Step into Andrew Jackson's former abode, a Greek Revival mansion, to see family mementos and artifacts from his time in the military and the White House. Tours of the 660-acre estate are available.

SEE THE PARTHENON

If you can't make it to Athens to see the real deal, Nashville offers a full-scale replica in Centennial Park. Just like the Greek Parthenon, this copycat has a 42-foot-tall statute of Athena, the goddess of wisdom, inside.

Meade was considered the greatest thoroughbred-breeding farm in the country. Get a glimpse of the elegance of late-19th-century Southern aristocrats in this 14-room Greek Revival mansion, which contains Empire and Victorian furnishings and an heirloom showcase with racing trophies and mementos. Also on the grounds are the Dunham Station log cabin and Carriage House, containing one of the South's largest carriage collections.

Admission: adults $16, seniors $14, students $10, children 6-12 $8, children under 6 free. Monday-Saturday 9 a.m.-5 p.m., Sunday 11 a.m.-5 p.m.

BELMONT MANSION

1900 Belmont Blvd., Nashville, 615-460-5459; www.belmontmansion.com

Built in the 1850s in the style of an Italian villa, this mansion was once considered one of the finest private residences in the U.S. It has original marble statues, Venetian glass, gasoliers, mirrors and paintings in the 15 rooms; gardens feature a large collection of 19th-century ornaments and cast-iron gazebos. Monthly garden tours are also available.

Monday-Saturday 10 a.m.-4 p.m., Sunday 1-4 p.m.

CHEEKWOOD BOTANICAL GARDEN AND MUSEUM OF ART

1200 Forrest Park Drive, Nashville, 615-356-8000; www.cheekwood.org

This one is for art lovers and garden fanatics. Cheekwood, once the private home and estate of the Cheek family, is now a cultural center set on 55 acres. The site, which opened to the public in 1960, includes a museum with a permanent collection of 19th- and 20th-century American art; a Botanic Hall with an atrium of tropical flora and changing plant exhibits; public greenhouses; and five major gardens specializing in dogwoods, wildflowers, herbs, daffodils, roses and tulips.

Admission: adults $10, seniors $8, students and children 6-17 $5, children under 6 free. Tuesday-Saturday 9:30 a.m.-4:30 p.m., Sunday 11 a.m.-4:30 p.m.

COUNTRY MUSIC HALL OF FAME AND MUSEUM

222 Fifth Ave. S. Nashville, 615-416-2001, 800-852-6437; www.countrymusichalloffame.com

A tribute to all things country music, this museum will give fans goose bumps, and even folks who aren't interested in the tunes will appreciate the history and American pop culture on display. Elvis's gold-leafed Cadillac is parked here, and visitors can gawk at a lyric sheet scribbled with Bob Dylan's signature. This $37 million complex includes displays with costumes and instruments donated by country music legends from Minnie Pearl to George Jones. You can also check out the restored Historic RCA Studio B, where more than 1,000 top 10 hits from Elvis Presley, Willie Nelson and other stars were recorded.

Admission: adults $19.99, children 6-17 $11.95, children under 6 free. Daily 9 a.m.-5 p.m.

ELLINGTON AGRICULTURAL CENTER

440 Hogan Road, Nashville, 615-837-5197; www.state.tn.us

This former horse barn sits on a historic estate. It's the oldest Agricultural Hall of Fame in the country. In it, you'll find farm tools, equipment and household items of the 19th century.

Monday-Friday.

ERNEST TUBB RECORD SHOP
417 Broadway, Nashville, 615-255-7503; www.etrecordshop.com

When Ernest Tubb wasn't out touring in a big silver bus with the Texas Troubadours, the country music star was tending to his other love, the Ernest Tubb Record Shop. Tubb died in 1984, but the store continues to sell nothing but country music releases. Offerings range from hard-to-find treasures to the newest smash hits. The store on **Music Valley Drive** *(2416 Music Valley Drive, 615-889-2474)* also features the Texas Troubadour Theatre, home of the Midnight Jamboree, every Saturday.

FORT NASHBOROUGH
170 First Ave. N., Nashville, 615-862-8400; www.nashville.gov

Patterned after the pioneer fort established several blocks from this site in 1779, the replica is smaller and has fewer cabins. There are stockaded walls and exhibits of pioneer implements.

Tuesday-Sunday.

GENERAL JACKSON SHOWBOAT
Opry Mills, Opry Mills Drive, Nashville, 615-458-3900; www.generaljackson.com

Named after the first steamboat working the Cumberland River as far back as 1817, this 300-foot paddlewheel riverboat—the world's largest showboat these days—offers lunch cruises featuring a buffet plus a country music show and elegant dinner cruises with a Broadway-style show.

GRAND OLE OPRY
2802 Opryland Drive, Nashville, 615-871-5043; www.opry.com

You haven't made it in Music City, USA, as a country star until you've graced the stage of the world's longest-running radio show. Every weekend, the Opry showcases the best of bluegrass, country, gospel, swing and Cajun. Part of the thrill for the audience is never knowing which stars will make surprise appearances.

Friday 7:30 p.m., Saturday 6:30 p.m. and 9:30 p.m.; also Tuesday in summer, 7 p.m.

GRAND OLE OPRY TOURS
2800 Opryland Drive, Nashville, 615-883-2211; www.gaylordhotels.com

One-hour, three-hour and all-day bus tours take visitors to houses of country music stars, Music Row, recording studios and on a backstage visit to the Grand Ole Opry House.

THE HERMITAGE
4580 Rachel's Lane, Nashville, 615-889-2941; www.thehermitage.com

Rebuilt after a fire in 1834, this Greek Revival residence of President Andrew Jackson is furnished almost entirely with original family pieces, many of which were associated with Jackson's military career and years in the White House. The mansion has been restored to its appearance from 1837 to 1845, Jackson's retirement years. Tours of the 660-acre estate are narrated by interpreters dressed in historical garb. The tour includes a museum; the Tulip Grove Mansion; the Hermitage Church; a garden with graves of Jackson and his wife, Rachel; two log cabins; a visitor center; and a biographical film on Jackson.

April-October, daily 8:30 a.m.-5 p.m.; November-March, daily 9 a.m.-4:30 p.m.

HIGHLIGHT

WHAT ARE THE TOP COUNTRY MUSIC ATTRACTIONS?

COUNTRY MUSIC HALL OF FAME AND MUSEUM

This country-music mecca showcases things such as Elvis's gold-leafed Cadillac and a lyric sheet signed by Bob Dylan. Be sure to pop into RCA Studio B, where greats like the King and Willie Nelson recorded music.

ERNEST TUBB RECORD SHOP

You'll only find country music at this shop, which was started by country star Ernest Tubb. E.T. is no longer around, but you can still scour the store for unusual finds or the hottest Nashville hit.

GRAND OLE OPRY

Any country singer who is worth his or her cowboy boots belts it out on stage at the Grand Ole Opry, the world's longest-running radio show. Expect surprise appearances by big-name stars.

RYMAN AUDITORIUM & MUSEUM

Everyone from Patsy Cline to Heart has performed at the historic Ryman. Check to see who'll take the stage at the "Mother Church of Country Music" when you're in town and stop by the museum to learn the venue's history.

WILDHORSE SALOON

If you love country music, you can't leave Nashville without doing some line dancing. Head to the Wildhorse Saloon to dance along to live music. Free line-dancing lessons are available to newbies.

NASHVILLE ZOO

3777 Nolensville Road, Nashville, 615-833-1534; www.nashvillezoo.org

At the Nashville Zoo, designers have gone to great lengths to make it seem as if you're simply walking through the woods and stumbling upon otters, cheetahs, apes, macaws and other animals. Make a stop at the African elephant savannah exhibit.

April-October, daily 9 a.m.-6 p.m.; November-March, daily 9 a.m.-4 p.m.

OLD HICKORY LAKE

Nashville, 615-822-4846; www.lrn.usace.army.mil

This 22,000-acre lake has 440 miles of shoreline, eight marinas and an abundance of water fowl and wading birds—a perfect place to spend a lazy day on the water. The lake also sees pleasure boats, sailboats, personal watercraft, fishing boats and commercial barges.

Daily.

THE PARTHENON

2600 W. End Ave., Nashville, 615-862-8431; www.nashville.gov/parthenon

The replica of the Parthenon of Pericles' time was built in plaster for the Tennessee Centennial of 1897 and later reconstructed in concrete aggregate. As in the original, there is not a straight horizontal or vertical line, and no two columns are placed the same distance apart. A 42-foot-tall statue of the goddess Athena stands inside; she is the tallest indoor statue in the country. It also houses 19th- and 20th-century artworks, changing art exhibits and replicas of Elgin Marbles.

October-March, Tuesday-Saturday 9 a.m.-4:30 p.m.; April-September, Tuesday-Saturday 9 a.m.-4:30 p.m., Sunday 12:30-4:30 p.m.

RYMAN AUDITORIUM & MUSEUM

116 Fifth Ave. N., Nashville, 615-458-8700; www.ryman.com

The Mother Church of Country Music is a National Historic Landmark. It hosts concerts and a museum that tells its story. Don't leave without buying a box of GooGoos in the museum gift shop. A tour of the auditorium is available.

Daily 9 a.m.-4 p.m.; evening show times vary.

SAM DAVIS HOME

1399 Sam Davis Road, Nashville, 615-459-2341; www.samdavishome.org

Described as "the most beautiful shrine to a private soldier in the U.S.," this stately house and 168-acre working farm have been preserved as a memorial to Sam Davis, a Confederate scout caught behind Union lines and tried as a spy. Offered his life if he revealed the name of his informer, Davis chose to die on the gallows. His boyhood home is restored and furnished with many original pieces; the grounds include a kitchen, a smokehouse, slave cabins and a family cemetery where Davis is buried.

June-August, Monday-Saturday 9 a.m.-5 p.m., Sunday 1-5 p.m.; September-May, Monday-Saturday 10 a.m.-4 p.m., Sunday 1-4 p.m.

STATE CAPITOL

600 Charlotte Ave., Nashville, 615-741-2692; www.state.tn.us

The capitol building is a distinguished reminder that Nashville is not just the capital of the country music world. Construction of the capitol began in 1845 and lasted until 1859, and it is built of local Tennessee limestone and marble quarried and cut by slaves and convicts. The architect, William Strickland, died before the building was completed, and his body was entombed within the building's northeast wall. The Greek Revival structure has an 80-foot tower that rises above the city, and columns grace the ends and sides. The building houses the governor's offices and the chambers of the state Senate and the

House of Representatives. During Union occupation of Nashville from 1862 to 1865, the capitol was used as Fortress Andrew Johnson.
Monday-Friday.

TENNESSEE STATE MUSEUM
Polk Cultural Center, 505 Deaderick St., Nashville, 615-741-2692, 800-407-4324; www.tnmuseum.org

This museum is one of the largest in the nation, with 60,000 square feet of exhibition space. It houses an awesome Civil War collection. The permanent exhibits illustrating life in Tennessee focus on the prehistoric, Frontier, Age of Jackson, Antebellum, Civil War and Reconstruction periods. Artifacts on display include Andrew Jackson's 1829 inaugural hat, an 1850s-style parlor, a steatite shaman's medicine tube and a hand-drawn map of the Shiloh battlefield prepared for Confederate General Beauregard. After visiting the main museum, walk across the street to check out the Military Museum in the War Memorial Building.
Tuesday-Saturday 10 a.m.-5 p.m., Sunday 1-5 p.m.

TENNESSEE TITANS (NFL)
LP Field, 1 Titans Way, Nashville, 615-565-4200; www.titansonline.com

Tennesseans have enthusiastically embraced their NFL team, the Titans (formerly the Houston Oilers). The 68,000-seat LP Field, an outdoor stadium set on the Cumberland River with a great view of downtown Nashville, regularly fills with rabid fans. If you stay downtown, the stadium is just a short walk across the river. Tickets can be tough to come by, so make sure to call well in advance.

TRAVELLERS REST PLANTATION AND MUSEUM
636 Farrell Parkway, Nashville, 615-832-8197; www.travellersrestplantation.org

This restored federal-style house belonged to Judge John Overton. Maintained as a historical museum with period furniture, records and letters, the building reflects the history and development of early Tennessee. The 11-acre grounds have formal gardens, a weaving house and a smokehouse.
Monday-Saturday 10 a.m.-4 p.m., Sunday 1-4 p.m.

THE UPPER ROOM CHAPEL AND MUSEUM
1908 Grand Ave., Nashville, 615-340-7200; www.upperroom.org

The chapel has a polychrome wood carving of Leonardo da Vinci's *The Last Supper*, said to be the largest of its kind in the world. The museum contains various religious artifacts, including seasonal displays of 100 Nativity scenes and Ukrainian Easter eggs.
Monday-Friday.

WILDHORSE SALOON
120 Second Ave. N., Nashville, 615-902-8200; www.wildhorsesaloon.com

Welcome to boot-scootin' paradise. The Wildhorse Saloon is the place to go line dancing in Nashville, and even if you have two left feet, you should go for the live music and celebrity sightings. Set in a three-level historic warehouse on Nashville's Music Row, the club features live country acts Tuesday through

HIGHLIGHT

WHAT IS THERE TO DO ON BEALE STREET?

Ever since W. C. Handy set up shop in the early 1900s, Beale Street has been known around the world as the home of the blues and the inspiration for rock 'n' roll. Blues legends such as B. B. King, Furry Lewis and Rufus Thomas got their starts here, and the street still attracts budding musicians to its nightclubs. Beale Street was a thriving commercial center for Memphis's African-American community for much of the 20th century and today, it is the city's prime entertainment district. Some say the strip lost its character in the transition from a gritty no-man's-land, but the folks dancing on the sidewalks to street musicians' tunes don't seem to mind a bit.

From the top of the hill at Second Street you can look down on all the action. Here you'll find B. B. King's club and Elvis Presley's, both upscale supper clubs with big name entertainment—sometimes even the King of the Blues himself. Stay on the lookout for the ghost of Elvis.

At Third Street and Beale, a statue of W. C. Handy stands in front of an amphitheater that is the venue for many local music festivals, concerts and other events. Down the street, the Orpheum Theatre hosts Broadway shows, and the New Daisy Theatre welcomes up-and-comers, and occasionally, artists who are their way back down

Saturday nights. A DJ supplements the acts, and the saloon offers free dance lessons for folks who aren't too shy to shake their hips with the experts. If all that dancing makes you hungry, the restaurant serves tasty Southern barbecue from 11 a.m. to midnight. Children younger than 18 are allowed entry with parents. *Restaurant: daily 11 a.m.-midnight; nightclub: until 2 a.m.*

WHERE TO STAY

★★★GAYLORD OPRYLAND RESORT AND CONVENTION CENTER

2800 Opryland Drive, Nashville, 615-889-1000, 888-777-6779; www.gaylordhotels.com

This impressive resort has a little bit of everything. The more than 20 restaurants and shops offer something to please everyone's taste, from the Southern grandeur of Old Hickory Steakhouse to the trendy Vegas-style fun of Fuse Nightclub. You can enjoy the outdoors year-round in the resort's lush gardens: The Garden Conservatory boasts 10,000 tropical plants, including towering palms and banana trees. The tropical Cascades Atrium features a 3½-story waterfall and abundant flowering trees and plants. The Delta River, the largest indoor river in the world, runs through the nearly 7 acres of gardens in the Delta Atrium. Guests touring the river on a Delta Flatboat might spot Donnie, the largest of the catfish that live in the river. The Delta Atrium also features an 85-foot fountain show every half hour at night. Country-music fans will be more interested in the hotel's location; the Grand Ole Opry is adjacent to the resort. Other nearby attractions include the award-winning, Scottish links-style golf course, Gaylord Springs Golf

Links, and outlet shopping at Opry Mills.

2,881 rooms. Restaurant, bar. Fitness center. Pool. Spa. Golf. $251-350

★★★★★THE HERMITAGE HOTEL

231 Sixth Ave. N., Nashville, 615-244-3121, 888-888-9414; www.thehermitagehotel.com

Channeling a more decadent age, the Hermitage is the grande dame of Nashville's hotels. Opened in 1910, this glorious downtown hotel offers white-glove service and plenty of opportunities to indulge. Your eyes can't help traveling upward when you step into the magnificent lobby and marvel at its vaulted stained-glass ceilings, arches decorated with frescoes and intricate stonework. The spacious guest rooms are filled with elegant traditional furnishings, creating a warm and welcoming atmosphere. Listed on the National Register of Historic Places, the hotel, which has hosted presidents and celebrities aplenty, was extensively renovated in 2003. On the lower level, you will find the Capitol Grille, domain of southern chef Tyler Brown, and one of Nashville's best restaurants. The adjacent Oak Bar, with its emerald-green club chairs and dark wood paneling, is a top spot for relaxing before or after dinner—be sure to try the signature bacon caramel popcorn, which may just be the best snack anywhere.

122 rooms. Restaurant, bar. Business center. Fitness center. Spa. Pets accepted. $251-350

★★★HOTEL PRESTON

733 Briley Parkway, Nashville, 615-361-5900, 877-361-5500; www.hotelpreston.com

Hotel Preston, Nashville's first boutique hotel, is near Nashville International Airport and within easy reach of the city's other attractions. The owner's affinity for art is readily apparent throughout the hotel, which is decorated in a distinctive Art Deco style. Amenities in the spacious rooms include a pillow menu (just pick your preferred pillow firmness), a spiritual menu (pick the religious book of your choice), bathrobes, Aveda bath products and flat-screen televisions. If you weren't able to bring your pet along, you can borrow a fish to keep you company during your stay. Rubber duckies and lava lamps are also available upon request. The trendy Pink Slip lounge features live bands Wednesday through Saturday evenings, and Café Isabella's menu is filled with Italian favorites and Southern-flecked fare.

190 rooms. Restaurant, bar. Business center. Fitness center. Pool. Pets accepted. $251-350

★★★HUTTON HOTEL

1808 W. End Ave., Nashville, 615-340-9333; www.huttonhotel.com

One of the most recent additions to Nashville's hotel scene, Hutton Hotel welcomes guests into a warm, inviting living room-style lobby featuring art by local college students. Green features are sported throughout the elegant hotel, from bamboo flooring and furniture in the hotel's rooms, to key-card–operated lighting. Attention to detail abounds with electric outlets at desk height, doorbells that make for a homier atmosphere and bathroom speakers so you can hear the morning's news while you're getting ready. Beautifully appointed spa rooms and a fitness center help you relax and stay in shape while away from home. The Java Bar and 1808 Grille restaurant provide what you need to keep you going during the day. Hutton Hotel's great West End location means you're close to everything.

247 rooms. Restaurant, bar. Business center. Fitness center. $151-250

Blackberry Farm:
On a 4,200-acre estate
in the foothills of
Tennessee's Great Smoky
Mountains, Blackberry is
one of the South's most
celebrated country inns
and a destination
onto itself.

The Hermitage Hotel:
The Hermitage is
the grande dame of
Nashville's hotels. The
glorious hotel offers
white-glove service and
plenty of opportunities
to indulge.

★★★LOEWS VANDERBILT HOTEL NASHVILLE
2100 W. End Ave., Nashville, 615-320-1700, 800-336-3335;
www.loewshotels.com

At Loews Vanderbilt Hotel there's no chance you'll
forget you're in Music City. From the jukebox playing
famous tunes in the lobby to the recorded wake-up calls
from your favorite Music City artists, you'll quickly
jump into Nashville's distinctive rhythm. This upscale
property, located between Vanderbilt University and
downtown, is close to everything. When you arrive
you'll be greeted by friendly valets and by an urban
exterior that's softened with attractive landscaping
and a soothing fountain. When you enjoy the hotel's
luxurious amenities, you'll feel just as pampered as
any of the hotel's celebrity guests. Comfortable guest
rooms, which offer views of either the campus or city,
feature quality bedding, mini-bars, plush robes and
Bloom toiletries. The works of Nashville artist Harold
Kraus, a renowned colorist, are featured onsite at the
Kraus Gallery.

*340 rooms. Restaurant, bar. Business center. Fitness center. Spa.
$151-250*

★★★RENAISSANCE NASHVILLE HOTEL
611 Commerce St., Nashville, 615-255-8400, 800-327-6618;
www.renaissancehotels.com/bnash

Business travelers will appreciate the Renaissance
Hotel's location; it's smack-dab in the business district
and the city's tourist area, and it's connected to the
Convention Center. The hotel offers great dining
options, but it's also within walking distance to all of
downtown Nashville's fine dining, shopping and favorite
attractions. Enjoy an evening stroll on the nearby Shelby
Street pedestrian bridge, which provides game-day
access across the Cumberland River to the Tennessee
Titans' LP Field. Ask for a room on one of the hotel's
upper floors and enjoy stunning views of the city.

*673 rooms. Restaurant, bar. Business center. Fitness center. Pool.
$151-250*

★★★SHERATON MUSIC CITY
777 McGavock Pike, Nashville, 615-885-2200, 866-716-8106;
www.sheratonmusiccity.com

A great option for those who prefer to stay near
the airport or away from the hubbub of downtown
Nashville, the Sheraton Music City is only three miles
from Nashville International Airport. It's also convenient to attractions on the east side of the Cumberland
River that runs through Nashville, Opry Mills outlet

mall and the renowned and historic Grand Ole Opry. Channeling a Deep South mansion, the hotel is appropriately welcoming and comfortable. Its oversized rooms feature either a balcony or patio, flat-screen televisions and Bliss toiletries. This is the hotel for you if you are an avid swimmer; the indoor heated pool is perfect for a dip when the weather's too cold to enjoy the hotel's outdoor pools.

410 rooms. Restaurant, bar. Business center. Fitness center. Pool. Spa. Pets accepted. $151-250

★★★SHERATON NASHVILLE DOWNTOWN HOTEL

623 Union St., Nashville, 615-259-2000, 800-447-9825; www.sheraton-nashville.com

This contemporary hotel is in the heart of downtown Nashville near the capitol building, a location that makes it popular with business travelers and legislators. Guests are offered a host of amenities and services, including room service, turndown service, plush robes and Sheraton's signature beds. Renovations were completed in 2010, providing a fresh, new finish throughout the hotel, from the lobby to the fitness center to the guest rooms.

474 rooms. Restaurant, bar. Complimentary breakfast. Business center. Fitness center. $151-250

★★★WYNDHAM UNION STATION HOTEL

1001 Broadway, Nashville, 615-726-1001; www.unionstationhotelnashville.com

Housed in a historic 1897 train station, the Wyndham Union Station is a National Historic Landmark. The lobby has marble floors, a vaulted ceiling of Tiffany-style stained glass and ornate carved woodwork. No two rooms are alike, but all have marble bathrooms with deep tubs or walk-in showers. With its downtown location only a few blocks from Second Avenue and Music Row, the Wyndham is close to much of the entertainment, dining and nightlife that Nashville has to offer, with complimentary shuttle service to nearby attractions.

137 rooms. Restaurant, bar. Business center. Fitness center. $151-250

RECOMMENDED

HOTEL INDIGO

1719 W. End Ave., Nashville, 615-329-4200, 877-270-1389; www.hotelindigo.com

Ensconced among Nashville's small but growing number of boutique hotel options, Hotel Indigo will appeal to those who like urban living. From its distinctive blue-indigo tower outside to the sleek stylings inside, Hotel Indigo manages to mix city and country in appropriate measures. For the country component, head to the hotel restaurant's lobby. On Tuesday through Friday evenings, you can enjoy some of Nashville's famous music live. Conveniently located on West End Avenue, which turns into Broadway, the hotel is a straight shot to all of downtown Nashville's attractions.

139 rooms. Restaurant, bar. Business center. Fitness center. Pets accepted. $150-250

WHERE TO EAT

★★★★CAPITOL GRILLE

231 Sixth Ave. N., Nashville, 615-345-7116; www.capitolgrillenashville.com

Located in the elegant Hermitage Hotel, the Capitol Grille offers an equally posh dining experience. Near the state capitol, the Grille hosts many a power lunch, but it's also a popular spot for theatergoers who want to enjoy a fine meal before a show at the nearby Tennessee Performing Arts Center. Executive chef Tyler Brown oversees the creative Southern cuisine; the menu is full of dishes like grilled pork chop with spring vegetables and smoked ham croquette, as well as pan-roasted flounder with fried Gulf oysters, crawfish étouffée broth and corn pudding. Truffle mac and cheese and spicy fried green tomato with spicy pepper relish are just a few of the restaurant's irresistible side dishes, and desserts such as chocolate Carolina Gold rice pudding with caramelized bananas end the evening on a perfect note.

American, Southern. Breakfast, lunch, dinner, late-night, Sunday brunch. $36-85

★★★F. SCOTT'S

2210 Crestmoor Road, Nashville, 615-269-5861; www.fscotts.com

This large restaurant gives off a friendly, elegant vibe, thanks to several small dining rooms. Popular jazz musicians play nightly, and chef Will Uhlhorn's frequently changing menu features French-influenced contemporary American dishes, such as duck breast with foie gras-bigarade sauce, roasted Emerald Glen chicken, and seared scallops with maple roasted local pumpkin.

American. Dinner. Closed Sunday. Bar. $36-85

★★★THE OLD HICKORY STEAKHOUSE

Gaylord Opryland Resort and Convention Center, 2800 Opryland Drive, Nashville, 615-871-6848; www.gaylordopryland.com

Located inside the Gaylord Opryland Resort, this special-occasion steakhouse offers refined dining in an atmosphere of dark wooden furniture and dimly lit rooms. Designed as a plantation-style house, the restaurant offers wraparound porch seating. Elegant table settings and beautiful indoor gardens complete the setting. The restaurant also offers occasional wine tastings. Watch out for the artisanal cheese cart with 25 varieties of cheeses and a large wine selection.

Steak. Dinner. $86 and up.

★★★THE PALM

140 Fifth Ave. S., Nashville, 615-742-7256; www.thepalm.com

A great spot for star-gazing—not the celestial kind—and beef-eating, The Palm is one of Nashville's most popular scenes. Serious-sized steaks, chops and seafood dishes grace the menu at this legendary steakhouse. Also found among the meaty menu selections are Italian-tinged dishes such as linguine and clams, penne with asparagus and sun-dried tomatoes, and a tomato capri salad. Going strong since 1926, The Palm has expanded its empire to 25 cities across the country, including Philadelphia, Las Vegas and Dallas.

Steak. Lunch, dinner. $36-85

★★★RUTH'S CHRIS STEAK HOUSE

2100 W. End Ave., Nashville, 615-320-0163; www.ruthschris.com

Born from a single New Orleans restaurant that Ruth Fertel bought in 1965 for $22,000, the Ruth's Chris Steak House chain has made it to the top of every steak lover's list. Aged prime Midwestern beef is broiled to your liking and served on a heated plate, sizzling in butter, a staple ingredient used generously in most entrées. Sides such as creamed spinach and fresh asparagus with hollandaise are not to be missed, and seven different potato preparations, including a one-pound baked potato and au gratin potatoes with cream sauce and cheese, are offered. The rich, dark wood walls and dim lighting give the dining room a cozy feel, making it perfect for special dinners.

Steak. Dinner. $36-85

★★★VALENTINO'S

1907 W. End Ave., Nashville, 615-327-0148; www.valentinosnashville.com

A popular spot for romantic dinners, Valentino's is set in a charming old house with several dining areas decked out in beautiful Old World décor. The menu features rustic Italian fare such as mushroom ravioli with truffles, farfalle with salmon and chicken Marsala.

Italian. Lunch, dinner. Closed Sunday. $36-85

RECOMMENDED

PARK CAFÉ

4403 Murphy Road, Nashville, 615-383-4409; www.parkcafenashville.com

Though it's not on one of Nashville's primary thoroughfares, Park Café is still easy to find in the city's Sylvan Park neighborhood and just as easy to love. The restaurant, created by owner/chef Guillermo "Willy" Thomas and his wife, co-owner Yvette, counts both its neighbors and Nashville's elite among its most loyal patrons. Enjoy such delicious dishes as green chili macaroni and cheese, grilled shrimp ratatouille or W.N. Farmers Market vegetable tian in the intimate and comfortable small rooms composing Park Café's dining room. The innovative cuisine is rooted in a commitment to simple preparations of high-quality, fresh ingredients from local farms and gardens, resulting in flavorful recipes that don't disappoint.

American, Southern. Dinner. Closed Sunday. $16-35

SUNSET GRILL

2001 Belcourt Ave., Nashville, 615-386-3663, 866-496-3663; www.sunsetgrill.com

A mainstay of Nashville's restaurant scene since 1990, Sunset Grill is a favorite in Nashville's trendy Hillsboro Village neighborhood, adjacent to Vanderbilt University. With Nashville's mild climate, the open-air patio provides delightful alfresco dining much of the year, while the attractive dining room is the perfect place year-round for enjoying delectable fare ranging from sautéed shrimp over Tennessee cheddar stone-ground grits for lunch to Cajun spiced duck breast for dinner and P.E.I. mussels from the late-night menu.

Californian, Southern. Lunch (Tuesday-Friday), dinner, late-night. Outdoor seating. $16-35

THE YELLOW PORCH

734 Thompson Lane, Nashville, 615-386-0260; www.theyellowporch.com

Loved by locals, The Yellow Porch is as pleasant as its name. Tucked away from Nashville's major tourist attractions and taking up residence in the charming Berry Hill neighborhood of bungalows-turned-eclectic-shops-and-recording-studios, the restaurant is owned by Gep and Katie Nelson, two of the forces behind Nashville's earth-to-table movement. Featuring a bright and cheery dining room by day, The Yellow Porch adopts a darker, cozier, more romantic ambiance by night. The small restaurant's excellent wine program is complemented by equally excellent fare that uses the freshest of fresh ingredients: produce and herbs grown in a garden in front of the restaurant. Favorite entrées include the seafood-laden paella served with saffron rice, onions, peppers and tomatoes. Specials change regularly.

Contemporary American. Lunch, dinner. Closed Sunday. Outdoor seating. $16-35

SHOPPING

DOWNTOWN FRANKLIN

www.downtownfranklintn.com

Located approximately 17 miles south of Nashville on Interstate 65, historic Franklin boasts a walkable, picturesque, downtown shopping district that attracts visitors from all over. The 15-block area along Main Street retains the charm of Franklin's bygone days. From home accessories to clothing, from jewelry to art, from furniture to gifts and antiques, the shops of downtown Franklin will delight window-shoppers and fashionistas alike. Check out Whats-In-Store (www.whats-in-store.com) for affordable high-fashion accessories, Franklin Tea (www.franklintea.com) for everything you need for a cuppa, and the delightful Landmark Booksellers (www.landmarkbooksellers.com) for that out-of-print book you've been searching for everywhere. If you tire of shopping, walk or drive through the surrounding tree-lined streets, which boast many beautifully preserved historic homes that give clues to Franklin's Civil War history. Downtown Franklin hosts several annual festivals, including Main Street Festival in the spring and Dickens of a Christmas in December.

HILLSBORO VILLAGE

21st Avenue, between Wedgewood and Edgehill avenues, Nashville; www.hillsborovillage.com

Hillsboro Village, located on the southern edge of Vanderbilt University's campus, is loved by locals and visitors alike. Bounded by active neighborhoods, residents walk to "The Village" to eat, watch movies and even do their banking. Mostly they come to peruse places like A Thousand Faces, an art, jewelry and knickknack store; Pangaea, an eclectic gift shop; BookMan/BookWoman, a used bookstore; POSH Boutique, a clothing retailer; and Zeitgeist Gallery, a gallery/architecture and design studio. Just a few blocks long, Hillsboro Village can provide a welcome daytime respite from the nightlife in Nashville's honky-tonks. When you need to recharge for more shopping, grab some coffee at Fido, a former pet store that's become a see-and-be-seen coffee shop, or grab lunch at one of the Village's numerous restaurants.

THE MALL AT GREEN HILLS

2126 Abbott Martin Road, Nashville, 615-298-5478; www.themallatgreenhills.com

Located in one of Nashville's ritziest neighborhoods, The Mall at Green Hills is the city's most upscale shopping mall. The mall recently began offering complimentary valet parking to help you begin your shopping excursion in style before you even step inside. The completion of a major renovation and expansion in 2005 attracted luxury retailers, who were often opening their first retail location in the state. Anchored by Dillard's and Macy's, the mall features more than 100 shops and eateries, including such fine specialty stores as Tiffany & Co., Louis Vuitton, Burberry, Juicy Couture, Kate Spade, Sephora and Brooks Brothers. The mall's biggest coup is that it snagged the Mid-South's first Nordstrom department store, which is slated to open in fall 2011.

OPRY MILLS
433 Opry Mills Drive, Nashville; www.simon.com
A favorite Nashville shopping destination, Opry Mills is adjacent to the Grand Ole Opry and the Gaylord Opryland Resort and Convention Center. With nearly 200 restaurants and stores, the expansive shopping and entertainment facility could keep you busy for days. But it's best known for the retail outlet locations in its midst, like BCBGMaxAzria Final Cut and the Gap Outlet. While you shop, you can catch a concert here. Its Music City location allows the mall to attract both up-and-coming and celebrated Nashville talents to perform on its grounds.

MIDDLE TENNESSEE

Best known as the home of Nashville, Middle Tennessee is more than just a paradise for country music fans. It's part of the historic soul of the South, with antebellum homes, whiskey distilleries and historic towns dotting the landscape. Middle Tennessee was first settled by non-Native Americans with land grants in and around Clarksville from the new U.S. government, which couldn't afford to pay Revolutionary War veterans. Clarksville features a cooperative visual arts community and is not far from beautiful parks and outdoors attractions, a fitting tribute to the Revolutionary War heroes. History is for sale in well-regarded antique stores in Clarksville, Gallatin and in the Cookeville area of the state's upper Cumberland region.

The best bet for history buffs is Franklin, where visitors can retrace the Battle of Franklin, a decisive battle that took place in 1864. The Confederates lost more than 6,000 men and six generals, while the Union lost another 2,300 troops at the Carnton Plantation. Many of the wounded were brought to the plantation and blood still mars the floor there today. If that's enough to make you want a drink, Middle Tennessee is also the base of two of the best American distilleries, the George Dickel Distillery in Normandy and Jack Daniel's in Lynchburg. Both offer tours and tastings of these classic American brands. You can easily stay in Nashville and make day trips out to any of these places.

WHAT TO SEE

CLARKSVILLE
BEACHHAVEN VINEYARD & WINERY
1100 Dunlop Lane, Clarksville, 931-645-8867; www.beachavenwinery.com
Tour the vineyard and winery and then hit the tasting room. There is also a picnic area on the grounds.

HIGHLIGHT

WHAT ARE THE TOP THINGS TO DO IN MIDDLE TENNESSE?

EXPLORE THE BURGESS FALLS STATE NATURAL AREA

Burgess is said to have one of the most beautiful waterfalls in the state. The 130-foot waterfall cascades from a gorge on the Falling Water River.

VISIT LORETTA LYNN'S RANCH

Country music fans will swoon at the chance to visit the superstar's home. You'll also get to tour her Butcher Holler Home and a simulated coal mine, all in honor of the coal miner's daughter.

DRINK UP AT THE JACK DANIEL'S DISTILLERY

Jack Daniel's is the country's oldest registered distillery. Go on a guided tour of the limestone spring cave and grounds and see what goes into making Tennessee's finest whiskey.

DUNBAR CAVE STATE NATURAL AREA

Clarksville, five miles southeast via Highway 79, 931-648-5526; www.tennessee.gov

This 110-acre park with a small scenic lake was once a fashionable resort; the cave itself housed big-band dances. The old bathhouse has been refurbished to serve as a museum and visitor center.

PORT ROYAL STATE HISTORIC AREA

Five miles east via Highway 76, near Adams, 931-358-9696; www.state.tn.us

At the confluence of Sulphur Fork Creek and the Red River, Port Royal was one of the state's earliest communities and trading centers. A 300-foot covered bridge spans the river.

COLUMBIA

ANCESTRAL HOME OF JAMES K. POLK

301 W. Seventh St., Columbia, 931-388-2354; www.jameskpolk.com

Built by Samuel Polk, father of the president, the federal-style house is furnished with family possessions, including furniture and portraits used at the White House. Gardens link the house to an adjacent 1818 building once owned by the president's sisters. There's also a visitor center.

April-October, Monday-Saturday 9 a.m.-5 p.m., Sunday 1-5 p.m.; November-March, Monday-Saturday 9 a.m.-4 p.m., Sunday 1-5 p.m.

THE ATHENAEUM

808 Athenaeum St., Columbia, 931-381-4822; www.athenaeumrectory.com

These Moorish buildings were used as a girls' school after 1852. During the Civil War, the rectory became headquarters of Union Generals Negeley and Schofield.

February-December, Tuesday-Sunday.

COOKEVILLE

APPALACHIAN CENTER FOR CRAFTS

1560 Craft Center Drive, Smithville, 615-597-6801; www.tntech.edu/craftcenter

The center is on 600 acres overlooking Center Hill Lake. Operated by the Tennessee Technological University, it has teaching programs in fiber, metal, wood, glass and clay. There are also exhibition galleries.

Daily 9 a.m.-5 p.m.

BURGESS FALLS STATE NATURAL AREA

4000 Burgess Falls Drive, Sparta, 931-432-5312;
www.state.tn.us/environment/parks/BurgessFalls

The scenic riverside trail leads to an overlook of a 130-foot waterfall, considered one of the most beautiful in the state, in a gorge on the Falling Water River.

Daily dawn-dusk.

CENTER HILL DAM AND LAKE

158 Resource Lane, Lancaster, 931-858-3125; www.smithvilletn.com

This 250-foot-tall dam controls the flood waters of the Caney Fork River and provides electric power. The lake has a 415-mile shoreline. It provides ample opportunities for swimming, waterskiing, fishing, boating, hunting, picnicking at six recreation areas around the reservoir and camping.

CROSSVILLE

CUMBERLAND MOUNTAIN STATE PARK

24 Office Drive, Crossville, 931-484-6138; www.state.tn.us

This park, along the Cumberland Plateau, is 1,820 feet above sea level. It stands on the largest remaining timberland plateau in America and has a 35-acre lake. The park also provides a pool, a bathhouse, fishing, boating (rentals), nature trails and programs, tennis, picnicking, a playground, a snack bar, a dining room, camping, tent and trailer sites and cabins.

Daily 7 a.m.-10 p.m.

HOMESTEADS TOWER MUSEUM

96 Highway 68, Crossville, 931-456-9663

The tower was built in 1938 to house administrative offices of the Cumberland Homesteads, a New Deal-era project. A winding stairway leads to a lookout platform at the top of the octagonal stone tower. At the base of the tower is a museum with photos, documents and artifacts from the 1930s and 1940s.

March-December daily.

HIGHLIGHT

WHAT IS THERE TO DO AT THE CHEROKEE NATIONAL FOREST?

This 630,000-acre forest, cut by river gorges and creased by rugged mountains, lies in two separate strips along the Tennessee-North Carolina boundary, northeast and southwest of Great Smoky Mountains National Park. A region of thick forests, streams and waterfalls, the forest takes its name from the Native American tribe. There are more than 700 miles of hiking trails, including part of the Appalachian Trail. The forest's 30 campgrounds, 30 picnic areas, eight swimming sites, 13 boating sites and seven white-water rivers practically guarantee that visitors will find outdoor adventure and scenic beauty on this expanse of land. Hunting for game, including wild boar, deer and turkey, is permitted under Tennessee game regulations. Fees may be charged at recreation sites.

FRANKLIN

CARTER HOUSE
1140 Columbia Ave., Franklin, 615-791-1861; www.carterhouse1864.com

The house served as the command post for the Union forces during the Battle of Franklin. It now houses a Confederate museum with documents, uniforms, flags, guns, maps and Civil War prints. Go on a guided tour of the house and grounds and see a video presentation.
Monday-Saturday 9 a.m.-5 p.m., Sunday 1-5 p.m.

HERITAGE TRAIL
North and south on Highway 31, Franklin

The trail provides a scenic drive along the highway from Brentwood through Franklin to Spring Hill, an area that was plantation country in the mid-1800s. Southern culture is reflected in the drive's many antebellum and Victorian houses; Williamson County was one of the richest areas in Tennessee when the Civil War broke out.

HISTORIC CARNTON AND MCGAVOCK CONFEDERATE CEMETERY
1345 Carnton Lane, Franklin, 615-794-0903; www.carnton.org

This federal-type house was modified in the 1840s to reflect Greek Revival style. Built by an early mayor of Nashville, the house was a social and political center. At the end of the Battle of Franklin, which was fought nearby, four Confederate generals lay dead on the back porch. The nation's largest private Confederate cemetery is adjacent.

HISTORIC DISTRICT
First Avenue and North Margin Street surrounding the Town Square and the Confederate Monument, Franklin

See the earliest buildings of Franklin, dating back to 1800; those along Main Street are exceptional in their architectural designs and are part of a historic preservation project.

GALLATIN
CRAGFONT
200 Cragfont Road, Castalian Springs, 615-452-7070; www.tennesseeanytime.org

This late Georgian-style house was built for General James Winchester, Revolutionary War hero, by masons and carpenters brought from Maryland. It is named for the rocky bluff on which it stands. It has a galleried ballroom, a weaving room, a wine cellar and federal-period furnishings. There are also restored gardens that are worth a gander.

Mid-April-November, Tuesday-Saturday 10 a.m.-5 p.m., Sunday 1 p.m.-5 p.m.

TROUSDALE PLACE
183 W. Main St., Gallatin, 615-452-5648;

The two-story brick house built in the early 1800s was the residence of Governor William Trousdale. Inside is period furniture and a military history library.

WYNNEWOOD
210 Old Highway 25, Castalian Springs, 615-452-5463; www.sumnercountytourism.com

Considered the oldest and largest log structure ever built in Tennessee, this log inn was originally constructed as a stagecoach stop and mineral springs resort. President Andrew Jackson visited here many times.

April-October, daily; November-March, Monday-Saturday.

HURRICANE MILLS
LORETTA LYNN'S RANCH
44 Hurricane Mills Road, Hurricane Mills, 931-296-7700; www.lorettalynn.com

Tours take you through the country music star's house, a museum, Mooney's Ranch Office, the Butcher Holler Home and a simulated coal mine. Plus, you'll get a peek at Western and general stores and Loretta Lynn's Record Shop. The ranch also offers swimming, fishing, hiking, tennis and camping.

April-October, daily.

NOLAN HOUSE
375 Highway 13 N., Waverly, 931-296-2511

This restored 12-room Victorian house offers period furnishings, a redoubt trail, a dog-trot and a family graveyard. Overnight stays are available.

Tours: Monday-Saturday.

JAMESTOWN
HISTORIC RUGBY
Highway 5517, Rugby, 423-628-2441, 888-214-3400; www.historicrugby.org

Social reformer Thomas Hughes founded this English colony in the 1880s in hopes of creating a utopian society founded on cooperative enterprise and Christian values. Residents enjoyed natural parks, recreation and cultural activities such as literary societies. Financial problems, a typhoid epidemic and unusually severe winters contributed to the community's demise, but much has been preserved for visitors' pleasure today. Of 17 original Victorian buildings remaining, four are open to the public. Hughes Public Library, unchanged since opening in 1882, contains a unique 7,000-volume collection from the

Victorian era. A visitor center is in Rugby Schoolhouse; guided walking tours are available. There is also picnicking and hiking in surrounding river gorges on trails built by the original colonists.

Monday-Saturday 9:30 a.m.-5:30 p.m., Sunday noon-5:30 p.m.

PICKETT STATE RUSTIC PARK
4605 Pickett Park Highway, Jamestown, 931-879-5821; www.state.tn.us

The park covers 14,000 acres in Cumberland Mountains. It offers unusual rock formations, caves and natural bridges. There's much to do: a sand beach, swimming, fishing, boating, nature trails, backpacking, picnicking, concessions, a recreation lodge, camping and cabins.

Daily dawn-dusk.

MANCHESTER
JACK DANIEL'S DISTILLERY
280 Lynchburg Highway, Lynchburg, 931-759-4221; www.jackdaniels.com

This is the nation's oldest registered distillery. Eighty-minute guided tours include a look at the rustic grounds, limestone spring cave and old office.

Daily 9 a.m.-4:30 p.m.

NORMANDY LAKE
Eight miles west, two miles upstream from Normandy; www.tva.gov

Completed in 1976, the dam that impounds the lake is 2,734 feet high. Controlled releases provide a scenic float way (28 miles) below the dam with public access points along the way. During the summer, the pool is open; in the spring and fall, there's excellent fishing. Picnicking and camping are available as well. Daily.

OLD STONE FORT STATE ARCHAEOLOGICAL PARK
732 Stone Fort Drive, Manchester, 931-723-5073; www.state.tn.us/environment

The 600-acre park surrounds the earthen remains of a more than 2,000-year-old walled structure built along the bluffs of the Duck River. Fishing, picnicking, a playground and camping are available.

Daily dawn-dusk.

EAST TENNESSEE

This region is the birthplace of country music and home to some of the best attractions in the state, including the Tennessee Aquarium, Dollywood, and the Smoky Mountains. Visitors should begin in Chattanooga, one of the South's most beautiful natural settings and the area that gave the name to the Chattanooga Choo Choo. Not far from the famed Appalachian trail, Chattanooga has a variety of attractions, from the first Coca-Cola bottling plant to the first miniature gold location to one of the world's largest freshwater aquariums and a beautiful lakefront in the shadows of the Appalachians.

Drive northeast 100 miles along into the Smoky Mountains, one of the nicest drives in the South, and you'll find yourself in Knoxville. Along the way, stop in

Gatlinburg, which features the Great Smoky Mountains National Park, deservedly the country's most visited national park. Afterward, stop in Knoxville, which began as a frontier outpost and worked hard to maintain its reputation as both a commercial center and for whiskey and wild times. Now, those wild times find a better outlet in the form of the orange-face-painted fans cheering on the University of Tennessee football team. Of course, no mention of Eastern Tennessee is complete with a tip of the hat to Dollywood, located in the shadow of the Smokies and offering the best theme park attractions outside of Disney. Walland is home to one of the best hotels in the country—Blackberry Farm—a destination unto itself.

WHAT TO SEE

CHATTANOOGA
BATTLES FOR CHATTANOOGA MUSEUM
1110 E. Brow Road, Lookout Mountain, 423-821-2812; www.battlesforchattanooga.com
An automated, 3-D display re-creates the Civil War Battles of Chattanooga using 5,000 miniature soldiers, flashing lights, smoking cannons and crackling rifles. Also here are dioramas of area history prior to the Civil War.
June-August, daily 9 a.m.-5 p.m.; September-May, daily 10 a.m.-5 p.m.

CHATTANOOGA AFRICAN-AMERICAN MUSEUM
200 E. Martin Luther King Blvd., Chattanooga, 423-266-8658; www.caamhistory.com
This educational institution highlights African-American contributions to the growth of Chattanooga and the nation.
Monday-Friday 10 a.m.-5 p.m., Saturday noon-4 p.m.

CHATTANOOGA CHOO-CHOO
Terminal Station, 1400 Market St., Chattanooga, 423-266-5000, 800-872-2529; www.choochoo.com
The song made it famous, but the Chattanooga Choo-Choo began chugging through the South and Midwest in the 1880s. The converted 1909 train station contains a hotel and restaurants. It also boasts formal gardens, fountains, pools, turn-of-the-century shops and a model railroad museum.
Daily 8 a.m.-10 p.m.

CHATTANOOGA NATURE CENTER AT REFLECTION RIDING
400 Garden Road, Chattanooga, 423-821-9582; www.reflectionriding.org
This park is meant for leisurely driving. It offers winding three-mile trips with vistas: historic sites, trees, wildflowers, shrubs, reflecting pools. It's also a wetland walkway, with a nature center, hiking trails and outdoorsy programs.
Monday-Saturday.

CRAVENS HOUSE
Chattanooga, 423-821-7786
The house is the oldest-surviving structure on the mountain, restored with period furnishings. The original house, which was the center of the "Battle Above the Clouds," was destroyed; the present structure was erected on the

HIGHLIGHT

WHAT ARE THE TOP THINGS TO DO IN EAST TENNESSEE?

CHECK OUT THE VIEW AT LOOKOUT MOUNTAIN
Head to this mountain, which rises more than 2,100 feet above the city, to get an amazing view. You'll be able to spy Tennessee, Georgia, North and South Carolina and Alabama from the top.

HIT THE RAPIDS AND GO WHITEWATER RAFTING
Adventure seekers will get a thrill on these white-water rafting trips through the Nolichucky Canyon and some of the deepest gorges this side of the Mississippi River. Be prepared to get soaked.

PLAY AT DOLLYWOOD
This grand amusement park calls itself "the friendliest town in the Smokies." It's certainly the most fun town in the Smokies, with 40 musical shows daily and more than 30 rides and attractions.

SPEED OVER TO THE SMOKY MOUNTAIN CAR MUSEUM
Car lovers will drool over the more than 30 specialty vehicles on display here. You'll see James Bond's "007" Aston Martin, Al Capone's bulletproof Cadillac and Elvis Presley's Mercedes, among others.

SPELUNK IN FORBIDDEN CAVERNS
Tennessee boasts more caves than any other state. Check out this excellent tour, which will bring you through dazzling formations, towering natural chimneys, various grottos and a crystal-clear stream.

original foundations in 1866.
Mid-June-mid-August, daily.

CREATIVE DISCOVERY MUSEUM
321 Chestnut St., Chattanooga, 423-756-2738; www.cdmfun.org
Kids will have a ball playing instruments, climbing through a replica of a riverboat and creating art, among other hands-on activities at this learning museum. Exhibit areas include the Artist's Studio, Inventor's Clubhouse,

Musician's Studio and Excavation Station.
Daily 10 a.m.-5 p.m.

HUNTER MUSEUM OF AMERICAN ART

10 Bluff View, Chattanooga, 423-267-0968; www.huntermuseum.org

Built on a bluff overlooking the Tennessee River, the museum has an outdoor beauty that's rivaled only by its art collection. The offerings include paintings, sculpture, glass, drawings, a permanent collection of major American artists and changing exhibits.

Tuesday-Saturday 9:30 a.m.-5 p.m., Sunday noon-5 p.m.

LOOKOUT MOUNTAIN

Chattanooga, 800-825-8366; www.lookoutmountain.com

The mountain towers more than 2,120 feet above the city, offering clear-day views of Tennessee, Georgia, North Carolina, South Carolina and Alabama. During the Civil War, the "Battle Above the Clouds" was fought on the slope.

LOOKOUT MOUNTAIN INCLINE RAILWAY

3917 St. Elmo Ave., Chattanooga, Lower Station, 423-821-4224; www.lookoutmountain.com

The world's steepest passenger incline railway climbs Lookout Mountain to a 2,100-foot altitude. Near the top, the grade reaches a 72.7-degree angle; passengers ride glass-roofed cars to witness the steepness. The Smoky Mountains can be seen from Upper Station observation deck.

NICKAJACK DAM AND LAKE

3490 TVA Road, Jasper

The Tennessee Valley Authority dam impounds the lake with 192 miles of shoreline and 10,370 acres of water surface. Fishing and boat launches are available.

POINT PARK

110 Point Park Road, Lookout Mountain, 423-821-7786

Get a view of Chattanooga and Moccasin Bend from the observatory. Monuments, plaques and a museum tell the story of battle. There's also a visitor center, which is part of Chickamauga and Chattanooga National Military Park.

RACCOON MOUNTAIN CAVERNS AND CAMPGROUND

319 W. Hills Drive, Chattanooga, 423-821-9403, 800-823-2267; www.raccoonmountain.com

More than 5½ miles of underground passageways offer views of beautiful rock formations. Opt for the Crystal Palace Tour for an overview of the cave's history and geology, or get a little dirty on one of the "wild" cave expeditions that give visitors a chance to examine undeveloped parts of the caverns. Several of these expeditions offer overnight stays in the cave. It's also a full-facility campground.

ROCK CITY GARDENS

1400 Pattern Road, Lookout Mountain, 706-820-2531; www.seerockcity.com

Among these 14 acres of mountaintop trails and vistas, visitors will find unique rock formations (including one called Fat Man's Squeeze), a 180-foot "swing-a-long" bridge and a critter classroom, where visitors learn about the creatures that live on or near Lookout Mountain. Daily.

SPECIAL EVENT

RIVERBEND FESTIVAL

180 Hamm Road, Chattanooga, 423-756-2211; www.riverbendfestival.com
This international award-winning festival along the Tennessee River features five stages and draws more than 600,000 people a year, in just nine days. The Riverbend Festival showcases performers from genres across the board. If you want to be a bit more active during this musical week and a half, there is the annual bluecross Riverbend Run and Walk featuring a 10K, 5K, and a one-mile fun run. With top artists (Sheryl Crow or Alison Krauss) performing, tickets can sell out quickly.
Mid-June.

RUBY FALLS-LOOKOUT MOUNTAIN CAVERNS

1720 S. Scenic Highway, Chattanooga, 423-821-2544; www.rubyfalls.com
Under the battlefield are twin caves with onyx formations, giant stalactites and stalagmites of various hues; at 1,120 feet below the surface, Ruby Falls is a 145-foot waterfall inside Lookout Mountain Caverns. Get a view of the city from the tower above the entrance building. Guided tours are available.

SIGNAL POINT ON SIGNAL MOUNTAIN

Chattanooga; www.sigmtn.com
This mountain was used for signaling by Cherokees and later by Confederates. By looking almost straight down to the Tennessee River from Signal Point Military Park (off St. James Boulevard), visitors get a glimpse of the "Grand Canyon of Tennessee."

TENNESSEE AQUARIUM

1 Broad St., Chattanooga, 423-265-0695, 800-262-0695; www.tnaqua.org
The aquarium was the first major freshwater life center in the country, focusing primarily on the natural habitats and wildlife of the Tennessee River and related ecosystems. Within this 130,000-square-foot complex are more than 9,000 animals in their natural habitats. The aquarium re-creates riverine habitats in seven major freshwater tanks and two terrestrial environments and is organized into five major galleries: Appalachian Cove Forest; Tennessee River Gallery; Discovery Falls; Mississippi Delta; and Rivers of the World. The highlight of the aquarium is the 60-foot-high central canyon, designed to give visitors a sense of immersion into the river.
Daily 9:30 a.m.-6 p.m.

TENNESSEE VALLEY RAILROAD

4119 Cromwell Road, Chattanooga, 423-894-8028; www.tvrail.com
The South's largest operating historic railroad has steam locomotives, diesels and passenger coaches of various types. Trains take passengers on a six-mile ride, including through a tunnel. There's an audiovisual show and displays.
June-August, daily; September-May, Monday-Friday.

GATLINBURG

GATLINBURG SPACE NEEDLE
115 Historic Nature Trail, Gatlinburg, 865-436-4629; www.gatlinburgspaceneedle.com
A glass-enclosed elevator takes you to a 342-foot-high observation deck for a view of the Smoky Mountains.

SKY LIFT
765 Parkway, Gatlinburg, 865-436-4307; www.gatlinburgskylift.com
The double-chairlift ride up to Crockett Mountain is 2,300 feet. Get a view of the Smoky Mountains en route and from observation deck at the summit. A snack bar and gift shop are available.
Daily, weather permitting.

GREENEVILLE

DAVY CROCKETT BIRTHPLACE STATE PARK
1245 Davy Crockett Park Road, Limestone, 423-257-2167;www.state.tn.us
The 100-acre site overlooking the Nolichuckey River serves as a memorial to Crockett—humorist, bear hunter, congressman and hero of the Alamo. A small monument marks Crockett's birthplace; nearby is a replica of the log cabin in which he was born in 1786. The park also has a swimming pool, picnicking, camping, a museum and visitors center.

JOHNSON CITY

APPALACHIAN CAVERNS
420 Cave Hill Road, Blountville, 423-323-2337; www.appalachiancaverns.com
When it is hot, caving will cool you off. These giant underground chambers—made colorful by deposits of manganese, copper, calcium and other elements—served Native Americans in need of shelter, hid soldiers during the Civil War and protected moon shiners during Prohibition.
Monday-Saturday 9 a.m.-6 p.m., Sunday 1-6 p.m.

HANDS ON! REGIONAL MUSEUM
315 E. Main St., Johnson City, 423-434-4263; www.handsonmuseum.org
The museum showcases more than 20 hands-on exhibits designed for children of all ages. Traveling shows also stop by.
Monday-Friday 9 a.m.-5 p.m., Saturday 10 a.m. -5 p.m., Sunday 1-5 p.m.

HISTORIC DISTRICT
Visitors Center, 117 Boone St., Jonesborough, 423-753-5961
This four-by-six-block area through the heart of town reflects 200 years of history. See private residences; commercial and public buildings of federal, Greek Revival and Victorian styles; brick sidewalks; and old-style lampposts.

JONESBOROUGH
Jonesborough, six miles west off Highway 11 E., 423-753-1030; www.jonesboroughtn.org
It's the oldest town in Tennessee and the first capital of the state of Franklin, prior to Tennessee obtaining statehood.

SPECIAL EVENTS

SMOKY MOUNTAIN LIGHTS & WINTERFEST

107 Park Headquarters Road, Gatlinburg, 865-453-6411; www.smokymountainwinterfest.com
The winter celebration includes Yule log burnings, more than 2 million lights and other special events. The festival spans over three towns—Gatlinburg, Pigeon Forge and Sevierville—and is sponsored by local businesses to make it one of the most festive holiday celebrations. Yes, all the lights are pretty, but there is more to Winterfest than the twinkling towns. It is the perfect time to hit the slopes in the Smoky Mountains. Enjoy parades from town to town, sales at a variety of stores for last minute shopping, and even a few chili cook-offs. There are usually discounts at the local hotels. Events vary by town, creating another reason to visit all three.
Late November-February.

SPRING WILDFLOWER PILGRIMAGE

Gatlinburg Chamber of Commerce, 888-898-9102; www.springwildflowerpilgrimage.org
After almost 60 years, the Spring Wildflower Pilgrimage is still taking people's breath away. The two-day event began with four hundred pilgrims from 20 different states showcasing their photography, plant arrangements and paintings. It also offered tours, field trips and evening sessions. Today, more than 1,000 pilgrims travel to Gatlinburg for 150 indoor and outdoor programs. The event has numerous wildflower, fauna and natural history walks, seminars, art classes and a variety of other programs. It is held outdoors at the Great Smoky Mountains National Park, as well as in a variety of indoor venues around Gatlinburg.
Late April.

JONESBOROUGH HISTORY MUSEUM
117 Boone St., Johnson City, 423-753-1015; www.jonesboroughtn.org
Exhibits highlight the history of Jonesborough from pioneer days to the early 20th century.

ROCKY MOUNT HISTORIC SITE & OVERMOUNTAIN MUSEUM
200 Hyder Hill Road, Piney Flats, 423-538-7396; www.rockymountmuseum.com
The log house, territorial capitol under Gov. William Blount from 1790 to 1792, is restored to original simplicity with 18th-century furniture, a log kitchen, a slave cabin, a barn, a blacksmith shop and a smokehouse. Costumed interpreters reenact a day in the life of a typical pioneer family; the 1 ½-hour tour includes the Cobb-Massengill house, kitchen and slave cabin, as well as a self-guided tour through the adjacent Museum of Overmountain History.
Monday-Saturday.

TIPTON-HAYNES HISTORIC SITE
2620 S. Roan St., Johnson City, 423-926-3631; www.tipton-haynes.org
This was the site of the 1788 Battle of the Lost State of Franklin. Six original buildings and four reconstructions span American history from pre-colonial days through the Civil War.

WATAUGA DAM AND LAKE
About 20 miles east of Johnson City off Highway 321, Hampton
Surrounded by the Cherokee National Forest and flanked by the Appalachian Mountains, Watauga Reservoir is arguably one of the most beautiful in the world and boasts excellent fishing. Below Watauga Dam is a wildlife observation area, where visitors can view waterfowl. The Appalachian Trail passes nearby.

WHITEWATER RAFTING
Cherokee Adventures, 2000 Jonesborough Road, Erwin, 423-743-7733, 800-445-7238; www.cherokeeadventures.com
A variety of guided white-water rafting trips blast through the Nolichucky Canyon and some of the deepest gorges east of the Mississippi River and along the Watauga and Russell Fork rivers.
March-November.

KINGSPORT
BAYS MOUNTAIN PLANETARIUM
853 Bays Mountain Park Road, Kingsport, 423-229-9447; www.baysmountain.com
The plant and animal sanctuary covers 3,000 acres and offers 25 miles of trails. On the grounds you'll also find a nature interpretive center; an aviary; a deer pen; otter, bobcat and wolf habitats; nature programs; an ocean pool; a planetarium; an exhibition gallery and library. Stop by the observation tower and the 19th-century farmstead museum and take a barge ride on the 44-acre lake.
Daily.

BOATYARD PARK
151 E. Main St., Kingsport, 423-246-2010; www.kingsportparksandrecreation.org
On the banks of the north and south forks of the Holston River, the park offers the Netherland Inn museum, picnic areas, playgrounds, boating, fishing and footpaths along the river.

EXCHANGE PLACE
4812 Orebank Road, Kingsport, 423-288-6071; www.exchangeplace.info
The restored 19th-century farm once served as a facility for exchanging horses and Virginia currency for Tennessee currency. There's also a crafts center onsite.
May-October, weekends or by appointment.

NETHERLAND INN
2144 Netherland Inn Road, Kingsport, 423-335-5552; www.netherlandinn.com
The large frame and stone structure on the site of King's Boat Yard was a celebrated stop on the Great Stage Road and was operated for more than 150 years as an inn and the town's entertainment center. U.S. presidents Andrew Jackson, Andrew Johnson and James K. Polk visited the inn during its heyday, between

HIGHLIGHT

WHAT'S THE BEST WAY TO TOUR THE COPPER BASIN?

For a look at some of Tennessee's most beautiful landscapes, take a drive along Highway 64 east of Chattanooga. You'll cruise through the scenic Cherokee National Forest, alongside the churning Ocoee River and through the badlands of the Copper Basin.

From Chattanooga, take Interstate 75 north toward Cleveland and then take Highway 64 east to the Georgia border (take the bypass around Cleveland). From outside the town of Ocoee, Highway 64 runs east through 24 miles of the Cherokee National Forest alongside the Ocoee River.

The river, which hosted the 1996 Olympic Whitewater Competition, lures daring paddlers to one of the premier white-water runs in the country. A series of Class III and IV rapids with nicknames like "Broken Nose," "Diamond Splitter," "Tablesaw" and "Hell Hole" hints at the river's reputation as one of the Southeast's greatest white-water runs. The acclaimed white water lies between two dams built and managed by the Tennessee Valley Authority (TVA) for hydroelectric power. The TVA can dry up or "turn on" the white water as easily as turning a spigot. Two dozen outfitters around Ocoee lead guided rafting expeditions downriver for half-day or full-day excursions; try Nantahala Outdoor Center (800-232-7238), Ocoee Outdoors (800-533-7767) or Southeastern Expeditions (800-868-7238). Connect with the outdoors in a more laid-back fashion at the Parksville Lake Recreation Area, 11 miles from Ocoee off Highway 64. The park offers a nice spot for picnics, boating or camping in stands of pine and dogwood trees. Enjoy a few leisurely hours here before continuing on to the Copper Basin.

Between Ducktown and Copperhill at the Georgia border, the Copper Basin gets its name from the copper mines that flourished here in the 1800s. Unfortunately, the industry clear-cut the forest and generated copper sulfide fumes that devastated what was then left of the local environment, creating a stark desert out of the once-lush forested terrain. In the 1930s, the Civilian Conservation Corps was sent in to restore the area, and after five forgiving decades and active land reclamation, the Copper Basin is beginning to recover. The Ducktown Basin Museum, 1/4 mile north of Highway 64 on Highway 68 (423-496-5778), tells the story of the copper industry. The remains of the town's first copper mine are nearby, as are the towns of Copperhill, Tenn., and McCaysville, Ga., both of which have historic districts worth a visit. From downtown Copperhill, the Blue Ridge Scenic Railway (800-934-1898), an antique locomotive with a red caboose, takes passengers to Blue Ridge, Ga. There are several restaurants and cafés right across the street from the depot.

1818 and 1841. Now a museum with 18th- and 19th-century furnishings, the complex includes a well house, flatboat, garden, log cabin, children's museum and museum shop.

May-September, Saturday-Monday; April, October, Saturday-Sunday.

WARRIORS' PATH STATE PARK

490 Hemlock Road, Kingsport, 423-239-8531; www.state.tn.us

A swimming pool, a water slide, a bathhouse, fishing and boating, nature bridle trails, 18-hole golf, a driving range, disc golf, a playground and concessions keep this park busy. The campground is on the shores of Patrick Henry Reservoir on the Holston River. The first-come, first-served wooded sites have picnic tables and grills. But plan ahead—the sites are usually full by Tuesday of race week.

KNOXVILLE

BECK CULTURAL EXCHANGE CENTER-MUSEUM OF BLACK HISTORY AND CULTURE

1927 Dandridge Ave., Knoxville, 865-524-8461; www.discoveret.org/beckcec

The center preserves the achievements of Knoxville's African-American citizens from the early 1800s. The gallery features changing exhibits of local and regional artists.

Tuesday-Saturday.

CONFEDERATE MEMORIAL HALL

3148 Kingston Pike S.W., Knoxville, 865-522-2371; www.knoxvillecmh.org

The antebellum mansion with Mediterranean-style gardens served as head-quarters of Confederate Gen. James Longstreet during the siege of Knoxville. Maintained as a Confederate memorial, the 15-room house is furnished with museum pieces, a collection of Southern and Civil War relics and a library of Southern literature.

Tuesday, Thursday-Friday.

CRESCENT BEND (ARMSTRONG-LOCKETT HOUSE) AND W. PERRY TOMS MEMORIAL GARDENS

2728 Kingston Pike, Knoxville, 865-637-3163

Here you'll find collections of American and English furniture, English silver and extensive terraced gardens.

March-December, Tuesday-Sunday.

EAST TENNESSEE DISCOVERY CENTER & AKIMA PLANETARIUM

516 N. Beaman St., Knoxville, Chilhowee Park, 865-594-1494; www.etdiscovery.org

Much more fun than high school biology, this museum has interactive exhibits that kids and adults will find fascinating. Displays include a live honey bee colony, an arthropod exhibit with giant Madagascar hissing cockroaches, a series that teaches about energy and a space shuttle with interactive control panels.

Monday-Saturday.

GOVERNOR WILLIAM BLOUNT MANSION

200 W. Hill Ave., Knoxville, 865-525-2375; www.blountmansion.org

The house of William Blount, governor of the Southwest Territory and signer of the U.S. Constitution, was the center of political and social activity in the territory. It's been restored to its condition of late 1700s with period furnishings, Blount memorabilia and an 18th-century garden. Tennessee's first state constitution was drafted in the governor's office behind the mansion.

April-mid-December, Monday-Saturday 9:30 a.m.-5 p.m.; January-March, Monday-Friday 9:30 a.m.-5 p.m.

JAMES WHITE'S FORT

205 E. Hill Ave., Knoxville, 865-525-6514; www.discoveret.org

The original pioneer house was built by the founder and first settler of Knoxville. Restored buildings include the smokehouse, blacksmith shop and museum.

March-mid-December, Monday-Saturday; January-February, Monday-Friday.

KNOXVILLE MUSEUM OF ART

1050 World's Fair Park, Knoxville, 865-525-6101; www.knoxart.org

The museum holds four galleries, gardens, a great hall and the ARTcade. See the impressive collection of graphics on display.

Tuesday-Saturday 10 a.m.-5 p.m., Sunday 1-5 p.m.

KNOXVILLE ZOO

3500 Knoxville Zoo Drive, Knoxville, 865-637-5331; www.knoxville-zoo.org

The zoo is home to more than 1,000 animals, including red pandas (which the zoo has had much success breeding), snow leopards, gorillas, elephants and about 100 species of reptiles. The African elephants Mamie, Jana, Edie and Tonka paint with their trunks, and their artwork has sold for as much as $1,350. Kids will enjoy the petting zoo.

MCCLUNG HISTORICAL COLLECTION

East Tennessee Historical Center, 500 W. Church Ave., 865-544-5744

More than 38,000 volumes of history and genealogy covering Tennessee and Southeastern U.S. are housed in the center.

RAMSEY HOUSE (SWAN POND)

2614 Thorngrove Pike, Knoxville, 865-546-0745; www.ramseyhouse.org

The first stone house in Knox County, built for Col. Francis A. Ramsey, was a social, religious and political center of early Tennessee. The restored gabled house with an attached kitchen features ornamental cornices, keystone arches and period furnishings. Picnicking is available.

April-October, Tuesday-Sunday; November-March, by appointment.

OAK RIDGE

AMERICAN MUSEUM OF SCIENCE AND ENERGY

300 S. Tulane Ave., Oak Ridge, 865-576-3200; www.amse.org

Much cooler than physics class, this museum is one of the world's largest energy exhibitions. Here you'll learn about fossil fuels, energy alternatives, resources and research through hands-on exhibits, displays, models, films, games and live demonstrations.

Monday-Saturday 9 a.m.-5 p.m., Sunday 1-5 p.m.

CHILDREN'S MUSEUM OF OAK RIDGE
461 W. Outer Drive, Oak Ridge, 865-482-1074; www.childrensmuseumofoakridge.org
Hands-on exhibits and displays include the International Gallery, Discovery Lab, Playscape, Nature Walk, Pioneer Living and Oak Ridge history. Performances, exhibits, seminars and workshops are also on offer.
September-May, Tuesday-Friday 9 a.m.-5 p.m., Saturday 10 a.m.-4 p.m., Sunday 1-4 p.m.; June-August, Monday-Friday 9 a.m.-5 p.m., Saturday 10 a.m.-4 p.m., Sunday 1-4 p.m.

FROZEN HEAD STATE PARK
964 Flat Fork Road, Wartburg, 37887, 423-346-3318; www.state.tn.us
The park takes up more than 12,000 acres in Cumberland Mountains. It offers trout fishing, hiking trails, picnicking, a playground, primitive camping and a visitor center.
Daily dawn-dusk.

INTERNATIONAL FRIENDSHIP BELL
Badger Avenue, Oak Ridge
A symbol of everlasting peace, the bell was designed to celebrate the dedication of Manhattan Project workers.

PIGEON FORGE
THE COMEDY BARN
2775 Parkway, Pigeon Forge, 865-428-5222; www.comedybarn.com
This entertaining family comedy variety show has magicians, jugglers, comedians and live music.
March-December, daily.

DOLLYWOOD
1020 Dollywood Lane, Pigeon Forge, 865-428-9488; www.dollywood.com
Dolly Parton's entertainment park is as big of a presence as its namesake. The park provides more than 40 musical shows daily. It also has more than 30 rides and attractions and 70 shops and restaurants.

FLYAWAY INDOOR SKYDIVING
3106 Parkway, Pigeon Forge, 877-293-0639; www.flyawayindoorskydiving.com
A vertical wind tunnel simulates skydiving. The instructor assists participants in the flight chamber and explains how to maneuver the body to soar, turn and descend. There's also an observation gallery.
March-November, daily.

MEMORIES THEATRE
2141 Parkway, Pigeon Forge, 865-428-7852, 800-325-3078; www.memoriestheatre.com
Each show is a tribute to musical legends of the past and present, such as Tom Jones, Cher, Elvis Presley, Kenny Rogers and Buddy Holly.
Monday-Saturday 8 p.m.

THE OLD MILL
2944 Middle Creek Road, Pigeon Forge, 865-453-4628; www.old-mill.com
This water-powered mill has been in continuous operation since 1830,

grinding cornmeal, grits, whole wheat, rye and buckwheat flours. The dam falls are illuminated at night.

April-November, Monday-Saturday.

SMOKY MOUNTAIN CAR MUSEUM
2970 Parkway, Pigeon Forge, 865-453-3433

This museum houses more than 30 gas, electric and steam autos, including Hank Williams Jr.'s "Silver Dollar" car, James Bond's "007" Aston Martin, Al Capone's bulletproof Cadillac and Elvis Presley's Mercedes.

May-October, daily.

SEVIERVILLE
FORBIDDEN CAVERNS
455 Blowing Cave Road, Sevierville, 865-453-5972; www.forbiddencavern.com

Tennessee has more caves than any other state, and the tour through the Forbidden Caverns is a spectacular show, even if it does get a little help from manmade additions, like lights and stereophonic sound presentations.

April-November, daily 10 a.m.-6 p.m.

NASCAR SPEEDPARK
1545 Parkway, Sevierville, 865-908-5500; www.nascarspeedpark.com

Raring for some time on the racetrack? You can get into the action here. Eight tracks offer levels ranging from the quarter-mile Smoky Mountain Speedway for drivers 16 and older, down to the Baby Bristol, a 200-foot starter track for kids. Or climb into a mock stock car and experience centrifugal forces, turns and crash impacts as you "drive" a full-motion NASCAR Silicon Motor Speedway simulator. Other attractions include a state-of-the-art arcade, kiddie rides, an indoor climbing wall, miniature golf and bumper boats.

WHERE TO STAY

CHATTANOOGA
★★★CHATTANOOGA MARRIOTT AT THE CONVENTION CENTER
2 Carter Plaza, Chattanooga, 423-756-0002, 800-228-9290; www.marriott.com

This high-rise hotel is in the heart of downtown, next to the convention center and near shopping, restaurants and great nightlife. Guest rooms feature contemporary furnishings and décor. Great downtown views can be seen from the third-floor outdoor pool area.

342 rooms. Restaurant, bar. Pool. $61-150

GATLINBURG
★★★EIGHT GABLES INN
219 N. Mountain Trail, Gatlinburg, 865-430-3344, 800-279-5716; www.eightgables.com

In a wooded setting that inspires tranquility, this country inn is perfect for a romantic getaway. Explore nearby attractions such as fly-fishing, golf and white-water rafting, or opt to spend the afternoon on the porch, admiring the grounds. Guest rooms are furnished with feather-top beds; suites have fireplaces and two-person whirlpool tubs. In addition to a five-course breakfast, the room rate includes nightly dessert and access to the inn's pantry. The inn serves candlelit dinners of regional Southern cuisine three days a week.

19 rooms. No children under 10. Complimentary breakfast. Restaurant. Spa. $151-250

KINGSPORT

★★★MARRIOTT MEADOWVIEW RESORT

1901 Meadowview Parkway, Kingsport, 423-578-6600, 800-228-9290;
www.meadowviewresort.com

Whether you decide to stick around the beautiful grounds of this vast resort or catch the excitement of a race at Bristol, the amenities and atmosphere here will not disappoint. For sporty types, the resort offers tennis, basketball, golf, mountain biking, freshwater fishing and volleyball; for those looking to relax, a dip in the outdoor pool.

195 rooms. Restaurant, bar. Pool. Tennis. Golf. $61-150

KNOXVILLE

★★★CROWNE PLAZA KNOXVILLE

401 Summit Hill Drive, Knoxville, 865-522-2600; www.crowneplaza.com

Located in the heart of downtown Knoxville, this hotel is convenient to many attractions, including the historic shopping district and the Old City. Rooms have been updated with down duvets and flat-screen TVs.

197 rooms. Restaurant, bar. Fitness center. $61-150

★★★HILTON KNOXVILLE

501 W. Church Ave., Knoxville, 865-523-2300; www.hilton.com

Located in downtown Knoxville and near the Tennessee River, this hotel offers great views from the upper floors. The University of Tennessee Conference Center is across the street, and many attractions and restaurants are nearby. The décor and furnishings are contemporary, and the lobby features a large granite fireplace with bookshelves on either side.

317 rooms. Restaurant, bar. Fitness center. Pool. $61-150

TOWNSEND

★★★RICHMONT INN B&B

220 Winterberry Lane, Townsend, 865-448-6751, 866-267-7086; www.richmontinn.com

Just 10 minutes from the entrance to Great Smoky Mountains National Park, this charming inn affords an elegant escape. The comfort and coziness of the rustic accents, such as wide-planked and slate floors, high exposed-beam ceilings and country furniture, are enhanced by the formal, attentive service.

14 rooms. No children under 12. Restaurant. Complimentary breakfast. $61-150

WALLAND

★★★★BLACKBERRY FARM

1471 W. Millers Cove Road, Walland, 37886, 865-984-8166; www.blackberryfarm.com

On a 4,200-acre estate in the foothills of Tennessee's Great Smoky Mountains, Blackberry is one of the South's most celebrated country inns. Those in the know commend its exquisite location, first-rate service and delicious food—the inn produces its own cheese, eggs, honey, vegetables and fruit for its guests. The property's two ponds and stream beckon anglers who travel here solely for the Orvis-endorsed fly-fishing; other diversions include horseback riding, swimming, hiking and tennis. Epicureans savor the regionally inspired haute cuisine. Housed in a charming 1870s farmhouse, the Aveda Concept Spa offers signature treatments using local blackberries to soothe and rejuvenate the body. *44 rooms. No children under 10. Restaurant. $251-350*

WHERE TO EAT

CHATTANOOGA

★★★212 MARKET

212 Market St., Chattanooga, 423-265-1212; www.212market.com

Local produce and meats are used in the frequently changing menu at 212 Market, a family-owned and operated restaurant in the heart of downtown Chattanooga. The brick exterior is set off with striped awnings and flower boxes, and the interior features contemporary Southwest décor, set off by colorful dinnerware, oak tables and chairs, local artwork and live plants. Guests can dine upstairs on the outdoor balcony, where there is seating at wrought-iron umbrella tables. A pianist performs every Friday evening, and a jazz band performs every third Sunday of the month.

Contemporary American. Lunch, dinner. $16-35

KNOXVILLE

★★★THE ORANGERY

5412 Kingston Pike, Knoxville, 865-588-2964; www.theorangeryrestaurant.com

A beautiful winding staircase is the first thing diners notice when they enter this elegant restaurant. Its interior is decorated with French provincial furnishings, chandeliers and antiques. A piano player entertains diners in the lounge, and large windows provide natural light and wonderful views of the beautiful gardens in the courtyard. The continental menu features specialties such as veal porterhouse, prime New York strip steak, buffalo with caramelized shallots, and elk chop with vegetable purée. Diners are sure to find perfect pairings for their meals on the restaurant's extensive wine list.

Continental. Lunch, dinner. Closed Sunday. $36-85

★★★REGAS

318 N. Gay St., Knoxville, 865-637-3427; www.connorconcepts.com

First opened as a stool-and-counter joint in 1919, Regas has since become one of Knoxville's most popular restaurants. The décor has a rich, Old World elegance with a cozy fireplace, beamed ceilings and brick-and-wood walls. The hearty lunch and dinner menus feature classic American cuisine, including steaks, chops, seafood and chicken. Save room for Regas' famous red velvet cake.

American. Lunch, dinner. Closed Sunday. $16-35

WALLAND

★★★★THE BARN

Blackberry Farm, 1471 W. Millers Cove Road, Walland, 800-648-4252; www.blackberryfarm.com

Designed in the same country-meets-luxury style that Blackberry Farm exhibits in its rooms, the visually stunning Barn restaurant allows guests to sample regionally inspired dishes on a nightly basis. Chef Adam Cooke uses the freshest ingredients from Blackberry Farm's onsite heirloom garden and its

housemade cheese, eggs and honey, and incorporates these ingredients into his unique Smoky Mountain "Foothills Cuisine." Diners choose from three menus: A chef's tasting menu, an à la carte menu or a garden tasting, featuring items such as seared foie gras with blackberries, frisee and toast.
American. Dinner. $36-85

GREAT SMOKY MOUNTAINS NATIONAL PARK

Half in North Carolina and half in Tennessee (with the state line smack in the middle), the Great Smoky Mountains National Park is renowned for its diversity of both flora and fauna. More than 95 percent of the park is covered in trees, and dense deciduous and spruce-fir forests blanket the area's valleys and ancient peaks, which range from 875 to 6,643 feet. The thick mixture of all this brush and trees creates a haze from the water and hydrocarbons thrown off by their leaves, resulting in a "smoky" appearance. These emerald-green stretches are dotted with numerous roaring waterfalls that help make every season—even winter—beautiful. More than 800,000 square miles became a National Park in 1934; they were designated an UNESCO World Heritage Site in 1983 and an International Biosphere Reserve.

The mountains were formed between 200 and 300 million years ago. As recently as the year 10,000 B.C., northern glaciers ground away the lands but stopped short of the Smokies, providing refuge for hundreds of different plant and animal species that can still be found here today. The Cherokee Nation first inhabited the region, and mountain people, whose ancestors came from England and Scotland, followed in the late 1700s. Remnants of their time here, including cabins, barns and mills, are still scattered throughout the park.

Whether to discover the historic abandoned buildings, hike, or just take in the dazzling fall foliage and amazing views, it's no wonder that 9 million visitors come here each year, making the Great Smoky Mountains one of America's busiest national parks.

WHAT TO SEE

A trip to the vast park is best begun at one of three main visitor centers. Serving the western corner of the park, the Cades Cove Visitor Center sits on the Caves Cove Loop. To the north, the **Sugarlands Visitor Center** *(Newfound Gap Road, 865-436-1291; open June-August, 8 a.m.-7 p.m.; April-May and September, 8 a.m.-6 p.m.; March and October, 8 a.m.-5 p.m.; November-February, 8 a.m.-4:30 p.m.)* is near Gatlinburg, Tennessee, and next to **Park Headquarters** *(107 Park Headquarters Road. Gatlinburg, 865-436-1200; www.nps.gov/grsm)*. The **Oconaluftee Visitor Center** *(828-497-1904; open daily 8 a.m.-7 p.m.; off-season schedule varies)* by Cherokee, North Carolina, provides access to the park from the south. In addition, there are four other visitor centers outside of the park in the towns of Gatlinburg, Sevierville and Townsend. Depending on your starting point, you can choose from two major loops through the park that give a great overview and allow you to see numerous sites: Cades Cove Loop Road and Newfound Gap Road.

If you begin at the Sugarlands Visitor Center, the Cades Cove Loop Road runs

11 miles west through forests and valleys to Cades Cove. The road has a number of stop-off sites that provide a glimpse of the rich history of the area through its buildings. The John Oliver Place is the first stop. Don't miss your chance to explore an early 19th-century log cabin nestled in a large valley. The white-frame Primitive Baptist Church and graveyard, Methodist Church and Missionary Baptist Church are good examples of pre–Civil War churches, and the Rich Mountain Road has great views of Cades Cove. The John Cable Mill is near the Cades Cove Visitor Center, where you can examine a wide variety of artifacts and learn about the history of early Great Smoky settlers.

The Newfound Gap Road runs about 45 miles southeast from the Sugarlands Visitor Center in the north to the Oconaluftee Visitor Center in the south. Passing from lowland cove hardwood pine-oak and northern hardwood forests to thick spruce-fir forests, don't be surprised if your ears pop as you ascend nearly 4,000 feet. Be sure to stop at the Chimney Tops Overlook, where the Sugarland Mountains' steep, tree-covered peaks jut up through fog-laced valleys. In the middle of the park, the Appalachian Trail cuts through the 5,048-foot Newfound Gap that sits on the Tennessee-North Carolina border. A trip from the visitor center to the gap is said to be equivalent to traveling from Georgia to Maine in terms of ecosystem variety. From climate to elevation to wildlife, the journey offers many different habitats along the way. A seven-mile detour on Clingmans Dome Road off the Newfound Gap Road is worth the trek, as it brings you to a half-mile trail that reaches the lookout tower at Clingmans Dome. Take in the amazing 360-degree views from here, the highest point in the park at 6,643 feet. It also has the distinction of being both the highest point in Tennessee and the third-highest mountain east of the Mississippi River.

Off the beaten paths of the north and western Smokies, the Cataloochee Valley lies in the rugged Balsam Mountains in the park's far eastern section. Soaring 6,000-foot peaks look down on this picturesque valley, which was once home to farms, orchards and early settlements. Today, visitors who make the long trip down the well-maintained gravel roads can see the remaining historic buildings as well as wildlife, including elk and bears.

Whether you're driving, hiking or biking the trails of the park, you will want to stop to view at least one of the many waterfalls. The Great Smokies' 85 inches of yearly rainfall and steep elevations make for spectacular falls and smaller cascades. Waterfalls are located throughout the park (maps are available at visitor centers and www.nps.gov/grsm/planyourvisit/waterfalls.htm), and most, like the popular Ramsey Cascades (the tallest waterfall in the park at 100 feet), are accessed by hiking trails. If you're not in the mood to walk, Meigs Falls (Little River Road, 13 miles west of Sugarlands Visitor Center) and Place of a Thousand Drips (Roaring Fork Motor Nature Trail, stop 15) are both accessible by car.

WHAT TO DO

HIKING

Hiking is extremely popular throughout the park, and there are more than 900 miles of trails and 170 miles of roads to explore, including 70 miles of the Appalachian Trail. For information on backcountry hiking, call 865-436-1297.

EASY

LAUREL FALLS

2.6 miles round-trip

Trailhead: From Sugarlands Visitor Center, turn toward Cades Cove on Little River Road and drive 3.5 miles.

This very popular paved trail will take you to the 80-foot waterfall. The trail is bordered by the evergreen laurel shrub, which blooms in May.

ANDREWS BALD

3.6 miles round-trip

Trailhead: Follow Clingmans Dome Road to the end (20 miles from Gatlinburg). Just before the restrooms, the Andrews Bald trailhead drops to the left.

This trail provides you with stunning views of the Smokies from one of only two grassy balds in the park, perfect for an afternoon picnic surrounded by sky. Just don't skimp on the carbs as the return trip requires a slight uphill climb.

MODERATE

RAINBOW FALLS

5.4 miles round-trip

Trailhead: Drive on Historic Nature Trail past the Noah "Bud" Ogle homesite to the clearly signed Rainbow Falls parking area.

This spectacular and popular trail climbs 1,500 feet to reach the 80-foot Rainbow Falls, whose mist creates a rainbow on sunny days. The adventurous can take the trail another four miles to Mount Le Conte.

STRENUOUS

ALUM CAVE BLUFFS TRAIL

10.4 miles round-trip

Trailhead: Alum Cave Bluffs parking area, approximately nine miles south of the Sugarlands Visitor Center or four miles north of Newfound Gap.

This trail follows the steepest path up Mount Le Conte. It climbs gently through old-growth forest until reaching the Arch Rock landmark. Continuing more steeply along rocky footing, which gets slick when wet, it also passes Gracie's Pulpit, named for Gracie McNichol who hiked this trail on her 92nd birthday. On the 6,000-foot plateau is the Le Conte Lodge and spur trails to the four peaks of Le Conte. The Alum Cave Bluffs Trail joins the Rainbow Falls trail at this point.

CHARLIE'S BUNION

12.8-mile loop

Trailhead: Newfound Gap parking area.

A 1925 wildfire that razed the slopes of this promontory, named for a hiker's inflamed big toe, created an exceptional view. The total elevation gain is over 4,500 feet, so you'll want to start early and dedicate a day to this trail, but the panoramas are worth it.

CHIMNEY TOPS

4 miles round-trip

Trailhead: Chimney Tops parking lot off Newfound Gap Road.

This trail starts gently but becomes rugged as it takes you on a 1,350-foot ascent to a breathtaking view—and a rock face, which is the Chimney. The daring and fit can use hands and knees to climb a crack in the Chimney and reach the summit.

HIKING AND NATURE STUDY ADVENTURES

Want to take an overnight backpack trip with experienced guides or have a scientist point out and explain black bears and other wildlife? A great way to learn about the park is through programs offered by the **Great Smoky Mountains Institute at Tremont** (9275 Tremont Road, Townsend, TN, 865-448-6709; www.gsmit.org) or the **Smoky Mountain Field School** (313 Conference Center Building, Knoxville, 865-974-0150; www.ce.utk.edu/smoky). Both offer programs and classes for adults, and kids will love the multiday summer youth camps with hands-on activities from canoeing to field research.

FISHING

More than 2,115 miles of streams and 40 species of fish make for superb angling in the Great Smoky Mountains National Park. From coldwater smallmouth bass streams to headwater trout streams, fishing is allowed year-round in most waters. Fishing is permitted from 30 minutes before sunrise to 30 minutes after sunset; check visitor centers for off-limits areas. Tennessee or North Carolina fishing permits are required for anglers over 12 in Tennessee and over 15 in North Carolina and are available in area towns.

HORSEBACK RIDING

Riding is allowed on 550 miles of trails within the park. Five horse camps (Anthony Creek/Cades Cove, Big Creek, Cataloochee, Round Bottom and Towstring) provide easy access to backcountry trails April to mid-November, 10 a.m.-10 p.m. Reservations are required (877-444-6777). For visitors without their own animals, the **Cades Cove Riding Stables** offers guided horseback tours ($15 an hour) as well as hay and carriage rides April to October (10018 Campground Drive, Townsend, 865-448-6286). Horses can also be rented from **Smoky Mountain Riding Stables** (Highway 321 four miles east of Gatlinburg, 865-436-5634; www.smokymountainridingstables.com) and the **Sugarlands Riding Stable** (1409 E. Parkway, Gatlinburg, 865-436-3535).

BIKING

While there are no mountain biking trails in the Great Smoky Mountains, cycling is permitted on the gravel Gatlinburg Trail, Oconaluftee River Trail and Lower Deep Creek Trail. The Foothills Parkway, 11-mile one-way Cades Cove Loop Road and Cataloochee areas also offer decent routes. You can bring your own bike or rent one from the Cades Cove Store (near Cades Cove Campground, 865-448-9034).

WILDLIFE

Smoky the Bear never actually lived here (the bear who inspired the safety campaign was from New Mexico), but plenty of other black bears reside in the park. You may even see some elk. The Great Smoky Mountain region is also a top destination for birdwatchers.

BEARS

Perhaps the animal most associated with the Smokies is the black bear. Up to about six feet in length, the females usually weigh around 100 pounds and males about 250, but both can double their weights as they prepare for winter. Black bears are omnivores, and 85 percent of their diet consists of plants, berries and nuts. There are currently about 1,600 living throughout the park. Bears in this region usually re-emerge from their slumbers in late March or early April and remain most active through the spring and summer months. You have the best chance of spotting a black bear in open areas like Cades Cove or Cataloochee Valley.

FISH

Fishing is a popular sport in the park, but surprisingly, only about 800 out of the 2,100 miles of streams here actually contain fish. There are more than 60 species represented, including bass, suckers and lampreys. The park has one of the few remaining wild trout habitats left in the eastern United States, and an aggressive park initiative has restored the native brook trout.

ELK

Weighing in at up to 700 pounds, elk are the park's biggest mammals. They mostly inhabit the Cataloochee area, where they feed on grasses, bark, buds and leaves. Until 2001, these animals hadn't been seen in the Great Smoky Mountains for nearly 200 years, but thanks to an experimental release program, more than 50 elk were brought to the park. (River otters and peregrine falcons are two other examples of animals that the National Park Service has successfully reintroduced to the area.) The best time to try to see an elk is in the early morning or late evening.

BIRDS

About 240 species of birds have been spotted in the park. Of those, 60 live in the park year-round, 120 breed here and the remaining species use the forested region as a layover on their migratory routes. Because the mountain chain's upper ridges so closely resemble Canada's boreal forests, the region's saw-whet owls, Canada warblers, black-capped chickadees and winter wrens, among other birds, use the spruce and fir trees as breeding grounds. The middle and lower elevations are the best places to see birds. Downy woodpeckers, American goldfinches, song sparrows and belted kingfishers are just a few species that flit through the hardwoods, while red-tailed hawks, wild turkeys and eastern meadowlarks prefer the park's open fields.

WHERE TO STAY

Gatlinburg is just minutes from Great Smoky Mountains National Park, and many hotels offer trolley access to area attractions. Townsend, located at the gateway to Great Smoky Mountains National Park, also offers convenient lodging options for those visiting the park and other east Tennessee attractions. If you're interested in camping, there are ten campgrounds scattered throughout the park. Smokemont, Elkmont, Cades Cove and Cosby take reservations *(mid-May to October, 877-444-6777; www.recreation.gov)*, while the other seven are first-come, first-served. Each has restrooms and water but no showers. Stays are limited to seven days in summer and fall and 14 days off-season. Fees range from $14 to $23 per night. Backcountry camping is permitted with reservations and permits, which are available at ranger stations and visitor centers *(865-436-1231, daily 8 a.m.-6 p.m.)*. Check *www.nps.gov/grsm/planyourvisit/carcamping.htm* for more information.

WHERE TO EAT

RECOMMENDED
GATLINBURG

MAXWELL'S STEAK AND SEAFOOD
1103 Parkway, Gatlinburg, 865-436-3738; www.maxwellssteakandseafood.com

Maxwell's is a nice change of pace from the chain restaurants that dominate the area. Seafood fans will appreciate the Smoky Mountain rainbow trout, a local favorite, while beef lovers can choose from a wide selection, including prime rib, charbroiled filet mignon and rib-eye steak. Desserts include homemade cheesecake.
American menu. Dinner. Bar. $16-35

THE PARK GRILL STEAKHOUSE
110 Parkway, Gatlinburg, 865-436-2300; www.parkgrillgatlinburg.com

This rustic log cabin–style restaurant is located on the main street in downtown Gatlinburg. Its whimsical decorations include antler fixtures, bird sounds and an outdoor waterfall. The menu mostly focuses on steaks and seafood, including area favorites like ribs and trout. There is also an impressive salad bar for diners to try while listening to the live piano music (offered six nights a week).
American menu. Dinner. Bar. $16-35

THE PEDDLER RESTAURANT
820 River Road, Gatlinburg, 865-436-5794; www.peddlergatlinburg.com

Literally constructed around the cabin of one of Gatlinburg's first pioneer families, this restaurant is within the park boundaries. The dining room has a cozy atmosphere, with cedar paneling and furniture, and covered porch seating gives diners extra-special views of the river. The menu offers favorites such as steaks, ribs, chicken and trout, all in generous portions. Be sure to leave room for the monstrous mud pie or hot blackberry cobbler for dessert.
American. Dinner. Bar. $16-35

PIGEON FORGE

OLD MILL
164 Old Mill Ave., Pigeon Forge, 865-429-3463; www.old-mill.com

Located in an old mill on a river (ask for a window seat), this popular tourist restaurant is conveniently situated off a parkway in the heart of Pigeon Forge with specialty shops nearby. The charming and cozy interior features wood floors and ceiling beams, antique furniture and accents and an open kitchen. The menu includes a great selection of Southern-style homemade meals.
American, Southern. Breakfast, lunch, dinner. $16-35

SEVIERVILLE

APPLEWOOD FARMHOUSE RESTAURANT

240 Apple Valley Road, Sevierville, 865-428-1222; www.applewoodfarmhouserestaurant.com

Acres of apple trees and a wraparound porch with comfortable rockers greet diners at this downtown Sevierville restaurant. The interior features a country-cozy décor with double fireplaces, oak tables and chairs, and other antiques. Fritters and juleps are served when seated—a preview of the delicious Southern country cuisine to come. It's a great choice for authentic down-home cooking.

American, Southern. Breakfast, lunch, dinner. $15 and under

INDEX

Numbers

21C Museum Hotel
  Louisville, 61
212 Market
  Chattanooga, 222
1886 Crescent Hotel & Spa
  Eureka Springs, 44

A

Abita Brew Pub
  Abita Springs, LA, 150
Abita Mystery House/
    UCM Museum
  Abita Springs, LA, 148
Abita Springs
  Abita Springs, LA, 148,
    150
Acadian Village: A
    Museum of Acadian
    Heritage and
    Culture
  Lafayette, LA, 96
Adventure Science
    Museum
  Nashville, TN, 189
Aidan Gill
  New Orleans, LA, 147
Alabama Constitution
    Village
  Huntsville, AL, 12

Alabama Gulf Coast Zoo
  Gulf Shores, AL, 36
Alabama Music Hall of
    Fame
  Tuscumbia, AL, 15
Alabama Shakespeare
    Festival
  Montgomery, AL, 26
Alabama Sports Hall of
    Fame Museum
  Birmingham, AL, 16
Allstate Sugar Bowl
    College Football
    Classic
  New Orleans, LA, 130
Alum Cave Bluffs Trail,
    225
American Museum of
    Science and Energy
  Oak Ridge, TN, 218
American Printing House
    for The Blind
  Louisville, KY, 57
American Rose Center
  Shreveport, LA, 91
American Saddlebred
    Museum
  Lexington, KY, 76
Ampersand
  New Orleans, LA, 108

Ancestral Home of James
    K. Polk
    Columbia, TN, 204
Anchuca Historic Mansion
    and Inn
    Vicksburg, MS, 165
Anchuca
    Vicksburg, MS, 168
Andrews Bald, 225
Annie Miller's Swamp &
    Marsh Tours
    Houma, LA, 94
Antoine's
    New Orleans, LA, 139
Appalachian Caverns
    Blountville, TN, 213
Appalachian Center for
    Crafts
    Smithville, TN, 205
Appalachians
    Appalachians, KY, 56, 81
Applewood Farmhouse
    Restaurant
    Sevierville, TN, 229
Arkansas, 3
Arkansas Alligator Farm &
    Petting Zoo
    Hot Springs, AR, 46
Arkansas Arts Center
    Little Rock, AR, 49
Arlington Antebellum
    Home and Gardens
    Birmingham, AL, 16

Arlington Resort Hotel
    and Spa
    Hot Springs, AR, 48
Arnaud's
    New Orleans, LA, 139
Ashland
    Ashland, KY, 83
    Lexington, KY, 76
Ashley's
    Little Rock, AR, 53
The Athenaeum
    Columbia, TN, 205
Audubon Aquarium of the
    Americas
    New Orleans, LA, 110
Audubon Nature Institute
    New Orleans, LA, 110
Audubon Zoo
    New Orleans, LA, 110
The Austin Hotel &
    Convention Center
    Hot Springs, AR, 49
Avery Island, 97
Azalea Trail Run Festival
    and Festival of
    Flowers
    Mobile, AL, 34

B

Bacco
    New Orleans, LA, 139
The Barn, 187
    Walland, TN, 222

Bastrop, 89

Baton Rouge, 89, 101

Battlefield Park
Jackson, MS, 155

Battles for Chattanooga
Museum
Chattanooga, TN, 209

Battleship Memorial Park,
USS Alabama
Mobile Bay, AL, 31

Bay Fest
Mobile, AL, 34

Bayona
New Orleans, LA, 139

Bayou Barriere Golf
Course
Belle Chasse, LA, 110

Bays Mountain
Planetarium
Kingsport, TN, 215

BBQ
Uptown, LA, 141

Beachaven Vineyard &
Winery
Clarksville, TN, 203

Beale Street, 183
Memphis, TN, 179

Beale Street Music Festival
Memphis, TN, 184

Beaumont Inn
Harrodsburg, KY, 79

Beauregard-Keyes House
and Garden
New Orleans, LA, 110

Beau Rivage by Mirage
Resorts
Biloxi, MS, 174

"Beauvoir"-Jefferson Davis
Home and Presi-
dential Library
Biloxi, MS, 171

Beaver Lake
Rogers, AR, 43

Beck Cultural Exchange
Center-Museum of
Black History and
Culture
Knoxville, TN, 217

Behringer-Crawford
Museum
Covington, KY, 68

Beignets
French Quarter, LA, 141

Belle Meade Plantation
Nashville, TN, 189

Bellingrath Gardens and
Home
Mobile, AL, 31

Belmont Mansion
Nashville, TN, 191

Bennett's Mill Bridge
Ashland, KY, 83

Bible Museum
Eureka Springs, AR, 40

Biedenharn Family House
  Monroe, LA, 91
Biedenharn Museum of
    Coca-Cola
    Memorabilia
  Vicksburg, MS, 165
Bienville National Forest
  Mendenhall, MS, 160
Big Spring Jam
  Huntsville, AL, 14
Biking, 226
Biloxi, 171
Biloxi City Center
  Biloxi, MS, 171
Birmingham, 16
Birmingham Botanical
    Gardens
  Birmingham, AL, 16
Birmingham Civil Rights
    Institute
  Birmingham, AL, 16
Birmingham International
    Festival
  Birmingham, AL, 22
Birmingham Jefferson
    Convention
    Complex
  Birmingham, AL, 17
Birmingham Museum Of
    Art
  Birmingham, AL, 17
Birmingham Zoo
  Birmingham, AL, 18

Birthplace of the Frog
    Exhibit
  East Leland, MS, 154
Black Belt
  Black Belt, AL, 11, 24
Blackberry Farm, 198
  Walland, TN, 221
Black Heritage Tour
  Selma, AL, 28
Blanchard Springs Caverns
  Mountain View, AR, 43
Blessing of the Fleet
  Biloxi, MS, 172
Blue Dog Cafe
  Lafayette, LA, 100
The Bluegrass Region
  Lexington, KY, 71
Bluegrass Region
  Lexington, KY, 56
Blue Heron Mining
    Community
  Cumberland, KY, 85
Blue Licks Battlefield State
    Resort Park
  Mount Olivet, KY, 69
Blue's Week
  Baton Rouge, LA, 105
Boatyard Park
  Kingsport, 215
Bon Secour National
    Wildlife Refuge
  Gulf Shores, AL, 36

Booker T. Washington
    Monument
  Tuskegee, AL, 29
Bouligny Plaza
  New Iberia, LA, 97
Bourbon Street
  New Orleans, LA, 111
Bragg-Mitchell Mansion
  Mobile, AL, 31
Brec's Baton Rouge Zoo
  Baton Rouge, LA, 101
Brec's Magnolia Mound
    Plantation
  Baton Rouge, LA, 101
Brennan's
  New Orleans, LA, 140
Bridge City Gumbo
    Festival
  New Orleans, LA, 130
Brigtsen's
  New Orleans, LA, 140
Brimstone Historic
    Society Museum
  Sulphur, LA, 96
Brooks Shaw & Son Old
    Country Store
  Jackson, TN, 178
Broussard's
  New Orleans, LA, 140
The Brown Hotel
  Louisville, KY, 62
Bry Hall Art Gallery
  Monroe, LA, 91

Buck's Pocket State Park
  Guntersville, AL, 20
Burgess Falls State Natural
    Area
  Sparta, TN, 205
Burns Park
  North Little Rock, AR, 49
Burritt Museum & Park
  Huntsville, AL, 12

C

The Cabildo
  New Orleans, LA, 111
Cahawba
  Selma, AL, 28
Cajun Country, 89, 93
Canal Street Depot
  Natchez, MS, 161
The Capital Hotel
  Little Rock, AR, 52
Capital/River, 160
Capitol Grille,
      Nashville, TN, 187,
    199
Carmichael's Bookstore
  Louisville, KY, 65
Carroll Chimes Bell Tower
  Covington, KY, 67
Carter Caves State Resort
    Park
  Olive Hill, KY, 84
Carter House
  Franklin, TN, 206

Casey Jones Home and
  Railroad Museum
Jackson, TN, 178, 180
Casey Jones Village
Jackson, TN, 178
Cathedral Basilica of the
  Assumption
Covington, KY, 67
Cathedral Garden
New Orleans, LA, 111
Cathedral of the
  Immaculate
  Conception
Mobile, AL, 31
Cave Hill Cemetery
Louisville, KY, 57
Cave Run Lake
Morehead, KY, 83
C. Bickham Dickson Park
Shreveport, LA, 91
Cedar Grove
Vicksburg, MS, 165
Cedar Grove Mansion Inn
Vicksburg, MS, 168
Cemetery & Voodoo
  History Tour
New Orleans, LA, 111
Center Hill Dam and Lake
Lancaster, TN, 205
Central Cities
Central Cities, AL, 11, 15

Chapel, Tuskegee
  University
Tuskegee, AL, 29
Charlie's Bunion, 225
Chateau Bourbon, A
  Wyndham Historic
  Hotel
New Orleans, LA, 129
Chattanooga, 209, 220,
  222
Chattanooga African-
  American Museum
Chattanooga, TN, 209
Chattanooga Choo-Choo
Chattanooga, TN, 209
Chattanooga Marriott at
  the Convention
  Center
Chattanooga, TN, 220
Chattanooga Nature
  Center at
  Reflection Riding
Chattanooga, TN, 209
Cheaha State Park
Delta, AL, 22
Cheekwood Botanical
  Garden and
  Museum of Art
Nashville, TN, 191
Chemin-A-Haut State Park
Bastrop, LA, 89
Chez Philippe, 187
Memphis, TN, 187

The Children's Museum of
    Memphis, 180
    Memphis, TN, 179
Children's Museum of
    Oak Ridge
    Oak Ridge, TN, 219
Chimney Tops, 225
Chitimacha Cultural
    Center
    Franklin, LA, 94
The Chophouse Vintage
    Year
    Montgomery, AL, 30
Chretien Point Plantation
    Lafayette, LA, 96
Christ Of The Ozarks
    Eureka Springs, AR, 41
Chucalissa Archaeological
    Museum
    Memphis, TN, 179
Churchhill Downs
    Louisville, KY, 57
City Park
    New Orleans, LA, 111
Civil Rights Memorial
    Montgomery, AL, 26
Clarksdale, 153
Clarksville, 203
Clinton Presidential
    Library and
    Museum
    Little Rock, AR, 50
Coastal Region, 169

Cochon Butcher
    New Orleans, LA, 145
Coleman's Crystal Mine
    Jesseville, AR, 47
Colonel Harland Sanders'
    Original Restaurant
    Corbin, KY, 85
Columbia, 204
The Comedy Barn
    Pigeon Forge, TN, 219
Commander's Palace
    New Orleans, LA, 140
Conde-Charlotte Museum
    House
    Mobile, AL, 32
Confederate Memorial
    Hall
    Knoxville, TN, 217
Constitution Square State
    Shrine
    Danville, KY, 73
Contemporary Arts
    Center
    New Orleans, LA, 112
Cookeville, 205
Corbin
    Corbin, KY, 85
Cottage Plantation
    Francisville, LA, 101
Country Music Hall of
    Fame and Museum
    Nashville, TN, 191, 193
Covington, 148

Covington (Cincinnati Airport Area)
Covington, KY, 67
Cragfont
Castalian Springs, TN, 207
Cravens House
Chattanooga, TN, 209
Creative Discovery Museum
Chattanooga, TN, 210
Creole Nature Trail National Scenic Byway
Sulphur, LA, 96
Crescent Bend (Armstrong-Lockett House) and W. Perry Toms Memorial Gardens
Knoxville, TN, 217
Crescent City Farmers Market
New Orleans, LA, 112
Crossroads, 89
Crossville, 205
Crowne Plaza Knoxville
Knoxville, TN, 221
The Crystal Dining Room
Eureka Springs, AR, 45
Crystal Shrine Grotto
Memphis, TN, 179
Cumberland Mountain State Park
Crossville, TN, 205

Cumberland Gap National Historical Park
Corbin, KY, 85
Cuvee
New Orleans, LA, 140
Cypremort Point State Park
Franklin, LA, 94
Cypress Grove Nature Park
Jackson, TN, 178

D

Daisy International Airgun Museum
Rogers, AR, 43
Daniel Boone Country
Corbin, KY, 85
Daniel Boone's Grave
Frankfort, KY, 74
Danville
Danville, KY, 73
Dauphine Orleans Hotel
New Orleans, LA, 132
Dauphin Island
Dauphin Island, AL, 35
Dauphin Island Campground
Dauphin Island, AL, 35
Davy Crockett Birthplace State Park
Limestone, TN, 213
Delta, 153

The Delta, 153

Delta Blues Museum
  Clarksdale, MS, 153

Derby Region, 56

De Soto National Forest
  Wiggins, MS, 173

Desoto State Park
  Fort Payne, AL, 20

Destrehan Plantation
  Destrehan, LA, 112

Dexter Avenue King
    Memorial Baptist
    Church
  Montgomery, AL, 26

Dixon Gallery and
    Gardens
  Memphis, TN, 179

D'Lo Water Park
  Mendenhall, MS, 160

Dollywood
  Pigeon Forge, TN, 219

Domenica
  New Orleans, LA, 145

Doubletree Guest Suites
    Lexington
  Lexington, KY, 79

Downtown Franklin
  Franklin, TN, 202

Duff Green
  Vicksburg, MS, 165

Duff Green Mansion
  Vicksburg, MS, 169

Dunbar Cave State Natural
    Area
  Clarksville, TN, 204

Dunleith Plantation
  Natchez, MS, 167

E

East Tennessee, 177, 208

East Tennessee Discovery
    Center & Akima
    Planetarium
  *Knoxville, Chilhowee
    Park, TN,* 217

Eight Gables Inn
  Gatlinburg, TN, 220

Ellington Argicultural
    Center
  Nashville, TN, 191

Elsong Gardens &
    Conservatory
  Monroe, LA, 91

Elvis Presley International
    Tribute Week
  Memphis, TN, 184

Emerald Mound
  Natchez, MS, 162

Emeril's Restaurant
  New Orleans, LA, 142

Empress Of Little Rock
  Little Rock, AR, 53

The English Grill
  Louisville, KY, 62

Entergy Imax Theatre
  New Orleans, LA, 112
E.P. "Tom" Sawyer State
  Park
  Louisville, KY, 57
Erling Jensen
  Memphis, TN, 188
Ernest Tubb Record Shop,
  193
  Nashville, TN, 192
Eufaula National Wildlife
  Refuge
  Eufaula, AL, 20
Eureka Springs
  Eureka Springs, AR, 40
Eureka Springs Historial
  Museum
  Eureka Springs, 41
Eureka Springs & North
  Arkansas Railway
  Eureka Springs, AR, 41
European Antique Market
  Louisville, KY, 65
Evangeline Oak
  Martinville, LA, 98
Exchange Place
  Kingsport, TN, 215

F

Fair Grounds Race Course
  New Orleans, LA, 113

Farmington Historic
  Home
  Louisville, KY, 58
Festival of the Bluegrass
  Lexington, KY, 77
F & F Botanica
  New Orleans, LA, 112
First White House Of The
  Confederacy
  Montgomery, AL, 27
Fishing, 226
Floral Clock
  Frankfort, KY, 74
Flyaway Indoor Skydiving
  Pigeon Forge, TN, 219
Fontainebleau State Park
  Mandeville, LA, 148
Forbidden Caverns
  Sevierville, TN, 220
Fordyce Bathhouse
    Museum & Hot
    Springs National
    Park Vistor Center
  Hot Springs, AR, 47
Fort Gaines
  Dauphin Island, AL, 35
Fort Morgan
  Gulf Shores, AL, 37
Fort Morgan Museum
  Gulf Shores, AL, 37
Fort Morgan Park
  Gulf Shores, AL, 37

Fort Nashborough
  Nashville, TN, 192
Fort Pike State Commem-
    orative Area
  Slidell, LA, 150
Fort Toulouse/Jackson
    Park National
    Historic Landmark
  Montgomery, AL, 27
Frankfort
  Frankfort, KY, 74
Franklin, 94, 206
French Market
  New Orleans, LA, 113
Frenchmen Street
  New Orleans, LA,
    119
French Quarter
  New Orleans, LA,
    113
French Quarter Festival
  New Orleans, LA, 130
French Quarter Walking
    Tours
  New Orleans, LA, 113
The Friendship Oak
  Pass Christian, MS, 174
Frog Fantasies Museum
  Eureka Springs, AR, 41
Frozen Head State Park
  Wartburg, TN, 219
F.Scott and Zelda
    Fitzgerald Museum
  Montgomery, AL, 27
F. Scott's
  Nashville, TN, 200

G

Gatlinburg, 213, 220
Gatlinburg Space Needle
  Gatlinburg, TN, 213
Galatoire's
  New Orleans, LA, 142
Gallatin, 207
Gallier House
  New Orleans, LA, 113
The Garden District
  New Orleans, LA, 114
Gatlinburg, 228
Gautreau's
  New Orleans, LA, 142
Gaylord Opryland Resort
    and Convention
    Center
  Nashville, TN, 196
General Jackson Showboat
  Nashville, TN, 192
Georgetown
  Georgetown, KY, 75
George Washington
    Carver Museum
  Tuskegee, AL, 29
Germantown Museum
  Minden, LA, 90
Governor's Mansion
  Baton Rouge, LA, 101
  Jackson, MS, 155
Gov. William Blount
    Mansion
  Knoxville, TN, 217

Graceland, 183
  Memphis, TN, 180
The Grand Dining Room
  Point Clear, AL, 34
Grand Casino Hotel Biloxi
  Biloxi, MS, 174
Grand Circuit Meet
  Lexington, KY, 77
Grand Gulf Military Park
  Port Gibson, MS, 164
Grand Hotel Marriott
    Resort, Golf Club
    & Spa
  Point Clear, AL, 33
Grand Ole Opry, 193
  Nashville, TN, 192
Grand Ole Opry Tours
  Nashville, TN, 192
Grand Village of The
    National Natchez
  Natchez, MS, 162
Gratz Park Inn
  Lexington, KY, 80
Gray Lines Bus Tours
  New Orleans, LA, 114
Grayson Lake State Park
  Olive Hill, KY, 84
Greater New Orleans, 148
Great Smoky Mountains
    National Park, 223
Greenbo Lake State
    Resort Park
  Ashland, KY, 83

Greeneville, 213
Grevemberg House
  Franklin, LA, 94
Griffin Gate Marriott
    Resort and Spa
  Lexington, KY, 80
The Grill Room
  New Orleans, LA, 143
Grill 83
  Memphis, TN, 188
Gulf Coast Towns
  Gulf Coast Towns, AL,
    11, 35
Gulfport, 171
Gulf Shores
  Gulf Shores, AL, 36
Gulf State Park
  Gulf Shores, AL, 37
Gumbo
  Treme, LA, 141

H

Hadley Pottery Company
  Louisville, KY, 65
Hammond Museum Of
    Bells
  Eureka Springs, AR, 41
Hampton Inn & Suites
    Birmingham-
    Downtown-
    Tutwiler
  Birmingham, AL, 23

Hands On! Regional
    Museum
    Johnson City, TN, 213
Harrah's New Orleans
    New Orleans, LA, 114
Harrison County Sand
    Beach
    Biloxi, MS, 171
Harrodsburg
    Harrodsburg, KY, 75, 79
Hattiesburg, 173
Hazel's Seafood Restaurant
    Orange Beach, AL, 38
Headley-Whitney Mu-
    seum
    Lexington, KY, 76
Hensley Settlement
    Corbin, KY, 86
Herbsaint
    New Orleans, LA, 145
Heritage Museum And
    Village
    Baker, LA, 102
Heritage Trail
    Franklin, TN, 206
Hermann Grima House
    New Orleans, LA, 114
The Hermitage
    Nashville, TN, 192
The Hermitage Hotel
    Nashville, TN, 197, 198
Herrington Lake
    Danville, KY, 73

Highlands
    Birmingham, AL, 24
Highlands Museum &
    Discovery Center
    Ashland, KY, 83
Hiking, 224
Hiking And Nature Study
    Adventures, 226
Hillsboro Village
    Nashville, TN, 202
Hilton Birmingham Pe-
    rimeter Park
    Birmingham, AL, 23
Hilton Jackson
    Jackson, MS, 158
Hilton Knoxville
    Knoxville, TN, 221
Hilton Lafayette And
    Towers
    Lafayette, LA, 100
Hilton Memphis
    Memphis, TN, 186
Hilton New Orleans
    Airport
    Kenner, LA, 150
Hilton New Orleans
    Riverside
    New Orleans, LA, 132
Hilton Shreveport
    Shreveport, LA, 92
Hilton Suites Lexington
    Green
    Lexington, KY, 81

Historic Arkansas
  Museum
  Little Rock, AR, 50
Historic Carnton and
  McGavock Confed-
  erate Cemetery
  Franklin, TN, 206
Historic "Charpentier"
  Lake Charles, LA, 96
Historic District
  Franklin, TN, 206
  Jonesborough, TN, 213
Historic Districts
  Old Louisville, KY, 59
Historic Jefferson College
  Washington, MS, 162
Historic New Orleans
  Collection
  New Orleans, LA, 114
Historic Rugby
  Rugby, TN, 207
Historic Springfield
  Plantation
  Natchez, MS, 162
Historic Washington
  Washington, KY, 69
Homesteads Tower
  Museum
  Crossville, TN, 205
Homochitto National
  Forest
  Natchez, MS, 162
Horseback Riding, 226

Horse Farms
  Lexington, KY, 78
Hotel Indigo
  Nashville, TN, 199
Hotel Le Cirque
  New Orleans, LA, 132
Hotel Monteleone
  New Orleans, LA, 133
Hotel Preston
  Nashville, TN, 197
Hot Springs Mountain
  Tower
  Hot Springs, AR, 47
House of Blues
  New Orleans, LA, 115
Houma, 94
Houmas House
  Burnside, LA, 103
The House on Ellicott Hill
  Natchez, MS, 162
The Howlin' Wolf
  New Orleans, LA, 115
Hunter Museum of
  American Art
  Chattanooga, TN, 211
Hunt-Morgan House
  Lexington, KY, 78
Huntsville Depot
  Huntsville, AL, 12
Huntsville Marriott
  Huntsville, AL, 15
Huntsville Museum of Art
  Huntsville, AL, 12

Hurricane Creek Park
Vinemont, AL, 20
Hurricane Mills, 207
Hutton Hotel
Nashville, TN, 197
Hyatt Regency Lexington
Lexington, KY, 81
Hyatt Regency Louisville
Louisville, KY, 62

I

Imperial Calcasieu
Museum
Lake Charles, LA, 97
Indian Mounds
Baton Rouge, LA, 103
Intercontinental New
Orleans
New Orleans, LA, 133
International Friendship
Bell
Oak Ridge, TN, 219
International House
New Orleans, LA, 133
International Motorsports
Hall Of Fame
Talladega, AL, 22
Irvin Mayfield's Jazz
Playhouse
French Quarter, LA, 119
Ivy Green
Tuscumbia, AL, 15

J

Jack Daniel's Distillery
Lynchburg, TN, 208
Jackson, 153, 155, 178
Jackson Brewery
New Orleans, LA, 115
Jackson Square
New Orleans, LA, 115
Jambalaya
New Orleans, LA, 141
Jamestown, 207
James White's Fort
Knoxville, TN, 218
Jean Bragg Antiques &
Gallery
New Orleans, LA, 115
Jefferson County
Courthouse
Louisville, KY, 59
Jennings, 95
Jenny Wiley State Resort
Park
Prestonsburg, KY, 84
John C. Stennis Space
Center
Gulfport, MS, 171
John James Audubon
Riverboat
New Orleans, LA, 117
Johnson City, 213
Jonesborough, 213

Jonesborough History
    Museum
  Johnson City, TN, 214
Josephine Tussaud Wax
    Museum
  Hot Springs, AR, 47
Joe Ley Antiques, Inc.
  Louisville, KY, 65
Juban's
  Baton Rouge, LA, 107
Jungle Gardens
  Avery Island, LA, 97

K

Kenner, 149, 150
Kentucky, 3
Kentucky Center for the
    Arts
  Louisville, KY, 59
Kentucky Derby Museum
  Louisville, KY, 59
Kentucky Fair And
    Exposition Center
  Louisville, KY, 59
Kentucky Historical
    Society
  Frankfort, KY, 74
Kentucky Horse Park
  Lexington, KY, 78
Kentucky Vietnam
    Veterans Memorial
  Frankfort, KY, 74
Kingsport, 215, 221

Knoxville, 217, 221, 222
Knoxville Museum of Art
  Knoxville, TN, 218
Knoxville Zoo
  Knoxville, TN, 218
Konriko Rice Mill and
    Company Store
  New Iberia, LA, 97

L

Lacombe, 150
Lafayette, 96
Lafayette Hotel
  New Orleans, LA, 134
Lafayette Museum
  Lafayette, LA, 96
Lafayette Square
  New Orleans, LA, 117
Lafitte Guest House
  New Orleans, LA, 134
Lafitte's Blacksmith Shop
  New Orleans, LA, 117
Lake Bistineau State Park
  Minden, LA, 90
Lake Charles, 96
Lake Guntersville State
    Park
  Guntersville, AL, 20
Lake Pontchartrain
  New Orleans, LA, 117
Landrum's Homestead
  Laurel, MS, 173

La Provence
  Lacombe, LA, 150
Laurel, 173
Laurel Falls, 225
Laurel River Lake
  London, KY, 86
Lauren Rogers Museum
    of Art
  Laurel, MS, 173
Laurens Henry Cohn Sr.,
    Memorial Plant
    Arboretum
  Baton Rouge, LA, 103
Le Chat Noir
  New Orleans, LA, 117
Le Meritage
  New Orleans, LA, 146
Le Pavillion Hotel
  New Orleans, LA, 134
Le Relais
  Louisville, KY, 63
Le Richelieu in the
    French Quarter
  New Orleans, LA, 134
Leroy Percy State Park
  Hollandale, MS, 154
Lexington
  Lexington, KY, 76, 79
Lexington Cemetery
  Lexington, KY, 78
Liberty Hall
  Frankfort, KY, 74

Lichterman Nature Center
  Memphis, TN, 181
Lilette
  New Orleans, LA, 146
Lilly's
  Louisville, KY, 63
Little Rock
  Little Rock, AR, 40, 49
Little Rock Zoo
  Little Rock, AR, 51
Locust Grove
  Louisville, KY, 59
Loews Vanderbilt Hotel
    Nashville
  Nashville, TN, 198
Longfellow-Evangeline State
    Commemorative
    Area
  Martinville, LA, 98
Longue Vue House &
    Gardens
  New Orleans, LA, 117
Longwood
  Natchez, MS, 163
Lookout Mountain
  Chattanooga, TN, 211
Lookout Mountain Incline
    Railway
  Chattanooga, TN, 211
Loretta Lynn's Ranch
  Hurricane Mills, TN, 207
Louis Armstrong Park
  New Orleans, LA, 117

Louisiana, 3
Louisiana Art & Science
    Museum
  Baton Rouge, LA, 103
Louisiana Purchase
    Gardens and Zoo
  Monroe, LA, 91
Louisiana Children's
    Museum
  New Orleans, LA, 118
Louisiana State Exhibit
    Museum
  Shreveport, LA, 92
Louisiana State Library
  Baton Rouge, LA, 103
Louisiana State Museum
  New Orleans, LA, 118
Louisiana Superdome
  New Orleans, LA, 118
Louisiana Swampfest
  New Orleans, LA, 130
Louisville
  Louisville, KY, 56
Louisville Science Center
    & Imax Theatre
  Louisville, KY, 60
Louisville Slugger
    Museum & Bat
    Factory
  Louisville, KY, 60
Louisville Zoo
  Louisville, KY, 60
LSU Tigers
  Baton Rouge, LA, 103

M

Madison Hotel
  Memphisv, 186
Magazine Street
  New Orleans, LA, 120
Magnolia Hall
  Natchez, MS, 163
Maifest
  Covington, KY, 68
Mainstrasse Village
  Covington, KY, 68
Maison Lemonnier
  New Orleans, LA, 120
Malbis Greek Orthodox
    Church
  Daphne, AL, 32
The Mall At Green Hills
  Nashville, TN, 202
Manchester, 208
Mandeville, 151
Manship House
  Jackson, MS, 155
The Mansion at Griffin
    Gate
  Lexington, KY, 81
Mardi Gras
  Biloxi, MS, 172
Mardi Gras Celebration
  Gulf Shores, AL, 38
Mardi Gras Festival
  New Orleans, LA, 130
Mardi Gras World
  New Orleans, LA, 120

Marie Laveau's House of
        Voodoo
    New Orleans, LA, 147
Marriott at Rivercenter
    Covington, KY, 70
Marriott Baton Rouge
    Baton Rouge, LA, 106
Marriott Birmingham
    Birmingham, AL, 23
Marriott Meadowview
        Resort
    Kingsport, TN, 221
Marriott Memphis
        Downtown
    Memphis, TN, 186
Marriott Memphis East
    Memphis, TN, 186
Martha Vick House
    Vicksburg, MS, 165
Mary Mahoney's Old
        French House
    Biloxi, MS, 175
Mary Todd Lincoln House
    Lexington, KY, 78
Maxwell Air Force Base
    Montgomery, AL, 27
Maxwell's Steak and
        Seafood
    Gatlinburg, TN, 228
Maysville
    Maysville, KY, 69
McClung Historic
        Collection
    East Tennessee, TN, 218

McDowell House and
        Apothecary Shop
    Danville, KY, 73
McIlhenny Company
    Avery Island, LA, 97
McRaven Home
    Vicksburg, MS, 165
McWane Science Center
    Birmingham, AL, 18
Meeman-Shelby Forest
        State Park
    Millington, TN, 181
Melrose Estate Home
    Natchez, MS, 163
Memorial Hall-
        Confederate
        Museum
    New Orleans, LA, 120
Memorial Tower
    Baton Rouge, LA, 103
Memories Theatre
    Pigeon Forge, TN, 219
Memphis, 179
Memphis Botanic Garden
    Memphis, TN, 181
Memphis Brooks Museum
        of Art,
    Memphis, TN, 180
Memphis in May Interna-
        tional Festival
    Memphis, TN, 184
Memphis Pink Palace
        Museum and
        Planetarium
    Memphis, TN, 181

Memphis Queen Line
   Riverboats
  Memphis, TN, 182
Memphis Rock 'n' Soul
   Museum
  Memphis, TN, 183
Memphis Zoo
  Memphis, TN, 182
Mena, 48
Mendenhall, 160
Metairie Cemetery
  New Orleans, LA, 120
Mid-American Science
   Museum
  Hot Springs, AR, 47
Middle Tennessee, 203
Mignon Faget
  New Orleans, LA, 147
Mila
  New Orleans, LA, 143
Minden, 90
Mississippi, 3
Mississippi Agriculture &
   Forestry Museum
   and National Ag-
   ricultural Aviation
   Museum
  Jackson, MS, 156
Mississippi Museum
   of Art
  Jackson, MS, 156
Mississippi Petrified Forest
  Flora, MS, 156

Mississippi Sandhill Crane
   National Wildlife
   Refuge
  Pascagoula, MS, 173
Mississippi Sports Hall of
   Fame And Museum
  Jackson, MS, 156
Mobile
  Mobile, AL, 11, 31
Mobile Medical Museum
  Mobile, AL, 32
Mobile Museum of Art
  Mobile, AL, 33
Monmouth
  Natchez, MS, 163
Monmouth Plantation
  Natchez, MS, 167
Monroe and West
   Monroe, 91
Monte Sanso State Park
  Huntsville, AL, 13
Montgomery
  Montgomery, AL, 26
Montgomery Museum of
   Fine Arts
  Montgomery, AL, 27
Montgomery Zoo
  Montgomery, AL, 27
Moonwalk
  New Orleans, LA, 121
Morehead
  Morehead, KY, 83

Morehead State University
  Morehead, KY, 83
Morgan Row
  Harrodsburg, KY, 75
Mountain Arts Center
  Prestonsburg, KY, 85
Mountain View, 43
Mount Locust
  Natchez, MS, 163
Mr. B's Bistro
  New Orleans, LA, 143
Mr. John's Steakhouse
  New Orleans, LA, 146
M. S. Rau Antiques
  New Orleans, LA, 118
Mud Island River Park
  Memphis, TN, 182
Muffuletta
  New Orleans, LA, 141
Musee Conti Historical
      Wax Museum
  New Orleans, LA, 121
Museum of Discovery
  Little Rock, AR, 51
Museum of Mobile
  Mobile, AL, 33
Museum of Natural
      Science
  Baton Rouge, LA, 104
  Jackson, MS, 156
Museum of Zoology
  Monroe, LA, 91

Muth's Candy
  Louisville, KY, 66
Mynelle Gardens
  Jackson, MS, 156
The Myrtles Plantation
  Francisville, LA, 104

N

Napolean House
  New Orleans, LA, 146
NASCAR Speedpark
  Sevierville, TN, 220
Nashville, 177, 188
Natchez, 161, 167
Natchez State Park
  Natchez, MS, 163
Natchez Vistor Center
  Natchez, MS, 163
National Civil Rights
      Museum, 180
  Memphis, TN, 185
National D-Day Museum
  New Orleans, LA, 121
National Park Duck Tours
  Hot Springs, AR, 47
National Shrimp Festival
  Gulf Shores, AL, 38
National Voting Rights
      Museum and
      Institute
  Selma, AL, 28
Netherland Inn
  Kingsport, TN, 215

New Holy Land
  Eureka Springs, AR, 41
New Iberia, 97
New Orleans, 89, 108
New Orleans Botanical
  Garden
  New Orleans, LA, 121
New Orleans Ghost Tour
  New Orleans, LA, 121
New Orleans Historic
  Voodoo Museum
  New Orleans, LA, 121
New Orleans Hornets
  (NBA)
  New Orleans, LA, 123
New Orleans Jazz &
  Heritage Festival
  New Orleans, LA, 131
New Orleans Museum of
  Art
  New Orleans, LA, 123
New Orleans Opera
  New Orleans, LA, 123
New Orleans Pharmacy
  Museum (LA Phan-
  macie Francaise)
  New Orleans, LA, 123
New Orleans Saints
  (NFL)
  New Orleans, LA, 123
New Orleans School of
  Cooking & Louisi-
  ana General Store
  New Orleans, LA, 124

New Orleans Steamboat
  Company
  New Orleans, LA, 124
Newport on the Levee
  New Port, KY, 69
Nickajack Dam and Lake
  Jasper, TN, 211
Noccalula Falls Park
  Gadsden, AL, 21
NOLA
  New Orleans, LA, 143
Nolan House
  Waverly, TN, 207
Normandy Lake
  Normandy, TN, 208
Northern Cities
  Northern Cities, AL, 12
Nottoway Plantation
  White Castle, LA, 104
Nottoway Plantation
  Restaurant & Inn
  White Castle, LA, 107

O

Oak Alley Plantation
  Vacherie, LA, 124
Oak Harbor Golf Course
  Slidell, LA, 150
Oaklawn Manor
  Plantation
  Franklin, LA, 94
Oakley House
  Francisville, LA, 104

Oak Mountain State Park
  Pelham, AL, 19
Oak Ridge, 218
The Oaks House Museum
  Jackson, MS, 158
Oak Square Plantation
  Port Gibson, MS, 164
Oktoberfest
  Covington, KY, 68
The Old Hickory
    Steakhouse
  Nashville, TN, 200
The Old Mill
  Pigeon Forge, TN, 219
The Old State House
  Little Rock, AR, 51
The Old U.S. Mint
  New Orleans, LA, 124
Old Alabama Town
  Montgomery, AL, 28
Old Arsenal Museum, 104
Old Capitol
  Jackson, MS, 158
Old Court House Museum
  Vicksburg, MS, 167
Old Depot Museum
  Selma, AL, 29
Old Fort Harrod State
    Park
  Harrodsburg, KY, 75
Old Governor's Mansion
  Baton Rouge, LA, 104
  Frankfort, KY, 74

Old Hickory Lake
  Nashville, TN, 194
Old Mill
  North Little Rock, AR, 51
  Pigeon Forge, TN, 228
Old Spanish Fort And
    Museum
  Pascagoula, MS, 173
Old State Capitol
  Baton Rouge, LA, 104
Old State Capitol Building
  Frankfort, KY, 75
Old Stone Fort State
    Archaeological Park
  Manchester, TN, 208
Old Town Historic
    District
  Selma, AL, 29
Old Mud Meeting House
  Harrodsburg, KY, 76
Olive Hill
  Olive Hill, KY, 84
Omni Royal Crescent
    Hotel
  New Orleans, LA, 135
Omni Royal Orleans
  New Orleans, LA, 135
Opry Mills
  Nashville, TN, 203
Orange Beach
  Orange Beach, AL, 37
The Orangery
  Knoxville, TN, 222

Orlando Brown House
  Frankfort, KY, 75
Ouachita National Forest
  Hot Springs, AR, 48
Ouachitas, 45
Ozark Folk Center State
    Park
  Mountain View, AR, 44
Ozarks, 40

P

Paddle Wheeler Creole
    Queen and River-
    boat Cajun Queen
  New Orleans, LA, 124
Palace Cafe
  New Orleans, LA, 144
The Palm
  Nashville, TN, 200
Panoply Arts Festival
  Huntsville, AL, 14
Pariange Plantation
  Baton Rouge, LA, 105
Paramount Arts Center
  Ashland, KY, 83
Park Cafe
  Nashville, TN, 201
The Park Grill Steakhouse
  Gatlinburg, TN, 228
Park Headquarters and
    Vistor Center
  Hot Springs, AR, 48
The Parthenon

  Nashville, TN, 194
Pascagoula, 173
Pass Christian, 174
The Peabody Little Rock
  Little Rock, AR, 53
The Peabody Memphis
  Memphis, TN, 187
Pea Ridge National
    Military Park
  Garfield, AR, 43
The Peddler Restaurant
  Gatlinburg, TN, 228
The Piedmont Art Gallery
  Augusta, KY, 69
Pelican Club
  New Orleans, LA, 144
Pentagon Barracks
    Museum
  Baton Rouge, LA, 105
Perdido Beach Resort
  Orange Beach, AL, 37
Perlis
  New Orleans, LA, 147
Perryville Battlefield State
    Historic Site
  Perryville, KY, 73
Petit Paris Museum
  Martinville, LA, 98
Phoenix Fire Museum
  Mobile, AL, 33
Pickett State Rustic Park
  Jamestown, TN, 208
Pigeon Forge, 219, 228

The Pillars
  Mobile, AL, 35
Pinnacle Mountains State
    Park
  Roland, AR, 51
Pinnacle Overlook
  Corbin, KY, 87
Pinson Mounds State
    Archaeological Area
  Pinson, TN, 178
Pioneer Playhouse Village-
    of-the-Arts
  Danville, KY, 73
Pitot House
  New Orleans, LA, 126
Pivot Rock and Natural
    Bridge
  Eureka Springs, AR, 41
Plum
  New Orleans, LA, 148
Po-boys
  Irish Channel, LA, 141
Point Mallard Park
  Decatur, AL, 21
Point Park
  Lookout Mountain, TN,
    211
Pontalba Building
  New Orleans, LA, 126
Pontchartrain Vineyards &
    Vinery
  Bush, LA, 148

Poor Boy's Riverside Inn
  Lafayette, LA, 100
Port Gibson, 164
Port Hudson State
    Historic Site
  Jackson, LA, 105
Port Of Gulfport
  Starkville, MS, 172
Port Royal State Historic
    Area
  Adams, TN, 204
Presbytere
  Martinville, LA, 100
The Presbytere
  New Orleans, LA, 127
Preservation Hall
  French Quarter, LA, 119
  New Orleans, LA, 127
Prestonsburg
  Prestonsburg, KY, 84
Proof On Main
  Louisville, KY, 63
Pyramid Arena
  Memphis, TN, 185

Q

Quapaw Quarter Historic
    Neighborhoods
  *Little Rock and North
    Little Rock, AR*, 51
Queen Wilhelmina State
    Park
  Mena, AR, 48

R

Raccoon Mountain Caverns and Campground
Chattanooga, TN, 211
Race-On Driving Experience
Memphis, TN, 185
Radisson Hotel Cincinnati Riverfront
Covington, KY, 71
Rainbow Falls, 225
Ramsey House (Swan Pond)
Knoxville, TN, 218
Regas
Knoxville, TN, 222
Renaissance Montgomery Hotel & Spa at the Convention Center
Montgomery, AL, 30
Renaissance Nashville Hotel
Nashville, TN, 198
Renaissance Pere Marquette Hotel
New Orleans, LA, 135
Restaurant August
New Orleans, LA, 144
Richards-Dar House
Mobile, AL, 33
Richmont Inn B&B
Townsend, TN, 221

Rickwood Caverns State Park
Warrior, AL, 19
Rinaldo Grisanti and Sons
Memphis, TN, 188
Rip Van Winkle Gardens
New Iberia, LA, 98
The Ritz-Carlton, New Orleans
New Orleans, LA, 135
Riverboat Excursion
Louisville, KY, 60
River Cruises
New Orleans, LA, 127
Riverfest
Covington, KY, 68
Riverfront Streetcar Line
New Orleans, LA, 127
River Valley, 40
Riverwalk
New Orleans, LA, 127
Rock City Gardens
Lookout Mountain, TN, 211
Rocky Mount Historic Site & Overmountain Museum
Piney Flats, TN, 214
Rodes
Louisville, KY, 66
Rogers, 43

Rogers Historical Museum
(Hawkins House)
Rogers, AR, 43
Rolex Kentucky Three-
Day Event
Lexington, KY, 77
The Roosevelt New
Orleans
New Orleans, LA, 138
Rosalie
Natchez, MS, 164
Rosalie House
Eureka Springs, 42
Rosedown Plantation and
Gardens
Francisville, LA, 105
Rosemont Plantation
Woodville, MS, 169
Rosswood Plantation
Lorman, MS, 164
Royal Sonesta Hotel
New Orleans
New Orleans, LA, 136
Royal Spring Park
Georgetown, KY, 75
R. S. Barnwell Memorial
Garden and Art
Center
Shreveport, LA, 92
Ruby Falls-Lookout
Mountain Caverns
Chattanooga, TN, 212

Ruffner Mountain Nature
Center
Birmingham, AL, 19
The Ruins Of Windsor
Port Gibson, MS, 165
Rural Life Museum
Baton Rouge, LA, 106
Ruth's Chris Steak House
Baton Rouge, LA, 107
Lafayette, LA, 100
Mobile, AL, 35
Nashville, TN, 200
R. W. Norton Art Gallery
Shreveport, LA, 92
Ryman Auditorium &
Museum, 193
Nashville, TN, 194

S

Sam Davis Home
Nashville, TN, 194
Sam Houston Jones State
Park
Lake Charles, LA, 97
San Francisco Plantation
Garyville, LA, 127
Scranton Nature Center
Pascagoula, MS, 173
Seafood Festival
Biloxi, MS, 172
The Seelbach Hilton
Louisville
Louisville, KY, 62

Selma
  Selma, AL, 28
Sevierville, **220, 229**
Shadows-On-The-Teche
  New Iberia, LA, 98
Shaker Village of Pleasant
    Hill
  Harrodsburg, KY, 76
Sheltowee Trace Outfitters
  Somerset, KY, 87
Sheraton Baton Rouge
    Convention Center
    Hotel
  Baton Rouge, LA, 107
Sheraton Birmingham
    Hotel
  Birmingham, AL, 23
Sheraton Casino and
    Hotel
  Robinsonville, TN, 187
Sheraton Music City
  Nashville, TN, 198
Sheraton Nashville Down-
    town Hotel
  Nashville, TN, 199
Ship Island Excursions
  Gulfport, MS, 172
Shops at the Canal Place
  New Orleans, LA, 128
Shreveport, **91**
Signal Point On Signal
    Mountain
  Chattanooga, TN, 212

Silk Stocking District
  Talladega, AL, 22
Singing River
  Pascagoula, MS, 174
Six Flags Kentucky
    Kingdom
  Louisville, KY, 60
Sky Lift
  Gaitlinburg, TN, 213
Slidell, **150**
Sloss Furnaces National
    Historic Landmark
  Birmingham, AL, 19
Small Craft Harbor
  Biloxi, MS, 171
Smith Robertson Museum
  Jackson, MS, 158
Smoky Mountain Car
    Museum
  Pigeon Forge, TN, 220
Smoky Mountain Lights &
    Winterfest
  Gaitlinburg, TN, 214
Snyder Memorial Museum
  Bastrop, LA, 89
Soniat House Hotel
  New Orleans, LA, 136
Southdown Plantation
    House/Terrebonne
    Museum
  Houma, LA, 94
Southern Museum of
    Flight/Alabama
    Aviation Hall of

Fame
Birmingham, AL, 19
Southern Repertory
        Theatre
New Orleans, LA, 128
The Spa at The Ritz-Carl-
        ton, New Orleans
New Orleans, LA, 146
Speed Art Museum
Louisville, KY, 60
Sportsman's Paradise, 88
Spring Fiesta
New Orleans, LA, 131
Spring Wildflower Pil-
        grimage
Gatlinburg, TN, 214
Stanton Hall
Natchez, MS, 164
State Capitol
Baton Rouge, LA, 106
Frankfort, KY, 75
Jackson, MS, 158
Little Rock, AR, 52
Nashville, TN, 194
Stax Museum of American
        Soul Music, 183,
        185
St. Bernard State Park
Braithwaite, LA, 128
St. Charles Avenue
        Streetcar
New Orleans, LA, 128

St. James Hotel
New Orleans, LA, 136
St. John's Episcopal
        Church
Montgomery, AL, 28
St. Louis Cathedral
New Orleans, LA, 128
St. Louis Hotel
New Orleans, LA, 137
St. Martin of Tours Catho-
        lic Church
Martinville, LA, 98
St. Martinville, 98
Sturdivant Hall
Selma, AL, 29
Sunset Grill
Nashville, TN, 201
Sun Studio, 183
Memphis, TN, 185
Superior Grill
Shreveport, LA, 92

T

Talimena Scenice Drive
Mena, AR, 48
Talladega
Talladega, AL, 22
Talladega National Forest
Montgomery, AL, 22
Talladega Superspeedway
Eastaboga, AL, 23
Tammany Trace
Covington, LA, 149

Tennessee, 3

Tennessee Aquarium
  Chattanooga, TN, 212

Tennessee State Museum
  Nashville, TN, 195

Tennessee Titans (NFL)
  Nashville, TN, 195

Tennessee Valley Railroad
  Chattanooga, TN, 212

Tennessee Williams New
    Orleans Literary
    Festival
  New Orleans, LA, 131

Thomas Edison House
  Louisville, KY, 61

Thorncrown Chapel
  Eureka Springs, AR, 42

Tipton-Haynes Historic
    Site
  Johnson City, TN, 215

T.O. Fuller State Park
  Memphis, TN, 185

Toltec Mounds
    Archeological State
    Park
  Scott, AR, 52

Townsend, 221

Toyota Blue Grass Stakes
  Lexington, KY, 77

Travellers Rest Plantation
    and Museum
  Nashville, TN, 195

Treasure Chest Casino
  Kenner, LA, 149

Trey Yuen
  Mandeville, LA, 151

Trousdale Place
  Gallatin, TN, 207

Tuscumbia
  Tuscumbia, AL, 15

Tuskegee
  Tuskegee, AL, 29

Tuskegee Institute
    National Historic
    Site
  Tuskegee, AL, 30

Tuskegee National Forest
  Tuskegee, AL, 30

Twickenham Historic
    District
  Huntsville, AL, 13

U

University of Lousville
  Louisville, KY, 61

University of South
    Alabama
  Mobile, AL, 33

The Upper Room Chapel
    and Museum
  Nashville, TN, 195

Upperline
  New Orleans, LA, 144

U.S Custom House
  New Orleans, LA, 129

USS Kidd
  Baton Rouge, LA, 106

U.S. Space and Rocket
  Center
  Huntsville, AL, 14

V

Valentino's
  Nashville, TN, 201
Vaughan's Lounge
  Bywater, LA, 119
Vent Haven Museum
  Fort Mitchell, KY, 69
Veranda
  New Orleans, LA, 144
Vicksburg, 165, 168
Vicksburg National
  Military Park &
  Cemetery
  Vickburg, MS, 167
Victorian Square
  Lexington, KY, 79
Victorian Village
  Memphis, TN, 186
Von Braun Center
  Huntsville, AL, 14
Vulcan
  Birmingham, AL, 19

W

Walland, 221, 222
War Eagle Cavern
  Rogers, AR, 43
Warrior's Path State Park
  Kingsport, TN, 217

Washington Artillery Park
  New Orleans, LA, 129
Watauga Dam And Lake
  Johnson City, TN, 215
Waterfront
  Covington, KY, 71
Water Tower
  Louisville, KY, 61
Water Town USA
  Shreveport, LA, 92
Waveland State Historic
  Site
  Lexington, KY, 79
W. C. Handy's Home
  Memphis, 179, 183
West Baton Rouge
  Museum
  Port Allen, LA, 106
Westin New Orleans Canal
  Place
  New Orleans, LA, 138
West Tennessee, 177
Wheeler National Wildlife
  Refuge
  Decatur, AL, 21
White Linen Night
  New Orleans, LA, 131
Whitewater Rafting
  Erwin, TN, 215
The Whitney
  New Orleans, LA, 137

W. H. Tupper General
   Merchandise
   Museum
   Jennings, LA, 95
Wildhorse Saloon, 193
   Nashville, TN, 195
Wildlife, 226
Wild River Country
   North Little Rock, AR, 52
William B. Bankhead
   National Forest
   Double Springs, AL, 21
William S. Webb Museum
   of Anthropology
   Lexington, KY, 79
Windsor Court Hotel
   New Orleans, LA, 137
Withrow Springs State
   Park
   Huntsville, AR, 42
W New Orleans
   New Orleans, LA, 137
W New Orleans French
   Quarter
   New Orleans, LA, 138
Woldenberg Riverfront
   Park
   New Orleans, LA, 129
Woodville, 169
World Of Sports
   Florence, KY, 69

World Trade Center Of
   New Orleans
   New Orleans, LA, 129
Wyndham Union Station
   Hotel
   Nashville, TN, 199
The Wynfrey Hotel
   Birmingham, AL, 24
Wynnwood
   Castalian Springs, TN,
   207

Y

The Yellow Porch
   Nashville, TN, 201

Z

Zachary Taylor National
   Cemetery
   Louisville, KY, 61
Zigler Museum
   Jennings, LA, 96
Zydeco Festival
   Memphis, TN, 184

ALABAMA

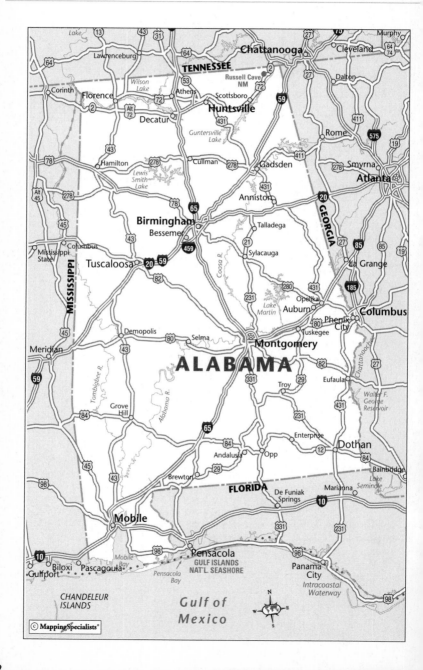

ARKANSAS

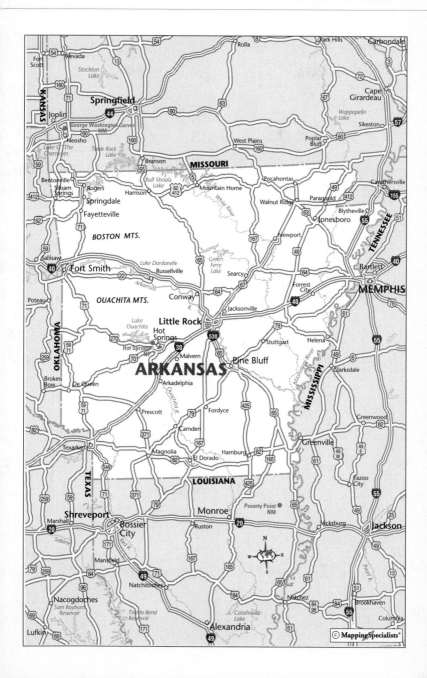

© MappingSpecialists®

TENNESSEE

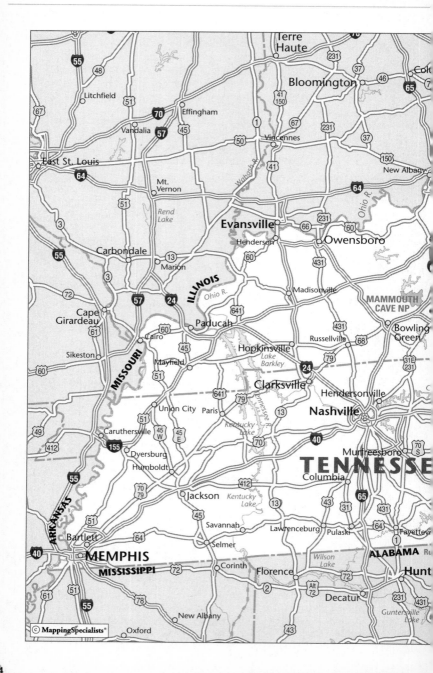

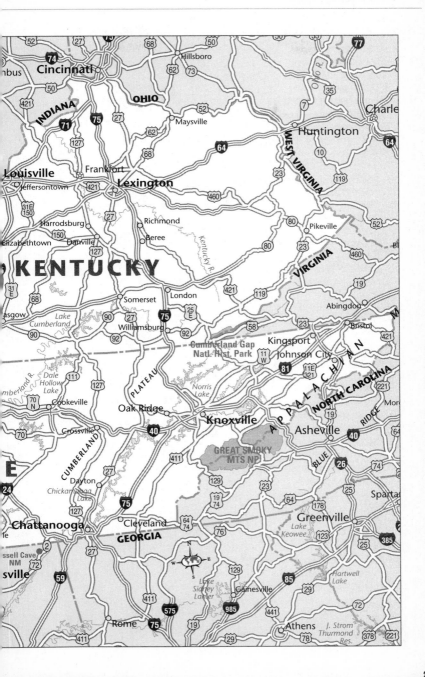

LOUISIANA

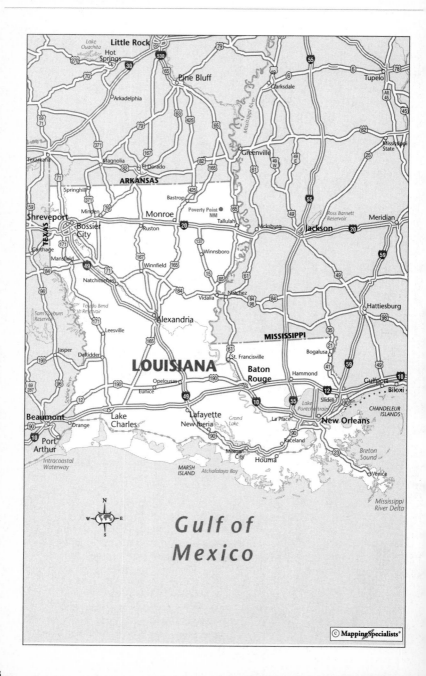

MISSISSIPPI

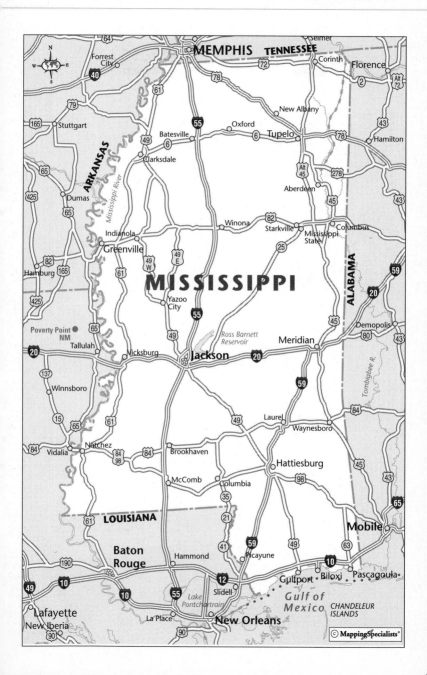

NOTES

NOTES

NOTES